AF608041

TEACHER EDUCATION IN A TRANSNATIONAL WORLD

Teacher Education in a Transnational World

EDITED BY ROSA BRUNO-JOFRÉ
AND JAMES SCOTT JOHNSTON

UNIVERSITY OF TORONTO PRESS
Toronto Buffalo London

© University of Toronto Press 2014
Toronto Buffalo London
www.utppublishing.com

ISBN 978-1-4426-4934-7

Library and Archives Canada Cataloguing in Publication

Teacher education in a transnational world / edited by Rosa Bruno-Jofré and James Scott Johnston.

Includes bibliographical references and index.
ISBN 978-1-4426-4934-7 (bound)

1. Teachers–Training of–Cross-cultural studies. I. Bruno-Jofré, Rosa del Carmen, 1946–, editor II. Johnston, James Scott, editor

LB1707.T43 2014 370.71′1 C2014-905016-X

University of Toronto Press acknowledges the financial assistance to its publishing program of the Canada Council for the Arts and the Ontario Arts Council, an agency of the Government of Ontario.

University of Toronto Press acknowledges the financial support of the Government of Canada through the Canada Book Fund for its publishing activities.

Contents

Focal Point 2: Paradigmatic Changes in Teacher Education

Focal Point 3: Aboriginal Teacher Education in the Globalizing Context

Focal Point 4: The European Setting: Erasmus, Bologna, and the European Higher Education Area

Figures and Tables

Figures

Tables

TEACHER EDUCATION IN
A TRANSNATIONAL WORLD

Introduction: Emerging Critical Issues in Teacher Education in a Globalizing and Transnational World

ROSA BRUNO-JOFRÉ AND
JAMES SCOTT JOHNSTON

The contents of this volume are representative of disparate, yet informed, ways of thinking about teacher education within the current parameters of globalization, differentiated historically from what has gone before by its supranational character. This is clearly expressed in developments such as the impact of the Bologna Accord, the role of the Organization for Economic Cooperation and Development (OECD), international testing such as those undertaken by the Programme for International Student Assessment (PISA), and ranking processes (Dale, 2003). Teacher education programs remain remarkably under-theorized with respect to this context, though there are a few examples to the contrary (Adora-Hoppers, 2000; Spring, 2001; Stromquist, 2002; Cook, 2004; Cole, 2005; Spring, 2006; Biesta & Peters, 2007; Peters & Besley, 2008; Popkewitz, 2008; Tan & Whalen-Bridge, 2008; Taylor, Scheirer, & Ghiraldelli, 2008; Torres, 2009; Zadja, 2010).

Much more prevalent are arguments supporting models of teacher education, essays on practical wisdom, position papers, governmental publications, and minutes of meetings and conferences, together with prescriptions for curricula, policy, and legislation to embrace (and in some cases, combat) the burgeoning transformation of teacher education. However, the absence of a unified document bringing together analysis of programs, practices, and theories on teacher education with respect to what we are calling a "globalizing and transnational world" is telling. Analysts of teacher education programs and those who theorize them are evidently not yet in a position to put forth a comprehensive discussion of the issues involved in what, to many, seems an inevitable transformation.

This volume seeks to understand and locate teacher education in relation to international influences, international agreements, and national policies and processes of reception at the national and local level. It does so without neglecting the non-affiliated discursive practices and political presences – such as the case of the Aboriginal peoples – within the context of what Roger Dale[1] calls a globalizing and, we will add, a transnational process. In line with this major aim, the book is organized according to five focal points: (1) Socio-political and Intellectual Spaces Where Teacher Education Is Located: A Historical, Sociological, and Philosophical Approach; (2) Paradigmatic Changes in Teacher Education; (3) Aboriginal Teacher Education in a Globalizing Context; (4) The European Setting: Erasmus, Bologna, and the European Higher Education Area; and (5) Transnationalization and State Policies. We, the editors, have selected strands that not only cut across various chapters, but are implicit throughout all the chapters.

We identify in the chapters recurring themes in history, sociology, and philosophy and raise foundational questions of historical causation and relation – and, in the case of philosophy, ontological and epistemological commitments – that are not often addressed. Historical explanations prevent presentism, a positioning that neglects processes, continuities and discontinuities, and ruptures – in other words, the temporal and spatial dimensions that may indeed lead to a rich connection with the present. The historical explanation is central to chapter 3, where Rosa Bruno-Jofré and Josh Cole analyse the insertion of teacher education in Ontario universities, and the conditions of possibility that facilitated that insertion. It is also key in chapter 5, with Anne Rohstock and Daniel Tröhler showing the decline of history of education in the teacher education program as a consequence of the cognitive shift that led to an ahistorical and decontextualized understanding of teacher education. It is the thread that runs through Sylviane Toporkoff's analysis (chapter 12) of the Erasmus Programme, exploring continuities and discontinuities in mobility programs from medieval times. Carlos Martínez Valle, in chapter 13, uses a historic-comparative analysis of the German and Spanish cases regarding the implementation of the Bologna Accord and local idiosyncratic answers to reform. Andrew Robinson (chapter 16) returns to the past to imagine the future, and disputes the strength of the concept of globalization.

An implicit idea emerging in some chapters is that globalization has its own "mode of historical consciousness" and, in particular, that the notion of Europeaneity can be construed as a special kind of historical consciousness. This is also the case for Aboriginal education, and if we press hard enough, we can find elements of historical consciousness in many (if not most) of the narratives global players provide. In chapter 1,

Roger Dale leads us in a sociologically grounded discussion of globalization and its impact on teacher education, raising questions regarding the pressures on teacher education from international organizations and the ever-tighter regime of accountability.

On the philosophical side, questions of ontology and epistemology arise in any theoretical examination of teacher education in a globalizing and transnational world. By "ontology" we mean the essential or basic stance of human beings towards themselves, each other, and the world. By "epistemology" we mean their theories of knowledge, what they claim in the way of knowing, and how they prove or demonstrate this. Of course, there is much taken-for-grantedness on the part of theorists with respect to these matters; we don't very often pause to consider what we take as basic, or what theory of knowledge we are happening to invoke. But these questions are nevertheless relevant ones, particularly in the setting of transnationalization, because there can be no taken-for-grantedness in what is basic in the way of our being and our knowledge when we transcend our culturally specific educational domains. It is a fallacy to assume that, across cultures, peoples have the same basic beliefs about being and knowledge.

This leads us to a very important question: which, if any, among our current philosophical schools of thought, serves best in attending to questions about being and knowledge? Of course, there are a variety of schools of thought to choose from, to put it quite cavalierly, yet not all will suffice. Specifically, those premised on an essentialist way of understanding the world, which requires a very particular account of being and knowledge, are not well disposed to aid in theorizing transnationalization for teacher education. We will need a less essentialist – or ideally, non-essentialist – school of thought to aid us in understanding transnationalization for our purposes. James Scott Johnston, Chris Beeman, and Nel Noddings give us three examples of this route. Johnston (chapter 2) argues for the consideration of pragmatism, rather than critical theory or post-structuralism, to be of benefit for transnationalization. This is so, he argues, because the latter two are metaphysically essentialist, whereas pragmatism is rooted in an openness to the world and to the results of inquiry. Beeman (chapter 9) argues for a metaphysics in which the human being is firmly situated in place. As such, he eschews the dominant, subjectivist modes of understanding human as primary. Noddings (chapter 4) argues for an irreducible ecological ethic of cosmopolitanism, one that does not attempt to isolate or abstract the person from common domains of living.

Another powerful theme of relevance in globalized contexts that appears in various chapters is the issue of aims responding to various conceptions of education and its function, including political educational aims linked to neoliberalism such as human capital theory and efficiency, environmental/ecological aims, ontological aims (deep knowledge), humanism, notions of self and social recognition, and wisdom. The question of aims for education in a globalizing, transnationalized context has received a great deal of attention, some of which is evident in the chapters of this volume. The question of arbitrating among aims when they seem to be in conflict – or, alternatively, prioritizing aims – is revealed when we contrast them with no clear path to decide which is best.

Political aims such as efficiency in the context of human capital theory and neoliberalism run up against cultural and scientific aims, such as ecology and humanism. They also run up against philosophical aims, such as social recognition and wisdom – aims which, at least in the cultures of the West, are very often prized. How do we adjudicate these aims? This will be a constant concern for teacher education programs in a transnationalized world. How will we balance, if at all, the competing aims of the political economy and the cultural aims specific to various contexts? Should some aims trump others? When and why (and how)? Or perhaps we will have to negotiate these aims through deliberation, debate, and compromise. The question of local and national versus international context is also raised: what will be the factors in the decision to favour more local and national aims over international aims, and vice versa? How, and by whom, will these decisions be made?

Questions such as these cannot be answered through traditional philosophic deliberation such as deductive processes, nor can they be answered through top-down governmental or legislative fiat. But neither can they be answered through detached quantitative analysis. At least, they cannot if what is wanted is a deliberative approach involving good reasons and arguments, but also representation from stakeholders including not only those directly affected by teacher education programs (such as teacher candidates, faculty, teachers, administrators, boards, districts, and state/provincial and national governing bodies), but those indirectly affected by them as well (parents, businesses, and municipal government officials). This requires, at a minimum, an open deliberation with plenty of opportunity for interested parties to have a voice. However, good arguments are essential to this deliberative process, good arguments that in turn rely upon reasons that can be defended.

The question "Which aims for education?", although a deliberative one, requires a strong foundation, itself rooted in traditions of the past, with respect to the reasons we give for our decisions. Thus, any consideration of Aboriginal issues, for example, requires an understanding of ontologies and epistemologies with regard to Aboriginal peoples in order to propose educational aims. This is a task that Beeman takes on in his chapter, making an inward turn and thinking of education as a way of being in the world. Situating aims in a historical continuum gains significance when explaining major shifts in teacher education in light of new educational and political aims, playing a role in the insertion of teacher education in universities in Ontario, or, for that matter, when dealing with teaching competences, as Toporkoff does (chapter 12). It is also significant in the quest for wisdom and the call for creativity and ethical commitment at the crossroad of competences as aims and a pluralistic notion of wisdom, as discussed by Gonzalo Jover and José Luis González Geraldo in chapter 15.

Various chapters in this collection unravel questions regarding technology and globalization in relation to paradigmatic changes in education and teacher education, within alternative configurations of time and space and lack of consent on globalization. It is a truism to say that technology has transformed the world. Far more interesting are the many subtle ways in which this transformation has occurred. The obvious way is certainly through the invention and development of the Internet and associated networks. If, as many assert, we are truly a part of a "global village," in Marshall McLuhan's seemingly prescient opinion, then we must ask what this means for us. Does it mean, for example, that political-economic issues take a backseat to this new status quo? To believe some experts, the answer is (a qualified) yes (Bontis & Fitz-enz, 2002; Healy & Cote, 2001; Lin, 1999).

Others, however, are uncertain. Indeed, the range of responses varies from cautious optimism to outright cynicism.[2] While some claim that systemic disenfranchisement and violations of human rights will cease in the context of a globalized technological imperative, others warn that this technology is being used in the service of further disenfranchisement. Still others worry that an uncritical uptake of technologies will hasten the demise of proven pedagogies and traditionally valuable subjects. Yet, a diverse and intense relationship with knowledge and new ways of learning have emerged, along with new forms of social communication that – positioned at the core of the globalizing process – redefine even formal education beyond conventional boundaries. Furthermore, technology as a set of practices has its own logic, not necessarily in tune with formal education, and in particular public education.

What role might teacher education have to play? Obviously, teacher education programs will be using, and in some cases benefiting from, global technology. Thus, the question of ethics in the taking up and use of this technology comes to the fore. The question of whether it is an educational need that requires attention *within* teacher education programs must be broached. It is not at all certain that it must, if we believe those who insist that attention to technology's present and possible consequences be made part of the assessment of its worthiness to individual programs. Far more reasonable might be a cautious approach , one that recognizes technology's utility but also its capacity to obscure or even worsen disenfranchisement, or move us away from subjects and pedagogies that we deem important. The issue of technology cuts across various chapters. In chapter 8, Nicholas C. Burbules addresses the issue of ubiquitous learning, while the complexities permeating the uptake of reforms at the intersection of the supranational and the local are reflected in Martínez Valle's chapter (13) on harmonizing the disparate systems of higher education in Germany and Spain.

A major theme involving various chapters is the working of educational policies at the crossroads of supranational forces, bloc forces, and local idiosyncrasies and asystemic forces. It touches on issues such as the Bologna and other accords, the place of teacher education in relation to university policies and the educational system, and local cultures and efforts at standardization and uniformity. Perhaps the largest set of accords affecting education globally is the Bologna Process. In 1999, twenty-nine education ministers from across Europe signed an accord at the University of Bologna. This was subsequently opened to other countries that had signed the European Cultural Convention. Subsequent meetings have been held a number of times in various cities across Europe, and the process now has forty-seven countries as signatories. Key to the process is access to higher education through streamlined admissions and course equivalents (EAQAHE, 2005). This has resulted in changes to degree requirements for programs, standardization of courses across nations, and changes in the role of faculty in maintaining professional autonomy in light of the push for standardization of course requirements and course content. Needless to say, there has been a good deal of pushback.[3] This has been most frequently seen in France and Germany, where (full or ordinary) professors are given much leeway in the control of their curricula.

What role has, and will, the Bologna Process play with regard to teacher education programs? Unfortunately for some, it means more uniformity of requirements, more standardization of curricula, and more portability of criteria for admission, acceptance, and course selection. And while this may be a benefit to the overall efficiency of the teacher education system, it does not bode well for the preservation of local teacher education cultures and practices. Specifically, a "way of life" is threatened – and it is through a way of life, after all, that meaning is conferred upon humans in their relationships with others and with the world. Therefore, a great deal is at stake in the disruption and reconstruction of ways of life in the context of teacher education, its faculty, students, and socio-cultural practices. This leads us to think about the role of uniformity in hindering reflective practice and the cultural context of reflective practice, a major issue discussed by Tom Russell in chapter 7.

Finally, there is the question of the effect of international accords such as the Bologna Process on the public. By "public," we mean the community of persons who work together to solve social problems through communication and (social) inquiry. This roughly corresponds with Dewey's notion of the "great society" (Dewey, 1982, p. 315). A public takes upon itself to judge the utility and validity of programs with respect to their (mutual) interests. A public manifestly does not succumb to the authoritarian, top-down imposition of programs and policies. This extends to institutions of higher education, including, for our context, teacher education programs. For this "public" to be sufficiently autonomous to make judgments regarding its practices, resistance to Bologna-styled processes seems necessary. But this is unlikely to happen, even though significant pushback on the part of higher education institutions is occurring. The political power required to resist the incursion of these programs, together with the generous benefits they offer, is lacking. Thus, teacher education programs must find ways of displacing the imposition of Bologna-style processes through various means, if they are to keep their "ways of life" intact.

Various chapters explore how local and systemic issues as well as cultural practices thwart the implementation of cross-national accords. Cristián Cox, Lorena Meckes, and Martín Bascopé's analysis of teacher education in Chile (chapter 17) shows that the market's powerful presence as a regulator of quality is a reflection of neoliberal economic policies overriding the professionalization of teaching. Chapter 6 by LeRoy Whitehead, on the transnationalization of teacher education, poses questions on how teacher education can generate the dispositions dealing with open-mindedness and flexibility that would characterize teachers' working in a transnationalized setting, while simultaneously attending to the needs of special populations. There is still the role of the state and its policies in relation to the internationalization of higher education in terms of fees and regulations, a topic addressed in chapter 18 by Snowdon in reference to the Ontario experience.

Last, but not least, a major theme in this collection is the question of Aboriginal education – or educating Aboriginally, as Beeman puts it; this topic is also addressed by María Eugenia Merino-Dickinson and Te Tuhi Robust in chapters 10 and 11. The question of the "ownership" of education – including not only the "texts" but the contexts (institutions and governmentalities, as well as pedagogies) – is a fraught one and has led to much debate.

Another major theme crossing the chapters is the disenfranchised, with respect to teacher education programs in the transnationalized context. It is also important to consider how to develop models of education that are sensitive to issues of social justice (including minority rights to self-government). The chapter by Andrew Robinson offers an educational model sensitive to social equity within the globalizing context that could be inspiring to faculties of education. The effects of these programs remain to be seen. But the concerns are already building, such as concerns that teacher education will be unable to implement strategies for social justice and other anti-oppressive and enfranchising programs within a standardized context. While it may be true that general programs such as UNESCO insist on the practice of human rights, this may not take into consideration the unique characteristics and challenges of local contexts. More disturbing is the scenario in which attention shifts from social justice to solely economic concerns, such as those of employment and human capital.

On one hand, existing theorizing on globalization in education has attempted to integrate social justice issues into their various conclusions regarding programs. This is largely an attempt to "stem the tide" of what looks to be a wholesale focus on market-driven economic understandings of globalization and their attendant human-capital theories. It is also an attempt to integrate UN-sponsored legislation regarding human rights with the flourishing of local cultural and linguistic practices. On the other hand, it seems that the dominant imperative of globalization is economic, and that human capital theory (and rational choice theory) is the intellectual driver of the powerful political and economic institutions in support of this imperative. For many committed to social justice education, this bodes badly for the future of teacher education and the institutions in which teacher education is practised. For these, the concern is the hollowing out of programs, including the reduction of commitments to social justice education and humanistic concerns for the welfare of those least able to weather the incursion of market forces into their local contexts.

It is our contention that the five focal points discussed earlier represent central issues in undertaking research on teacher education in a transnationalized world. Below, we defend our choice of these five points, for – while we do see them at play in the chapters – we also believe they operate on their own as powerful points of departure for our overall topic.

At every turn, scholars are confronted with the social, historical, and philosophical contexts of the peoples and systems they study and attempt to articulate. These often have a long pedigree and are bound up with practical concerns (norms) that make them impossible to understand if there is no attempt to examine the context. Too often, educational reforms fail through being historically and philosophically insensitive to this context. Scholars of globalized or globalizing teacher education can ill afford to take this context for granted. Furthermore, the socio-economic, political, and intellectual spaces where peoples and systems of education operate must be treated with the utmost respect, as decisions on globalized or globalizing policy are made in such spaces. From the scholar's point of view, these spaces are where transformations take place. Both the boundaries of the spaces and their content (e.g., the particular speech acts as well as legislations that construct the policy) are important sources for scholarship.

Paradigmatic changes in teacher education can be local ("on the ground") or systematically instituted. Here, we consider both. While it may seem that only a systematically instituted change could be of benefit to teacher education in a global world, the converse is likely the case for two reasons: (1) it is difficult to imagine, wholesale, a teaching program, and any program instituted must be tested and reconstituted as needed; and (2) local, "on the ground" changes often take place according to actual, not anticipated, needs, and better serve those communities that have those needs. Regardless, as children (and adults) from multiple nations enter our school systems, changes that are in keeping with mandates of human rights and social justice will be made and will be paradigmatic, for the converse will be seen as mistreatment and perhaps even a human rights violation.

Aboriginal education is taking on more and more significance, partly through human rights legislation, both international and national, and through local and regional minority initiatives. In some cases there is pushback, on the part of minority populations, against dominant educational systems; in others there is a desire to acquaint the world with minority culture, language, and history. It will increasingly become impossible to do global education, to say nothing of national education, in ignorance of minority issues. International attention, and particularly international human rights laws and organizations that administer them (the United Nations, national and regional human rights commissions, parliaments, and legislators) will continue to focus further and further on the rights of minorities in respect of their land, their languages, and their cultures.

The European setting is where the effects of the Bologna Accords are most keenly felt. It may not seem – from the vantage point of North America – a matter of great concern, but wholesale attempts at streamlining the accords for American and Canadian schools of higher education are under way. South America has felt the effect more strongly than North America, and many schools there are already set up to receive European students (and vice versa). The particular accords aside, what is at issue is the devolution of education faculties (for they have progressively less and less say over how to grade their classes, or who to consider for admission), the loss of individual institutional identity, and (especially for certain European countries) the loss of a national identity that operates through the university system. The concern is that this model is to be transported across the ocean.

Aligned with this is the issue of state policies. While Bologna may be the largest multi-state policy of hegemony, it is by no means the only one. Increasingly, states are ratifying agreements to consolidate or merge with other systems, in a process tantamount to one state controlling another's education systems. This is often done through international organizations, particularly the World Bank. At the base of some of these initiatives are multinational corporations, some of whom have a vested interest in the educational systems of particular nations or regions. No less relevant is the how jurisdictions approach the process; a case in point is Ken Snowdon's chapter on Ontario, Canada.

While the chapters in this volume do not definitively answer all these concerns, they do address them. In what follows, we summarize the chapters and then suggest a strategy to understand them in communication with one another over these central concerns. The chapters are organized around five focal points where themes converge, which we will discuss at the introduction to each main section, which serves as an interlude. Next, we will present the main claims of the chapters conforming to each focal point.

Focal Point 1 is entitled "Socio-Political, Cultural, and Intellectual Spaces Where Teacher Education Is Located: A Historical, Sociological, and Philosophical Approach." It includes the following chapters: "Globalization, Higher Education, and Teacher Education: A Sociological Approach," by Roger Dale (University of Bristol, UK); "Theorizing Globalization: Rival Philosophical Schools of Thought," by James Scott Johnston (Memorial University of Newfoundland, Canada); "To Serve and Yet Be Free: Historical Configurations and the Insertions of Faculties of Education in Ontario," by Rosa Bruno-Jofré and Josh Cole (Queen's University, Canada); and "Cosmopolitanism, Patriotism, and Ecology," by Nel Noddings (Stanford University, USA).

Roger Dale explores the relationship between the university, teacher education, and globalization. He finds that the association of teacher education with the university has taken on new dimensions of risk and threat through the incorporation of quality assurance and risk management regimes, under the umbrella of accountability; these developments are rooted in current changes in the global political economy. The pressures deriving from these regimes are generating changes in the conception of teaching and the work of teachers. Teacher education programs and faculties and schools of education are under pressure from private organizations in tandem with the globalization drivers in international organizations, and while there is recognition of the significance of the teacher's work, as Dale puts it, it is "of dubious pedigree and purpose." The somewhat Janus-faced position of teacher education, looking simultaneously into the university and out to the world of schools, and to a degree connecting them to each other, enables the development of several fascinating lines of inquiry.

Johnston's chapter discusses the rival philosophical approaches to globalization that are currently in vogue. Johnston attempts to distil the existing theories of globalization down to two philosophical varieties: critical theory and post-structuralism. Both critical theory and post-structuralism share a common theme, and this is a criticism of subjectivism. Subjectivism is the view that the "I" is the central feature of knowledge. This is a Cartesian view, in which a metaphysical claim about the centrality of the self as subject is put forward. Critical theory and post-structuralism thus share, along with a number of other philosophies of the nineteenth and twentieth centuries, a critique of Cartesianism. However, critical theory and post-structuralism have fatal flaws. In the case of critical theory (here, Johnston discusses Theodor Adorno), there is a turn away from the subject to the object, with no further connecting of the two. In the case of post-structuralism (here, Johnston discusses Jacques Derrida), there is an essentialist philosophy of dispersion that denies unities, totalities, and syntheses. Rather than distinguishing unities from differences, these glorify differences at the expense of unities. This is problematic because – if we are to transcend extant understandings and practices – programs that attempt to understand and change existing structures of global practices seem to require an understanding and acceptance of both differences (the local, the particular, the margin, the minority) and unities (the structure, the whole, the system, the forces of change and stability). Pragmatism, Johnston argues, is better suited for discussing and theorizing both differences and unities. Pragmatism is better because it recognizes both differences and unities, and attempts a synthesis of the two, while at the same time avoiding the extreme subjectivity characterized by Cartesian programs of the subject. This intersubjective theory of self and other provides the theorist with an account of self and community, which is requisite for any further account of globalization, whether economic, political, or social.

Bruno-Jofré and Cole's chapter examines the complex relationship of teacher education and universities, using as thread the two foundings of the Faculty of Education at Queen's University (1907 and 1965). This relationship is treated within the major configuration generated by the educational state and the need to produce the modern Canadian subject, as well as the intellectual developments that led to a respectable body of scholarship on education and gave tools for new rhetorical claims on the necessary conditions for teaching and learning. The tension between liberal education and theoretical issues and practice was present in the first period analysed here, in which elementary teachers had limited preparation. The period after the the Second World War dramatically changed the educational aims and motivated a redirection of teacher education. It introduced the Cold War elements at the core of the formative understanding of the subject, the notion of human capital, discussion about the interplay between liberal education and a utilitarian education, and socio-economic changes including a new demographic reality. The elementary teacher in Ontario (other provinces had moved teacher education to the universities or were in the process of doing so) needed a different formation, a university education. This coincided with the developing of the multiversities and their eclectic mission. The second founding of the Faculty of Education at Queen's (called the College of Education at the time) is situated in this emerging context, without disregard for the economic prosperity of the time and the increasing number of students.

Cosmopolitanism has developed as a major trend in the attempt to deal with categorical fragmentation and keep a concern with our shared humanity; this is certainly a theme of renewed interest in teacher education. Nel Noddings deals with cosmopolitanism – belonging to the world rather than to a nation, tribe, or region – using the United States as an example. She argues that patriotism is the major obstacle to the teaching and understanding of cosmopolitanism. Patriotism advocates national pride and has an emotional effect on people, whereas cosmopolitanism does not. Noddings relies on Benjamin Barber and Jean Bethke Elshtain to recommend a notion of "chastened patriotism" that would induce a concern for goodness and an openness to critique acts that were later regretted. Furthermore, a narrow notion of patriotism and not teaching the ways of others may lead to reinforcement of a notion of superiority. After exploring Martha Nussbaum, Noddings makes the case that, to encourage cosmopolitanism, we need to start in some domain other than the political. She then discusses ecological cosmopolitanism and moves from the notions of nation and a collection of nations, to the earth as a natural community and countries as interconnected home-places.

While not addressing teacher education programs directly, Noddings nevertheless suggests that this cosmopolitanism should be part of the teacher education curriculum. The benefits of an ecological cosmopolitanism are many, including connection, interdependence, and sustainability, together with balance and diversity. Most important, she claims that an ecological cosmopolitanism is best suited to help us solve our social problems. In line with Dewey, Noddings thinks that this is best accomplished in the curriculum through attention to history and geography. However, political history, which she believes has been overemphasized in the curriculum, should at least be tempered with the history of common living – homes, childhood, and parenthood – for common living far better represents our shared understandings and practices of life. She looks for an integration with nature and manual work and the physical and emotional dimensions of life.

Focal Point 2, entitled "Paradigmatic Changes in Teacher Education," contains four chapters: "From the Sacred Nation to the Unified Globe: Changing Leitmotifs in Teacher Training in the Western World, 1870–2010," by Anne Rohstock (Universität Tübingen, Germany) and Daniel Tröhler (University of Luxembourg); "Transnationalization of Teacher Education: A New Paradigm for Ontario?" by LeRoy Whitehead (Queen's University); "Paradigmatic Changes in Teacher Education: The Perils, Pitfalls, and Unrealized Promise of the Reflective Practitioner," by Tom Russell (Queen's University); and "Ubiquitous Learning and the Future of Teaching," by Nicholas C. Burbules (University of Illinois, USA).

For Rohstock and Tröhler, a significant cultural shift of the eighteenth century was the educationalization of the social world, having as a central element nation building and the modern citizen. The two world wars led to questioning of the notions of the nation state and generated quests for unity. Each period had a leitmotif characterizing teacher training: in the nineteenth century, it was national uniqueness and supremacy; in the post–Second World War period, it was internationalization and global standardization. While history of education dominated teacher education before the wars and in particular before the Second World War, in the period after 1945, the cognitive revolution displaced history in teacher education and ended up promoting a decontextualized educational ideal while moving to an international context. They explain the shift as part of a new international paradigm of scientification/scientization in Western societies, that provided the foundations for a transnational program of social engineering and a tendency to promote interdisciplinarity and international cooperation ("educational multilateralism"). It was necessary to make teacher education more academic; this paved the way for the insertion of teacher education at universities in Germany and similar attempts in the United States.

However, the major shift towards internationalization and scientification of teacher preparation took place after 1945. Progressive education was made responsible for the plight of education since it did not generate intellectual life, and scientists had played a central role in the war effort. It was not only an intellectualization and scientification of classroom teaching, but a cognitive turn moving away from behaviourism and focusing on research on mental abilities. Problem solving, logical operations, and general understanding of the subject would take precedence over its mastery. Jerome Bruner called this process "scaffolding," as he wanted to transfer his engineering model into pedagogical practice; the school was expected to transform the human mind into a decoding system. Universally applicable and future-oriented ways of thinking suppressed traditional and present-oriented spatially, historically, and culturally contextualized subject matter. The teacher became a technician using new means. Cognitive psychology became dominant in teacher training in the 1980s with the application of scientific knowledge about teaching, cognitive guided instruction, and reflective teaching practice. The notion of a teacher-researcher with a repertoire of thinking and problem-solving skills grew. The role of the OECD fell in line with a systematic reform of teacher education. The teacher relying on his or her metacognitive skills underwent a kind of self-monitoring process; individual internalization of control mechanisms meant a better control of the overall system.

Russell's chapter is premised on an unfulfilled hope: putting the notion of reflective practice into action has yet to be achieved. Russell draws on Donald Schön's development of the notion of the reflective practitioner, and it is this notion, Russell thinks, that has been misunderstood, misdirected, and bent for purposes other than and beyond the original ones. The problem for Russell is located in the move from theory to practice, or action. In the taking up of the notion of the reflective practitioner, the required transition from theory to action has resulted in a loss of the original intentions of the notion. Russell provides us with a summary view of six important papers detailing reflective practice in teacher education, and notes the limitations of each. All of these in some way manage to misinterpret or misunderstand the basic intentions of Schön's original thinking on reflective practice.

Whereas Schön made manifest the importance of learning from experience, problem solving, and listening and conversing in one's practice, these essential aims of reflective practice seem to have gotten lost in the uptake of his thinking. Indeed, in some cases, Schön is bypassed completely, with the result that the notion of reflective practice bears little resemblance to his original understanding. While Schön has had an influence on the articulation of reflective practice in education, it has not been pervasive, with the result that researchers have neglected the importance of attending to how teachers can learn from their own experiences to improve their professional action. Russell laments this neglect, and presses for a re-engagement of both Schön and the importance of attending to teachers' experiences. This is particularly important for teacher educators, the audience Russell has in mind here.

Teacher educators are not generally the individuals who observe teacher candidates, nor are they necessarily reflective practitioners in their own right. There is a disconnect between the development of reflective practice regarding teacher candidates and the teacher educators who supervise them, and this contributes to the theory-practice divide rampant among faculties of education, and the resultant complaints of teacher candidates that the theoretical program bears little resemblance to practice and to practical needs.

Russell does not discuss the issue of reflective practice in the context of a globalized teacher education. But it is not a stretch of the imagination to conclude that he would think of reflective practice as a concern of all teacher education programs, everywhere. The question for teacher education in a global context concerns not the ubiquity of the need for reflective practice, but the particular shapes reflective practice will take in the varied contexts in which it arises, and the role that a streamlined and uniform structure and set of curricular aims and outcomes would have on privileging or thwarting this practice. If reflective practice is for teacher candidates to develop (and follow through on), what role does the increasing uniformity of educational standards and curricula play in helping (or hindering) the student to achieve this practice?

Whitehead's case study presents an informal assessment of the degree to which concepts of transnationalization are present in the pre-service teacher education program of one faculty of education in the province of Ontario, Canada – in particular, at the Faculty of Education at Queen's University. The author situates the issue in relation to a constellation of concepts such as multiculturalism, pluralism, globalization, and cosmopolitanism, and assumes that ideally the cadre of teacher candidates selected for the program would be multicultural in its make-up. He identifies salient themes of a transnationalized professional setting, such as a cosmopolitan and inclusionary environment and the cultivation of teacher dispositions such as open-mindedness and flexibility, as well as a passion for borderland education. The analysis of the literature of the transformation of legal education at McGill University in Montreal leads Whitehead to identify the incorporation of transnationalism in the curriculum, moving it beyond jurisdictional and systemic boundaries and creating a cosmopolitan educator – something difficult to achieve in teacher education, given its links to the state.

Whitehead also finds other guiding principles, such as the use of comparative studies and the study of philosophical traditions. The analysis of the Vision Statement of the pre-service teacher education program at Queen's and the features of the program favouring transnationalization leads Whitehead to refer to the factors affecting further transnationalizations, including the length of the program (eight months), the failure to have a transnationalized cadre of teacher candidates, the difficulties in linking underlying values and philosophical traditions to current and alternative teaching practices, and the integration of comparative inquiry in courses to promote a deeper understanding. However, he concludes on an optimistic note.

For Burbules, ubiquitous learning is anywhere/anytime learning; it is bound up with interaction, and with structured opportunities in real time. It increasingly places learning in the hands of the learner, and it is highly context-sensitive, grounded in the purposes of the moment. These alone mandate the utmost attention to learning in the "digital age." No doubt, there are also concerns. These include equality of access to technology, the need for an "off-switch" to pause the constant streaming of information, and the question of what of "traditional" learning is left in the digital wake. But there are other challenges as well, challenges that must be faced if we are to successfully navigate ubiquitous learning for and in our schools.

One is the basic place of learning transformed as ubiquitous; learning is no longer a realm unto its own. Rather, it is synonymous with the flow of human activity. The barrier between learning and other practices of human activity breaks down. A second is its irreducibly contextual feature; it is thoroughly situated. And while this is the case, some learning needs to be systematically developed so that the richness of contextual learning can take place. Third, ordinary events are learning moments in ubiquitous learning, such that facts are no longer isolated, but continuous with other facts. This requires the development of metacognitive awareness in sorting out the precise roles facts are to play in making judgments and other, associated cognitive acts. Fourth, ubiquitous learning emphasizes collaborative communities. These communities are increasingly distributive, and involve both teacher and students.

Fifth, the teacher comes to resemble more a tutor, a facilitator, than a lecturer or all-knowing authority. Indeed, students are often more aware of the technologies available and how to operate them than the teachers, and this augurs for more of a partnership or collegial relationship. The teacher comes to resemble a planner, designer, and manager, rather than a pedagogue. Ubiquitous learning equalizes the relationship between teachers and students. But, sixth, the teacher now has a more manifest role of ensuring equality among students with regard to access to and ability to navigate technologies. While ubiquitous learning equalizes relationships between teachers and students, it does not necessarily equalize the relationships between haves and have-nots in the context of the classroom and across school districts and other divisions. This is the responsibility of teachers and administrators.

Seventh, it requires the breaking down of existing theories of space, time, and location into those that are more coordinated, less temporal, and more global. Here is the connection, it seems, to the global context. Ubiquitous learning requires new configurations of space, time, and location to take advantage of the changes in human relationships that the digital age demands. Political configurations such as nations, or even micro-locations such as classrooms, need to be rethought in view of these changes. Finally, eighth, that teachers see themselves as participants in ubiquitous learning is demanded. This not only dehierarchizes teachers, but also makes them more responsible than in the past for their own learning.

Focal Point 3, "Aboriginal Education in a Globalizing Context," contains three very different contributions: "Autochthonous Ed: Deep, Indigenous, Environmental Learning," by Christopher Beeman (Queen's University); "Exploring Teacher Education Programs and Policies in Chilean Universities and Their Commitment to Intercultural Acknowledgment," by María Eugenia Merino-Dickinson (Catholic University at Temuco, Chile); and "Indigenous Spaces in Contemporary Learning Institutions: Theoretical and Methodological Frameworks in Approaching Māori Education," by Te Tuhi Robust (Te Whare Wananga o Awanuiarangi [Northlands], New Zealand). These essays are among the most unique and disparate of the collection. With these chapters (and particularly those by Beeman and Robust), we see the tension between integration of systems and autonomy of lifeworlds; "space" and "place" become central terms in this enterprise. These terms are, in Beeman's mind at least, invested with ontological significance: inhabiting the "space" and "place" of another is a deeply significant act. Ways to get at this significance might include Merino-Dickinson's understanding of "interculture" (done well), or Robust's development of *kaupapa* – indigenous spaces. In all these cases, there is an ontological commitment involving the uniqueness of the other and that other's place. Read carefully, these emerge as the most philosophical of the essays collected here.

What is the difference, if any, between Aboriginal Education and Indigenous Education? While Aboriginal Education is often construed as an education for, and by, Aboriginal members of society, this does not convey the connotation Beeman wishes to get at – the deep, ontological commitment of human and world, or place. This ontological commitment is not merely human; it is other-than-human, in that it does not make the human the essential feature of the basic relationship between human and place or world. Beeman says Aboriginal Education, while attempting to preserve cultural, linguistic, and social practices of Aboriginal peoples, does not go far enough. What is required is an Indigenous Education that digs down to the root of our basic being-in-the-world, the fundamental relation between human and place. Beeman thinks this Indigenous Education might serve Westerners well, if they can peel back the social and institutional practices (including those of colonization keeping us enslaved to a manifestly impoverished way of thinking) that keep them from seeing that the fundamental commitment to the world is not primarily human, but more-than-human, or human and place or world. We have much to learn from Aboriginal peoples, though not through the extant institutions of education; we will need to deconstruct these in order to get back to the ontological relationship we have with the world, to see the world with Aboriginal eyes. This move from "indigenous" as an ethnic term to an ontological term is a move to a deep environmental ethic – deep, because it is ontological.

Merino-Dickinson studies the degree of incorporation of indigenous culture knowledge in the curricula of nursery and elementary teacher education programs in Chile. Her chapter is distinctive among the range in this collection, in that it is a case study focused on three universities located in the regions of Tarapacá in the north, Valparaiso in the centre, and Araucanía in the south of the country. Chile does not have a strong working notion of multiculturalism in the context of existing political and cultural ideology. In fact, its understanding is both broad and nebulous. As a result, Merino-Dickinson draws on the prevailing notion of interculturality, which understands itself as a dynamic, cultural process in which two or more cultures define themselves and each other through extant cultural institutions in the context of historical processes. The resultant dialogue then depends on the orientations and strategies of the actors involved. Unfortunately, this understanding of interculturality takes place in the context of the commodification of education, brought about by the turn to efficiency on the part of nations in the current global context. To remedy this, an overt emphasis on the teaching of social justice is required.

Thus, an analysis of the presence of interculturality and the teaching of social justice in the nursery and elementary teacher education programs is due. Curricula, course programs, and professional profiles are analysed together with the voices of the students who study in these programs. The main findings show that the curricula do not incorporate ancestral knowledge of the Chilean indigenous groups (Aymara, Quechua, Pascuense, and Mapuche) that inhabit the regions mentioned above. Neither do they prepare students to interact and act pedagogically in intercultural class contexts, nor do they consider indigenous knowledge as an intercultural option to enrich teacher education programs and policies. Social justice is thus thwarted in nursery and elementary teacher education programs by the near-absence of indigenous knowledge and pedagogies.

For Robust, the inclusion of Māori ancestral houses – *marae* – on university campuses in New Zealand has been a significant development since the mid-1980s. This initiative provided indigenous space for Māori to meet, teach, and study in a culturally appropriate environment, and has since been added in other schools and educational entities. The examination of two ancestral houses in Canadian and New Zealand universities provides insight into the implementation and maintenance of policies to ensure that cultural observances are ongoing. The University of Auckland ancestral meeting house, Tane-Nui-A-Rangi, and Sty-Wet-Tan, the ancestral Longhouse at the University of British Columbia, are considered examples of indigenous infrastructure and space development within university settings. Within the context of *kaupapa Māori* – Māori principles and philosophies – the development of indigenous "space" is examined. Space is not a mere dwelling; as does Beeman, Robust asserts that space consists in and confers ontological commitment to those inhabiting.

Robust has attempted to provide a snapshot in time of the creative intent of two internationally recognized, research-led universities that have continued to seek to improve the delivery of their business. In this case, what has been described is a transformative strategy within existing resources and infrastructure. The chapter concentrates on the theoretical and methodological issues involved in carrying out a comparative case study of the two institutions. Specific attention is given to the role of critical theory and associated theoretical frameworks in the setting of understanding the context of indigenous "space," as well as the interpretation, validity, and analysis of data in the context of methods and methodologies in comparative case study research. This investigation will be of benefit to those who wish to undertake similar comparative case studies, or who are interested in the theoretical and methodological issues of similar research.

Focal Point 4, entitled "The European Setting: Erasmus, Bologna, and the European Higher Education Area," consists of the following chapters: "The European Program Erasmus on Mobility and Its Impact on the European Dimension of Higher Education," by Sylviane Toporkoff (Institut d'études européennes, Paris, France); "Harmonizing the Disparate? Bologna's Implementation in Secondary Teachers' Education in Germany and Spain," by Carlos Martínez Valle (Universidad Complutense de Madrid, Spain); "The Bologna Process and Teacher Education Reforms in Eastern Europe: The Changing Policy Terrain in Ukraine," by Benjamin Kutsyuruba (Queen's University); "Transnationalization of Higher Education Teaching and Learning at European Universities: Rethinking the Way to Wisdom," by Gonzalo Jover (Universidad Complutense de Madrid, Spain) and José Luis González Geraldo (Universidad de Castilla–La Mancha, Albacete, Spain); and "Guilded Youth? The Returns of Practical Education," by Andrew Robinson (Jean Monnet European Centre of Excellence, University of Leeds, UK).

Toporkoff traces mobility to the period of antiquity, well before universities were founded. The universities were the result of students' and teachers' need to regroup into university corporations, but as students attended various universities, there were no boundaries at the beginning. The core idea was a discovery of knowledge that was broader, more "universal," and personal, an academic *peregrinatio* (using a trans-historical language). In the fourteenth and fifteenth centuries, the universities began to lose their international character when they started to be funded based on recruitment. The idea was sponsored again in the sixteenth century by learned humanists. Toporkoff explores the European space for higher education, taking the Second World War as a landmark, and traces the history of the creation of the higher-education space. Some key points include 1976, when the European Commission revisited the idea of developing European citizenship banking on youth, and the 1980s, when the notion of studying in foreign countries developed with the onset of a European educational policy. The focus in the chapter is on mobility: the Erasmus Programme allows 200,000 students each year to study and have a training period abroad. Erasmus was created upon the realization that, while there were six million students attending university, only one in a hundred studied in another country's university. The Declaration of the Sorbonne in 1998 centred on the economy of knowledge and gave birth to a European space of higher education.

The Europe of knowledge is understood as social and human development to consolidate European citizenship, capable of giving its citizens the competences to face the challenges of the new millennium. Mobility was conceived as a means to reinforce European cohesion, to encourage transnational cooperation, and to support the emergence of a European citizenship. Mobility includes mobility of studies, mobility of experience, and mobility of teachers. The idea behind this was that students needed an experience of Europeaneity; the advantages would be the development of communication skills and cultural sensitivity. The last part of Toporkoff's chapter deals with other European programs and also with the problems emerging from the evaluation process, in part due to differences in the functioning of transnational mobility and understanding the factors of success.

Jover and González Geraldo's chapter discusses the re-instantiation of a wisdom society as (part of) the response to the disenchantment First World nations have with global projects such as the Bologna Process, and brings re-instantiation to bear on the issue of teacher education. The authors structure their argument along the lines of dialectic: an initial encounter with the Bologna Process, a disencounter from the process, and a final re-encounter with the process, though of a different form or shape than initially. The initial encounter is one of excitement and agreement. The disencounter is one of questioning and even scepticism; the re-encounter, the authors claim, must be one of wisdom. The initial encounter absorbs the rhetoric of the knowledge society put forth by the Bologna Process and other similar bureaucratic mechanisms. This is a process driven by standards (not standardization), and it is implemented through instrumental objectives, especially economic competitiveness. The student is viewed as a client or consumer in this understanding. Issues of student competence rise to the fore. The disencounter is manifest in the increasing calls for attention to other aspects of pedagogy and the student, specifically creativity and ethical commitment. This has somehow been lost in the rush to competence and information processing. The re-encounter emerges in the bridging or bringing together of the aims of competence and what the authors call "wisdom."

The authors have a pluralistic notion of wisdom, drawn from such figures as Aristotle, Montaigne, Dewey, Hutchins, Jaspers, Marcel, Arendt, Freire, and David Hansen. Central to the notion, however, is the place of Being. Being – variously described as consciousness, as attitude, as *sagesse* – is not mere contemplation, nor is it a scientific and technical adjustment of the person. Wisdom is embodied, and resides in the (older) idea that deep knowledge cannot be transmitted, but must be self-achieved. This returns the teacher to the role of a Socratic *maieusis* that seeks to cultivate a capacity for a questioning life, rather than a purveyor of facts or disseminator of knowledge. Wisdom is also manifest in self-growth, and this is a chief aim of the wisdom society. We must aid one another to grow into ourselves, as it were, through connecting knowledge to the surrounding culture. Oddly enough, this wisdom is thought to be utopian, suggesting it is more of an ideal than a live possibility.

In his chapter, Martínez Valle argues that the Bologna Process aimed from its inception at creating a European Higher Education Area that would harmonize superior education and foster mobility of students and the labour force within Europe. He believes it could be construed as a perfect example of the Stanford neo-institutional conception of globalization. This paradigm maintains the existence of a world-level educational culture and ideology that supports the diffusion or globalization of models – or what Martínez Valle calls "rationalized myths" – leading to educational isomorphism across the world. However, multilayered decision instances, new governance, and vagueness or contradictions in the objectives allowed doubt about the achievement of the desired homogenization. The maintenance of heteromorphism is evident in one of the arguably central objectives of the reform: secondary-school teacher training (SSTT). As the historic-comparative analysis of the German and Spanish cases shows, different political constellations, regional and national academic cultures, and institutional inertia reproduced the differences in SSTT both between countries and within the German states. In practice, the SSTT reforms implemented under the aegis of Bologna, rather than the diffusion of a global model, could be understood as local-idiosyncratic answers to the reforms of secondary school that took place in both countries during the previous decades.

What is particularly salient for Martínez Valle are the extra-systemic "conditionings" that remain unchanged by the agreements – the resistances and mis- or un-appropriations of practices mandated or strongly suggested. The resultant SSTT systems have, paradoxically, resulted in an even more nationally specific set of practices, requirements, and contents, often on the basis of the use of national myths, common educational values, and the prerogatives of the elite universities (especially in Germany). Also paradoxical are some of the unintended effects of the Bologna Process; in Germany, for example, rather than increasing mobility, it has served to decrease it. And whereas the attempt to harmonize disparate education systems is the goal of the process, in practice, these mandates have served to institutionalize students (especially in Germany) even further.

Robinson, relying on both his practical experience and his recent scholarship, uses the financial burnout of the global economy to outline a timidly emerging model that has its roots in the very history of Europe, generating a model sensitive to social equity within the context of globalization and harnessing new communication technologies. The implications for education are powerful; in his views, elites in the Western world are facing a crisis of re-examination of the types of higher education and further education adapted to a flawed economic and social construct based on inequality. He writes that "the mantra of the knowledge economy has been shown to be insufficient by itself, when over-focused on an unregulated financial service sector, to build, and now re-build, Western economies in the face of a multipolar world." His thesis is that the adaptive learning cultures and instruments of manufacture and capufacture – a combination of practical skills and intelligence – will need to be harnessed in domestic markets, and from there, compete and collaborate in cross-border regional and international arenas. The local, modest, citizen-centric approach to growing the skills base gives the best chance to citizens, but this cluster-based approach should be balanced and strong, with an active engagement to work with other communities of practice, in both the private and public sectors, beyond the domestic market.

Robinson's chapter gives examples of current educational developments, mainly in Germany. Blending classroom with onsite experience, Germans, in his view, were able to understand commerce in a world which remained stubbornly but understandably differentiated by culture, history, language, and traditions. It is not a globalized economy, but a connected set of very different economies and societies. At the same time, he argues that given the influence of Continental power blocs and the human capital needed for the future, smaller economies should not retreat to narrow, technical, and provincial specialization, thinking only of domestic demands. Instead, they should "blend a new local resilience with active strategies to utilize the resources from wider labour pools and ecosystems." Robinson elaborates on examples of revival of the *métiers nobles* in Europe, particularly in France in the form of the Compagnons du Devoir program based on mobility. The United Kingdom has already felt the influence of the Compagnons. Recruiting colleges, companies, and organizations are seeing the value of cultivating practical intelligence and linking apprentices to the skills and technologies of tomorrow. The Compagnons model demonstrates how a Europe-wide medieval tradition of mobility and skills, revived in France and transmitted to the United Kingdom, forms the basis for a new tradition that will benefit not only local young people, but also their communities as well as the ambitions of giant multinationals.

Robinson sees an incoming need to adapt the ethos of education, curricula, and benchmarks of success to the nurturing of students as smart, self-managing learners, ready to widen their portfolio of skills regularly and open to the benefits of international experience and practice. Focusing in Europe, he foresees teacher education – currently narrowly national with a small cohort of teachers of teachers – as having a worldly mindset, preparing a cohort of people for the real European economy, and paying attention to projects which show how cross-border learning stimulates smart thinking as well as teaching and learning with an active sense of social justice and participation. He calls for the integration of older forms of training and fellowship, such as apprenticeship, and the enactment of transnational efforts to stimulate the labour market more efficiently than the one operating only within national boundaries. It is important, in his view, to harness both the technological opportunities of e-learning and the structural changes needed in local, national, and international educational provision and attitudes.

Focal Point 5, "Transnationalization and State Policies," includes two case studies: "Teacher Education Policies in Chile: From Invitation to Prescription," by Cristián Cox, Lorena Meckes, and Martín Bascopé (Pontificia Universidad Católica de Chile, Chile); and "Internationalization in Canadian Higher Education: The Ontario Experience, by Ken Snowdon (Snowdon & Associates, Toronto, Canada).

Teacher education in Chile is a reflection of neoliberal educational policies and the consequent process of privatization. The offering of teacher education – and in particular, initial teacher education with low entrance requirements – was fed by a process of upward social mobility and privatization of education. The massification of higher education took place through the private sector and the offering of new professional programs, including teacher education. The growth has been at the expense of academic selectivity in the choice of applicants. The chapter by Cox, Meckes, and Bascopé analyses the evolution of policies regulating the offering of teacher education that aim at improving the programs and set requirements for institutions. Since 2008, the Ministry of Education adopted a more active role in the implementation of policies moving towards normative regulation. Between 2004 and 2012, diverse commissions and external reviews made public the insufficiency of teacher education in Chile, particularly in relation to the demands of the new curriculum. The most crucial and consequential was the 2004 OECD review of Chilean educational policies that concluded that there was a capacity gap in the teaching force. There were also the reports of the National Commission of Deans of Faculties of Education (2005) and the Presidential Advisory Council on Education (2006). The latter was convened after a protest movement among secondary students demanding quality and equity in education. The OECD report, *Teachers Matter* (McKenzie et al., 2005), was in line with the critiques and with the recommendation of a graduating or exit exam. The policy measures – including introduction of standards for teachers finishing their course of studies, exit tests, mandatory accreditation, and entrance scholarships for education students – are part of international trends.

However, Chile exhibits a hybrid set of policies reflecting an ambivalence: the standards are orientations, weakening their implementation. All the regulatory policies reveal competing advocacy coalitions for and against the policies. The ambivalence is evident in the exit exam for new graduates willing to teach in schools that receive public funding. The exam is still voluntary for both institutions and their graduates, although the results are published and may serve as a form of market regulation. The programs that were closer to the requirements for the selectivity of students joined the program that would allow them to apply for full tuition grants, but those that had traditionally set the bar lower for their applicants did not. The latter institutions instead put emphasis on programs not reached by regulations.

The accreditation programs are, in effect, not implemented by a national agency, but by a market of agencies. Accreditation bodies are not allowed to close programs that are not accredited, leaving the regulating role to the market. In this way, the economic interests of the higher education institutions that offer these low-quality teacher preparation programs are protected, and the demands for social mobility are not frustrated. It is a hybrid approach with some structural shift of policy options.

Snowdon examines the trends in international student enrolment in Ontario, first, through a summary of major trends from the 1960s to the present and, second, through a brief analysis of the aims of higher education institutions and the Ontario government. This allows Snowdon to make some comments regarding the "state" of internationalization in higher education in Canada and, specifically, Ontario. For Snowdon, human capital and the expansion of the capital asset base are at stake in the programs for internationalizing education in Canada, and the government and the higher education institutions themselves have been, and continue to be, major players in this asset base. Snowdon is cautious with respect to the government, in terms of both its history of regulation of international education and its effects on the higher education institutions. Indeed, it is not too much of a stretch to say that government intervention in this regard has been for the most part mixed, and often baleful, as it has served to hinder the flexibility of the higher educational institutions to raise their student base and set their own fees. In this regard, the deregulation of fees for international students has been a boon for higher educational institutions and for international enrolment generally.

It is clear for Snowdon that higher educational institutions are now financially stretched and can no longer serve to increase international enrolment without a change in government regulation. While Canada generally has had stepwise increases in international enrolment, Ontario has sometimes lagged behind, and PhD and masters-level enrolment has run 20 per cent and 15 per cent respectively – numbers not much better than in the mid-1980s. International tuition is topped out in Ontario, and a so-called head tax on these students will only drive costs higher. Snowdon seems pessimistic regarding the capacity of government to develop long-range visionary policy over and against short-term gain. While Snowdon does not pause to discuss what this vision should be, it seems likely that it will be one generated not from the Ontario government but from the higher educational institutions themselves.

Conclusion

We have collected in this volume a set of studies that we have sorted according to five focal points. These points are certainly helpful for delineating what is of utmost concern regarding teacher education in a transnational world. Each of these chapters bears on a focal point; some bear on more than one. All testify to the complexities of educating globally. We should see these points as intersections, indeed, as configurations in which a nesting of themes (historical, philosophical, sociological, political, economic, public) is evident. For, while these points can be separated, in practice they operate together. We should therefore see these points not merely as heuristic devices for organizing trends, terms, and ideas, but as markers for the actual practices of transnationalization. They are the ideas made concrete in the context of teacher education in the world in which we currently live and breathe. Thus, we can usefully trace back from these points the practices to which they give shape. That this is so will be made clearer in reading the chapters.

NOTES

1 See Dale, this volume.
2 For an example of this cynicism, see Olsson, 2004.
3 One major source of the pushback has been the International Student Movement; see http://www.emancipating-education-for-all.org/forum/39.

FOCAL POINT 1

Socio-Political, Cultural, and Intellectual Spaces Where Teacher Education Is Located: A Historical, Sociological, and Philosophical Approach

This focal point, interdisciplinary in character, situates the development of teacher education mainly under the conditions of globality. It opens with a sociological analysis by Roger Dale addressing the relationship between the university, teacher education, and the globalization of teaching; in particular, it emphasizes the new characteristics and pressures shaping teacher education. Then, James Scott Johnston engages the reader in intellectual discussions of globalization in a critique of both critical theory and post-structuralism. He makes a case for pragmatism as a framework that provides a theory of self and other that would lead to a theory of self and community – a better way to understand and change structures of global practices. Next, Rosa Bruno-Jofré and Josh Cole engage the reader in a grounded historical case of global and national interactions at various levels that framed the insertion of teacher education in the university. The chapter describes how skilled communities construed responses to economic and political projects and negotiated both intellectual and ideological claims. The focal point closes with a chapter by Nel Noddings that describes a view of cosmopolitanism and its limits in the American context, and opens avenues for a critique and proposals of aims alternative to those that are hegemonic, such as ecological cosmopolitanism. In the last instance, the goal is to attempt to bring together different communities, social practices, cultural understandings, and local economies in a larger understanding of overarching practices.

1 Globalization, Higher Education, and Teacher Education: A Sociological Approach

ROGER DALE

The enormous range and depth covered in this volume is testimony to the richness and spread of the issues raised by a transnationalizing – or as I shall suggest, globalizing[1] – world. What is especially intriguing and original about the book is its focus on teacher education, which sometimes feels like the neglected child of education – unloved by practising teachers, who rarely are strongly supportive of their training; marginalized in the university, where it plays a kind of Cinderella role (though one that is as lacking in a Prince Charming as it is replete with ugly sisters); and frequently identified as the most obvious, or easiest, scapegoat for a plethora of education's failings. My aim in this paper is to try to indicate the bases of the shallowness of such understandings by examining what might be revealed through the relatively new lens of the relationship between the university, teacher education, and globalization.

Teacher Education (TE) in one sense stands in the centre of a confluence of distinct but mutually influential forces, all of which shape it in multiple ways, but none of which wholly determines its shape and purpose. However, this position is a very interesting one analytically, since it provides a valuable and unique place from which to observe the ways that the relationships between these various forces are realized in a particular instance. We can also see that the playing out of the forces in this case provides insights into their operations individually, as well as more broadly into the wider relations of power in the current era, not only in teacher education itself but also in the governance of education systems, including the university sector. In particular, the somewhat Janus-faced position of teacher education – looking simultaneously into the university and out to the world of schools, and to a degree connecting them to each other – enables the development of several fascinating lines of inquiry, through which it may be possible to expose the nature of its lowly status.

In this chapter, I will discuss briefly the relationships of these different forces, and then try to come to some conclusion about how we might understand more clearly the nature of teacher education in a transnational world. At the centre of my argument is the idea that the forces and practices of globalization have shaped – in novel, sometimes independent and sometimes overlapping, ways – all the major elements of the relationship between the significant "players" in teacher education and the university. This includes the two principals themselves, and their mutual relationships, but also the changing nature of the work of teaching and schooling more broadly. My aim is therefore rather theoretical; I shall not be considering issues of the techniques and "effectiveness" of teacher education so much as the consequences for teacher education of different and changing conceptions of its roles, processes, and contributions.

I will consider first the relationship between globalization and the university, then the relationship between globalization and TE, with a final section on the relationship between TE and universities. My focus will be mainly on England and the United States, though I will also refer at times to understandings that may be gained from considering the development of relevant aspects of the Bologna Process in European higher education.

Globalization and the University

Theoretically, the argument is set at a very broad level. It suggests that the current state of the universities, like other institutions of Western modernity, is fundamentally a reflection of and a response to the changing nature of the relationship between capitalism and Western modernity. In developing the fundamental argument, I follow Boaventura de Sousa Santos in suggesting that it is crucial to the understanding of the current global predicaments to distinguish between the trajectories of capitalism (as found currently in the form of neoliberal globalization) and of Western modernity, and to examine the relationships between them. As he puts it:

> Western modernity and capitalism are two different and autonomous historical processes ... [that] have converged and interpenetrated each

> other ... It is my contention that we are living in a time of paradigmatic transition, and, consequently, that the sociocultural paradigm of modernity ... will eventually disappear before capitalism ceases to be dominant ... partly from a process of supersession and partly from a process of obsolescence. It entails supersession to the extent that modernity has fulfilled some of its promises, in some cases even in excess. It results from obsolescence to the extent that modernity is no longer capable of fulfilling some of its other promises. (Santos, 2002, pp. 1–2)

He goes on: "Modernity is grounded on a dynamic tension between the pillar of regulation ([which] guarantees order in a society as it exists in a given moment and place) and emancipation ... the aspiration for a good order in a good society in the future" (p. 2). Santos describes modern regulation as "the set of norms, institutions and practices that guarantee the stability of expectations"; the pillar of regulation is constituted by the principles of the state, the market, and community (typically taken as the three key agents of governance; see Dale, 1997). Modern emancipation is the "set of oppositional aspirations and tendencies that aim to increase the discrepancy between experiences and expectations" (Santos, 2002, p. 2). However, he continues, "what most strongly characterises the sociocultural condition at the beginning of the century is the collapse of the pillar of emancipation into the pillar of regulation, as a result of the reconstructive management of the excesses and deficits of modernity which ... were viewed as temporary shortcomings and as problems to be solved through a better and broader use of the ever-expanding material, intellectual and institutional resources of modernity."

The central argument of this chapter will be that universities do offer a very good example of Santos's argument. It does not seem too far-fetched to see in the recent history of the university just the kind of fusing of emancipation and regulation to which Santos refers. Historically, I will argue, the modern university could be seen as much more attached to the pillar of emancipation than to the pillar of regulation. However, more recent experience points to, first, the increasing involvement of the university with the pillar of regulation and, second, the increasing absorption of that pillar by the rules and practices of the market. In particular, the changes to the university might also be seen as forms of "reconstitutive management" of the deficits of modernity, as they have been exposed by the demands of neoliberal capitalism.

We can give some flesh to these arguments by considering some key ways in which they have had an impact on the university as an institution, all of which have consequences for its relationship with TE. The broad nature and effects of those changes for the university have been succinctly set out by Mary Henkel. Writing in the context of England, but concerned with globally generated conditions that have come to affect all universities (considering how they come together in the all-pervasive rankings that now embrace most universities in the world), she suggests:

> The changing relationships between the State, the market and higher education created new restrictions and new freedoms for higher education institutions. Higher education had acquired a new political salience, as knowledge and learning were defined as key economic and social drivers. At the same time, governments sought to reduce the State's share in the sum of resources supplied to higher education institutions (HEIs) and to shift the relationship within which money was allocated towards one of contract. In the context of a general drive in advanced economies towards new public management, HEIs were required to increase their efficiency and to subscribe to various forms of quality assurance. Before long, income maximisation became an institutional imperative driving them to compete both for more restricted and conditional public funding and in a range of markets. Like commercial organisations they had to find ways of combining participation in global, national, regional and local markets. Unlike commercial organisations, they were also endeavouring to sustain academic values and forms of knowledge. (Henkel, 2002, pp. 30–1)

These pressures have been reflected in, for instance, the "massification" of university study, which has seen massive increases in the number of university students, with several countries now enrolling close to half of each age cohort in universities. This has been accompanied in many places by the development of cost-sharing measures. Despite the wide diversity of national and subnational funding patterns, universities all over the world have been forced to find new sources of funding, all of which both altered and increased universities' funding bases. This was most directly experienced via students' contribution to the cost of their higher education in the form of fees. This had a transformative effect on the relationship between the university, academics, and students, in that it presented universities with new forms of risk to manage, in the shape of the student as client or consumer, especially for teacher education.

A third element of these qualitative changes has been the requirement for universities to contribute directly and indirectly to the development of "knowledge-based economies," which have become a global phenomenon. The range of the global knowledge economy (GKE) discourse is evident in the World Bank's Knowledge Assessment Methodology, through which every country in the world can work out how close it is to being "knowledge-based," and the steps it needs to take to reach that status (World Bank, 2012).

This new mantra has very different implications from the human capital theory assumptions that underlay the accumulation problem twenty years ago. The same could be said about "promoting competitiveness." The state's role is no longer confined to providing an infrastructure that will underpin the productive economy, but rather expands and shifts to become concerned with the promotion of nationally based industries on the world market (competition state). Nor is it any longer confined to providing research infrastructure; the state's role includes active involvement in the funding and direction of research. Perhaps the most frequently noted consequence, certainly in contexts like higher education (HE), is that the state itself becomes directly involved in processes of capital accumulation. The most widely recognized example of this, certainly in studies of HE, is the development of HE as a crucial "export industry," where the contribution of teacher education is via the production of students with the knowledge, skills, and competences to drive the knowledge economy.

However, the most important and pervasive of these impacts on universities has been that delivered through the influence of what is referred to as New Public Management (NPM). NPM appears to have provided a kind of template for reforms to university governance. A great deal has been written about the NPM, but for present purposes it may be sufficient to point to its critique of the poor performance of the public sector, the latter's lack of responsiveness to clients, its lack of accountability, and its tendency towards "provider capture," which were taken to characterize the public sectors of all Western countries. Four aspects of the NPM are important here. First, the NPM was equally applicable to all sectors; it was a set of principles for public management that held irrespective of whether the sector was the police or health or education. Second, the NPM was both prescription and diagnosis, solution and framing of the problem. It embodied and was the mechanism through which key elements of neoliberalism were installed in public sectors around the world. Third, it involved the replacement of a relationship of trust between the university and what are now (and in consequence of this shift) typically referred to as its stakeholders, with a relationship of contract. Finally, the NPM was concerned with the formal relationship between process and outcomes (or, more narrowly, outputs), not with outcomes themselves.

Three major consequences have occurred as a result of this, all of which have had considerable repercussions for teacher education in the university. These have been to prioritize issues of process over issues of substance, which were to a degree to be met through proxies of performance, rather than established through explicit policy; to demonstrate, frequently quantitatively, the achievement of "quality" across all activities of the university; and to demonstrate "excellence," especially in the form of research excellence, also to be demonstrated quantitatively. Even more important, this last consequence enabled a competitive element to be introduced.

From Quality Assurance to Reputational Risk

The most succinct means of indicating the nature and consequences of these changes for universities as a whole, including TE within them, is to examine briefly the relationships between and consequences of quality assurance and reputational risk, especially those generated by competitive ranking systems, which are key media through which the consequences of neoliberalization of the university have been delivered. The terms quality and rankings lead us along somewhat different paths, which themselves point to and reflect the emergence of new expectations of universities as institutions and of higher education as a sector. Fundamentally, we may see "quality" – in the form of quality assurance mechanisms – as fulfilling two key functions for the new university. On the one hand, it was a key element of the audit regime that had been imposed on universities as part of the NPM, which extended to all parts of their operation, including, very importantly, their students. On the other, it provided an evidential basis for membership of a national, and often more importantly, an international higher education community; this was of particular importance for TE in the university.

At the same time, ratings and indicators, especially of research performance, were being transformed into the basis for universities' claim to individual excellence based on competitive comparison on a world scale, through the medium of such ranking mechanisms as league tables. Quality assurance (QA) provides elements of consumer – and funder and other stakeholder – protection against inadequate products or service, or against cheating. In doing so, QA creates, by categorizing and reifying in various and multiple particular ways, the very "tofu-like"[2] concept of quality. Here, the societal requirement for a reliable and trustworthy form of protection for two particular sets of consumers and beneficiaries of human capital at a national level – but also, with the growing emphasis on the international mobility and migration of people, at a transnational level – generates institutional responses in the form of mutually compatible QA systems.

However, in recent years we have witnessed a significant shift from QA as providing "benchmarks" of national (and increasingly international) collective *consumer protection*, to providing global *competitive comparison* between regions, national systems, and individual institutions. This is an instance of the growing gap among the institutions of what had been, until the last quarter of the twentieth century, a fundamentally nationally based version of capitalism, and those which have subsequently taken a neoliberal form with the ambition of minimizing the influence of borders both between and within countries. That shift may be viewed as one that sees universities move along a continuum that runs from national human capital producers to key players in the emergence of *a global knowledge economy*. Different universities in different countries are at different stages of this shift, but we may observe an increasing "globalization" of the bases and criteria against which their "progress" is measured.

This is not all to play down the importance of international agreements on QA (e.g., see Hartmann, 2010). Comparability itself represents a very important tool of governance of the sector internationally. For instance, in the Bologna Process of harmonizing HE in Europe (and not just in the European Union, as around half the members of the Bologna Process are not members of the EU), QA issues become central. As Saarinen (2005) points out, "the quality policy goals are set jointly in transnational settings, requiring different kinds of negotiations and discursive strategies" (p. 200). In other words, international influences find their way into national policies persuasively rather than authoritatively, which also strengthens the local (institutional) level over the national one. However, as she goes on to add, this is a rather different conception of QA than the one we have associated with the NPM: in the case of Bologna, "the motive behind quality work is to ease the recognition and comparison of higher education systems and degrees for the purposes of mobility and employability. The few mentions of 'academic quality' or 'quality of higher education and research' have been subordinated to the comparability and attractiveness of European higher education" (Saarinen, 2005, p. 201).

However, one major area of change resulting from these shifts is that in a sense QA has been absorbed by, and into, what are increasingly seen as at least three new major *risks* for universities. These have become more severe since 2007–8, though they existed in some form before that. Crucially, these risks all threaten the reputation of (individual) universities, and their consequences reverberate through all aspects of institutions' work. In addition, universities have been increasingly governed by the creation of competitive rankings, which put them into direct comparison with each other. These risks are those contained in university rankings; student consumer responses, especially the ways that these are deployed for commercial purposes; and financial risks, as assessed by credit rating agencies.

The difference between quality and rankings is that benchmarks of quality are (1) threshold, not comparative, concepts; (2) in effect zero-sum – you either have them or you don't; (3) are by intention a framework for action that can be met in diverse ways; (4) subject to formal audit – how do we know that you did what you said you would do?; and (5) not subject to quantification, and hence not available for ranking. "Quality" itself has a homogeneous quality; it is signalled "clerically," rather than "performatively."

What all these different mechanisms have in common is a press towards the *quantification* of difference – and hence, its comparative measurement. Consequently, this has resulted in the transformation of benchmarks into rankings, or of quality into quantity, which at the same time dialectically transforms quantity into quality, in the process shifting the basis of risk and multiplying it; as we will see, this is directly experienced in TE. This *quantifiability* is a key aspect of what makes other forms of risk qualitatively different from QA, where the risk is much more to institutions as a whole – for QA is by no means confined to the academic activities and personnel of the university. Thus, risk management becomes a matter of central importance to universities, individually as well as (or rather than) collectively. One aspect of this is that reputational rankings call forth *performative* responses, rather than the ticking of boxes, a very significant shift. In essence, we may see QA as setting the rules for institutional survival in the sector, while rankings construct, reveal, and reflect reputational risks for individual institutions.

The importance of risk management to universities was made most apparent in 2000, when the Higher Education Funding Council for England (HEFCE) – the body charged with overseeing the demands for increased accountability for the use of public funds and good governance – required all universities to introduce risk management as a governance tool; this was based on a private-sector model. HEFCE guidance "directs the governing body towards a high level, risk-based approach to establishing a sound system of internal control, covering all types of risk" (HEFCE, 2001). This in itself creates a new kind of risk for HEIs in the form of their reputation with HEFCE (see also Huber, 2011).

What this implies is that, as two German authors write, "risk management is part of a broader set of transformations of universities from being ungovernable and idiosyncratic collections of individuals to being accountable organisations with clear missions, formal structures, professional management and an 'appetite' for risk" (Krücken & Meier, 2006).

So, the rationale behind risk management becomes a dominant one as it is reproduced through internalization (Power et al., 2009). The organization has no other means to see itself but through the lens of risk management: "As an increasingly explicit managerial category [risk] is both a specific symptom of late modern intensification of organizational and individual concern with appearances, and plays a *performative* role in shaping managerial behaviour" (ibid., p. 302). However, this also means that particular forms of events, experiences, outputs, and so on need to be *defined as* ***risks***, not as "an unfortunate position on an arbitrary data sheet" (Huber, 2009, p. 85), and in this way, "reputation" has emerged as the key and dominant currency of risk to universities worldwide. The basis of these "calculative representations of reputation" is increasingly the research output, based on international rankings of universities which acquire increasing prominence as they acquire recognition. As Power et al. (2009) put it, "they generate self-reinforcing behaviours and shift cognitive forms and values, motivations and missions" (p. 311). They not only order but determine the basis of order, and thereby construct reputation so that reputation is produced by the forms that measure it.

Crucially, too, rankings transform organizational reputation and "constitute it as a managerial object" that pervades most areas of the institution (Power et al., 2009, p. 302), and thus "perpetuate the internal organizational importance of externally constructed reputation," so that "organizational performance indicators for internal purposes come to be reactively aligned with those which inform an evaluation or ranking system" (p. 312) – and also vice versa. Thus, "reputation" as a perceptual construct may be one component of a ranking metric in the first instance, but the rank itself has come to influence the perceptions of key constituencies, such as clients, potential students, and potential sponsors.

However, lest we assume that all elements of risk to the university are to be found in the ranking league tables, we should recall the other two components mentioned earlier. The first of these was student assessments of their university experience, which may be especially important in the field of TE. These include such in-depth analyses as those carried out by the HEFCE-backed National Student Survey,[3] to say nothing of "Rate My Professors," which claims to have collected 13 million opinions on over 1.5 million professors.

The other risk component mentioned above was universities' credit ratings, which have become increasingly important as sources of funding for universities are diversified. According to a 2003 report by the Observatory on Borderless Higher Education (OBHE):

> In a context of long term decline in government funding per student, and increased national and international competition, Standard & Poor's (S&P) [a leading international credit rating agency] gives the best outlook to universities with diversified income streams, which it argues better enable institutions to ride out / take advantage of changing external conditions … Ratings form an additional layer of "quality assurance" and public information about the standing of higher education institutions, and are another example of the growing role of third parties in the running and assessment of higher education. As many universities gradually reduce their dependence on public funding, ratings will be a useful way to secure private capital, but this reduced dependence will equally open institutions to greater vulnerability. (OBHE, 2003)

One fundamental mechanism propelling the kinds of shifts we are referring to as reputational risk management is the work of transnational organizations seeking to instantiate a basis for a GKE. The central feature of all these bases of reputational risk from the present perspective is that they are indeed "transnational" rather than "international." The chief objective of international quality assurance mechanisms is to facilitate comparability of national systems, for the purpose of enabling greater mobility, for instance. However, as we will see in the case of the Bologna Process, the chief objective of the international organizations, and the ends towards which the efforts of the rankings agencies are bent, is essentially the creation of a supranational set of criteria for ranking the performance of individual universities in a burgeoning GKE.

It could be objected that TE is relatively immune from such risks because it has not been, and is rarely expected to be, a major contributor to the university's research ranking. However, that would underestimate the power and prevalence of risk management in the university, since, in effect, "the organisation has no other means to see itself but through the lens of risk management" (Huber, 2009, p. 85), as all its different component agencies are drawn into it, for the "reputation" itself embraces all of a university's component departments and activities – administrative as well as academic, teaching as well as research – so that it is "held" by the responsibility of all of them. Reputation enables, but has to be enabled.

The extent and significance of the penetration of the university by reputational risk management can be seen most significantly in the effect it has on a critical condition of the flourishing of the liberal university. The liberal university is based on the idea, possibility, even necessity, of "loose coupling" or mutual insulation of different elements in order for it to develop in the ways and in the directions which it has been able to do. Above all, perhaps, the insulation of academic activities from other demands on the university is what enables and acts as the basis for academic freedom.

Globalization and Teacher Education

Concerns about the nature and state of TE have historically centred on the best ways to do it, to whom, and its costs. However, as Marilyn Cochran-Smith (2005) points out, it has more recently become a much more general and high profile "policy problem" (p. 4). It is a problem that "all developing and developed countries must deal with," where "the goal is to determine which of its broad parameters that can be controlled by policymakers is most likely to enhance teacher quality and thus have a positive impact on desired school outcomes." Our argument here is that this policy problem is both globally relevant, as "a new national preoccupation with the supply and quality of teachers is now almost universal" (Furlong, Cochran-Smith, & Brennan, 2009, p. 7), and globally generated, by the increasingly high stakes attached to education systems, as well as by the responses of international organizations such as the OECD and the World Bank to these issues. As the OECD claimed in its publication *Teachers Matter* (McKenzie et al., 2005), teachers, "as the most significant and costly resource in schools" (p. 1), are crucial to implementing the school improvement agenda. In addition to the global high-stakes agenda, TE is affected by the changes in the work of teachers and the nature of the teaching profession that are associated with the high-stakes accountability focus, and also by the direct intervention of the OECD and the World Bank, as well as major multinational firms, in issues of teacher education.

Beyond the consequences mediated through its effects on the university as a whole, neoliberal globalization has had notable direct effects on teacher education across the world. Most important, it has reinforced, at transnational levels, the mantra that in a global knowledge economy all countries need effective education systems that will ensure the production of appropriately skilled and "knowledged" students. It has also reinforced the notion that the effectiveness of those forms of education is due in considerable degree to the effectiveness of teachers, which is in turn closely associated with the effectiveness of teacher education. And of course, since this is a global message, about the high economic stakes involved, it involves countries and systems being in competition with each other, which places teacher education at the forefront of the global battle. This competition necessarily produces more losers than winners, which partly accounts for the denunciation of national teacher education systems for their contribution to lack of national economic success.

It is also important to note that these changes and expectations have led to changes in the expectations of the teaching profession and its organization, which themselves have direct repercussions for teacher education. This has led to considerable "restructuring of the teacher workforce" in many countries (see B. Carter et al., 2010; Compton & Weiner, 2008). Christian Maroy (2009) argues that this involves the supersession of what he calls the "bureaucratic-professional" model of teaching by an "evaluative state" or "quasi-market" model (p. 71). This is clearly closely linked to the striking increases in the accountability demands placed on teachers (e.g., see Cochran-Smith, 2005, pp. 16–17). Perhaps most directly impinging on the work of teacher education has been the pervasive shift in how "quality" is defined and appraised in teacher education – from its meaning of "cultural competence, ethical practice, and responsiveness to learners within a broad definition of curriculum" – as two New Zealand teacher educators put it – to "definitions that seem set to feature test scores and value-added measures of literacy and numeracy" (Ell & Grudnoff, 2013, p. 82), which typically take the form of post-hoc evaluation of teaching through forms of high-stakes testing.

Teacher education has also been directly affected in many countries by the ideology that the market is always and necessarily superior to public provision, and that competition necessarily leads to superior performance. This has introduced the idea that competition will lead to the improvement of teacher education, and the encouragement of alternatives to the traditional university-based form, from both public and private suppliers. One of the more interesting and pervasive of these initiatives has been the "Teach for …" movement. The "Teach for …" initiatives are social-enterprise-based organizations, claiming to recruit outstanding graduates to teach in schools where the majority of pupils come from the poorest families. They typically receive abbreviated forms of training and are expected to teach in disadvantaged schools for two years, before moving into "leadership" positions in education or in the wider business world. They originated in the United States (Teach for America), but are now found all over the world, including India, Malaysia, and Australia. This movement constitutes a broad critique of teachers and teacher education. It implies that teaching is not a job that requires careful training and induction, and is not a career that the "best" graduates would want to stay in for more than two years, though it may provide good training for a more lucrative leadership role in business.

The Representation of the Teacher by International Organizations and Firms

One easily overlooked aspect of the internationalization of teacher education is the construction of the good teacher and good teaching practices by international organizations, through exhortations about the importance of education and the pressing need to improve it. As noted above, there seems to be a form of a global causal sequence with respect to the importance of teachers' work: national prosperity depends on an active and effective knowledge economy, which in turn depends on a thriving higher education sector, which itself is dependent on successful students, who are themselves dependent on being taught by good teachers, who are in turn dependent on effective teacher education. Though this script takes very different forms in different places, it consistently and increasingly informs the work of international organizations working in education. Thus, while it might be excessive to claim that it has a major influence in advanced countries, one would also be remiss to ignore the effects of such powerfully backed discursive interventions on the work of teacher educators everywhere – not least because many of them are involved in teacher education beyond their own shores, or their own continents. Two recent examples are especially important. They both frame the parameters of the modern teacher's work, and the forms of preparation for it.

The first of these is the World Bank's System Assessment and Benchmarking for Education Results (SABER), which documents "teacher policies for public schools in developed and developing countries in order to inform policy choices and promote policy dialogue, globally" (Klees et al., 2012). However, according to Steiner-Khamsi (2012), "both the language and the policy goals used in SABER-Teachers clearly depict a negative image of teachers" (p. 15). This "should be read as an invitation to decision-makers to come up with reforms that police and sanction the masses of underperforming teachers and provide material incentives to a small group of teachers who perform well. Without any doubt, the programmatic conditionality of the World Bank in the area of teacher policies is teacher accountability." However, she notes that "judging from the list of 'best practices' presented in the publication, the portfolio of eligible projects for World Bank funding are contract tenure reforms, pay-for-performance reforms, and other types of accountability reforms that, if implemented globally, make a profession that already suffers from universal shortage and low prestige even less attractive" (ibid., p. 15).

Similarly, Robertson (2012) sees SABER as a response to "what the Bank regards as chronic teacher incompetence" (p. 584), and as "represent[ing] a significant intervention into shaping governing frameworks aimed at teachers in national education systems" (p. 585). Again, while these may not be models that the majority of teacher educators would endorse – and the uptake of SABER seems to have been far less than enthusiastic (as noted by Robertson) – they do contribute to the broader framing of the issues of concern to teacher educators.

The World Bank is not the only international organization to involve itself directly in teacher policy. As we noted above, the OECD has also concerned itself with challenges facing the teaching profession, including recruitment, uncredentialed teachers, high levels of attrition, and low social status. The findings of their report "were used to launch a major benchmarking project on teachers, the *Teaching and Learning International Survey* (TALIS), which reported in 2009" (Robertson, 2012). The TALIS findings "were used to frame the first *International Summit on the Teaching Profession* in 2011 hosted by the US Department of Education, the OECD, and the global teachers union, Education International. A feature of this event was the cast of sponsors: a mix of philanthropic foundations and corporations,[4] all with an interest in the governance of teachers" (ibid.).

It is not only international organizations who have been presenting diagnoses and remedies for the problems of teachers. As Cochran-Smith (2009) shows, "education is big business, as evidenced by the sharp rise in for profit education providers, and stunning increases in production and profit in the text book industry" (p. 16). Robertson (2012) also refers to a report carried out by the international consulting firm McKinsey and Co., whose central argument was that "the quality of the education system cannot exceed the quality of its teachers," highlighting "the centrality of effective teachers and systems to support the development of teachers' pedagogical practices." This led Robertson to argue that "the mechanisms of global governance of teachers are being transformed from 'education as (national) development' and 'norm setting,' to 'learning as (individual) development' and 'competitive comparison.'" This change is being "orchestrated by key global agencies who argue there is a crisis in the teaching profession, and have sought to colonize the field of symbolic control over teacher policy," with "tendencies toward a convergence of agendas amongst these global actors, and the creation of a visible epistemic community amongst global teacher policy entrepreneurs" (Robertson, 2012, p. 586). However, she notes that important differences exist among these actors, as well as among "the national settings they seek to influence."

However, and by contrast, if we consider the particular case of TE in Europe, and in particular the reforms introduced under the Bologna Process, we find that TE is among the areas of university activity that is least affected by it. A report on the impact of the Bologna Process on curricular reform in universities found that "in all European countries, the structure of teacher training is strongly bound and shaped by national context and history. The state as the main employer of graduates tends to have a strong influence on the structure and content of teacher training, and the related requirements generally tend to lower the flexibility of provision in this field. The programmes cater mainly for national labour markets" (Centre for Higher Education Policy Studies [CHEPS], 2008, p. 39).

This does not mean that the European Union has not had ambitions to be involved in teacher education, or has been inactive in the field. There have been a number of attempts at bringing greater coherence to teacher education in Europe, but these efforts have amounted to very little, for two reasons in particular. On one hand, "there is no consensus on what school education is about, on the priorities for curriculum, on the skills and qualities required to be a teacher, or the responsibilities to be undertaken" (Sayer, 2009, p. 159). On the other, the constitutional position – which limits the EU to assisting member states to improve quality in the area of education (see Dale, 2009 for a fuller and more detailed account) – has essentially precluded it from direct involvement. Thus, its activities have been largely confined to exhortation, pointing out to member states the importance of good teaching and of teacher education as a means to bring this about, with actual activities essentially confined to the sharing of good practice and peer learning activities.

The area where the EU has had the most impact has probably been that of upgrading status ("universityfication") of teacher education in newer member states (Zgaga, 2008, p. 41). However, despite its limited ability to directly influence teacher education in member states, the EU's message has essentially been the same as that of the other international organizations which have begun to involve themselves in the area: improved educational performance is crucial in driving forward the global knowledge economy, and improving the quality of teaching is central to achieving this, which means that teacher education must do better at the national level. However, it would be unwise to assume that because there has been little direct EU involvement in teacher education, it has had no effect on the university context in Europe. There are linkages discernible between various forms of European cooperation in higher education, through the Bologna Process, as well as the EU's "Lisbon agenda" – essentially its framing of what is required to make Europe into the most competitive, dynamic, knowledge-based economy in the world. This common agenda inevitably influences the institutional contexts within which the (albeit rather different) national forms of teacher education find themselves operating.

The Relationship between Teacher Education and the University

In order to register the nature and extent of the changes being brought about by some of the shifts discussed so far, it will be helpful to consider how they relate to earlier changes in TE. To this end, we can draw on a very thoughtful account of the historic relationship between teacher education and the university in the United States. David Labaree (2005) explores the historic and contemporary relationship between teacher education and the university as one where "the university provides status and academic credibility" and "teacher education provides students and social utility" (p. 297). Two main tensions[5] in these relationships, Labaree argues, are what he refers to as "education's status problem" and "the consequences of using university status to overcome this problem." I will spell out briefly his accounts of these issues, and then attempt to consider how they may be changed as a result of changing relationships between globalization and the university.

Labaree attributes teacher education's low status to three things in particular. First, he notes the legacy of the market pressures that shaped the normal school in the United States.[6] According to Labaree (2005), the legacy of this history has been that teacher education retained its "reputation for being an academically weak program produced on the cheap for students of modest intellect" (p. 297). Further, the evolution into a university "meant that the normal school lost both its professional mission and its control over the education of teachers." Teacher education "seemed responsible only for the vocational side of things," which "put education on the lowest tier" of the university's status hierarchy (p. 298). Second, its "bad company" reputation came from serving stigmatized populations, recruiting mainly lower-class students, and working with undistinguished and undifferentiated populations (in contrast to graduates of other professional schools, such as medicine and law). Third, the nature of teachers' work is such that their skills appear "transparent and ordinary" (p. 299).

In weighing up the balance of costs and benefits to teacher education and to the university, Labaree (2005) points on the one hand to the status and expertise boosts that accrued to teacher educators in the university and, on the other, to the potential loss of teachers' professional mission. From the side of the university, the benefits came in the form of both large numbers of low-cost students, as well as the claims it was able to make of being "useful" and making a relevant contribution to the solution of social problems. The potential cost to the university lay in undercutting its own academic credibility, so that "as a weak program with benefits it is useful to have around as long as it is not embarrassing, but its position in the university is never completely secure" (p. 302). He goes on to indicate that this threat is what divides the responses of more and less prestigious universities.

What differences to this account, if any, might we see as resulting from the kinds of forms of globalization we have been discussing in the chapter? In terms of TE's status, it may appear that little has changed, but in reality we are able to point to two quite different bases for the current stigmatization of teacher education. On one hand, TE has suffered a very great loss in its ability to shape, contribute to, or control its professional mission and the forms it might take. On the other hand, the examples provided to support the low-status arguments are now perhaps somewhat different, largely as a result of the hugely increased stakes attributed to the outcomes of teaching and teacher education, and the much wider consequences of their alleged failures, referred to at several points above.

In terms of the company it keeps, the status of traditional teacher education has been distinctly reduced by the emergence – often with official encouragement – of alternative forms, all of which seek to reduce both the costs and teacher educators' claims to special and necessary expertise. One particular form we have noted above is the emergence of the "Teach for ..." programs, with their explicit suggestion that teaching is not a job that requires a great deal of preparation for those with better degrees, who should also not consider it as a career, but rather as a means of fast-tracking themselves into careers more suitable to their talents.

Labaree's discussion about the nature of teacher educators' work as an issue in thinking about their status led me to think about the discussions of the proletarianization of teachers' work that were so prominent in the 1980s and 1990s in the sociology of education. These discussions were largely based on Braverman's proletarianization thesis that centred on the separation of the execution and conception of work. That separation seems to be becoming even more pronounced in teacher education, as states seek to lay down "scripts" of various kinds and introduce post-hoc accountability regimes of increasing degrees of severity. However, another basic element of the current condition of teacher education that derives from the NPM should be recognized: the replacement of trust by contract. This is, of course, not confined to teacher educators – indeed, it may be relatively new to their profession, but the audit accountability that pervades the public sector is a feature of the changing regime under which they operate in an era of globalization.

If we turn to the balance of benefits that Labaree sketched out, it may seem that on the surface little has changed in terms of the benefits accruing due to teacher educators' association with the university. However, the increasing centrality of research achievement in the calculation of institutional reputation does tend to weaken their status within the university rather than strengthen it, while what could have been seen as strength – involvement in the solution of social problems – has become both more mandated and expected than in earlier times. Also, more significantly, this has become an area where they are more likely to be pilloried than praised, blamed rather than appreciated.

Finally, there is one additional aspect of teacher education's affiliation with the university that should be mentioned. With the profile of reputational risk in the university, and especially its pervasiveness across all its areas of activity, teacher education becomes more tightly coupled to the university as a whole. It therefore loses the benefits of partial detachment, and is involved in further responsibilities over which it has little control.

Conclusion

The changing conditions of existence of both HE and TE in an era of neoliberal globalization, and the consequent complex changes in the relationships between them and their separate practices, have major implications for TE in particular. It is possible to point to five of these, which emerge from the analysis briefly sketched out above.

First, TE is now assailed from even more sides and in qualitatively different ways. Its association with the university, always a little rocky as Labaree shows, has taken on new dimensions of risk and threat, as it becomes incorporated more deeply into the university (though without much evidence of this raising its stature) through involvement with quality assurance and risk management regimes.

Second, while TE may have become more tightly coupled to the university, it has at the same time, as part of the same set of processes, become more loosely coupled with both education policymaking and with schools themselves, as they, too, come under increasing accountability pressures. These includes shifts from responsibility for outcomes to accountability for outputs, and changes in the conception of the work of teaching from "professional" to technician.

Third, the great apparent paradox here is that, as Robertson's work shows, the importance of the work of teaching is very clearly recognized by the international organizations who act as drivers of globalization. However, in this changing recognition there is a changing conception of teaching, and of the role of TE. Thus, as Cochran-Smith argues, TE has itself become a policy problem, and one that international as well as national organizations seek to shape.

Fourth, a further crucial aspect of these changes, as again Robertson's work shows, is that the university's role as key provider of TE is under pressure from private organizations that claim to do the job more quickly, cheaply, and effectively – though what that "job" is, requiring only minimal qualifications and training, is clearly very different from that which TE has traditionally assumed.

Fifth, and associated with this, TE is clearly perceived by many international actors, including for-profit companies, as in itself a potentially commercial and private rather than public enterprise. Thus, all three elements of the authority of the state, as the "traditional" funder, provider, and regulator of TE, are beset by the forces of globalization and their drivers in international organizations.

In conclusion, while there are few who would dispute the significance of the relationships between globalization and education, it is important to resist the tendency to simplify those relationships – that "this happened because of globalization" – or to reduce the many dimensions of complexity that are implied by those relationships. It is hoped that this brief account does indicate something of the nature and consequences of those complexities in the field of TE.

NOTES

1 Transnationalization is certainly an improvement on internationalization as the term through which to label the enormous range of changes we have seen in the governance and organization of education, but it still retains a sense of "the national" at the centre of the stage, even as it seeks to register the inadequacy of the national to capture the nature of the changes. However, it can lead to neglect of forces and discourses that shape the national, for instance, but have no recognizable national affiliations. An interesting recent account that follows the paradigm of internationalization as it is quite narrowly defined here comes from Sieber & Mantel (2012), who argue that "internationalisation is largely about 'foreign' influences

on developments in teacher education" (p. 7). They go on to discuss the phenomenon as essentially a form of educational "transfer," which suggests identifiable transferers and transferees. For a critique of such conceptions of policy transfer, see Dale & Robertson (2012).

2 By "tofu-like," I refer to concepts that have no intrinsic meaning in themselves, but take their meaning from the particular environment.

3 The NSS is a high-profile annual census of nearly half a million students across the UK. It is an established survey and produces influential higher-education public information, giving students a powerful collective voice to help shape the future of their course and university or college. The survey asks mostly final-year undergraduates to provide feedback on their courses in a nationally recognised format. The NSS offers the opportunity to provide honest feedback on the learning experience. It asks twenty-three core questions, relating to six key aspects of the student learning experience, overall student satisfaction, and satisfaction with the students' union, association, or guild. Students are also given the opportunity to give positive and/or negative comments on their whole learning experience at their university/college. http://www.thestudentsurvey.com/your_voice.html#.Uzam2F5upN0.

4 Metlife, National Education Association, Simons Foundation, the Ford Foundation, Pearson Foundation, American Federation of Teachers, Bill and Melinda Gates Foundation, Carnegie Corporation of New York, Google, W.K. Kellogg Foundation, the William and Flora Hewlett Foundation, Adobe Foundation, Intel Corporation, Noyce Foundation, Scholastic Inc., and National Public Education Support Fund.

5 Although not directly germane to the discussion here, Labaree (2005) also considers a third tension, that of the role and place of teacher education in elite and regional universities in the United States.

6 Again, this is rather different from the history of teacher education in much of Europe, for instance, but there are sufficient similarities between the trajectories Labaree describes and those of many of those countries to make the comparison worthwhile.

2 Theorizing Globalization: Rival Philosophical Schools of Thought

JAMES SCOTT JOHNSTON

Globalization Theory and Philosophies of Education

Read a manuscript discussing educational theory in light of globalization. What *philosophical* lenses are you likely to find? If you range back through the past twelve years or so, chances are it will be the same two or three of the many possible lenses extant.[1] These are critical theory and post-structuralism (Burbules & Torres, 2000, p. 13).[2] More recently, pragmatism has come into vogue (Tan & Whalen-Bridge, 2008). There are obviously alternatives to these, but they seem to be underrepresented, to judge by a (cursory) review of the literature.[3] Now, what are we to make of this state of affairs? One might be tempted to say that (1) theory is in vogue, and that philosophies such as critical theory, but especially post-structuralism, are tailor-made for theory. One might also be tempted to say that (2) critical theory and post-structuralism take seriously political economy – a field of scholarship that is essential to, if not the ground of, the various theories of globalization. Finally, one might be tempted to say that (3) critical theory and post-structuralism are right and true – or if not true, at least the best philosophical accounts for any theory that purports to examine social relationships – and therefore are the right and true or best philosophical accounts to undergird theories of globalization.

I believe that (1) and (2) are correct, but that (3) is wrong. I will discuss why (3) is wrong in a further section. For now, I wish to concentrate on (1) and (2). I believe (1) to be correct on the basis of the sheer volume of studies devoted to globalization and education that are critical-theoretic or post-structuralist in philosophic persuasion. While not denying (3) here, I think the fact that the range of philosophical options from which theorists of globalization could have chosen is vast, and yet the choices made so narrow, accounts for more than just the "rightness" of these particular philosophies. It accounts for their fashionability, as well. I believe (2) to be correct because most of the scholarship on globalization does concern both the political-economic origins and consequences of national and multinational strategies. There is of course, much scholarship on groups, communities, and individuals involved, as these are often on the receiving end of the effects of globalization – but these relationships, too, are very often cast in a political-economic framework.

However, fashionability and the close alliance with scholarship on political economy are not the only, nor even the greatest, reasons why I think critical theory and post-structuralism are regnant. I think they are regnant because they have done an inestimable job of pressing the contradictions and confusions of what I will call *extreme subjectivity*. That is, I imagine that this feature of critical theory and post-structuralism invites theorists of globalization to take them seriously, and more seriously, perhaps, than other philosophies. Both critical theory and post-structuralism lay great emphasis on the denial of or opposition to strong notions of self, subjectivity, and self-consciousness. This is in contradistinction to earlier traditions of philosophy, and particularly the Cartesian tradition. The Cartesian tradition was the tradition of the irreducible "I" that thinks according to "clear and distinct ideas." René Descartes (1998) put it this way in the second Meditation:

> Therefore from the very fact that I know that I exist, and that meanwhile I notice nothing plainly different as belonging to my nature or essence except this alone, that I am a thinking thing, I rightly conclude that my essence consists in this one thing, that I am a thinking thing. And although perhaps, or rather … I have a body that is very closely conjoined to me, nonetheless because on the one hand I have a clear and distinct idea of myself insofar as I am only an unextended thinking thing, and on the other hand a distinct idea of my body insofar as it is only an extended non-thinking thing, it is certain that I am really distinct from my body, and can exist without it. (p. 56)

Extreme forms of subjectivity brought many philosophical puzzles, and these puzzles took the better part of three hundred years to unravel. The Cartesian germ ensconced itself in much modern philosophy and only in the twentieth century – partly through the efforts of both critical theorists and post-structuralists – has it been exposed and sidelined.

For example, the claim that we have unlimited and direct access to the contents of our minds has been steadily challenged since the time of Immanuel Kant. And the mind-body dualism that claims there is one substance but two kinds of properties (physical and mental) has taken a severe beating in the twentieth century. Beyond this, the claim that the self is the locus of consciousness, and even that the self is systematic and self-articulating, has come into question. Philosophies of otherness, or philosophies privileging strong accounts of the social, are preferred to philosophies that emphasize a strong, overly autonomous or individuated, self.

What is it about subjectivity that philosophies of otherness, in vogue in theories of globalization, decry? After all, strong accounts of autonomy are privileged in philosophies of subjectivity (accounts that at least imply a robust sense of individual freedom, dignity, and moral personality). But therein lies the problem: individuality or, more precisely, individualism. This understanding is closely allied to a classical liberal conception of the free and autonomous person who has inalienable rights to property. More recently, it is allied to a neoliberal conception of the individual – a veritable *homo economicus* whose relations with others are merely instrumental (Rizvi, 2008, p. 257). This particular political conception of the person is thought to be given further emphasis by accounts of autonomy, which are in turn bolstered by theories of subjectivity.

Thus, and despite the seeming differences between critical theory and post-structuralism, each shares (at least) one feature in common with the other: anti-subjectivism. By anti-subjectivism, I mean the disavowal of the Cartesian claim that the "I" is the central metaphysical mark of knowledge. This claim has been variously understood as the "philosophy of consciousness" and the "philosophy of the subject" (Habermas, 1992, p. 16). From German Idealism onward, and with varying degrees of success, philosophers have attempted to distance themselves from the extreme subjectivist standpoint. The first and common way was to recognize the central importance of the other for self-consciousness. This "counter-enlightenment project" was begun in earnest by Gottlieb Fichte, who developed rudimentary theories of the subject and recognition (Habermas, 1987; Henrich, 1992). Fichte asked two questions in *The Foundations of Natural Right* (1796). The first is how self-consciousness is possible. The answer is that the self posits itself as a not-self and this (Fichte tells us) is the Law of Freedom or Autonomy (Fichte, 2005, p. 21). However, this law concerns only the possibility of self-consciousness; self-consciousness, as it actually occurs, is a development that relies upon the recognition (*Anerkennung*) of another. Fichte calls this development "heteronymous nature," to distinguish it from his talk of autonomy (p. 94). Heteronymous nature consists in what Fichte calls "a summons" (*Aufforderung*) – the summoning of the other, who then recognizes herself as an agent (p. 95). Unfortunately, Fichte did not develop this account further; it was left to later idealists, and particularly G.W.F. Hegel, to offer a robust account of self-consciousness involving recognition.

Hegel did so in the *Phenomenology of Spirit* and later publications. For Hegel (1977), recognition of the other is central to overcome the conflict that our conceptual understanding of what he calls "consciousness" (*Bewusstsein*) brings upon itself when it attempts to adjudicate the role of self in regard to appearances and laws (forces) (p. 162). "Consciousness" is a form or shape of thought or Spirit in which the role of the self becomes evident in any understanding of the world. However, there is a rank solipsism in devolving thought on the self ("I") alone: the self cannot ground the claims of itself to understand the world without recourse to something other – at least, not without circularity. This other can only be another self (p. 178). The turn to the other in understanding our understandings of self is the operating premise of the shape of thought Hegel calls "self-consciousness" (*Selbstbewusstsein*), and is a premise taken seriously by many later philosophers – critical as they might be of Idealism.

Critical theory and post-structuralism accept, in part, the critique of subjectivism that German Idealism first brought forth. However, what this turn to the other means for them, differs. For critical theory, as I will maintain, the turn to the other manifests as a turn away from subjectivity towards the object. This is notable particularly in Adorno's project of conceiving a "negative dialectics" to rival and supplant what he sees as the Hegelian dialectics of synthesizing opposites. For post-structuralist theories such as Derrida's, this is done through essentializing difference, the metaphysical denial of something like a Hegelian unity, totality, or synthesis of the concept. But critical theory and post-structuralism are not the only – and in my opinion, not even the best – anti-subjectivist philosophies offering accounts of the other and otherness extant. I will argue that only pragmatism, and specifically the pragmatists Dewey and Mead, accomplished a turn to the other that refused to neglect the self. This was accomplished through positing a rival theory of the self, one that is naturalistic and immanent, rather than metaphysical or totalizing. Furthermore, pragmatism is the only viable philosophy offering a plausible account of problem solving, an account which can be tailored to the context of teacher education. I will discuss each of these attempts at overcoming subjectivism in order.

Rival Philosophies of Anti-Subjectivity: Critical Theory, Post-Structuralism, and Pragmatism

The Anti-Subjective Basis of Critical Theory

Critical theory has its roots in the early-twentieth-century project of criticisms of social institutions and culture famously undertaken by the so-called first generation of Frankfurt School researchers, especially Max Horkheimer and Theodor Adorno. The Frankfurt School for Social Research was an empirical-critical program, unlike the strictly ideological programs plentiful among Marxists in the early half of the twentieth century. Horkheimer in particular laid the most problematic element of these ideological programs – the rise of instrumental reason – at Kant's feet. For Horkheimer (1993), Kant's separation of science and morality (knowledge and faith) was tantamount to allowing scientific rationality unlimited access to culture (p. 20). For Adorno, Hegel's (and Kant's) legacy is more ambiguous. Adorno recognized the importance of Hegel to Marx's later theory of socialism and the importance of German Idealism generally to the project of the emancipation of the working classes; he was, however, critical of the supposed "tyranny of the concept" in Hegel's philosophical system. Hegel, Adorno claimed, left no room for the material, for matter, for the objective. Everything was sublated in spirit (Adorno, 1973, p. 7). Spirit, in turn, was Absolute Identity, the affirmation of all that is and is not. Characteristically, Adorno thought of Hegel's account of Absolute Identity as a failure:

> The principle of absolute identity is self-contradictory. It perpetuates non-identity in suppressed and damaged form. A trace of this entered into Hegel's effort to have non-identity absorbed by the philosophy of identity, indeed, to define identity by non-identity. Yet Hegel is distorting the state of facts by affirming identity, admitting non-identity as a negative – albeit a necessary one – and misconceiving the negativity of the universal. He lacks sympathy with the utopian particular [the "empirical content"] that has been buried underneath the universal – with that non-identity which would not come into being until realized reason has left the particular reason of the universal behind. (p. 318)

Against this abstractionism, Adorno famously countered with a "negative dialectics," which, as an anti-identity philosophy, would re-establish the primacy of the material: "To change this direction of conceptuality, to give it a turn toward nonidentity [the non-subject; the not-self; the not-I], is the hinge of negative dialectics. Insight into the constitutive character of the nonconceptual in the concept would end the compulsive identification, which the concept brings unless halted by such reflection. Reflection upon its own meaning is the way out of the concept's seeming being-in-itself as a unity of meaning" (Adorno, 1973, p. 12). It is debatable whether Adorno was successful in overcoming the Hegelian machinery of identity and unity.[4]

The Anti-Subjective Basis of Post-Structuralism

I will use the umbrella term post-structuralism for a distinctive Continental response to Martin Heidegger's call for an end to metaphysics. The concern here is the essentially dispersed nature of discourse, thought, and practice.[5] Post-structuralists do not deny truth, nor do they admit that their philosophical conceptions are relative among other conceptions. They defend their core ideas and ideals, and even posit an "ultimate reality" (Schroeder, 2005, p. 268).[6] In contradistinction to the history of Western philosophy, which stresses unity, wholeness, organicism, and centrality (particularly in the wake of Descartes), post-structuralism stresses fragmentation, disunity, diffusion, and difference. Often, the goal is to get back behind the claims to unity, to reveal the essentially fragmentary nature of various systems of truth and discourses (in Michel Foucault's terms). The fragmentary nature of these is best represented by notions such as Gilles Deleuze's rhizomes, Jacques Derrida's *trace* and critique of self-presence(s), and Foucault's "regimes of truth." Philosophies of the subject – which supposedly privilege a spectator theory of knowledge, truth, and subjectivity, and which in turn account for a privileged self-consciousness – are unmasked as totalizing narratives that conceal their essential lack of depth. Derrida (1993) asks:

> But what is consciousness? What does consciousness mean? Most often, in the very form of meaning, in all its modifications, consciousness offers itself to thought only as self-presence, as the perception of self in presence.[7] And what holds for consciousness holds here for so-called subjective existence in general. Just as the category of the subject cannot be, and

> never has been, thought without the reference to presence as *hupokeimenon* or as *ousia*, etc., so the subject as consciousness has never manifested itself except as self-presence. The privilege granted to consciousness therefore signifies the privilege granted to the present; and even if one describes the transcendental temporality of consciousness, and at the depth at which Husserl does so, one grants to the "living present" the power of synthesizing traces, and of incessantly reassembling them. (p. 68)[8]

If consciousness is the power of synthesizing (and reassembling) traces in the moment, post-structuralism (and Derrida's deconstruction) is the activity of setting them free.

Sometimes subjectivity is turned on its head. In this inversion, subjectivity connotes an extreme self-fashioning individual. Foucault's Nietzschean-inspired inward turn to aesthetic self-cultivation is the best example of this. His attempt to recuperate a quasi-Stoic care of the self for the contemporary context is the counterpart to his denial of subjectivity (Foucault, 1988). In Foucault's estimation, the self is constructed through habit, practice, and disposition, rather than reason, autonomy, or reflexive self-awareness. These practices Foucault famously labels "regimes of truth": "'Truth' is linked in a circular relation with systems of power which produce and sustain it, and to effects of power which it induces and which extend it. A regime of truth … is not merely ideological or superstructural; it was a condition of the formation and development of capitalism. And it's the same regime which, subject to certain modifications, operates in the socialist countries" (Foucault, 1980, p. 131). We are locked into practices inasmuch as we have no other means through which to conduct our discourse(s). Our only hope (and it is a dim one) is the Nietzschean-inspired endeavour to self-cultivate aesthetically – to will to be otherwise, by inculcating habits and attitudes that operate against the grain of the dominant.

The Anti-Subjective Basis of Pragmatism

The first Anglo-American school of thought historically critical of extreme accounts of subjectivity and the philosophy of consciousness is, of course, pragmatism.[9] This is particularly true of William James and John Dewey. James (1956) was famous for his dislike of "Hegelisms" and he saw German Idealism in particular as endlessly multiplying abstract ideas, culminating in a vacuous Absolute Spirit. To this James contrasted radical empiricism and pragmatism. James was an empiricist at heart;

questions of knowledge and truth were ascertained not by abstraction or idealization, but by experience and the outcome of experimentation. Nevertheless, James had in common with German Idealism (and particularly, Hegel) the criticism of phenomenalism and crude empiricism in favour of an understanding of knowledge tempered by time, place, sentiment, and circumstance. In many ways, James naturalized Hegel's notion of the developing self-aware self, particularly with his apt descriptions of the self as both material and personal.[10]

For his part, Dewey acknowledged the debt to Hegel. Dewey began as a neo-Hegelian and tried to unite spirit and nature in an overarching psychological account of self. He was unsuccessful at this; however, Dewey would eventually provide a hugely successful experimentalist account of psychology. He can be called a naturalized Hegelian: in place of subjective Spirit, Dewey has growth; in place of civil society, Dewey has community; in place of the state, Dewey has democracy.[11] Adjustment, adaptation, and other naturalistic metaphors serve as substitutes for Hegelian metaphors of alienation, rupture, sublation, and self-sundering. Dewey discarded subjectivism and, after his initial enchantment with neo-Idealism, was critical of the metaphysics he saw as all-too prevalent. Consciousness Dewey admitted, but it too was naturalized; in Dewey's estimation, there was no Absolute Spirit to which consciousness ascends. There were merely the relations of meanings built up through inquiry – itself an experimental accounting of mind and thought.[12] Here is Dewey discussing consciousness directly:

> The ties and bonds of associated life are spontaneous uncalculated manifestations of this phase of human selfhood, as the union of hydrogen and oxygen is natural and unpremeditated. Sociability, communication, are just as much immediate traits of the concrete individual as is the privacy of the closet of consciousness. To define oneself within closed limits, and then to try out the self in expansive acts that inevitably result in an eventual breaking down of the walled-in self, are equally natural and inevitable acts. Here is the ultimate "dialectic" of the universal and individual. One no sooner establishes his private and subjective self than he demands it be recognized and acknowledged by others, even if he has to invent an imaginary audience or an Absolute Self to satisfy the demand. (Dewey, 1981, p. 187)

More than any other recent thinker, Dewey rejected the dualism he thought lay at the heart of Cartesian and much post-Cartesian philosophy – a dualism he found pernicious because, as he argued, the world was carved up into non-natural entities and ideas that had to be fitted together again in a systematic, all-encompassing philosophical account. The dualism, however, existed only in the minds of philosophers.

Ranking Philosophies for Globalization Theory

Contemporary accounts denying subjectivity deny the relationships and connections between disparate phenomena and events. Contemporary accounts often do not have an account of unity and difference; instead, what they provide is an account of unending difference. Here we may think of post-structuralist attempts at deconstructing or otherwise unpacking claims of unity and identity and the various schools as gathered under the umbrella of a "philosophy of dispersion" (Schroeder, 2005, pp. 267–8). These argue that organic unity – ultimate reality – is endlessly fragmented and this is made evident through investigations into social institutions and the social sciences (Foucault), the metaphysics of self-presence (Derrida), and philosophy itself (Deleuze). Taken together, a very large swathe of what we consider intellectual thought (including history, politics, sociology, philosophy – indeed, all the human sciences or *Geisteswissenschaften*) consists in relations, linkages, and elements that are endlessly differentiated. This claim often gets expressed in the language of "heterogeneity" or "paralogy," or "multiplicity." We may also include Adorno's (1973) "negative dialectics" (pp. 12, 19). The equation of unity in unity and difference gives way to an essentialization of difference. And each difference is differentiated into further differences, seemingly ad infinitum. In no case can an account of identity in which "what is, is and what is not, is not" be construed from these attempts – for "what is" is always giving way to "what is not," with no opportunity for reconciliation or return.[13]

The problem with essentializing difference (and its *sequelae* of relations endlessly differentiated, de-centred, and fragmented ad infinitum) is twofold: first, we would need a conceptual understanding of unity in order to see the endlessly differentiated *as* endlessly differentiated. This was one of Hegel's points in the *Science of Logic* (1969): we can only see something for itself from the purview of its unity with something other than itself (something for other) (p. 63). Absent this unity, there can be no negativity, and no other from which to differentiate. In other words, a dynamic logic that conceptualizes unity and difference (contra

Adorno and Derrida) is required to represent endless difference, dispersion, or negation.[14] Second, and more important, each of the differences we elucidate in a deconstructive process is itself a unity; as difference is endlessly differentiated, so each alighting on difference is an alighting on some unity – even if this unity is further differentiated. It is not optional that we consider any particular idea or conception (or representation) a unity; in order for further differentiation to occur, we must infer back from the point we now occupy to the previous and claim *that this was a unity*. All accounts – post-structuralist included – must admit this, and this is why essentializing of difference ad infinitum is bound to failure.

There are further philosophical conundrums that arise. Without an account of unity and difference, we cannot say why, when, or under what circumstances we should consider phenomena, experiences, or ideas connected or unconnected; we cannot theorize the conditions under which these might or might not be related; and we cannot draw inferences regarding these connections or relations. We also have no explanatory power when it comes to events or situations because, absent a theory of unity and difference, we cannot draw relationships between occurrences. And if we cannot do that, we have no business making normative (including political) claims about the reasons why we prefer this or that program, or why one program should be preferable to another. We would not understand when phenomena or objects or ideas are to be brought together, under what circumstances they are to be brought together, or when phenomena or objects or ideas are to be differentiated from one another. We would be left with Hume's explanations for (causal) relations – association, proximity, and custom – with no understanding of how (or why) these operate in various moral contexts and situations.

In terms of the self, we would be unable to say how representations come together or what the relationships between representations are. As we would have recourse to neither descriptive metaphysical accounts of the self's unity (I am thinking here of Kant), nor immanent metaphysical accounts of the self's unity (such as Hegel's or Dewey's and Mead's, as I shall discuss), we would be left with the notion of the self as a "bundle or collection of different perceptions" (Hume's account of the self), but with no understanding of why the representations and meanings the self supposedly orders operate as they do (Hume, 1978, p. 253).

Pragmatism (at least, on Dewey and Mead's accounts) avoids these conundrums. Pragmatism has an answer to the question of the self's unity, and it is a positive answer. Unlike in critical theory (Adorno's) or post-structuralist accountings of self, there is no wholesale turn to the negative, or to essentialized difference. Consider again Dewey's account of how we recognize ourselves in recognizing others:

> The ties and bonds of associated life are spontaneous uncalculated manifestations of this phase of human selfhood, as the union of hydrogen and oxygen is natural and unpremeditated. Sociability, communication, are just as much immediate traits of the concrete individual as is the privacy of the closet of consciousness. To define oneself within closed limits, and then to try out the self in expansive acts that inevitably result in an eventual breaking down of the walled-in self, are equally natural and inevitable acts. Here is the ultimate "dialectic" of the universal and individual. One no sooner establishes his private and subjective self than he demands it be recognized and acknowledged by others, even if he has to invent an imaginary audience or an Absolute Self to satisfy the demand. (Dewey, 1981, p. 187)

G.H. Mead gives an even more robust accounting of the role of consciousness. He says,

> Our whole experiential world – nature as we experience it – is basically related to the social process of behaviour, a process in which acts are initiated by gestures that function as such because they in turn call forth adjustive responses from other organisms, as indicating or having reference to the completion or resultant of the acts they initiate ... The whole content of mind and of nature, in so far as it takes on the character of meaning, is dependent upon this triadic relation within the social process and among the component phases of the social act, which the existence of meaning presupposes. (Mead, 1934, p. 112)

Mead continues: "Consciousness or experience as thus explained or accounted for in terms of the social process cannot, however, be located in the brain – not only because such location of it implies a spatial conception of mind ... Consciousness is functional, not substantive; and in either of the main senses of the term it must be located in the objective world rather than in the brain – it belongs to, or is a characteristic of, the environment in which we find ourselves" (p. 112). It is enough, pragmatists will say, to claim that the self is self-aware at some level or in some sense, and that this is a condition for knowledge, communication, and associated living. Mead's naturalized, Hegelian alternative to mentalist approximations of consciousness makes Dewey's point even clearer and more forceful.

While all the accounts discussed here are anti-subjectivist, what should make Dewey and Mead's accounts more attractive to educators developing a theory of globalization than the critical theory and post-structuralist ones is that they have naturalized, immanent metaphysical accounts of self and others that rely on neither a *wholesale turn to the negative* nor an *essentialization of differences*. There is a dialectical movement, in other words, which proceeds from self to other and back again, whereas critical theory and post-structuralism *turn away from the self* and *remain fixed at the site of the other*. We can theorize how the self transforms itself through the other in these naturalistic accounts of pragmatism, a transformation that is denied to critical theory (Adorno) and post-structuralism through their reification of negativity, otherness, and difference.

Pressing Pragmatism's Advantage

Having an immanent, naturalized accounting of self and other allows for a dialectical understanding of the relationship of person to community, a relationship necessary to understand ideas of global community. Theories of globalization need such an account for two reasons: first, to explain how relationships among persons, cultures, and languages take place and how socio-economic differences come about and operate; second, to demonstrate why we ought to go about securing better ones in the face of problematic situations. I will discuss both of these reasons.

Communities establish themselves organically, not transcendentally – that is to say, communities come together over natural needs such as survival, trade, and economies, as well as the more familiar groupings of family, tribe, language, and state/nation. There is no transcendental sense in which a group is a group. There is thus nothing more unique about groups and communities than persons or individuals. They each have their natural, social existence and they are the other's point of departure. Second, an immanent and naturalized account of self and other operates on a model of transformation (what Dewey would call "growth") that is dialectical (Dewey, 1987, p. 21). Tensions between the relation of self(s) to other(s) – and other(s) to self(s) – serve as the point of departure for inquiry into the social conditions that manifest in the tension. Out of the solution to (social) problems a community of persons with shared interests and experiences derives.

This community is premised on experiencing and sharing problem solving, rather than a transcendental claim defining what a community is beforehand. Thus, a community's origins are traced to the shared experiences and problem solving of its individuals. This is both the site of origin for novel communities as well as the key to how to theorize the development of new communities from established ones (communities based in language, geography, kinship, economy, gender, and race, as well as political communities such as state and nation). Novel communities develop out of existing ones through persons' attention to shared experiences and social inquiry into social problems, and they do so without destroying the existing communities to which these persons already belong. Certainly, these existing communities transform, but they are transformed by becoming larger and fuller iterations of themselves, capable of not only housing the relations that form what they once were, but of expanding to include the new relations – the passage of community to what Dewey (1982) once called the "great community" (p. 360).

This is a naturalized variant of the Hegelian motif of "sublation" (*Aufhebung*) (Hegel, 1977, p. 29). Tensions internal to communities brought about by existing social problems bring on social inquiry; social inquiry transforms the community through novel relationships and resultant social practices. The older community is transformed: while maintaining many of its older relationships and practices, it takes on new ones and becomes a larger and more progressive iteration of itself. The key to transforming the community is social inquiry and social problem solving. Once tensions are identified within the community, those within must undertake inquiry of the conditions under which the community is experiencing problems, investigate these problems, propose solutions, and carry these out. The community, in other words, must operate experimentally to determine and to solve its problems.

Solutions to problems posed by globalization theory require a similar approach. Attention to the problems caused by "theorizing" theory, as either a wholesale turn to the other or an essentialization of negativity or difference, must be carried out. The one-sidedness of these approaches will readily be discovered, and their inflexibility and antagonism towards a dialectic involving persons (self and other) that ultimately privileges neither will be duly noted. Once the limitations of theory's own theorizing of the relationships between selves and others is recognized, a model of experimental problem solving needs to be put forth. This will include calls for earnest investigation into the existential problems arising from existing relationships between persons and organizations already in operation. These problems are context-bound, and require methods that are context-sensitive. Both problem-finding and problem-solving methods, as Dewey maintains, will be necessary at this beginning stage of inquiry (Dewey, 1986a, p. 109). This is perhaps the most important stage of inquiry in terms of investigation of globalization and its attendant consequences because it requires deliberate attention to the existential and experiential natures of the problem, from as many who experience the problem as can be found. Problems are felt, and felt problems remain unarticulated until adequately investigated and theorized. But to theorize a problem to the point of articulation means to undertake a deliberate investigation into its conditions, requiring the development of novel premises and conclusions, rather than any wholesale application of a metaphysical theory. Given the abundance of competing and contradictory theories of globalization, resisting this application is the most difficult challenge of all.

In one respect, programs of teacher education now beginning to confront the myriad complexities of globalization are in a good position. This is because they are only beginning to develop the concentrated relationships in which problems are manifest. They are therefore spared some of the difficulties in articulating problems in those environments. This is not to say that problems that already exist are fully articulated – they are surely not, and one of the reasons (the reason I am stressing here) is the poverty of existing theories to articulate them. Nevertheless, the unique position programs of teacher education find themselves in means that novel relationships can be examined for novel tensions that might develop – tensions leading to "felt problems" (often of a normative or moral nature), into which we can then inquire. This can be done at the faculty level. For example, faculties thinking of engaging in relationships with corporations for funding, or with organizations for teaching placements, or with exchanges with other universities, can identify potential problems and bring these to the point of articulation. These can be inquired into, in an experimental manner, through the postulation of "anticipated consequences" which, when carried through, either net a solution to the problem or require revision or replacement (Dewey, 1986b).

Conclusion

Teacher education programs will soon be faced with having to make normative decisions regarding their curricula, personnel, structure, and function, on the basis of changes wrought by globalization. I believe understanding what these changes are, why they present themselves as they do, and what (if any) choices can be made in regard to them, is vitally important if these programs are to survive in any recognizable form. This requires theory. What theories we adopt should not be a simple pick-and-choose affair; we should adopt those theories that do their best to articulate the sorts of problems we will face – problems that are not merely institutional or structural, but personal and experiential. We should be especially cautious of adopting theories that have behind them a metaphysical apparatus of difference, negativity, or otherness, or those that have no problem-solving methods embedded, or problem-solving methods that are tied so tightly to their metaphysics that they are inflexible. Such theories will be one-sided, and by definition will neglect important subjective elements of experiencing, problem solving, and relating. Nor will their accounts of problem solving be driven by the context or situations in which the problems occur; rather, they will be driven by a predetermined metaphysical program.

We will instead want a philosophy that privileges neither the self nor the other. We will want a philosophy that has an account of how the self and other interrelate, as well as how larger iterations of relations form and sustain themselves. Most of all, we will want a philosophy that has a cogent account of transformation. I submit that the best philosophy – the one that has accounts of each of these – is pragmatism. It is pragmatism that we should therefore choose.

When we press the advantage of pragmatism and, specifically, a Deweyan conception of inquiry that responds to "felt problems" arising from the immanent tensions in social relationships (though, obviously, a corresponding tension arises in the application of certain metaphysical philosophies to issues of globalization), we see that pragmatism has a natural, dialectical understanding of the person and community, together with an understanding of inquiry that accounts for (indeed, leads to) social transformation. It does so without recourse to essentializing differences, a turn to negativity, or the denigration of the self. This more flexible account of transformation makes it more adaptable to the "felt problems" of those in teaching communities broaching the numerous normative difficulties created by engaging head-on in globalization projects.

NOTES

1 I say this because the landmark text introducing theory of globalization in education is Burbules & Torres (2000). I say philosophical not to exclude other theoretical lenses, but to delineate just those lenses that draw on thinkers wholly a part of the philosophical tradition.
2 I do not include (most) feminist and postcolonial analyses here, because these are not, strictly speaking, philosophical programs unless they evidence a metaphysics; however, when they do emphasize a metaphysics, it is very often of critical-theoretic or post-structuralist design.
3 See P. A. Dhillon, A Kantian Conception of Human Rights Education, in K. Roth & E. G. Ze'ev (Eds.), *Education in the Era of Globalization* (Dordrecht, Netherlands: Springer, 2007).
4 Jürgen Habermas, for one, does not think so. See Habermas (1987), p. 128.
5 The notion of post-structuralism as essential dispersion comes from Schroeder (2005). "To be dispersed is to become scattered and diffused without pattern. Dispersion is a process as well as a resulting configuration of relationships … As a process, 'dispersion' suggests that the dividing, self-repelling operation is ongoing, unceasing. Things have not simply 'fallen apart'; they continue to fall further apart. Philosophies of dispersion conceptualize everything as skewed (in space and time); nothing coalesces or develops into organic unity" (p. 267).
6 Indeed, there would otherwise be little reason to take them seriously.
7 Of course, this was *not* Kant's understanding of self-consciousness. On Derrida's reading of self-consciousness, we are talking of the empirical self, not the "transcendental unity of apperception."
8 These traces are themselves ephemeral: disappearing images present then absent, never to return. There is no depth to presence; it is all surface. And there is no undergirding to the self; not even subconscious drives. The edifice of the self is supported only in *this* moment. Put this way, what we have here is a rejection of the accounts of Augustine, Locke, Hume, Descartes, Kant, *and* Hegel – indeed, of the history of Western attempts at construing the self.
9 Of course, other Anglo-American schools of thought were also critical of subjectivism; indeed, almost all the various schools that can be grouped together as "analytic" count in this regard. However, as the task here is to discuss schools of thought that have an influence on globalization theories, I will confine myself to pragmatism.
10 See W. James (1918), *Principles of Psychology*, vol. 1. (New York: Dover), p. 385. See also J. Dewey (1984), From Absolutism to Experimentalism,

in J. A. Boydston (Ed.), *John Dewey: The Later Works*, vol. 5 (Carbondale: Southern Illinois University Press), pp. 154–5.

11 See J. Good (2006), *A Search for Unity in Diversity: The "Permanent Deposit" in John Dewey's Philosophical Thought* (Lanham, MD: Rowman and Littlefield). See also J. Garrison (2006), The "Permanent Deposit" of Hegelian Thought in Dewey's Theory of Inquiry, *Educational Theory, 56* (1), 1–37.

12 Dewey rejected the Absolutism of self after his turn from Hegel to naturalism in the mid-1890s. The question for Dewey scholars is: What constitutes this Absolutism that Dewey turned away from? In Dewey's opinion, it was clear that Absolutism connoted a totalizing whole. However, this is a poor understanding of Hegel's Absolute Spirit, which behaved nothing like a totalizing whole. It is also surprising, given the parallels between Dewey's theory of inquiry and Hegel's logic and dialectic. Good has done much to dispel both this reading of Hegel and the distance between Dewey's organic method of inquiry and Hegel's social and political thought.

13 See also Aristotle, *Metaphysics*, book 7, part 17.

14 I say contra Adorno because this will likely require some attention to the logic of identity – the ability to correctly say of something "what is, is and what is not, is not," in Aristotle's terms. This is an essential feature of Kant's logic and Hegel's as well. Though Dewey quite rightly avers from a metaphysical claim regarding identity, he nevertheless admits we must have a functional understanding of the logic of identity to distinguish parts (of inquiry) from wholes (of situations) in order to experiment. See Dewey (1986b), p. 523.

3 To Serve and Yet Be Free: Historical Configurations and the Insertions of Faculties of Education in Ontario

ROSA BRUNO-JOFRÉ AND JOSH COLE

This chapter examines the developments that led to the insertion of teacher education into the university in Ontario, and the conditions of possibilities that mediated that process within a broader Canadian and international context. The historical problematic drawn from the two foundings of the Faculty of Education at Queen's University in Kingston, Ontario (1907 and 1965, opening in 1968), provides the historical thread for this chapter. The first part will address the educational contours of modernity – or rather, modernities – between the end of the nineteenth century and the beginning of the Second World War. It frames this analysis in relation to the development of the liberal educational state within an overall liberal framework (Curtis, 1988; McKay, 2000), and the intellectual configurations and educational ideas that began to coalesce at the turn of the nineteenth century. The second part focuses on those post–Second World War conditions that formed the groundwork for a fundamental rethinking of the relation between education and the creation of citizen subjectivities. Throughout, we pay particular attention – utilizing Daniel Tröhler's understanding of the formative "languages" underlying educational change – to how education as a set of practices is articulated with complex power relations tied to structural change and socio-economic transformation (Tröhler, 2011b).

The Educational Contours of Modernity: Teacher Education from the end of the Nineteenth Century to the Second World War

By the end of the nineteenth century – the fin de siècle – the primary elements of the educational state were in place in Canada, although its liberal hybridity was also reflected in regional adaptations and accommodations derived from ethnic and religious tensions. By 1916, eight provinces had compulsory-schooling laws: Ontario was the first in 1872, while Quebec and Newfoundland did not have legislation until 1942 (Axelrod, 1997, p. 36). Ontario's free, non-sectarian, compulsory public school model reflected a hegemonic consensus among the province's English-speaking population about what constituted a proper education, although separate schools existed to accommodate the province's Roman Catholic population. Ontario immigrants tried to recreate the Canadian West in the image of their own province (Mitchell, 1986a, 1986b).[1] The public non-sectarian school actually conveyed a Protestant educational language (Tröhler, 2011b).

Public schooling in English Canada was construed as the primary state agency for inculcating unity of thought in young citizens, and thus for creating a homogeneous nation based on a common English, imperial culture, and a governable polity. In other words, it aimed to create a self-regulated moral citizenry that could be more or less in line with the political and economic liberal model at the crossroads of British and American ideas and regional, ethnic, and religious differences. Normal and model schools held the responsibility for preparing teachers able to generate and foster this version of Canada as an "imagined nation," perpetuated through education (Anderson, 1991). It is not surprising to read that the official discourse on citizenship was not necessarily taught and learned in schools, which had their own contours nourished by the thousands of school districts, community agendas, and the limited preparation of elementary teachers. But teachers also mediated the curriculum, and in some cases could challenge official views; some, like Fred Tipping and Arthur Beach from Winnipeg and James Skene from Brandon – all of them industrial arts teachers – were active in the labour scene. Others had an involvement with feminist organizations, and yet others were related to the Grain Growers' Association, whose publications were critical of schooling and citizenship (Bruno-Jofré, 1998). Furthermore, the composition of the classroom reflected not only ethnic origins, but the political involvement of the pupils' parents: "Citizenship formation had in practice a dynamic relational character and was constantly conditioned by developments beyond school boundaries" (p. 31). Nonetheless, the rapid growth of the normal and model schools can be considered important components of the Canadian state's hegemonic, educative role, and the maintenance of the ideal for the English Canadian teacher remains an important marker of what those behind the school system viewed as important and worthy of perpetuation through education.

As historian Ian McKay (2010) argues, modern Canadian history can be understood as the result of what he calls a "liberal order" (p. 362). As he has it, beginning in the 1840s, a small band of activist, organic intellectuals (in the Gramscian sense) – dedicated to classic British liberal notions of individual liberty, formal equality, and the private possession of property – skilfully engaged the various "grids of power" available to them (including the "penitentiaries and criminal codes, schools and legislatures") in order to contain and control their ideological rivals (from Amerindians to Acadians), and instil liberal ideology as a form of hegemonic common sense throughout northern North America (McKay, 2009, p. 40; 2010, p. 362). What resulted was a powerful "conservative experiment in top-down liberalism," lasting until the end of the 1940s. During that time, it served as a "structured and structuring principle of both public and private life" (McKay, 2009, p. 42; 2010, p. 363). However, it is important to keep in mind that this is a broad interpretative framework, since, in practice, the official language of education was often challenged or resisted and even redirected.

Universities in Canada were also undergoing immense changes by the late nineteenth century. This period saw a shift in the mission of the province's universities – from being primarily vehicles dedicated to preserving Christian ideals and training elites for leadership positions in society, to hybrid institutions that would fulfil this role while also beginning to meet the industrial needs of the province. These included the exploitation of natural resources in the northern reaches of the province, and the preparation of scientists, engineers, pharmacists, and social workers, as well as secondary-school teachers (Axelrod & Reid, 1989). This process, tied to the rising influence of the science of political economy, would only accelerate with the onset of the First World War.

The ideas informing educational discourse – and thus teacher preparation in English Canada and Ontario – drew, as they did in the United States, from the work of Johann Pestalozzi, Friedrich Wilhelm Froebel, Johann Friedrich Herbart, Friedrich Hegel, Charles Darwin, and Herbert Spencer. The impact of German experimental psychology and the child study movement, and the resolute emergence of the scientific method, generated complex configurations that influenced policies and teacher education. Kliebard has identified four major currents at the end of the nineteenth century in the United States that are also applicable to Canada: the humanists promoting Western cultural heritage and three kinds of reformers, the child study movement, the social efficiency educators, and the social meliorists (Kliebard, 1986, p. 28). It is important to note the contextual place of religion, which intersected with the forces at play and the various educational projects. In fact, as Bruno-Jofré and Jover (2011) found, in the last years of the nineteenth century a collection of sixteen pedagogical creeds was published – including John Dewey's "My Pedagogic Creed" as well as Canadian James L. Hughes's creed – working out the intersection of religion and the notion of God and belief with the centrality of the child, evolution, and the concept of progress. Meanwhile, reformers such as the Social Gospel advocates fully embraced progressive education and John Dewey's ideas and understanding of democracy. The influence of Dewey's educational theory grounded in pragmatism, and in particular in his theory of experience, already had a presence in Canada. The various and often conflicting strands of progressive education that took shape at the beginning of the twentieth century – from behaviourism to progressive pedagogy – represented an eclectic response to modernity, albeit tainted by various modalities. It was at once forward-looking, but also riddled with blind spots: gender and race (not least the colonizing role of education in the case of Aboriginals in Canada) remained unaddressed.

These intellectual developments, processes of reception of circulating ideas, and the state agenda itself are reflected in the biographies of Canadian educational leaders, as well as in the policy directions they tried to enact. For instance, James L. Hughes – a graduate himself from the normal school, a Grand Master of the Orange Lodge, and Sunday school teacher – became the chief inspector of the Toronto school system, where he promoted the Froebelian kindergarten and manual work. He had a fluid relationship with American pedagogues such as the neo-Hegelian advocate of Froebel's ideas William Torrey Harris.[2] Meanwhile, John Dewey's ideas became well known after the publication of "My Pedagogic Creed" and *School and Society*, and his texts started to be included in advanced teacher preparation programs, including that of the first faculty of education at Queen's University. Comments about Dewey's work appeared in the *Chicago Tribune* and in the *Globe and Mail* (Toronto). The engagement of Queen's philosopher John Watson, an idealist, with Dewey's pragmatism is well documented.[3]

In Ontario and in Canadian provinces, the rapid growth of the number of normal schools and model schools in the later nineteenth century reflected the need for a large number of teachers in the growing education system, as well as the need to create and sustain self-regulating, model liberal citizens in light of a rapidly changing, increasingly dynamic, hybrid modern Canada. So, mass education and teacher preparation served at one and the same time educational and state-formational needs, while Canadian universities fell into line with "nation building" and a discourse grounded in the notion of public service to Canada and to the larger British Empire, of which Canada was still very much a part.[4] The relevance of the mission to produce the modern Canadian subject was in contrast with the limited preparation of elementary teachers and the lack of attention paid to the professionalization of teaching in the country at this time. In the United States, as David Labaree has pointed out, early in the twentieth century state legislatures started to transform normal schools into teachers' colleges able to grant bachelor's degrees, which gave academic and professional credibility to their programs. From the 1920s, these colleges diversified their programs and started to become state colleges, while the process of institutional evolution to acquire the status of university programs started in the 1950s (Labaree, 2008).

In the late nineteenth century, prestigious universities established chairs in pedagogy or education not only in the United States (universities of Iowa, Ohio, Michigan, Columbia, Berkeley, Chicago, Stanford, and Harvard) but also in Europe. The focus was the preparation of a small number of high school teachers and administrators, as well as those equipped to conduct educational research (Labaree, 2008, p. 295). The creation in 1893 of a degree in pedagogy at the University of Toronto, the creation of their Faculty of Education in 1906, and the founding of the Faculty of Education at Queen's University in 1907 were all in line with the drive to professionalize teaching, in particular at the secondary level. The programs were directed towards high school teachers and graduate work (Editorial Notes, 1894). A body of scholarship had begun to develop, in particular in psychology and educational theory. New rhetorical claims regarding teacher education and the "necessary conditions" for teaching and learning then flowed from these developments. In 1893, the *Educational Journal*, which consolidated the *Educational Weekly* and the *Canada School Journal* and was published in Toronto, welcomed the university degrees in pedagogy at the University of Toronto:

> If there is any doubt as to the inherent right of teaching to be regarded as one of those [learned] professions, that doubt arises mainly from the fact

> there are necessarily many grades of teachers, and that hitherto extensive learning has not been regarded as necessary except for the higher of those grades. The day will, we venture to predict, come, though we fear it is yet in the far-off future, when this opinion will have been changed, and high educational qualifications [will] be deemed as indispensable for the lower as for the higher departments of educational work. Indeed, it might not be hard to show that a thorough knowledge of the mind and its workings is even more essential for those who have to do with its training in its earlier stages of development. (p. 56)

Queen's University was founded in 1842 in Kingston, Ontario, as a Presbyterian "Bible college." Its early years are particularly associated with the principalship (1877–1902) of George Monro Grant. Under Grant, Queen's became a major national university (Neatby, 1978). Like other institutions descended from the Scottish university tradition, Queen's had a utilitarian slant, and a preoccupation with undergraduate work and the applied sciences (Fallis, 2007, pp. 31–6). Thus, it is not surprising that Queen's would be interested in offering new degrees in the growing "scientific" field of modern pedagogy.[5] In 1907, the *Queen's University Journal* announced that the Ontario Normal School College at Hamilton would be closed by the Ontario government, and superseded by a faculty of education located at the University of Toronto. This generated "a feeling" that "she too, Queen's, should have a Faculty of Education established by government aid since she was doing great in Western Ontario and was supplying the province with a large percentage of its High School Teachers" (Faculty of Education, 1907, p. 65).[6] It did not address teacher education at the elementary level. Other articles in the *Journal* praised Queen's for recognizing the educational needs of the province and responding promptly to them (School of Pedagogy, 1906). Importantly, changes in scholarship, along with the overall political and economic context, played a critical role in making teacher preparation within the university setting plausible, desirable, and seemingly necessary.

The new Bachelor of Pedagogy degree – as seen through 1907–8's "Preliminary Announcement" – sought to balance the philosophical, historical, and psychological literature with professional tools for teaching and learning. Thus, part 1 included the history of education and educational systems, principles of education underpinned by new developments in philosophy, psychology, school administration and law, school management, general methods, and special methods. Part 2 consisted of what we today call curriculum, with an emphasis on public and high school courses of instruction. Part 3 was devoted to observation and practice teaching in Kingston high schools, and observation in the area's ungraded rural schools (Preliminary Announcement, 1907).[7] Regular students were required to have (a) obtained a university degree in the arts from any university in the British dominions; or (b) have attained senior teachers' academic standing according to the regulations of the Education Department of Ontario.

This curriculum fully embraced the pedagogical tendencies of the time, while having a degree of eclecticism. It included John Dewey and William James, thus highlighting pragmatism, William Kilpatrick in the line of Dewey, but also Herbert Spencer and Edward Thorndike. Friedrich W. Froebel was conveyed through the work of James Hughes, and Johann F. Herbart, who interestingly stressed the development of character through literature and history and the rational use of the will ("a good man commands himself"), was studied through his major American exponent, DeGarmo. Other readings included Stanley Hall, a major figure in the child study movement, and William Torrey Harris, neo-Hegelian and humanist, who represented a transition between the new ideas on education and the traditional ones. The degree of Doctor of Pedagogy (D.Paed.) also embodied the intellectual spectrum of the time (Preliminary Announcement, 1907).

This points to some important questions. Why did the Faculty of Education at Queen's fail? Why could it not survive? Two things became clear after the insertion of teacher education within Queen's. One was the intervention of Ontario's educational state in the process (via curriculum parameters set by the Department of Education), as well as the abrogation of university's duty (via the superintendent of education) by demanding to approve faculty appointments.[8] The other was an increased tension between academic and professional knowledge, a point made by David Labaree (2008) when tracing the history of teacher education in the United States. This tension was clearly expressed in another article published in the *Queen's University Journal* on the supposed value of a B.Paed. degree. In the opinion of the writer, the teaching profession held this new degree in low esteem because of what was being taught in the new program – mostly psychology, history of education, and the science of education. This was considered by teachers to be of no use in actual teaching since teachers were thought to be born, not made. The article goes on to say: "Of course, experience proves the falsity of both of these contentions – though some people could never be made teachers" (New Degrees, 1907, pp. 212–13). In the end, the ambiguity of the latter statement gave "experienced" teachers licence to discount the new knowledge offered by the Queen's experiment in university-based teacher preparation for secondary teachers.

The new faculty struggled with poor registration. In a memorandum apparently written in 1917, Superintendent of Education John Seth expressed serious concern with the enrolment numbers in the faculty: in its first five years, the enrolment average was 36 students per year. It peaked at 76 students in 1915–16 (Seth, 1917). He also questioned the qualifications of the staff and the unwillingness of Queen's to incur expenses beyond its governmental grant, and even pointed toward the "uneconomical use of funds" by the program. Further, he drew attention to what he considered the unsympathetic Kingston Board of Education, and the city's schools themselves, which provided poor-quality teacher educators to the faculty. Seth, like others in the province at the time, was inclined to support the closure of the faculties of education in both the University of Toronto and Queen's, in favour of a centralized College of Education in Toronto related to the University of Toronto.

According to the Principal's Report of 1919–20, the faculty's enrolment numbers had not improved by that time. In that report, Dean H.T.J. Coleman expressed his concern with the idea of centralizing teacher preparation in an Ontario College of Education. He described the proposal as "a retrograde movement of a most serious kind." The faculties were providing, he said, a more acceptable type of instruction to both students and the public than the one to be offered by the new college. Further, he argued for more, not less, decentralization in university-based teacher preparation. To this end, he took pains to point out the faculty's lack of freedom in appointing professors and organizing and delivering courses (Coleman, 1920, pp. 36–9). Despite such criticism, by the spring of 1920, the move had taken place. The faculties of education in both Toronto and Kingston were closed and replaced by the Ontario College of Education. The new arrangement, the principal said in his 1920–1 report, would impact Queen's more than the University of Toronto, since the college would be more or less under the influence of the latter institution (Queen's University, 1921, p. 9).

The closing of the faculties of education coincided with two key junctural points in education. The onset of the First World War in 1914 spurred a renewed concern with character education, service, and citizenship, and a focus on Western civilization in the United States and Canada. As Ken Osborne (1998) wrote: "After the War citizenship was defined not only in terms of Canadian and British heritage, but of membership in a wider Western civilization" (p. 7).[9] The postwar period also spurred a repositioning of the universities. While the schools were used to shore up imperial sentiment and a culture of war (not least in expunging the German language from the Ontario school system), the university's role was much more direct (Stamp, 1982, pp. 91, 95). University administrators and professors eagerly contributed to the war effort, by appealing to "patriotic instinct, to imperial sentiment, to democratic values, to the lessons of history and the words of the poet, and to religious convictions" to mobilize students to enlist (McKillop, 1994, pp. 255–6). Queen's University, for instance, contributed its own well-trained student militia, who had long been engaged in rifle and infantry drills (p. 265). In addition to these human resources, the universities contributed scientific knowledge to the war effort, making particularly notable contributions in chemistry and metallurgy (pp. 283–4). These efforts helped to end the Canadian university's image as "a cloistered, almost monastic community," divorced from the practical world (p. 284). This new status would benefit the universities greatly during the Second World War, and into the Cold War as well, as Canada eagerly joined the burgeoning North American "Military Industrial Complex."

The 1920s witnessed the flourishing of new education in Europe and progressive education in the United States, as well as the resurgence of international educational networks which had provided sustenance to educational thought and practice since the 1840s. These networks were reconstituted in the 1920s, after a break occasioned by the First World War, as organized institutions rather than the loosely affiliated form they took before 1914 (Fuchs, 2007, p. 207). For instance, the League of Nations established the Liaison Committee of the Major International Associations as an umbrella organization for those networks involved in furthering international understanding, peace education, and humanitarianism. It was a rich period for the international circulation of (at times, radical) ideas. Meanwhile, the education of elementary teachers took place in normal and model schools, there were various levels of certification, and hundreds of school districts in rural areas that preferred teachers drawn from their local communities.

After the First World War, education came to be seen as a means of instilling (select) political subjectivities in children and young people. Tom Mitchell has made the case that the First World War invoked a new sense of national identity among Anglo-Canadians. While this was happening, Canada as a country remained fragmented along ethnic, class-based, and regional lines (Mitchell, 1996). In analysing the National Conference on Character Education in Relation to Canadian Citizenship (which took place in Winnipeg in 1919), Mitchell argues that middle-class Canadians sought to cast "the post-war order in a particular idiom of nationalism informed by a common Canadianism rooted in Anglo-conformity and a citizenship framed in notions of service, obedience, obligation and fidelity to the state" (p. 21). The notions of diversity that would come to consume Canadian educational discourse after the 1960s were nowhere to be found, despite the increasingly diverse nature of Canadian society. Even more, the delegates from Quebec tried with little success to make participants aware that there was another vision of Canada. This is not surprising given the emphasis on "Englishness," a form of subjectivity deeply sedimented in Canadian institutions, including schools and universities.

The emergence of teachers' federations in the 1920s added a new dimension to the articulation of education, citizenship, and the professionalization of teaching. There were contradictions between the federations' discourse and its level of sophistication, and the reality of most elementary teachers' formation and work in one-room rural schools, although women teachers with university degrees were often hired as elementary teachers first (Bruno-Jofré, 1993). In the mid-1920s and in particular the 1930s, teachers' magazines all over the country expounded a discourse imbued with John Dewey's language of democracy and education (education as part of life itself) and the understanding of education as a means of protecting and perpetuating Western civilization, along with a renewed emphasis on the importance of the British Empire in Canadian life. In fact, the discourse was imbued with a justification of colonialism and the suppression of the Aboriginal peoples, and also failed to deal with women's rights. The latter was evident in salary disparities between male and female teachers and other issues (Bruno-Jofré, 1993).

In 1937, in a move reflecting the new education movement in Europe as well as recent progressive interventions in Alberta education, Ontario's Ministry of Education produced the *Program of Studies for Grades I to VI of Public and Separate Schools*, containing pedagogically progressive curriculum proposals that promised more autonomy for teachers. A new, more active inquiring subject then emerged within this liberal, Canadian framework, reflecting a "new knowledge archive in the system of schooling" in the 1930s (Milewski, 2008).[10]

Normal schools carried out their work across the country during the thirties and through the Second World War within the context of an earlier process of feminization of the teaching profession, particularly at the elementary level. Fuelled by the rise of the politically far-right ideology of National Socialism in Germany and of Fascism in Italy and Japan, the Second World War far exceeded its predecessor in destructive power (Hobsbawm, 2004, pp. 23–4, 36–7). Canada, with Britain, entered into the fray in September 1939. As was the case with the First, the Second World War was projected as a limited engagement – "a controlled effort that would not bankrupt the nation, produce high casualties, or strain the delicate balance between French and English Canada" (Granatstein, 2004, p. 572). Only the first proved true, as Canada's government took control of industry and propelled it forward, laying the groundwork for the country's postwar Golden Age economy in important ways.

During the Second World War, the Allies considered themselves to be fighting Fascism in the name of liberal democracy, and the classrooms – particularly in English Canada[11] – dwelled on unity, patriotism, and service through the war efforts. The pedagogical progressive reforms of 1937 in Ontario were upset by a conservative turn in 1945, which brought a more utilitarian approach – and thus, cadet training, after dying on the vine in the interwar period, was again made mandatory by the Toronto Board of Education in 1939 (Stamp, 1982, p. 172). Ontario schools pressed "chins up" messages from King George VI and Winston Churchill upon their students, as Red Cross work, air raid drills, and scrap metal drives became a part of everyday school life. The war provided a temporary death knell for progressive education in the province. The new school readers, the new social studies reforms, and the non-traditional "situational ethics" they fostered would not do for a public and a political class that demanded firm and absolute values in the face of Fascism and world war (pp. 171, 173, 175).

Canada's universities were considerably more prepared for war than they were in 1914. Both the Canadian military and the government insisted that those associated with higher education could serve the common good by contributing their expertise in scientific research and development to the war effort. Professors did research in radar, long- and short-wave radio, electronics, chemical warfare, submarine detection, and nuclear fission. As Principal Wallace of Queen's declared, "This is a war which may well be won or lost in the laboratories" (quoted in McKillop, 1994, p. 531). Students who worked in these subjects were given special status, and subjects that had "practical value" rose as others – the arts and humanities – fell (pp. 529, 535). This trend would not be reversed until the 1960s, as we will see. The postwar period signalled a new era for education and a reformulation of the educational state, the aims of education, and the notion of citizenship; with these multi-variant changes, teacher education had to be revisited.

Teacher Preparation and the University, Post-1945

Like all countries, Canada underwent major political, military, demographic, and educational shifts after 1945. Among these were transformations in the liberal order that had underpinned the Canadian state for over a century. While the emphasis on liberty, equality, and property remained intact, a shift towards collective social goals became evident as well. As Eric Hobsbawm argues, after 1945, capitalist economies around the world welcomed a degree of state intervention that would have been unthinkable before the war. For those involved in postwar reconstruction, the future was not with laissez-faire capitalism, but rather with hybrid, mixed economies, part capitalist and part socialist (Hobsbawm, 2004, p. 272).

Canada, reluctantly at first, followed this line and bowed to pressure from postwar "new liberal" reformers and leftists alike. Thus, the Canadian state introduced some Keynesian controls over the economy, and began to create social welfare programs as well (McKay, 2010, p. 373). Canada's liberal order – its "political unconscious" – came to encompass a degree of collectivism, and even a globalized cosmopolitanism (reflecting changes in mass communications, as well as developments in global manufacture and trade, of which Canada was a major beneficiary) (Edwardson, 2008, p. 16). However, Canada's foundational conservatism remained strong as well. As Ian McKay points out, the British king and queen still served as Canada's heads of state, and its welfare programs were hobbled by notions of "less eligibility." And – as ever – "peace, order, and good government" (as enshrined in the British North America Acts from 1867 forward) remained the rule, not the exception, in Canadian political life (McKay, 2010, pp. 363, 373).

When the Cold War commenced, it became clear that it was not only a military struggle, but a cultural struggle as well, one which increasingly focused on pedagogy. Despite misgivings among many Canadians over about the importation of US-style Cold War tactics – including the abrogation of civil liberties, anti-communist screenings of public servants, and harassment of immigrants and refugees – Canada was a largely enthusiastic Cold War ally. Like the United States, it also articulated military security, liberal democracy, and capitalism as core "Western values" (Fahrni & Rutherdale, 2008, p. 4; Whitaker & Marcuse, 1994). Following the launch of the Soviet Sputnik satellites into outer space in 1957, which was seen in the West as iron-clad proof of Soviet technological and educational superiority, education in Canada (as in the United States) became a matter of security policy (Rudolph, 2002; Urban, 2010). The situation generated a particular pressure regarding the need to restructure educational administration and teacher education.

No less important were the demographic changes in Canada created by the "baby boom," postwar immigration, and the arrival of 160,000 displaced persons between 1946 and 1953. Educating the school population that resulted required a new, massive expansion of the educational state, unprecedented before or since. Immediately after 1945, nearly every province launched major reviews of their educational systems and the "aims and objectives" of education. As Hugh Stevenson (1971) has succinctly put it, in Canada after 1945, "there was no thought of merely relying on the educational institutions which existed before the war" (p. 386).

The demographic changes alone proved a daunting challenge for the educational state. From the late 1940s to the mid-1960s, Canadian children entered school in larger numbers, and stayed longer as well – not least because their parents encouraged them to take advantage of conditions that they never enjoyed, and because the "Golden Age" economic boom entailed the creation of 'white collar' work, which required more education (Gidney, 1999, p. 27). What resulted was a helter-skelter expansion of the school plant. Between 1946 and 1961 alone, the number of classrooms in Ontario doubled, and in 1950s Quebec, a new school was opened every day (Gidney, 1999, p. 28; Owram, 1996, p. 120).

The postwar era in Canada, as in the United States, was characterized by the notion of economic growth and so-called human capital. Education would come to play a crucial role in fostering human capital through the production of knowledgeable workers for an increasingly technological economy (Schultz, 1961). In Canada, this revolutionized thinking about education. As the economic historian K.J. Rea (1985) points out, governments such as Ontario's went from being chronically reluctant to spend on education to "enthusiastically promoting" it at every turn (p. 103).

Canada's school systems did not only need to get bigger, they also had to become more centralized, complex, and bureaucratic. They simply could not operate with thousands of school districts, potentially acting in an improvised manner. The profile of the student as a productive and governable subject, a citizen, was permeated by the ethos of education as human capital, progressive international competition, and a notion of rights that started to amend, if not surpass, pre-1945 notions of citizenship.

Postwar developments in higher education in Canada were initially less of a priority than those of schooling, but by the 1960s, they too came to be seen as part of the postwar educational continuum – what one historian has described (in the Ontario context) as "the educative society" (Fleming, 1971). Coming out of the Second World War, Canada's universities were in an enviable position. Professors, administrators, and students won a new level of public prestige by producing trained personnel for the war effort, for their role in scientific and technological advances, and, after the war, for educating veterans in Canada's version of the American G.I. Bill (McKillop, 1994; Sheffield, 1971, p. 386). In line with the idea of an "educative society," universities developed a practical social role, and the insertion of teacher education would help to fulfil the vocational professional role while keeping research.[12]

This period also saw the development of the "multiversity" in Canada. The multiversity was an American invention, specifically designed to meet the (perceived) needs of a "post-industrial," knowledge-based society. As the name indicates, the multiversity served several purposes. It offered both liberal and professional education at the graduate and undergraduate levels. It functioned as both a teaching and a research institution, enjoying links to government and the private sector alike (Fallis, 2007, pp. 49–50). It was meant to be both conservative and radical. As its principal theorist, the American political economist and school administrator Clark Kerr, put it in 1961, the multiversity would serve "eternal truths" by fostering "the improvement of service wherever truth and knowledge of high order may serve the needs of man." He then tellingly added that the multiversity "must ever be improved in a competitive dynamic environment" – in other words, it would be open to the creative destruction of the capitalist marketplace (Kerr, 1982, p. 38). By the mid-1960s, Kerr's ideal was actively reshaping Ontario universities such as the University of Toronto and Queen's. It was also built directly into the DNA of the province's new universities, including York, Trent, and Brock. And it would prove a natural home for postwar teacher preparation – itself a liminal subject of study, hovering between the liberal arts, professional practice, and postwar utilitarian demands.

The perceived inadequacy of the normal school within the context of these dynamic postwar changes was solved in some provinces in the 1950s through the creation of teachers' colleges, following the American model that had developed from the early 1900s. In addition to this, elementary teacher preparation started to be moved to the universities: in Alberta in 1945, in Newfoundland in 1946, in British Columbia in 1956, in Saskatchewan in 1964, in Manitoba in 1965, in Ontario in 1965, and in Quebec in 1969 (Sheehan & Wilson, 1994).[13] This influenced national cultural policies, academia, and public schooling (Dewar, 2006). It was a decade when royal commissions and provincial commissions on education sprang up across the country. Schooling, teacher preparation, the social, political, and economic functions of schooling, and educational aims were all at stake.

Of particular importance in this respect was the 1951 report of the Royal Commission on National Development in the Arts, Letters and Sciences, also known as the Massey commission. The commission sought to extend elite culture as a form of moral education to all postwar Canadians. As they had it, universities were the "nurseries of a truly Canadian civilization and culture, which would arm Canadian society" against communism, as well as the excesses of American materialism – thus, the committee pressed for permanent, federally-derived financial security for higher education (quoted in McKillop, 1994, p. 563). The government acquiesced to this idea with great fanfare. Though the commissioners were essentially Cold Warriors in their staunch support of liberal-democratic culture, they were also fiercely anti-American (Edwardson, 2008, chapter 2). Within this frame of mind, they addressed teacher preparation and asked: "How many Canadians realize that over a large part of Canada the schools are accepting tacit direction from New York (Columbia University) that they would not think of taking from Ottawa?" (Massey, 1951, pp. 15–16).[14] The reference here is to pedagogical progressive ideas on education and their influence on teachers. Critics such as the Massey commissioners called for a home-grown Canadian alternative to American university teacher education; the commissioner Hilda Neatby (1953) would take this topic up again in her bestseller *So Little for the Mind*.

There is one more factor to consider. The business and political leaders who supported the expansion of the educational state in the 1960s stressed to governments that they did not want students educated in a strictly utilitarian fashion. As historian Paul Axelrod (1989) argues, what they wanted instead was "intensive student exposure to the liberal arts," which they saw as "vital" to the postwar economy (p. 192). The ideal student would be critical, creative, and crucially flexible – able to adapt to new, ever-more complex work environments. This is what constituted human capital in the complex, dynamic, increasingly international postwar economy. Within the context of the "educative society," it did the university no harm to become involved with the schools – for both were now seen as part of the same pedagogical continuum – and it did the schools no harm to benefit from the status of the university.

All these multi-variant relations came together in Ontario's new approach to teacher education, considered to be "the perennial backwater of the Ontario educational system" before 1945 (Fleming, 1971, p. 209; Stamp, 1982). Teaching's intellectual reinvention as a serious, advanced profession can be pinpointed to the Minister's Committee on the Training of Elementary School Teachers, convened in 1964. The report the committee produced – known as the MacLeod report, after the Windsor school inspector who chaired it – was delivered in 1966. The Honourable William Davis, minister of education, greeted the report with enthusiasm and began to implement it immediately (Fleming, 1971, pp. 59–60). In it, the committee argued that teacher preparation in the province was deeply out of sync with American and British efforts to modernize teacher education after the Second World War (Ontario Department of Education, 1966). Further, they asserted that teacher preparation in Ontario was out of step with larger social, cultural, and economic changes. As the report had it, education in the province was designed to prepare children and young people to live in an "economic structure based largely upon agriculture and in a society which was relatively simple." Yet those conditions had been radically superseded, due to "improvements in transportation and communications," "acceleration of automation in commerce and industry," "the rapid pace of invention and discovery, and the great expansion of knowledge in recent years." This, in turn, transformed patterns of thought, views of society, and values (p. 9). If Ontario was going to keep up with the postwar world, and with the pedagogical work being done in other countries, teacher preparation in the province would have to be improved from the ground up, and this meant integration with the university.

The revamped program would feature a foundation of "academic education"; this would provide the potential teacher with a thorough knowledge of the subjects they would eventually teach. The program would impart loftier qualities as well, by increasing "the capacity of the teacher to live an enriched life, to gain an insight into social issues, and to choose between good and bad, truth and falsehood, the beautiful and the ugly, the worthwhile and the trivial" (Ontario Department of Education, 1966, p. 23). All of this would take place within the university, so as to ensure the "academic integrity" of the knowledge acquired.

Within the professional program, the foundations of education would include educational psychology, so that the candidate could become familiar with "child development," the "nature of the learning process," and ultimately the "needs and interests of children" (p. 24). Educational philosophy would immerse candidates in the "philosophical background" of the Western educational tradition. This would enable them to formulate a personal approach to pedagogy, while establishing "suitable goals and purposes" within the classroom (pp. 24–5). Educational sociology would "sharpen the student's awareness of the problems that grow out of the socio-cultural realities of the world – past, present, and future" (p. 25). Such an approach was crucial in an era characterized by the "explosion of scientific and technological knowledge," in which "cultural values and social institutions are undergoing such rapid change" (pp. 24–5). Of course, the program would involve more practical matters as well. Courses in teaching techniques, school management, and school administration would be part of the program. Practice internships in actual classrooms would be undertaken. But mere technique was not the end goal of the program: "Overemphasis on teaching patterns and techniques insufficiently related to the foundations of education" would be avoided (Ontario Department of Education, 1966, p. 25; Fleming, 1971).

The moral leadership that the teacher was expected to exercise in the classroom brought the notion of teacher candidate "selection" to the fore in the MacLeod report. The potential teacher must be the right sort of person for the job, before any training would begin. As the committee put it: "Assuming adequate scholarship, the finest people undoubtedly make the best teachers." The "finest people" would have a high standard of physical and mental health and "good personal qualities." They would have a wholesome character and a "pleasing personality." In addition, they would be creative, enthusiastic, fair, and self-controlled. Finally, they would be genuinely interested in young people and public service (Ontario Department of Education, 1966, p. 39). These people would be identified by "carefully chosen committees of selection" (pp. 39–40). These committees would "collate all significant information" regarding the candidate, and then conduct interviews in order to arrive at a "sound appraisal" of their suitability for the program (p. 40). Committees would consist of the stakeholders "most vitally concerned in teacher education" – including representatives from schools, universities, and the Department of Education. While the MacLeod committee admitted that such a process would be difficult and even subjective, the importance of teacher education made its existence necessary (pp. 39, 41).

In order to comply with the recommendations from the MacLeod report, teachers, in particular elementary teachers, would have to undergo more education and teacher education would have to be moved in its entirety to the university setting. Those with pre-1945 qualifications would be phased out, and new teachers, equipped with mandatory university degrees, would be brought in. Thus, the Canadian summer programs that had been used for years to train teachers quickly (but often sloppily) were transformed into permanent institutions, nested in the university (Clifford & Guthrie, 1988, p. 172; Stamp, 1982, p. 199). So, in this way, the Queen's summer program established in 1960 became the McArthur College of Education in 1968. The introduction of teacher education into the university led to a more serious preparation for primary school teachers, as the length, intensity, and academic requirements were increased for the first time (Gidney, 1999, pp. 54–5).

By the end of the 1960s, faculties of education would become sources of pedagogical expertise. In the Ontario Institute for Studies in Education (OISE) – a degree-granting graduate school associated with the University of Toronto created in 1965 – the province even had its own research and development "think tank" to study "problems relating to or affecting education" and to disseminate those findings to teachers, administrators, and the public (Fleming, 1971, p. 212). OISE would provide the new faculties of education in the rest of the province with cutting-edge educational knowledge, and highly trained educational administrators as well.

The creation of the College of Education (later on, Faculty of Education) at Queen's University needs to be interpreted as part of this complex reorganization of the educational system, itself a reaction to reformulated postwar socio-economic aims. On 28 August 1964, Principal J.A. Corry reported to the board of trustees that Kingston had been under serious consideration for the establishment of a college of education in Eastern Ontario, but that there had been a delay due to the inability to find a suitable location close to the university. He also recommended the sale of a portion of the Palace Road Property to the college of education. The location of the college in Kingston, he argued, would be an advantage to the university. As he wrote, "the relative importance of Queen's in relation to the schools of Ontario has been decreasing for many years and the association of a College of Education with Queen's should definitely strengthen our position" (Queen's University, Board of Trustees, 1964a, p. 180). Corry also argued that certain college courses could be taught by university faculty, but this would be done at the college's cost (p. 181). The idea was approved in October 1964 (Queen's University, Board of Trustees, 1964b, pp. 8, 189). When he presented the text of the proposed agreement between the Minister of Education for the Province of Ontario and Queen's University at Kingston at a special meeting of the Senate, Corry made clear that the governance of the college of education would be carried out by the university, and that the internal administration would be similar in form to that of existing faculties (with a faculty board and representation on the senate).[15] The senate requested that the phrase "subject to the approval of the Minister" be deleted from various sections, including those for designating the dean and the appointment of the teaching staff (Queen's University, Senate, 1965, p. 93). The request was granted and the phrase "after consultation with the Minister" was substituted. The foundations of the college of education (later on faculty) were then set.

At the time, it was referred to as the College for the Professional Training of Teachers. By May 1965, Corry stated that consideration had been given to naming the new college of education in honour of Duncan A. McArthur: a graduate of Queen's in 1907, a professor of history, Deputy Minister of Education for Ontario between 1934 and 1940, and then Minister of Education until his death in 1943. The naming was important, as McArthur represented a powerful link to the progressive pedagogical tradition in education that was now joined with an emphasis on liberal arts training in the new faculty, which began offering the new programs in September 1968. Importantly, the citation read when he was granted the degree of Doctor of Laws *honoris causa* at Queen's in 1935 referred to McArthur's innovative ideas in education. Indeed, the changes he spearheaded, including the 1937 Program of Studies created under his watch, were considered radical at the time, and remain so today.

By October 1965, Vernon Ready had been appointed dean of the McArthur College of Education, but the location one mile from the university was questioned in the senate by Professor H.M. Estall, who argued that the distance would have academic implications (Estall, 1965, p. 32). The agreement between the Minister of Education for the Province of Ontario and Queen's University makes clear that the minister agreed "that acceptance by the University of full responsibility for operation of the College must carry assurance of as wide a range of discretion in the said operation as is compatible with the final responsibility of the Minister for policy and for adequate preparation of teachers."[16]

The college started its B.Ed. degree program in September 1968. Students were required to have a university degree to be admitted into the program at McArthur College of Education to become either an elementary or a secondary teacher, and were required to have forty-five credits in Arts, Science, or Commerce subsequent to Grade 8 or equivalent. The program's first academic calendar recreated the history of teacher preparation at the university, in a move tantamount to myth making. It asserted that though the current status of teacher education in some universities "varies widely," Queen's was different and, further, had always been so. As the creators of the calendar wrote: "McArthur College is particularly fortunate to be a part of Queen's University because Queen's role in the province's school system has been 'long and honourable'" (Queen's University, McArthur College of Education, 1968, p. 9). They continue: "Actually, during the period 1907–1920, Queen's University had its own faculty of education." Further, "it seems perfectly in keeping with this old tradition that so many faculties and departments of the University have extended friendly assistance and positive support" to the new faculty. This "old tradition" was an invented one, for the former experiment lasted a mere thirteen years, and as we have seen, was fraught with the troubles that led to its closure in 1920. In the later 1960s, however, it was important to stress the synergy between the university, the schools, and teacher preparation.

Within the calendar, we can also see a number of threads we have been considering come together, including a commitment to teacher preparation within the university setting. As the calendar reads, "McArthur holds the view that an institute of teacher education must foster the intellectual outlook," and, as they stress, "a teacher who is not learning constantly, is not teaching adequately." Clearly for the leaders of the faculty, as expressed in the calendar, the continued pursuit of academic study was a key part of the teacher's character, and all members of the college – faculty and students alike – were encouraged to persevere with their private studies (Queen's University, McArthur College of Education, 1968, p. 7). The program was strongly student-centred.

It also evoked the intellectual idealism expressed in a commitment to liberal learning: "McArthur College is committed to the traditional objectives of liberal education respecting the broad development of human personality, character, and mind" (ibid.). The foundations of education – including a strong philosophical component, history, and sociology – and, later on, comparative education courses, would have a strong place in the program. As for utilitarianism in education, the calendar contained a cautionary statement with a Massey-esque tone: "Recognizing the tendency for educational institutions especially professional schools, to adopt purposes and functions which are mainly utilitarian, we will not allow education for utility to supplant education for wisdom" (ibid.). It also indicated a critical approach to instructional methodology: "We need to be on guard against the tyranny of technique. It is obvious that practices which are grounded in research and verified by experience should be accredited. But it is also true that we are confronted by the miracle of life, which is incalculable" (ibid.).

Most of the professors at the new college did not have doctoral degrees and were not involved in intensive research. Thus, this faculty, like many others, went through a painful process of adjustment to their new life in the university (Acker, 2000). The program would undergo changes after the 1960s, particularly in the 1990s, when the tensions between the liberal arts components and professional components, along with new intellectual and socio-political configurations, were resolved through a rethinking of the relationship between theory and practice, and a turn to the notion of the teacher as reflexive professional.

Conclusion

The fin de siècle brought to North America and Canada a preoccupation with curriculum and teacher preparation within the context of a modern liberal educational state. It happened at the crossroads of regional, ethnic, and religious tensions (the Catholic question made clear the need for accommodation), and the general need to shape the political and moral subject. The latter would be imbued with Englishness as a colonial core of character formation imparted through formal education. The scholarship on educational matters, in particular on psychology, and the international impact of progressive education in its various emerging strands made pedagogy or education a suitable and desirable emergent area in the universities. Chairs of pedagogy or education were established in the United States and various European countries, focusing on research and the preparation of high school teachers and administrators.

Both the University of Toronto and Queen's University opened faculties of education at the turn of the century. Both were closed in 1920. Regarding the Queen's Faculty of Education, our case in this chapter, the insertion – which was limited to the preparation of high school teachers – failed mainly due to the governance of the system that was expressed in overt state interference in the faculty's business, as well as the indifference from the teachers themselves. The end of the war along with labour unrest generated a renewed concern with citizenship formation and character education, as well as a redefinition of citizenship in terms of Canadian and British heritage and Anglo-conformity, but also with a renewed emphasis on Western civilization. The normal schools would continue preparing teachers during the 1930s and 1940s, but the break generated by the Second World War created the conditions of possibility for an administrative restructuring of the system and of teacher education. The conditions were generated by the Cold War and its construction of education as a matter of security, the demographic changes brought on by the baby boom and postwar immigration, the theory of human capital, and the development of the multiversity and its preoccupation with public usefulness. The MacLeod report provided the point of reference for changes in educational administration and in teacher education. The discourses of the time are embodied in the tensions regarding a utilitarian approach to education and the place of the liberal arts in teacher preparation. The second foundation of Queen's needs to be placed in relation to the MacLeod report and the conditions of possibilities developing after the Second World War.

NOTES

1 This was a powerful issue in Manitoba, as exemplified in the Manitoba School Question, a crisis that culminated with the elimination of the dual confessional system and declaring French just another language in a multilingual system. In 1916, the Norris government abolished the multilingual framework of the school system and made school attendance compulsory until age 14. The system became secular, unilingual, and

universal (public), though private schools were permissible.

2 See B. N. Carter, *James L. Hughes and the Gospel of Education: A Study of the Work and Thought of a Nineteenth Century Canadian Educator*, PhD dissertation, 1966, University of Toronto, Canada.

3 There are interesting manuscripts on Dewey dealing with "reality as experience" and an "ordinary view of truth," as well as many pages devoted to Dewey and to pragmatism available at Queen's University Archives, John Watson Fonds, 1064.1, box 6, file 2.

4 Michael Ignatieff described his great grandfather George Monro Grant, principal of Queen's University between 1877 and 1902, as follows: "Under the influence of Weil and his wife's strong religious belief, George came to conclude that the family's original faith – pious, earnest Presbyterianism – had been the spine that had sustained both its patriotic love of Canada and its insistence that Canada must resist the lure of American ideals and greed." M. Ignatieff, *True Patriot Love: Four Generations in Search of Canada* (Toronto: Penguin Group, 2009), p. 139.

5 Hilda Neatby wrote that "by about 1904 authorities at Queen's were considering the possibility of an institution offering teacher training at various levels by associating a university department of pedagogy with the model school, which had been revived, thanks to the help of two Queen's professors." Neatby (1978), p. 278. This is clear in the minutes of the board of trustees from 29 August 1905, the Report of Committee Re: Teachers Colleges, and the minutes of the board of trustees from 11 September 1905 (Queen's University Archives). It is stated in the latter that the general opinion was that it was desirable that a teachers' college be established in Kingston in close relation with the university for the purpose of carrying out the training of teachers in the three grades which were then represented by the models schools, the normal schools, and the Ontario Normal College. See also Queen's University Archives, Gordon Papers, Address by Principal Gordon, 1906, Kingston, Ontario.

6 See also Neatby (1978), 278–9.

7 The observation component involved the equivalent of 50 school lesson periods, and the practice teaching was the equivalent of 20 school lesson periods. Queen's University Archives (Kingston, Ontario) (see Preliminary Annoucement, 1907, p. 3).

8 There is strong evidence of that intervention. The most compelling was the need to retract the appointment of Mr Hector J. Anderson, from Glasgow, as associate professor in the new faculty. His appointment had been discussed with the superintendent of education, representing the ministry. However, in the end the appointment was objected to on the grounds

that Mr Anderson lacked familiarity with the educational conditions in Ontario. Principal Gordon wrote a letter to Mr Anderson rescinding the appointment and offering compensation. Gordon Papers, Gordon to Hector J. Anderson, Esq., M.A. Hillhead High School, Glasgow, 12 July 1907. See also Gordon Papers, Memorandum Re: correspondence with H.J. Anderson, n.d., manuscript. A letter to Principal R. Bruce Curtis signed by Dean Coleman described an incident in which a student of the faculty was doing her practicum and was pulled from the class in front of the students by an inspector. The dean says that the inspector had assumed the function of inquisitor. Queen's University Archives, Dean Coleman to Principal Taylor, 7 December 1918.

9 As Eric Hobsbawm (2004) has argued, the First World War marked both the end of the nineteenth century and the birth of the "age of total war" that marked the twentieth (p. 22). It was the first war for a century which drew in the European "Great Powers," aside from Spain, the Netherlands, the Scandinavian countries, and Switzerland. Troops from all corners of the British Empire were called into action. Thus, Canada found itself at war with Germany by August 1914. By October, 32,000 volunteers left the country to prosecute the war on England's behalf. (Morton, 2004, p. 225).

What most wagered would be a quick war quickly turned into the "bloody stalemate" of the Western Front, as all sides dug in for what would prove to be the modern equivalent of siege warfare (Hobsbawm, 2004, pp. 27–8). By 1915, defence spending in Canada was more than the entire government had spent in 1913. And yet, as the war proceeded, it lifted the country out of pre-war economic depression. Food production – particularly wheat – boomed during the war years, and the creation of the Imperial Munitions Board quickly became Canada's biggest business, supplying shells, ships, aircraft, explosives, and chemicals for the war effort and employing hundreds of thousands of workers (Morton, 2004, p. 225).

10 See also T. M. Christou, *Progressive Education: Revisioning and Reframing Ontario's Public Schools, 1919–1942* (Toronto: University of Toronto Press, 2012), chapter 7.

11 After the Allied victory, the spoils were divided up between the conflict's two primary victors, the USA and the USSR. The series of agreements reached between these newly minted "superpowers" had the USSR controlling its existing territory as well as much of Eastern Europe (which came to be known as the Eastern Bloc by the late 1940s), and the USA and its North Atlantic Treaty Organization (NATO) allies, including Canada, commandeering the western half of that continent (Hobsbawm, 2004,

p. 226). What came next was "forty years of an armed and mobilized confrontation, based on the always implausible, and in this case plainly baseless, assumption that the globe was so unstable that a world war might break out at any moment" (p. 230). In point of fact, it was much more stable than it had been at any time in the modern period.

12 David Labaree (2008) developed the most sophisticated argument regarding relevance and public usefulness (p. 301).

13 With reference to Quebec, in 1964 the Parent report recommended that teacher education be entrusted to universities. In December 1968, the Assemblée Nationale gave the public, province-wide network of the Université du Québec the power to provide teacher education. In the spring of 1969, autonomous campuses of the Université du Québec network were established in several cities such as Quebec, Montreal, Trois-Rivières, and Chicoutimi, and started operating in the fall of 1969. Pre-existing institutions were merged to create the autonomous campuses. A similar process occurred in the other Quebec universities. Personal communication (email) from Claude Corbo, 18 January 2013.

14 See also Dewar (2006).

15 Special meeting of senate, 13 February 1965, pp. 64–5. The draft of the proposed agreement was attached to the minutes.

16 Queen's University Archives, Agreement between the Minister of Education for the Province of Ontario and Queen's University at Kingston, attached to minutes of Senate, September 1965–May 1966, session of 3 December 1965, pp. 78–84.

4 Cosmopolitanism, Patriotism, and Ecology

NEL NODDINGS

The Idea of Cosmopolitanism

Cosmopolitanism, the idea of belonging to the whole world rather than one nation, tribe, or locality, is as old as the ancient Greeks, but it has always been overshadowed by the far more exciting idea of national patriotism. There are no uniforms, flags, parades, martial music, public pledges, or mock battles to celebrate cosmopolitanism. In times of peace and prosperity, we admire "cosmopolitans," highly cultured people who are "at home" anywhere in the world. But in times of national or group trouble, the committed cosmopolitan is likely to be criticized. In such times, "My country right or wrong" becomes the proud motto.

The experience of Thomas Paine is instructive. Although he was a lifelong advocate of non-violence, he strongly supported the American Revolution in the name of social justice and even criticized his Quaker colleagues for refusing to bear arms (True, 1995, pp. 11–15). American schoolchildren hear of Paine's influential pamphlet *Common Sense*, but they are unlikely to hear of his cosmopolitan motto, "My country is the world; to do good is my religion," or of anything he wrote in *The Age of Reason*. And they probably will not hear that, years later, Theodore Roosevelt called Paine "a filthy little atheist" (True, 1995, p. 14).

The story of Paine's life and travails is important for teachers when they try to encourage critical thinking about cosmopolitanism. Despite a lifetime of enmity towards violence, slavery, and injustice, Paine was called "a Judas, reptile, hog, mad dog, souse, louse, arch beast, brute, liar, and of course infidel" (Jacoby, 2004, p. 36). What generated such hatred and condemnation? Paine was critical of all three great monotheisms, although he never explicitly rejected the existence of a deity.

His two great sins were putting the welfare of all people above national loyalty and his rejection of the formal religions of Christians, Jews, and Muslims.

Even today, teachers may find it difficult to mention that several of America's founders were deists or secularists. Jefferson and Madison were secularists; Washington, Franklin, and John Adams were almost surely deists. Because cosmopolitanism and secularism have been so closely related, when one comes under criticism, the other is likely to suffer also. The current resurgence of conservative religious views, then, may stand in the way of a fair discussion of cosmopolitanism.

Patriotism, however, is the greater deterrent to acceptance of cosmopolitanism. When I speak of acceptance, I do not suggest that we try to convert students to cosmopolitanism through our teaching. Rather, I suggest that we teach for understanding and a fair evaluation of cosmopolitan views based on that understanding. Cosmopolitanism itself requires of its adherents that they *listen* to others and try to understand their intent and what they are going through. Unquestioned patriotism makes it difficult, even morally questionable, to engage in such listening.

Patriotism involves pride in national identity and dedication to the preservation and enhancement of that identity. Our schools have always been expected to instil and increase the spirit of patriotism in our children, and, as mentioned earlier, the culture promotes patriotism through an impressive variety of celebrations. As a result, patriotism has a powerful emotional effect on us. We are moved by the exploits of heroic patriots and by the call to solidarity in times of trouble.

In contrast, cosmopolitanism does not seem to have a great emotional impact on us. Benjamin Barber (1996) points to the "thinness" of the concept. It simply does not invite our passionate engagement. "Our attachments," he writes, "start parochially and only then grow outward" (p. 34). But without thoughtful encouragement, they may never grow outward and, even when they do, an over-zealous patriotism can call them back. Patriotism whipped into a frenzy can produce expressions of hatred that are hard even to imagine years later. Americans who were children during the Second World War look back incredulously to the hatred they were taught to feel towards the Japanese.

Is there a way to exercise some control over patriotism so that it does not overwhelm us and give comfort to blind hatred or prejudice? Barber concludes, "The question is not how to do without patriotism and nationalism but how to render them safe" (ibid., p. 36). Agreeing with this sentiment, Jean Bethke Elshtain (1987) recommends a move to what she calls "chastened" patriotism. She points out that thoughtful, chastened patriotism should induce deep concern for the character and goodness of our country – not simply pride in its successes.

In the spirit of this chastened patriotism, we must admit that our nation has sometimes committed acts that should be regretted, and we should educate our children not only about these acts but also about the serious disagreements that have followed them. The incident of the *Enola Gay* is an important example. The *Enola Gay* was the plane that delivered the atomic bomb that destroyed Hiroshima in the Second World War. The proposed exhibit of the plane and its mission at the Smithsonian Museum would have drawn attention to the 1945 bombing and all the horror of that event. Even though the bombing had taken place fifty years before the planned exhibit, emotions still ran high, and objections to any graphic reminder of what "we" did at Hiroshima were so strong that it was decided simply to exhibit the plane with no mention of its mission. The planned exhibit was criticized as anti-American, suggesting that the bombing was somehow morally questionable. Guided by a chastened patriotism, we might find a way to tell our children not only what happened but how memories and explanations differ. Differences of opinion and arguments occur not only before crucial decisions, but after them as well.

Michael Bess (2006) notes that two very different purposes clashed over the proposed exhibit of the *Enola Gay* – commemoration of the end of a horrible war that took the lives of so many Allied soldiers who should be honoured, and a moral regret about how the war was ended. He suggests that the two purposes must be kept separate, but he is ambivalent about this. Such separation might prevent the kind of uproar induced by the proposed exhibit, but the uproar itself is something students need to hear about. Why do feelings remain so high after fifty years? Why can we not accept the clash of memories and feelings as a lesson in itself?

There are many topics for critical examination in this one story. Must memorial ceremonies and exhibits be kept sharply separated from critique of any kind? Does insistence on the sacredness of memorials contribute to the continuance of war? For present purposes, however, the important thing to notice in this account is that those citizens who wanted to tell the full story of Hiroshima were accused of being anti-American, unpatriotic. During war, it is almost impossible to consider

Elshtain's chastened patriotism, and it continues to be very difficult years later, when the memories of war are aroused.

In the absence of war, schools might be able to move students towards a consideration of cosmopolitanism. Martha Nussbaum (1996) offers four arguments for focusing on cosmopolitanism in civic education. First, "through cosmopolitan education, we learn more about ourselves" (p. 11). Without the study of parenting and child-rearing practices in other parts of the world, Nussbaum suggests, we are likely to assume that our ways are "'normal' and 'natural' for all humans" (p. 12). I pause here to note that our schools teach nothing about parenting and child-rearing, and that neglect is likely to aggravate Nussbaum's concern. Because our students have heard almost nothing by way of critique of our own parenting methods, they are ill prepared to consider other practices. Unless teaching the ways of others is done carefully and in some depth, the conclusion is likely to be that our way is *superior* to others, and this conclusion may well support the current claim of American *exceptionalism.* With that claim widely accepted, it becomes a duty to convert the rest of the world to our ways.

Second, through cosmopolitan education, Nussbaum writes, "we make headway solving problems that require international cooperation" (p. 12). With an emphasis on the *listening* advocated by Marcus Aurelius earlier in her discussion, we might well make some headway. Receptive listening is a basic feature of care ethics, too (Noddings, 1984, 2006). This sort of listening is genuinely open; it does not start out with an attitude of judgment or evaluation. It seeks to learn what the other feels and needs. It encourages the listener to be moved by empathy (Slote, 2007).

Third, Nussbaum continues, "we recognize moral obligations to the rest of the world that are real and that otherwise would go unrecognized" (1996, p. 12). Nussbaum makes an especially important point here when she notes that the universalization of America's high living standards would likely lead to ecological disaster. Consideration of America's profligate consumerism and waste production is a main point in my argument for ecological cosmopolitanism (Noddings, 2012), and that idea will be discussed further below.

Nussbaum's fourth point is that through cosmopolitan education, "we make a consistent and coherent argument based on distinctions we are prepared to defend" (p. 14). Nussbaum worries that the "shared values" extolled by Richard Rorty and Sheldon Hackney seem to be confined to our national boundaries. Why, she asks, "should these values, which instruct us to join hands across boundaries of ethnicity, class, gender, and race, lose steam when they get to the borders of the nation?" (p. 14). In answer, we have to ask exactly which values we have selected and why Rorty and Hackney think that we should "join hands." The traditional, patriotic answer to this is that we want to preserve the distinctive political/social nature of America and the devotion of its citizens. Today, the answer is often stated in terms of keeping America # 1, first in the world economically and militarily. When American exceptionalism is the basic value underlying all others, then many other values *do* stop at our national borders.

If we are to have any chance to encourage cosmopolitan attitudes, I think we must start in some domain other than the political. One promising possibility is to concentrate on ecology, on the health of Earth itself. The well-being of every nation depends ultimately on the health of the Earth on which we all live. To address ecological cosmopolitanism in our schools will require that teachers cross disciplinary boundaries and make the connections central to ecological thinking.

Towards Ecological Cosmopolitanism

We think of our country as both a home-place and a nation. In the past three centuries, and especially in the twentieth century, American attention has been on the *nation*, a collection of people with distinctive civic values and a special form of government. Similarly, at the global level, we have tended to think of the world as a collection of nations. As we move towards ecological cosmopolitanism, we may experience a homecoming of sorts and begin to concentrate on Earth as a natural community and countries as interconnected home-places. This does not imply that we should ignore international politics and economics, but it does suggest a shift in emphasis.

Such a shift does not require that we believe in global warming and the role of human beings in producing it, but it does require that we take such warnings seriously. If global warming is not yet a scientifically proven fact (although many of us believe it is), it must be considered by all reasonable people as a potential disaster that should be prevented if possible. We begin our studies and global conversations with the aim of protecting the health of Earth. This is a common interest par excellence.

In our schools, the shift in emphasis would induce a corresponding change in curriculum that would concentrate more on geography and natural history than on political history. Again, this does not mean that we should abandon political history. The change in emphasis will require healthy coordination between social studies and science, making both areas of study richer and more meaningful.

A third shift in emphasis would move us from a concentration on wilderness (separating human residences and nature) towards one on ecology. The twentieth-century attention to the preservation of wilderness was admirable in many ways, and Americans are rightly appreciative of our great national parks. However, the focus of wilderness preservation was on satisfying human needs, and the parks were designed and maintained to promote the desire of people to enjoy the wilderness. The parks became recreation areas (Steinberg, 2002). Important as the wilderness movement has been, it has obvious limitations: it concentrates the protection of nature within designated wilderness areas, and says little about the overall condition of natural communities. The shift to an ecological approach began to gather steam with the publication of Rachel Carson's *Silent Spring* in 1962. Ted Steinberg writes:

> Although she used the word sparingly in her book, Carson helped to transform *ecology* into the rallying cry of the environmental movement. Unlike *wilderness,* conceived as a world apart, the word *ecology* suggested, in a sense, the reverse – that all life was bound up in an intricate, interconnected web. Human beings, she believed, were thus part of the balance of nature, not divorced from it in the way that some wilderness advocates implied. (Steinberg, 2002, p. 247)

An emphasis on ecology offers several benefits. First, it gives us a common global centre of interest. Second, it requires a move beyond twentieth-century faith in bureaucratic management. "Bureaucracy" has become a familiar pejorative, connoting red tape and all sorts of administrative congestion, but initially it described a system that would carefully match problems and solutions. The idea was to identify a problem and assign it to a designated agency for efficient solution. In addition to the "run-arounds" for which the system is so widely criticized, bureaucratic thinking often led to a proliferation of problems generated by the "solution" of a problem initially identified and assigned to one agency. Carson (1962) pointed out, for example, that spraying fruit trees with pesticides to preserve the fruit led to the depletion of food supplies for birds and, worse, the poisoning of birds through contaminated food – hence, a spring silent of birdsong. Moreover, with fewer birds – natural pest consumers – even more pesticides would be required. It has become apparent that bureaucratic thinking in both environmental and social domains must yield to a more holistic approach, a recognition of interdependence.

An ecological approach to environmental matters should also have a positive effect on social problems. Instead of looking for one cause of the problem of failing schools, for example, we are beginning to realize that we face not just one root cause but a whole tangle of related causes. Gradually, we are beginning to look at our educational problems ecologically – that is, with attention to the whole community and all its parts. We have to work on several fronts at once with careful attention to what is being done on each one.

In schools, students should have opportunities to study environmental problems in both oceanic and terrestrial settings. Following the emphasis on ecological thinking, marine scientists have established the importance of diversity (Safina, 2011). Studying the deterioration of coral reefs in the Caribbean, they found that heavy growths of seaweed blocked the sunlight needed for baby corals to live and grow. Why did seaweed grow out of control in the Caribbean, but not on the reefs around Palau in the Pacific? The answer is almost certainly that the large population of seaweed-eating fish was preserved in Palau but depleted in Belize by commercial fishing. Safina comments:

> The fish are why baby corals regained their foothold and have flourished. Because Palau decided not to let its fish get exported – and because its human population is small compared to their vast reefs – it now has: the fish, boatloads of paying tourists, and the highest coral-recovery rate ever recorded. (p. 285)

As students read about the dramatic recovery of the reefs of Palau and the importance of looking at the whole community of life, they may begin to worry about the "boatloads" of tourists. How did the tourists get there? How much air pollution is caused by airplanes? How do carbon emissions affect global warming? What has global warming to do with the rising seas and increasing likelihood that the islands of Palau will be inundated? And how do we preserve these wonderful, natural places without depriving their human populations of opportunities to grow more prosperous?

Ecological thinking emphasizes balance, and it recommends diversity. In agriculture as well as reef building, the maintenance of diversity and balance is crucial. Disasters of monoculture such as the Irish potato famine in the mid-1840s are usually avoided today by heavy applications of pesticides, but diversity of plants and insects could be effective and far less dangerous. Commenting on the practice of monoculture, Eric Grissell (2001) writes:

> A single type of plant is grown in controlled rows at specific distances in chemically altered soil that is weeded with discs and chemicals. The result is that not even two plants can interact very much. There is little or no diversity in such a system. Also, there are hundreds or thousands of acres under such constant supervision and under such a constant barrage of insecticides, miticides, fungicides, and herbicides ... [that] there is no natural or ecological balance at work. (p. 227)

How does diversity of species and habitats affect stability? How can a variety of insects be encouraged, and how might we use them to manage our gardens naturally?

Ecological thinking has also begun to exercise more influence over city planning. Instead of blank walls to separate people, planners now consider how to use the space between buildings to bring people together. Larry Ford (2000), writing about the spaces between buildings, comments that "we seek some sense of community, sense of place, sense of belonging, sense of history, or feeling of involvement and participation" (p. 208). Ecologically considered, alleys and spaces should connect, not create barriers and separation.

Similarly, the ecological approach is breaking down the sharp separation between city and country. Many cities have created garden strips and paths in between skyscrapers and train lines, and we have learned that front porches and well-maintained and lighted windows reduce the incidence of crime, perhaps by contributing to people's sense of being together in a community. Some might say that lighted front windows convey the sense that someone is watching, and it is this feeling of being watched that has helped to reduce the crime rate in some neighbourhoods, but it is just as plausible to argue that this openness increases our sense of community and the desire to maintain its security.

Although ecological thinking is now popular in city planning, controversy still exists (Christensen, McDonald, & Denning, 2012). Some ecological thinkers want cities to make room for parks, trees, small yards, and habitats for small animals, birds, and insects. Others (urbanists) insist that simply concentrating human life in cities will improve the entire environment by reducing automobile traffic and other sources of emissions. Concentrating residential life in cities would also reduce the harm done in maintaining large suburban lawns with their heavy use of water and fertilizers. The hope is that urbanists and new ecologists will continue to talk and work together to produce urban environments that are efficient, beautiful, and more supportive of health. Watchwords here, as in ecology itself, are *connection, interdependence,* and *sustainability.*

On a global level, students should be made aware of Earth's "hotspots" – areas where the threat of species' extinction is highest. E. O. Wilson notes that these twenty-five hotspots "take up only about 1.4 percent of the world's land surface. Yet, astonishingly, they are the exclusive homes of 44 percent of the world's plant species and more than a third of all species of birds, mammals, reptiles, and amphibians. Almost all are also under heavy assault" (Wilson, 2002, p. 61). This means that if we fail to protect these places, Earth would lose an incredible variety of life forms. It also means that, because the area is relatively small, preserving it should be a manageable task. However, because these places are already so badly damaged and, in most cases, so heavily populated, the task will actually be difficult.

Consider how rich and relevant geography lessons might become. Can students locate the Amazon forest, the Greater Antilles, the Congo forest, the Western Ghats of India, the Philippines, and New Caledonia? Can they name a few species at risk in these areas? What else is threatened when old forests are reduced or destroyed? But the lessons should not be confined to the terrestrial hotspots. Recall the mention of deteriorating coral reefs. Where are the reefs dying, and where are they thriving?

Notice, too, that a concentration on ecology leads necessarily to what might be called *disciplinary ecology* – that is, educators will have to consider how the disciplines now taught in our schools connect with each other and with life itself. We can no longer support a system that separates every school subject from every other subject. What point, other than scoring well on a test, is there to learning an interminable set of disjoint facts and skills? (Noddings, 2007, 2012).

The study of global ecology should be fascinating, but it may also induce a feeling of helplessness in pre-college-level students. What can they do about such huge problems? To answer this question, we should turn to a consideration of local ecology and how students can be usefully engaged in valuable environmental projects.

Ecological Homecoming

Because so many children today are not allowed to roam freely outdoors, it may be even more important for schools to encourage student contact with nature and, for that matter, with objects that need fixing and with material that can be used to create things. Wendell Berry has commented:

> I believe that for many reasons – political, ecological, and economic – the best intelligence and talent should be at work and at home everywhere in the country. And therefore, my wishes for our schools are opposite to those of present-day political parties and present-day politics of education and culture. Wes Jackson has argued that our schools – to balance or replace their present single major in upward mobility – should offer a major in homecoming. (Berry, 1995, p. xi)

Ecological thinking about the environment begins in our own backyards. After discussing the problems of our great rivers, Sara Stein advises us to look close up:

> But let's look at something smaller than the Colorado. Let's look at seeps, rivulets, sumps, hollows, bogs, ditches, frog ponds. Let's examine the face of the continent through a magnifying glass, noticing less the large protuberances and declivities than the fine texture of its skin, its pores, and little wrinkles. Let's get down to the minutiae of puddles. Let's look at our own back yards and ask where butterflies can drink. (Stein, 1993, pp. 175–6)

We are short-changing our children by separating them so early and so definitively from nature and manual work. By doing so, we also separate them from other human beings who work with their hands and from an important part of themselves. Matthew Crawford quotes the director of the California Agriculture Teachers' Association as saying, "We have a generation of students that can answer questions on standardized tests, know factoids, but they can't do anything" (Crawford, 2009, p. 12). Not only is this counterproductive for the kind of work central to ecological cosmopolitanism, it also undermines the development of whole human beings. Real-world, hands-on projects connect us with one another and with an essential part of ourselves. In recommending projects as part of learning in depth, Kieran Egan notes:

> I just want to add the observation about our catastrophic ignorance of the natural world, and its cognitive consequences, as another reason to consider the educational value of LiD [learning in depth]. Especially if we choose our topics from the natural world, we can enable every student to build up both a quantity and a richly meaningful intensity of knowledge, which might go some way toward saving us from our current inability to think well about the natural world and our place within it. (Egan, 2010, pp. 17–18)

Schooling should not separate us from the physical and emotional dimensions of our lives. Indeed, the watchword in ecology is *connection* – not only among life forms on Earth but also among the topics we study, the objects we use, the physical conditions in which we live, our houses and gardens, how and why we get from one place to another. This observation suggests that in schools we might profitably reduce the emphasis on political history and give more attention to the history of homes, parenting, and childhood. There need be no intellectual loss in making this change, because – as Dewey pointed out years ago – the intellectual power of a subject is not determined by its title but by the way it is studied. Algebra is not inherently more intellectual than cooking.

As we encourage students to care for their own backyards, tend gardens, and appreciate the variety of life forms around them, we should also help them to understand that people all over the world love their own natural places – inside and outside cities. Caring for our own part of the Earth should lead quite naturally to a desire to understand and protect the larger world, Earth itself.

Back to Earth

Education today should make it safe for students to proclaim themselves citizens of the world. Highly nationalistic patriotism is simply no longer healthy for either the Earth or the country we love. In addition to a change in emphasis from national patriotism to ecological cosmopolitanism, students should be invited to consider how nationalism is supported by music, uniforms, and celebrations. Contrast, for example, two patriotic songs that all American schoolchildren learn: "The Star-Spangled Banner" and "America the Beautiful." In the first, we sing of flags, rockets, ramparts, fighting, war's desolation, bravery, and triumph. In the second, we sing of spacious skies, amber waves of grain, mercy, self-control, success as nobleness, and brotherhood from sea to shining sea. Does the contrast describe a difference in how we might express our love of country? Suppose Arbor Day were celebrated with the enthusiasm of Independence Day?

We should return, finally, to an extension of Nussbaum's second benefit of teaching cosmopolitanism – making headway on solving problems that require international cooperation. Engagement in ecological cosmopolitanism can serve as an accompaniment or, often, as a prelude to political cosmopolitanism. As we work to solve environmental problems, we get to know one another better. We learn to exercise the central requirement of caring – listening. Working together, listening, we come to care not just about the problems and their solution. We come to care for those with whom we work; to hurt or destroy them has become unthinkable. It is at this stage that we may safely tackle political differences.

FOCAL POINT 2

Paradigmatic Changes in Teacher Education

This focal point brings to the fore the contextualized character of teacher education and its location in relation to complex globalizing connections. There is indeed a connection between international political and economic forces, the accompanying intellectual changes, and teacher education. Thus, after the Second World War, the prominence of science within the framework of the Cold War set the stage for what Rohstock and Tröhler refer to as the scientization and intellectualization of classrooms. The emphasis on mental activity went along with the popularity of cognitive psychology. The vision of education historically decontextualized, but focused in the future, became dominant.

But what are the conditions for a program to enact a transnational and cosmopolitan quality, in light of the confluence of so many political and economic agendas? Not less important are questions raised by Whitehead about the role of the teacher as a professional, and the poor connection between university-based classes and school-based practicum experience beyond the boundaries of technical rationality. The problematization of the reflective practitioner takes centre stage in this section, especially in the chapter by Russell. Furthermore, there is an embracing dimension at the core of the globalizing process; this is the ubiquitous learning, as described by Burbules, that developed as a product of dramatic technological changes. It signals the need to build human dispositions towards creativity and mastery, in line with the idea of expanding experience and knowledge which is part of the flow of human activities. Certainly, there is a need to articulate a renewed understanding of the role of education in building a learning society and critical citizens, and to think about the kind of teacher education program that would prepare teachers to relate goals to contexts and experiences, having ubiquitous learning as a resource.

5 From the Sacred Nation to the Unified Globe: Changing Leitmotifs in Teacher Training in the Western World, 1870–2010

ANNE ROHSTOCK AND DANIEL TRÖHLER

One of the most fundamental and lasting cultural shifts of the eighteenth century was the "educationalization" of the social world. Probably the most significant legacy of this educational turn was the establishment of the modern mass school system, a development connected to the abolishment of the feudal and divided societies of the Age of Absolutism and the rise of the modern nation state around 1800. Nation building and the creation of the modern citizen were viewed to a large extent as an educational project (Tröhler, Popkewitz, & Labaree, 2011) in whose context education as an academic discipline arose (Lagemann, 2000).

The world wars of the twentieth century led traditional notions of the nation state to be questioned, and fostered new institutions for ordering social and political life, including the League of Nations after the First World War (Fuchs, 2006) and the United Nations and other organizations of global governance after the Second World War (Chabbott, 2003). The Cold War, as well, brought about new educational projects in the Western world (Hartman, 2008; Tröhler, 2010). After the Second World War, global peace was soon linked to the need for a transnational sense of citizenship. Furthermore, in the context of the West's competition with the USSR, a larger emphasis was placed on science and mathematics in educational curricula (Erickson, 2006; Rudolph, 2002).

The educational turn of the late eighteenth century, nation building of the nineteenth century, and efforts to promote global unity after the two world wars had effects not only on educational organizations, policies, and materials, but also on the manner with which the major actors in the world of education – namely, teachers – were trained. The leitmotifs that emerged in teacher training reflected the major cultural concerns of each era: in the nineteenth century, this was national uniqueness and supremacy; in the postwar period, it was internationalization and global standardization. These leitmotifs were associated with the emergence of particular academic subfields and heavily shaped pedagogical ideals. In the era of nation building, the history of education dominated teacher education. In the context of the Cold War, teacher training was aligned with a new internationalist and scientific paradigm.

This chapter discusses these two leitmotifs in teacher education, which must properly be viewed as reflections of the dominant political and cultural aspirations of their time. In the first section, we will reconstruct the rise of the history of education as a major subject in nationalist and religiously inspired teacher education in Germany and France. In the second section, we will show how this leitmotif was supplanted by a "cognitive revolution" in the training of professional educators in the Cold War period that not only "slaughtered" the sacred cow of educational history in teacher training, but also promoted the rise of an ahistorical and fundamentally decontextualized educational ideology. The last section describes how this change in leitmotifs can be viewed as a transition from external to internal mechanisms of control in educational systems.

The Rise of Nation States and the Need for a Nationwide School System

Uniform and professional systems of teacher training did not exist until the nineteenth century. As we shall see, teacher training was an important element of the strategies pursued by rising European nation states. On one hand, teacher training was viewed as a means of integrating the population. On the other hand, it was seen as a way of advancing the nation and strengthening its competitive position on the international playing field.

In this way, the strategy of introducing a nationwide school system was closely linked to the idea of the nation state that emerged from the French Revolution, and, within Europe, particularly from the Congress of Vienna (1814–15). Most of the emerging new states – with the exception of archconservative Prussia – enacted constitutions that legally grounded the state's new sovereignty and transformed the inhabitants into legal subjects. Whereas the army had the mission of defending territorial sovereignty externally, it fell to the newly established school systems to integrate the citizenry into the constitutional state. This integrative task required a means of identification – the ideal of the nation – that interpreted society as an entity united not by being composed of identical individuals, but by similarities of history and language.

The first modern education laws in Europe were enacted in Western and Northern Europe, and by the end of the nineteenth century, such laws had spread across the entire continent. Typically, legal provisions for teacher training were enacted concurrently with new educational laws – for, ultimately, the newly created school systems needed appropriately qualified professional staff. Although the new nation states were primarily preoccupied with building their internal administrative structures during the first half of the nineteenth century, by the second half they were also exhibiting mounting levels of animosity and competitiveness towards other nations. The Franco-Prussian War (1870–1), which ultimately brought about the unification of Germany's northern and southern territories with the founding of the German Empire in 1871, was of particular significance for the history of pedagogy in the realm of teacher training. Under Chancellor Otto von Bismarck, the constitution of the German Empire was adopted on 16 April 1871, opening the way for the creation of a nationwide school system, whose development was financed, nota bene, through war reparations from France.

The Foundation of the German Empire and the Emergence of the "History of Pedagogy"[1]

The unification of the North German Confederation with the large southern German states of Württemberg and Bavaria under the domination of Prussia to create the German Empire was, above all, a cultural tour de force. Suddenly there was a pressing need to compel territories that had formerly been enemies to become a *single* nation. The foundation of the German Tariff Union in 1866 had already set in motion an economic unification process that predated political unification. And Johann Gottlieb Fichte's "Addresses to the German Nation," delivered in Berlin in 1808 as an expression of opposition to French military occupation, set the stage ideologically. Fichte proclaimed not only that German was the only language that enabled one to achieve true knowledge, but that a nation was essentially defined as a community of individuals who shared the same mother tongue (Craig, 1978; Fichte, 2008). The efforts to achieve political, economic, and ideological unification demanded cultural acceptance as well; only in this way could different territories ultimately be moulded into an "imagined community" (Anderson, 2006).

The dissemination of the knowledge necessary to foster this community was the mission assigned to schools, and especially to teachers, who would need to be specially educated for this lofty task. Accordingly, the education of the teacher could not be limited to the technical aspects of professional training. Rather, it would need to include subjects that the teacher would not actually teach in primary schools, such as psychology, didactic methods, and the history of pedagogy. In fact, teaching about the history of pedagogy had been in place for some time and not coincidentally can be traced back to the French occupation of Germany after 1805–6, although it only became a separate subject of study after 1871. It was at this time that the genre first took on its full dimension, and then spread to other nations.

This new field – that is, the general education of teachers – required its own teaching materials. Four new sets of teaching materials for teacher training were published in Germany in the three-year period between 1871 and 1873, all of which proved to be very successful:

Friedrich Dittes (1871): *Geschichte der Erziehung und des Unterrichts: für dt. Volksschullehrer* [History of Education and Instruction: For German Public School Teachers], reprinted eleven times through 1903.

Lorenz Kellner (1872): *Kurze Geschichte der Erziehung und des Unterrichtes mit verwaltender Rücksicht auf das Volksschulwesen* [A Brief History of Education and Teaching with Administrative Consideration of the Public Educational System], reprinted eleven times through 1899.

Joseph Kehrein (1873): *Überblick der Geschichte der Erziehung und des Unterrichts: für Zöglinge der Lehrerseminare und zur Vorbereitung auf die Allg. Bestimmungen angeordneten Prüfungen* [Overview of the History of Education and Instruction: For Students in Teachers' Colleges and for Preparation for General Examinations], reissued sixteen times through 1922.

August Schorn (1873): *Geschichte der Pädagogik, in Vorbildern und Bildern* [History of Pedagogy in Examples and Pictures], the absolute bestseller among all the history texts, reissued for the thirty-second time in 1922.

All these "histories of education" are markedly nationalistic, a fact clearly demonstrated by the pedagogues chosen for inclusion.[2] As figure 5.1

Figure 5.1 Authors cited in German histories of education, 1871–1873

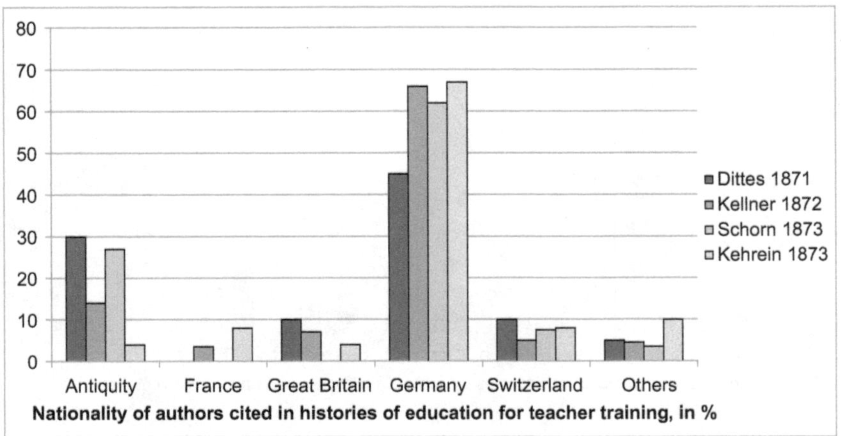

shows, the Germans primarily made reference to the great figures of German education. With the exception of Dittes, two-thirds of the quotations cited by the three other authors are from German educators, and sources from antiquity figure more prominently than authors from France or England. Thanks to Rousseau and Pestalozzi, Switzerland ranks ahead of the two other European great powers.

The French Facsimile

Following France's defeat at the hands of Prussia in 1871, we can recognize similar efforts to institute a nationwide educational system in France. Germany's western neighbour proceeded to develop its own national educational system, specifically focused on teacher training, although this occurred some ten years behind Germany. Education professorships dedicated exclusively to teacher training were not established until the 1880s. In France, as in Germany, teaching materials were needed, and the developed texts aimed at strengthening the nationalist and moral character of prospective teachers. The Law of 1882 established a legal foundation for the new system of teacher training in France, and in subsequent years various histories of education and instruction were published. The first of these proved the most successful: Gabriel Compayré's *Histoire de la pédagogie* [History of Pedagogy], which covered the period from antiquity to the present, was published

Figure 5.2 Authors cited in French histories of education, 1871–1891

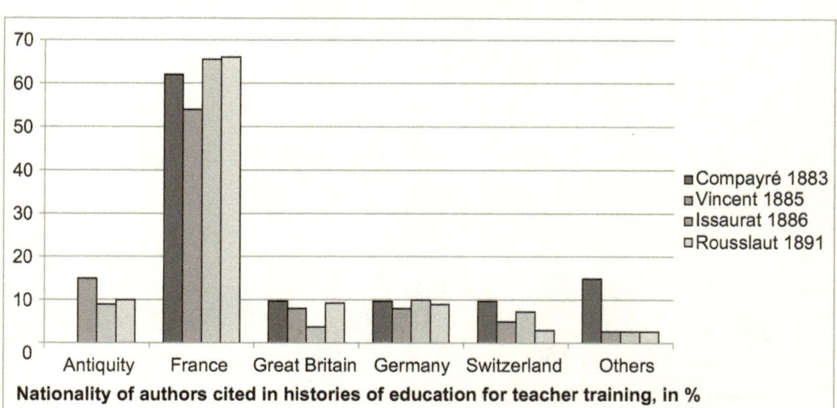

in 1883. Its twenty-eighth edition was released in 1917, and there is also reference to an undated thirty-third edition. In French histories of education, we find a similar situation concerning the selection of educators who were cited. French writers primarily cited French educators, thus proving themselves to be no less nationalistically oriented than their German neighbours.

As figure 5.2 shows, French writers accounted for between 60 per cent and 66 per cent of the authors who were cited; all other nations and antiquity are equally represented at around 10 per cent. If we combine the four histories from Germany and the four from France, we can see the parallel emphasis on national paradigms in figure 5.3.

These writers all agreed that teacher training should not be purely academic, but should have a practical benefit. Thus, as Compayré (1883) put it, one should study the history of education not merely in a "spirit of erudition," but rather on practical grounds "in order to search for enduring truths" (p. xiv). In comparable fashion, Dittes (1871) also sought to derive moral and practical benefit from the history of education: "Sojourning in this realm will fill the teacher with love and enthusiasm for a calling that is ennobled and sanctified by its glorious luminaries; with those ideas in which all attempts to improve mankind must find their true aims; through these greatest paragons of perseverance and self-sacrifice in the service of civilization" (p. 9f.).

However, "civilization" was conceived along national lines, as demonstrated by the selection of sources. The "love and enthusiasm"

Figure 5.3 Authors cited in French and German histories of education, 1871–1891

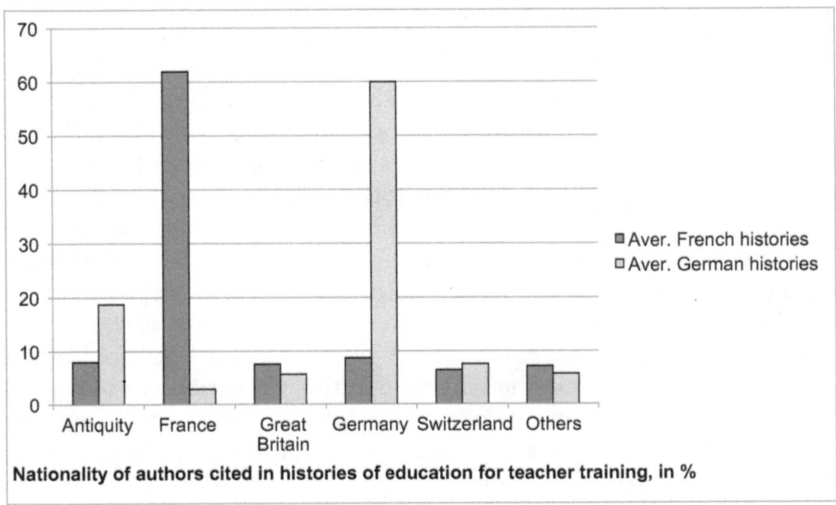

for his profession that was to be instilled in the teacher had to be evoked by national heroes – and not international ones, with the occasional exceptions of Rousseau in France and Pestalozzi in Germany. Furthermore, the love that was to be stimulated by these great historical figures was always meant to operate *prospectively*: the history of education had a distinct past that would lead to a goal situated in the present and the immediate future. In both countries, the historical texts are thus arranged chronologically according to epochs. Compayré differentiated between classical antiquity, the Middle Ages, the Renaissance, and modernity, while Dittes located the distinction as being between "ancient peoples" and the "Germans." He subdivided the "Germans" into five categories, the first two pre-Luther and the last three post-Luther. Compayré represents the epochs as embodied by "great figures" (p. xiii), or, as Dittes expressed it, "ground-breaking leaders of the human race," whom Dittes regarded as being primarily of ancient or German origin (p. 9f.). With this background, we can see that these authors did not view themselves as writing histories of education, but rather *the* history of education, which ultimately was equivalent to documenting cultural progress – only in one instance, progress had its epicentre in Germany, and in the other, in France.[3]

National-Religious Idealizations

The idea of the nation was not a rationalist project, but an idealistic and emotional one. As a result, there was a belief that merely educating students in various subjects would not be sufficient to unify the population and win its support for the nation state. Rather, it was necessary for future teachers to feel "love and enthusiasm" for their patriotic occupation and to imbue them with an ideological zeal for their mission. Accordingly, school curricula were nationally biased, and this was not only the case for subjects like history or geography. The goal of these various histories of education was nothing less than to inspire a quasi-religious identification with the nation on the part of the teacher.

This "missionary" aspect is readily apparent in the selected histories when one considers the ways the authors describe the historical sweep of progress they attributed, in part, to education. Compayré saw his work of history as "showing the progress of pedagogy as it gradually elevated itself from instinct to reflection, from nature to art." Pedagogy is capable of "revealing this beautiful spectacle to us of humanity growing without end" (p. xiii). The ultimate lessons of such historical progress were to be obtained through a "science of education" that was yet to be created. The closing passages from his *Histoire de la pédagogie* show how Compayré imagined historical progress. While he rejected an understanding of evolution that envisioned the emergence of a race of supermen, Compayré did believe in the power of proper education.

According to Compayré, the progress of mankind arose from reasoned reflection on what constituted an adequate education, and this reflection needed to be more comprehensive, broader, more earnest, and more liberal than ever before. Thus, Compayré thought it made sense to base this new form of education on empirical psychology, so as to create a *science de l'éducation* backed by historical examples, which could formulate a theory of education. This form of scientism was not rationalist or universal, but it mirrored the rationalist ideology to which France had been committed since the French Revolution. Rationality in this sense was not conceptualized in a universal sense, but as French. This is demonstrated by the final passage from Cyprien Issaurat's book: "Now, the philosophy of instruction that should prevail in national education, in state institutions, the one and only philosophy that is responsive to the needs of our epoch, to paraphrase the way that an academician expressed it, to meet those demands that every day demand more and more to be satisfied, this is the spirit of science in the broadest sense ... of an absolutely secular or materialistic science" (Issaurat, 1886, p. 493).

One can discern a comparable foundation that is even more clearly identifiable as religious in German historical writings. Dittes summed up his ideas as follows: "Not nearly all the essential requirements of pedagogy have been legally recognized as yet, and so many reforms we consider essential still exist only on paper. But if we compare the present with the past, we can rejoice with all our hearts about the progress that has been made ... Pedagogical science and art have not progressed so far that we can be complacent, but sufficiently for it to fulfil its mission" (Dittes, 1871, p. 216). The vocabulary of Christian salvation, as it appears here in the notion of "mission," is hardly coincidental. In keeping with this spirit, Kellner's history also concludes with an invocation: "Anyone who fails to awaken, elevate, and intensify religious sensibility in his educational program, who fails to deliberately place it at the forefront, in full awareness of existing conflicts, such a person, no matter how favourable circumstances or humanity may be, will never accomplish what is truly fruitful, pleasing to God, or permanent. This is and shall remain the lesson of educational history!" (Kellner, 1872, p. 261).

A Newly Ordered World: Teacher Education and Global Convergence

The nationalistic and historically grounded philosophy of education that dominated teacher training underwent a process of change after the First World War, one that accelerated after 1945. A new and essentially ahistorical educational ideology of a "harmonized educational globe" (Tröhler, 2010) ultimately fostered the cultural decontextualization of education policy in general and teacher training policy in particular. In the "new world" to be created, teachers were no longer expected to conduct their work in a moral or emotional way, but instead to be nonmoralizing, rational, and logical. Educational policymakers hoped that by elevating the scientific, cognitive, and technological aspects of education, it would be possible to create a world free of aggressive nation states and to fashion a peaceful world without a past or local particularities and constraints. Problems in this future world should instead be solved pragmatically with the help of scientific methods and scientific knowledge (Bell, 1960).

How can we explain such complex transformations in a relatively short time period? Three closely related developments were primarily responsible: the rise of a new international paradigm of scientification from the interwar period onward; the triumphal march of psychology and its "cognitive revolution" in education research and policy (beginning in America in the 1950s); and the ascendancy of a new view of human nature, one that sought the technological and systematic improvement of humanity based on the insights of cybernetics and artificial intelligence.

The Academization of Teacher Training following the First World War

In the wake of the First World War, we can observe pronounced tendencies towards internationalization and scientification in nearly every modern Western society; these tendencies formed the basic foundation for a transnational program of *social engineering*. Historical research reveals a clear effort to promote interdisciplinary and international cooperation among different scientific disciplines in order to foster new systems for ensuring the integrity of societies that were being subjected to the centrifugal forces of modernity. The principal driving force behind these plans was a transnational and elite cadre of scientifically qualified experts. In the realm of education, this led to ideas ranging from the "educational multilateralism" (Fuchs, 2006, p. 167) espoused by the League of Nations in 1919, to the scientific educational policy efforts of the fascist alliance that was active internationally (Bernhard & Rohstock, forthcoming).

The trends towards scientification and internationalization had a significant impact on teacher education. Driven by scientific progress in psychology and the associated elevation of pedagogy as science taught and researched in university settings, more and more academics and politicians from the United States and Europe campaigned for the professionalization of teacher training and for a reformulation of its subject matter (Nelles, 1995). The efforts towards scientification were initially reflected in the attempts in many Western nations to make teacher training more academic. The Weimar Constitution of 1919, for example, contained provisions for the nationwide reformulation of teacher training throughout Germany, which was to be oriented towards "principles that generally apply to higher education" (Weimar Constitution, 1919, article 143). This paved the way for teacher training to be integrated into the university. Similar attempts to make teacher training more academic can be seen in England and in the United States; in the latter country, there was a wave of restructuring in which formerly normal schools were transformed into teacher colleges or state colleges (Labaree, 2008, p. 295; Tyack, 1967).

Thus, the academization of teacher training became a phenomenon that spanned multiple nations, and its orientation to international themes was also reflected at an organizational and substantive level. In the first half of the twentieth century, international teachers' associations operating on a global scale were founded, such as the World Organization of Associations of Public School Teachers in 1926 and the World Organization of Teachers in Higher Education, which had already come into existence before the First World War (Fuchs, 2006). At the same time, internationally oriented academics and politicians placed the "international mind" (Butler, 1912) at the centre of their efforts for the transnationalization of teacher training. The "international mind" was defined as "that fixed habit of thought and action which looks upon the several nations of the civilized world as co-operating equals in promoting the progress of civilization, in developing commerce and industry, and in diffusing science and education throughout the world" (Butler, cited by Kuehl & Dunn, 1997, p. 65). A survey conducted on behalf of the League of Nations in 1929 came up with the surprising finding that practically all teacher training schools in the United States "are preparing their students to train their future pupils along the lines of world friendship" (World Federation of Education Associations, 1929, p. 76).

In the majority of cases, however, efforts to internationalize and academize teacher training in the 1920s and 1930s were confined to the purely discursive level. For example, in England and Germany, there was massive resistance to the integration of teacher training into the university (Schellack & Große, 2007; Thomas, 1990). In many nations, the process of complete formal incorporation of teacher education into the university would have to wait for some time. Efforts along these lines proceeded at a faster or slower pace in different countries, but they intensified noticeably in the 1960s and 1970s, and reforms ultimately were implemented in all Western nations by the first decade of the twenty-first century, at the very latest. "The intention was," as Hannu Simola (1998) outlined for Finland, "to transform teaching from 'a haphazard activity into a rational one'" (p. 343).

Science Makes the World Go Round: Internationalization and Scientification of Teacher Training since 1945

Society's understanding of science was transformed over the course of the Second World War, and this accelerated the process of academization. During the 1940s, there was a growing belief that science had the potential to solve all problems, a conviction that first arose in the United States but spread increasingly to Europe (Rohstock, 2012). This belief was visible first and foremost in the realm of politics. Contemporaries were in broad agreement that the Allied victory had been enabled by the technological advances of military research, such as that conducted at MIT (Leslie, 1993; Stewart, 1980). In light of growing tensions with the Soviet Union, science was once again called to arms by policymakers; research and technology were viewed as the keys to prevailing in this new competitive race (McDougall, 1985).

The experience of the Second World War also solidified the belief among researchers themselves in the universal capacity of science to solve all problems. Hardly any scientist in the public arena expressed the slightest doubt that rationality and the human intellect could chart the way to a better world, whether through technological progress or by the further evolution of mankind itself. Jerrold Zacharias, for example, a physicist in military service and a member of the American scientific elite during the postwar era, spoke for his colleagues when he expressed his unalterable belief that nearly every problem facing American society could be solved through "first-class intellect" (Zacharias, as cited by Rudolph, 2002, p. 90).

According to many in the US intellectual elite, a "crisis of education" had been gripping the country since the end of the Second World War. Numerous critics assigned responsibility for the plight of the educational system to progressive education and the life-adjustment movement. Entirely in keeping with the new paradigm of scientification, Jerome Bruner, a leading psychologist of the era, saw progressive education as characterized by a "discontinuity from the frontiers of knowledge" and a "disinterest in the intellectual structure of classroom activities" (Bruner, as cited by Olson, 2007, p. 33). Thus, it was not educators but scientists, especially from the disciplines that had previously been crucial to the war effort – psychology, mathematics, chemistry, physics, and biology – who played a dominant role in the debates about the future design of school curricula, new systems of teacher education, and the reform of universities. Their primary aim was the scientification and intellectualization of classroom teaching (Hartman, 2008; Rohstock, 2012; Rudolph, 2002).

Cognitive psychology figured significantly in this process. The so-called cognitive turn established a view of the educational system in general and on teacher training in particular that remains dominant today. With its promise of a total departure from the previously dominant behaviourist model of teaching and learning, its focus on research about mental activity as a form of information processing inspired by cybernetics, and its orientation towards premises derived from the natural sciences concerning the production of knowledge, cognitive psychology contained precisely the right dosage of revolution and science-inspired renewal to catalyse its rapid adoption in the world of research as well as in political realms.

Inspired by the "cognitive turn," the American philosopher of science Thomas Kuhn posited a thesis regarding the nature of scientific revolutions that soon achieved worldwide notoriety (Kuhn, 1962). American politicians, too, were mesmerized by the promise of a scientific renewal in the field of education. When two of the principal American protagonists for the cognitive turn, the psychologists and former military experts Jerome Seymour Bruner and George Armitage Miller, approached John Gardener, then-president of the Carnegie Corporation in New York, to urge him to provide start-up financing for a Center for Cognitive Studies, Gardener responded by immediately offering a quarter of a million dollars. Shortly thereafter, the Ford Foundation became aware of the project. It not only invested an additional $250,000, but soon shut down its program for the behavioural sciences, thereby turning off the spigot of financial support to an entire generation of behaviourist researchers (Bruner, 1983, pp. 122, 124). Support from representatives of the political elite, from Sargent Shriver to John F. Kennedy and Lyndon B. Johnson, showed that the American political elite had rapidly become persuaded of the potential offered by cognitive psychology for reforming the educational system. Supporters of cognitive psychology took advantage of these new opportunities that arose in the field of education: the fact that the US federal government began to involve itself in what the US constitution guaranteed was a system of locally administered schools – something that even Sargent Shriver had to admit constituted "political dynamite"– was due in no small part to individuals like Bruner and Miller (Shriver, as cited by Bruner, 1980, p. 136). In any case, there was a veritable wave of new initiatives emanating from the cognitive centre that Bruner and Miller had built up at the beginning of the 1960s. In ensuing years, similar institutions sprang up like mushrooms, and the prefix "cognitive" became a quality brand with high recognition value (Boden, 2006).

In the area of schools, the American proponents of cognitive psychology at first focused less on the training of teachers, but concentrated all their efforts on how to educate students. Their primary goal was reform of the curriculum. At the celebrated ten-day Woods Hole Conference in 1958, subject specialists, together with psychologists, developed new teaching plans and textbooks that had no less a goal than the complete reformulation of the curriculum. From now on, abstract problem-solving capabilities should be at the forefront of learning in each individual discipline, and logical operations and a general understanding of a subject should take precedence over its mastery; in the future, just as had taken place in scientific research after the Second World War, teaching would be oriented to mandatory target goals. Structure was the new magic word. Schools would have to subordinate themselves to this principle and the teacher would furnish the student with knowledge structures. Bruner called this process "scaffolding"; explicitly he wanted to transfer this engineering model into pedagogical practice. He believed that the future schools would enable the student to solve unfamiliar problems in contexts that were totally different from those already encountered (Bruner, 1960; Olson, 2007). According to this perspective, the function of the school was to transform the human mind into a decoding system that could break down every imaginable code that might arise in a future environment (Bruner, 2006). In this way, universally applicable and future-directed ways of thinking found their way into the American classroom, and suppressed traditional present-oriented, spatially, historically, and culturally contextualized subject matter.

Along the way to implementing this program, the teacher was regarded primarily as "an obstacle." As the actions of the scientific elite ultimately demonstrate, in the scientification of the classroom they were also engaged in a "depedagogization" of instruction. From the outset, these scholars had major doubts whether the "ordinary" teacher would rise to meet the intellectual demands of the new system of teaching or be able to impart the devised novel forms of learning. In fact, teachers had not been educated up to that time – as many scientists disdainfully noted – in "cutting-edge science"; rather, their studies had focused first and foremost on education (Rudolph, 2002, p. 66). The technologization of classroom teaching promised a solution to this dilemma. The use of teaching and learning machines and educational films could minimize the impact of the old teaching staff, as could handouts compiled in thick volumes that educators were to scrupulously go through during the class period (Rohstock, 2012). These measures were intended to limit the role of the teacher to an "effective instructional manager." Incorporating the teacher into "a systematic design of instruction should reduce the number of inefficient, ineffective and non-essential teaching-learning situations" (Razik, 1972, p. 60).

The Ascendency of Cognitive Psychology in Teacher Training since the 1980s

The fact that the planned rollback of the role of educators from classroom teaching was not only naive, but also fell short of what was required, became the increasing focus of criticism during the second half of the 1970s. The oft-recurring question that was raised was how students could engage in explorative learning "when the teacher was to be regarded as a mere technician" (Tanner & Tanner, 1987, p. 189). In addition, pedagogical research had found that teachers typically didn't use the lesson materials that had been developed by the scientific elite in the intended manner. Instead of applying the methods designed to promote abstract cognitive abilities, they continued to teach facts (Cohen, 1973, p. 33; Goodlad, 1966). For this reason, educational policymakers sought "radical changes" in teacher training as part of a comprehensive reform of the educational system (Yates, 1970). The OECD even saw the progress of the Western world as dependent on the systematic reform of teacher education, stating that "there is little hope of progress without programmes for systematic continuing training. The education of teachers will be at the centre therefore of any programme of educational reform" (OECD, 1974a, p. 9). Indeed, since the 1970s the OECD has devoted increased attention to the reform of teacher training (OECD, 1974b, 1977, 1971a, 1971b).

Within the scope of such reform efforts, one goal was to redesign curricula for teacher training. Despite all the rhetoric about scientification, the degree to which this effort was driven by the Cold War and the aim of denationalizing the Western world is evident when we take a look at the institutions involved in the reformulation of teacher training and the programs they put forth. The effort to mould educational systems in the image of defence systems that had been previously witnessed in the reform of the US curriculum (Rudolph, 2002) was now extended internationally. The North Atlantic Treaty Organization (NATO), an organization that had no mandate for educational policy, promoted a far-ranging international program for the reform of teacher training. NATO went so far as to construct an Atlantic Information Centre for Teachers (AICT) in London, which attempted to exert a direct influence on educators in European classrooms with a whole series of seminars, beginning at the end of the 1960s. In these well-attended courses, the aim first and foremost was to achieve American-European solidarity and the strategic unity of the West in a defensive community that encompassed all of society. Teachers and schools would be enlisted to accomplish this aim. The mindset of the NATO-financed conferences was that European teaching staff had a mission to educate young people about the "total dependency" of Europe on the United States such that they would "learn to treasure" the involvement of the Americans (Atlantic Information Centre for Teachers/AICT, 1969, pp. 18, 23).

The AICT clearly indicated that for this endeavour the national state should be regarded as the utmost evil: in 1971, James Becker, member of the AICT Advisory Committee, told numerous teachers and members of European cultural affairs administrations that the national state had not only been among the greatest enemies to world peace in the past, but that it continued to represent the greatest potential danger in today's world, and should even be regarded as an aggressive entity, one that could throw the world into anarchy at any time. Therefore, Becker proposed considering the establishment of a world government as a way of preventing the occurrence of this kind of anarchy. As might be expected, Becker's proposal to abolish the nation state encountered harsh criticism (AICT, 1971, pp. 10, 11). Nonetheless, the idea of a global government or centre for world planning was already widely disseminated at this time and had found major support in both the United States and Europe (Rohstock, 2012).

These visions of a unified world order contained a quasi-religious promise of salvation – that man could achieve "control over his destiny" through schools and education (US Senate paper, as quoted by AICT, 1971, p. 13). The work of teachers would no longer be related to the present, and certainly not to the past, but rather to the future: above all else, teachers had to prepare children for the world of tomorrow. This explicitly meant discarding one's own past along with "slaughtering" the "sacred cows" of teacher training, and especially the "history of education," as a UNESCO report literally stated (Cohen, 1973, p. 24). This intention can also be inferred from the fact that national history began to play an ever smaller role in teacher training programs beginning in the 1970s (Simola, 1998). The titles of the teacher training programs designed in the 1980s spoke volumes: in 1986, the Carnegie Corporation's Task Force on Teaching as a Profession published its report, *A Nation Prepared: Teachers for the 21st Century*. The same year, the Holmes Group presented its report, *Tomorrow's Teachers* (1986).

The scientists and politicians involved in teacher training wanted not only to transform its contents, but also to revolutionize the methods and techniques that teachers employed. Following the widespread failure of curriculum reform efforts that had focused on developing technologies for the classroom and on the students themselves (Dow, 1991; Rohstock, 2012), an enormous influence was exerted by cognitive psychology, which increasingly turned its attention to teacher training after the 1980s (Popkewitz, 1993). Its involvement in this area of education was celebrated, above all, as a process of scientification, as the "application of scientific knowledge about teaching" (Cochran-Smith et al., 2008, p. 1140; Husén & Postlethwaite, 1985). Whether in the form of micro-teaching (Klinzing, 2002), "cognitively guided instruction" (Fennema, Carpenter, & Peterson, 1989), expert-novice approaches, or metacognitive strategies in a reflective teaching practice (Cruickshank, 1987; Pickle, 1985; Shulman, 1986), the research literature on teachers' cognition has experienced an unprecedented boom since the 1980s (Bromme, 1992; Valli, 1992). That the issue here was – perhaps primarily – about securing research funding was clearly articulated by the researchers themselves: "We need continued federal support for cognitive research focused on issues relevant to … teacher education." For, as they put it, "our expertise in cognitive psychology is a national resource" (Linn, 1982, p. 6). Even Jerome Bruner had to admit that, in this respect, cognitive psychology was "full of clever moves," especially when it came to marketing itself as a scientific program with a direct impact on the social practice of education. "The basic trick was to state your findings in centimeters, grams and seconds," Bruner stated, thus unmasking the supposed scientification of psychology as a simple shift of emphasis to the quantification of one's research findings (Bruner, 1983, p. 107).

Compelled by the appeal of a supposedly rigorous, scientific, and objective curriculum, politicians rapidly jumped on board. The reports of the Holmes Group and the Carnegie Task Force in the United States "drew significantly on recent theory and research in the psychology of learning and teaching in portraying the ideal teacher" (Peterson, Clark, & Dickson, 1989, p. 2). In keeping with the goal of scientification, the ideal teacher had to be first and foremost a teacher-researcher with a broad repertoire of thinking and problem-solving strategies. Drawing upon his or her metacognitive capacities, the teacher should be able to reflect upon his or her own thinking and actions and undergo a kind of self-monitoring process so as to be able to help students develop "meaningful and coherent structures of knowledge and action." This, at least, was how the American Psychological Association described the benefits stemming from its "research during the last few decades on pedagogic practice" (Baer, 2000, p. 23).

Beginning in the United States, cognitive psychology has experienced a veritable triumphal march in connection with the reform of teacher training in many Western nations since the 1980s (Hudson & Zgaga, 2008). In Germany, France, and England, for example, we can observe very similar approaches to teacher training in place during the 1990s. Teacher training was aimed primarily at professionalization and certification, enhancement of teacher autonomy, and subject didactics, and also featured an increased emphasis on lifelong learning (Norman, 1995). An OECD study on the subject in 2010 came to the conclusion that the reform efforts inspired by cognitive psychology that had taken place in OECD member states had raised educators to the level of "experts in their precise field … with a strong critical sense, autonomy and professional problem-solving abilities" (Musset, 2010, p. 5).

Conclusion: From Government Domination to Self-Regulation in Teacher Training

The transformation of the recurrent themes in teacher training (as described in the two previous sections) can be summarized as follows. First, we can observe a shift in the geographic and ideological context in which teacher training has taken place over the last 150 years. While the central point of emphasis during the nineteenth century was the nation state and, by extension, the education of citizens, since the beginning of the twentieth century this focus has been replaced by an ideal increasingly oriented to an international context.

Second, there has been a discernible normative shift from moral and religious narratives towards scientific and rationalist ones. Whereas the education of young students in the nineteenth century was conducted with an emotional, and even missionary zeal, since the rapid rise of the paradigm of scientification during the interwar period, teaching methods have been coupled with an ideal that is precisely the opposite: the teacher should not appear as a religious moralizer, but should instead act according to strictly rational and scientific criteria. That this "rationalism of hopes" also has a fundamentally religious element is seldom recognized (Simola, 1993).

Third, there seems to be a permanent shift in temporal reference points. In the twentieth century, experts with international influence were explicit about committing their efforts to "slaughter" what had still been a "sacred cow" during the nineteenth century – the history of education. They sought to eliminate references to the past in teacher training and replace them with references to the future, a time when a world unified by standardization in education and science could promise to solve the increasingly interdependent problems of a globalized world.

Fourth, this shift also signified a turning away from a fixed educational canon towards an increasingly constructivist concept of knowledge. As a consequence of the constructivist ideal, cognitive structures and abstract, mathematical, and logical problem-solving abilities became privileged over historically and culturally bound knowledge concerning the world.

As fundamental as the transformation in teacher training between the nineteenth and twenty-first century might be at the discursive and ideal level of leitmotifs and plans for policy reform, the implementation of these changes at the level of classroom teaching practice is something entirely different. For one thing, there are large question marks concerning whether and how this international approach to teacher training curricula actually found its way into everyday teaching. Recently published research has found that despite all the rhetoric of Europeanization and internationalization, the most frequent point of reference in actual teaching practice across a variety of school subjects still remains the nation state (Schleicher & Weber, 2002).

Furthermore, it has been demonstrated that the reason-oriented anthropocentrism of cognitive psychology is quite difficult to impart to students in actual classroom practice. Curriculum projects from the 1960s, for example – in which students were asked to find answers to questions such as "What is uniquely human about human beings?", "How did human beings get that way?", and "What could be done to make them more so?" (Bruner, 1983) – failed without exception to yield positive results (Dow, 1991).

Furthermore, we cannot yet predict whether reforms in teacher training according to the premises of cognitive psychology are actually as universally applicable as the narrative of scientification suggests, and as politicians have propagated. The degree to which cognitive psychology was and is essentially Western, male-oriented, and rationalist – and thus culturally contextualized – is never more clearly expressed than in the positions taken by its proponents. For example, Jerome Bruner characterized the notion of emotional intelligence as "surely an absurd idea" (Orlofsky, 2001, p. 68). The fact that this entire way of thinking was conditional upon hierarchical differentiations that privilege a Western and rationalist culture was revealed in Bruner's characterization of Latin-American immigrant children: "Different cultures produce different types of minds," was his lapidary explanation for their lack of success in the United States school system (Bruner as cited by Olson, 2007, p. 23).

In the end, the quasi-religious element, particularly as it was manifest in the salvation rhetoric of numerous politicians and international organizations, played a significantly greater role than would be suggested at first glance by the narrative of the scientification of teacher training. Religiosity had enjoyed a particularly large boost in the anti-communist atmosphere of the McCarthy era (Rudolph, 2002). As a result, the American ideal of education, which had always been associated with Protestantism, became more profoundly attached to its religious roots, albeit with a new twist. As paradoxical as it may sound, in the context of the Cold War, the religious salvation thinking that was part of an American educational philosophy marked by Protestantism amalgamated with the scientistic ideology of the academic elite, generating a kind of global belief in salvation through science education (Rohstock, 2012; Tröhler, 2011a).

Last but not least, we should also be sceptical about the rhetoric of autonomy. Politicians all over the world often link cognitive approaches in teacher training to the enhancement of individual freedom. John M. Heffron from the University of Hawaii at Manoa made a contrary argument. In an extremely well argued 1995 essay, he wrote that the historically documented borrowings from cybernetics, which cognitive psychology had made during the course of its development, had merely led to a shift in educational control mechanisms from an external to an internal locus. Thus, it made no sense to speak of any gain in autonomy in the sense of freedom.

With regard to teacher training, government control and planning instruments in the nineteenth and twentieth centuries gave way to the individual's internalization of control mechanisms in the twenty-first century, a shift that ultimately guaranteed far more total control of the overall system. Like a servomechanism operating in an endless feedback loop, the teacher, now equipped with metacognitive abilities, would observe, control, and, if necessary, constantly readjust his or her activity in a self-referential and self-reflective cycle of optimization. That the proponents of the cognitive revolution already saw this in the 1960s as a step towards the desired refinement of the human mind is beyond question. Indeed, Jerome Bruner stressed the "liberating effect" that the computer would ostensibly have on psychologists' conceptions of what was humanly possible (Bruner, 1983, p. 104). Whether "liberating" is an apt term for an intrinsically deployed system of control – which, precisely because it is internal rather than imposed from the outside, functions as a potentially unopposable condition of human existence – remains to be seen.

NOTES

1 The material in both of the following subsections was previously included in Tröhler (2006).
2 Here, only the names of those persons listed in the table of contents were included, since it was assumed that such a listing provides an indication of the importance assigned to that person. This avoids the statistically misleading effect of cursory mentions within the text.
3 Nevertheless, one should note regarding French historiography that it validates English and American discourses of the nineteenth century, whereas in Germany, experience with "foreign" ideas in the nineteenth century was restricted to what was known as the Bell-Lancaster method.

6 Transnationalization of Teacher Education: A New Paradigm for Ontario?[1]

LEROY WHITEHEAD

In this chapter I will present a reflective, informal assessment of the degree to which concepts and themes of transnationalization are present in the pre-service teacher education program of one faculty of education in the province of Ontario, Canada. The purpose is to assess, in an informal and preliminary way, whether there is potential to move the paradigm of teacher education in Ontario further towards a paradigm of transnationalization. I will use the teacher education program of my own Faculty of Education at Queen's University in Kingston, Ontario, the one with which I am most familiar, as the focus of the case study. I make no claim that this program is notably unusual or better than other teacher education programs in Ontario. To the contrary, I believe the program is fairly representative of what is happening in pre-service teacher education in Ontario at the present time, though each of the extant programs does have its unique features and situations. I write not as a scholar or "expert" in either the field of transnationalism or in that of teacher education, for I am neither. Rather, I write from the perspective of one who was responsible for the management of day-to-day operations of a pre-service teacher education program for more than a decade.

This reflection purports to be nothing more than a modest attempt to begin a process of describing what themes and characteristics a transnationalized teacher education program would have, and the characteristics and dispositions its graduates would ideally possess. I hope that others will continue the conversation. Once consensus is reached regarding programmatic themes and characteristics, as well as the desirable characteristics and dispositions of graduates, later steps would include detailed discussion of program and course content – but that would be premature at this point.

I begin with the assumption that the purpose of a transnationalized, pre-service teacher education program would be to prepare teachers to teach in transnationalized settings. Such settings are becoming more common in Canada and elsewhere, so the question is a significant one. I also assume that, ideally, the cadre of teacher candidates selected for the program would be multicultural in its make-up, because a diverse group of teacher candidates would provide a rich resource for use in a program preparing the kinds of teachers that transnationalized settings would require.

The chapter will proceed as follows. First, I will briefly attempt to situate this chapter within the context of the literature relating to transnationalization, the transnationalization of education, and especially the transnationalization of teacher education (there does not appear to be a great amount of literature available with regard to the latter topic). I will only touch on the literature relating to inclusionary classrooms, of which there is an enormous amount. Second, I will review two articles that I have found especially useful for the purpose of identifying some salient themes of transnationalized professional education programs and dispositions or characteristics of effective professionals working in transnationalized settings. Third, I will identify which, if any, of these themes or characteristics are present in the test-case program. Finally, I will identify some factors that may either promote or impede further steps towards transnationalization of the program and draw some conclusions.

Transnationalization

The concept of transnationalism has become a key concept for the analysis of international migration (Brunner & Oester, 2010). It is closely related to a constellation of concepts that include multiculturalism, pluralism, internationalization, globalization, and cosmopolitanism. Definitional boundaries between internationalization, globalization, and transnationalization (and other related concepts) are not yet crisp and clear. The concept of transnationalization appears to have grown out of sociological studies of the lives of immigrants in receiving countries and cultures (e.g., Brunner & Oester, 2010), but for many scholars it has morphed into the study of how influxes of immigrants have led to institutional transformations, including but not limited to the transformation of education systems, in receiving countries. There is also some concern in the literature for the effects of emigration on countries of departure.

One institution that is undergoing decisive transformation is the institution of citizenship. Ease of travel and communication have changed perceptions of citizenship radically and made it far easier for people to move between and among nation states for business, work, education, and pleasure. New immigrants need no longer expect to remain in their new countries forever, nor do they find it necessary to cut ties to their former countries and relatives who remain there to the extent that they once did. This leads to changing conceptions not only of citizenship, but also of political community (Reisenauer & Faist, 2010).

Reisenauer and Faist (2010) quote Khagram and Levitt as follows to help explain the concept of transnationalism. The transnational world is one in which borders are becoming less relevant. Some observers have opined that transnationalism has rendered the nation state obsolete:

> By transnational, we propose an optic or gaze that begins with a world without borders, empirically examines the boundaries and borders that emerge at particular historical moments, and explores their relationship to unbounded arenas and processes. It does not take the existence of, or appropriateness of the spatial unit of analysis for granted ... A key component of the transnational approach, however, is to interrogate the territorial breadth and scope of any social phenomenon without prior assumptions. (Khagram & Levitt, 2008, p. 5)

Transnationalization of Education and Teacher Education

Harriss and Osella (2010) have provided a brief overview and critique of the literature of transnationalism as it relates to education in general. They include topics relating to education and transnational migration, ethnographic challenges to transnationalism, histories of transnational education, global production of educational regimes, and parents' and students' spatial strategies with regard to education. They "return frequently to the example of India, tracing the kinds of 'transnational' processes that are implicated in educational change" (p. 140). However, they make no mention of the effects of transnationalization on teacher education programs. They conclude, among other things, that "the unfolding project of transnational education has produced new forms of inequality … The promises of transnational education are therefore not always congruent with the realities" (p. 157).

Brunner and Oester (2010) studied identity management among migrant adolescents in a highly transnationalized urban area in Switzerland, where residential segregation resulted in the proportion of foreign pupils in local schools reaching as high as 76 per cent. They point out the sources of assimilative pressure placed on the adolescents, which include "the often unconscious middle class habitus of Swiss teachers," many of whom come from "politically conservative and ethnically homogenous rural areas, where assimilative concepts of integration prevail." They describe how the situation leads to educational disadvantage for the immigrant children (p. 4). Highlighting the inadequacies of the teachers' preparation for dealing with this type of situation, they observe:

> There is only one way to break out of this vicious cycle. As the French anthropologist Claude Lévi-Strauss puts it, one of the two main functions of a state's educational system is to reproduce the central values of a society. The other function, however, is to foster social change. In order to fulfil the second function, a teacher in a transnationalized environment has to become an ethnographer in his or her own society, "in which teaching methods learned are no longer applicable." (1993, p. 389)

In other words, as Oester et al. (2008) conclude, assimilative learning has to be completed with new learning forms and contents developed in and adapted to the pupils' transcultural environments, including multilingualism, migration experiences, and other aspects of the adolescents' everyday lives (p. 4). They conclude, in part, that

> many Swiss schools react to growing cultural diversity in their classrooms with increased assimilative pressure. As a result teachers often focus on the migrant learners' deficiencies instead of their resources. New learning strategies adapted to transnationalized environments, new contents and didactic methods inviting all pupils to contribute with their different language abilities, social and cultural backgrounds would increase the students' motivation and help them to succeed. (p. 9)

Kalekin-Fishman (2010), in her paper dealing with the dilemmas of cosmopolitan education in the context of transnationalism, observes that

> although there are papers on education that refer to "cosmopolitanism" and recognize the prevalence of transnationalism, remarkably few delineate clear criteria for discovering that one or another program is indeed an example of cosmopolitanism in education. Even fewer relate to the realities of schooling into which teachers must integrate cosmopolitanism. (p. 164)

She further argues that "the dilemmas of schooling that teachers face are ignored" (p. 164), and discusses state education as an obstacle to cosmopolitanism, using the state of Israel as a case study (p. 175). She writes that, "although cosmopolitanism is described as a form of consciousness, cosmopolitanism in education is possible only if framed in action" (p. 164). It requires, in other words, an activist pedagogy. Peace, human rights, democracy, and development appear to be the main areas of activist concern (p. 170). However, she sees the educational process that prepares teachers for state education systems as preparing teachers who will uphold the status quo. Her characterization of teacher education in Israel, as follows, would not be out of place if applied to many, if not most, other jurisdictions:

> Further obstacles to cosmopolitanism in education arise from the framework for professional education that prepares candidates for teaching. In Israel, the formation of the teacher is the responsibility of specialist professional schools or of professionally-oriented departments at the university. In their professional education, teachers acquire discipline-grounded pointers about how to get along with students in schools, along with repertoires of skills for imparting "pieces of knowledge" of different kinds. The teacher is led to see herself as an autonomous professional but she is taught how to limit her interventions to what is interpreted as needed by students – and what is needed to preserve community/state solidarity. In the professional preparation, the emphasis is on how to do teaching. Since teaching is purported to be a way of channelling knowledge and consensual values, i.e., the values that are taken for granted in the textbooks and acted out in the organization of schools; knowledge is assumed to be unambiguous and students in classes are assumed to be associated with universally agreed upon types ...

> The upshot of their professional education is that teachers are supposed to emerge as agents (not in the philosophical sense of autonomous actors, but in the insurance sense – representatives of organizational goals). They are, moreover, in the conceptualizations (metaknowledge) they hold, in their repertoires of patterns of behavior and in their intentions (habitus), the representatives of state ideology, the message (albeit evolving) that the state fosters as the "good life," for its perpetuation as an organization and institution. (pp. 179–80, 181)

Kalekin-Fishman then draws a distinction between the teacher as agent of the state and the teacher as educational, if not social, activist and seems to question whether truly cosmopolitan education can take place under the aegis of the state.

Inclusionary Classrooms

While there may be sparse literature about transnationalization in teacher education programs, there is much literature about inculcating inclusionary practice in elementary and secondary classrooms and in teacher education programs. In Ontario and many, if not most, other jurisdictions in Canada and the United States, teacher education programs typically give much attention to diversity of many kinds in the classroom. In North America since the Second World War, attention has moved from desegregation issues to special education and its attendant inclusion/mainstreaming issues to, more recently, issues of including increasing numbers of immigrants from a more diverse constellation of countries and cultures. With regard to teacher education programs, perhaps a look at a single, basic teacher education textbook can serve as a typical example of the kinds of instruction teacher candidates currently receive in pre-service teacher education programs. Lewis and Doorlag (2011), in their introductory textbook chapter on "Diversity in Today's Classrooms," explain the multicultural education approach in the following way:

> There have been many approaches to the education of students from groups diverse in culture, race and ethnicity. Kitano … described two major philosophical positions underlying these approaches: assimilation and pluralism. In assimilation, the goal is to move students away from their original culture and teach them the skills needed to compete in the macroculture. In *pluralism*, students are encouraged to retain

their original culture, and, to promote educational success, schools make accommodations based on students' experiential backgrounds. (p. 72, emphasis in original)

They identify multicultural education as being based on the pluralistic approach, and cite Gollnick and Chin (2006) as having identified six fundamental beliefs underlying the concept of multicultural education:

- Cultural differences have strength and value.
- Schools should be models for the expression of human rights and respect for cultural differences.
- Social justice and equality for all people should be of paramount importance in the design and delivery of curricula.
- Attitudes and values necessary for the continuation of a democratic society can be promoted in schools.
- Schooling can provide knowledge, dispositions, and skills – values, attitudes, and commitments – to help students from diverse groups learn.
- Educators working with families and communities can create an environment that is supportive of multiculturalism. (p. 7)

In the chapter mentioned, Lewis and Doorlag go on to discuss implications for the classroom, the promotion of acceptance of diversity, standards for effective pedagogy for diverse learners, and specific suggestions for teaching practice that promotes acceptance of diversity in the classroom. Other chapters discuss such concepts and topics as Response to Instruction (RTI), Universal Design for Learning (UDL), and Positive Behaviour Support (PBS) approaches to teaching and learning, and ways of working with students in various categories such as gifted and talented, English language learners, students with physical, intellectual, or learning disabilities, or those with attention and behavioural disorders.

There are a multitude of similar textbooks in print and in use in Canadian and American pre-service teacher education programs. Our teacher candidates are receiving foundational instruction to sensitize them to diversity in their future classrooms and to acquaint them with pedagogical concepts and strategies for working with diverse student bodies. If this is the case, then, what is the difference between the multicultural education approach of Lewis and Doorlag, Gollnick and Chin, and others, and a cosmopolitan or transnationalized approach?

I believe there might be two main distinctions. First, while the appearance (or perhaps the beginnings) of an activist pedagogy is present in Gollnick and Chin's formulation of six fundamental beliefs underlying the concept of multicultural education, the many references to US federal law in Lewis and Doorlag's textbook cause me to conclude that their textbook will prepare teachers who are – in Kalekin-Fishman's formulation above – agents of the state in the "insurance" sense, rather than pedagogical activists in the philosophical sense of agency. The difference, perhaps, is partly a difference in intensity and partly a difference in intent. Second, when I read Jukier's (2006) article and Cline and Necochea's (2006) article, both reviewed below, I see that the preparation we are giving our teacher candidates now is shallow and inadequate in comparison to what Jukier and Cline and Necochea are recommending.

"Transnationalizing the Legal Curriculum: How to Teach What We Live" (Jukier, 2006)

The literature of transnationalization is heavy with discussion of transnationalism as a socio-political phenomenon and with discussion of how this phenomenon has affected and will continue to affect school systems. However, as Kalekin-Fishman (2010) noted, it is light in terms of practical advice or insight as to what a transnationalist paradigm for teacher education might look like, or the kind of process one might put in place to transform an existing conventional program of teacher education into one that is more transnational in character. Interestingly, one of the most insightful and helpful articles I have found in the latter regard is not about professional teacher education, but about professional legal education. Jukier (2006) provides an articulate case study describing the transformation of one Canadian law faculty's legal education programs from conventional to transnational (or, as that faculty prefers, "trans-systemic").

Teacher education and legal education may be different in many ways. The transnationalization of legal education has much more to do with legal aspects of international business transactions than it does with the legal needs of recent immigrants within a country, for example. However, even given such differences, Jukier's documentation of the program transformation at McGill University in Montreal, Canada, merits careful consideration by teacher educators because there are several important ideas and guiding principles we can glean from it. I will not provide a lengthy summary of the article here, as it is easy to access online. But know this: the transformation at McGill was real and radical, not just rhetoric or the mere repackaging of old courses with new labels, nor was it a superficial rebranding with "cutesy" images and clever tag lines for advertisements to attract students who might otherwise go elsewhere. In my view, the first and perhaps most important idea or principle the teacher education community can learn from the McGill experience is this: if we want to offer genuinely transnationalized (or trans-systemic) teacher education programs, we must be prepared to undertake genuine program transformation. Mere repackaging or reshuffling of old memes will not suffice. Brunner and Oester's citation of Claude Lévi-Strauss (above) to the effect that "a teacher in a transnationalized environment has to become an ethnographer in his or her own society, 'in which teaching methods learned are no longer applicable'" certainly resonates here, as does Kalekin-Fishman's view (above) that the educational process that prepares teachers for state education systems typically prepares teachers who will uphold the status quo.

A crucial element in the McGill project provides the second key principle for teacher educators because it goes to the heart of the concept of trans-systemic professional education: the McGill faculty sought to "incorporate transnationalism into the curriculum by freeing the study of law from jurisdictional or systemic boundaries" (p. 174). This idea will resonate strongly, either positively or negatively, with teacher educators who are long accustomed to tailoring their teacher education programs to specifications laid down by their respective government ministries of education. Jukier continues: "The ambition is to create cosmopolitan jurists. The curriculum is designed to expand the perspectives on legal education so as to develop more agile minds in our students, and more outward-looking and more broadly trained lawyers and legal professionals in our graduates" (p. 174).

Can teacher educators really hope to free professional teacher education from jurisdictional or systemic boundaries and create cosmopolitan educators with expanded professional perspectives and agile minds, who are more outward looking and broadly trained? Again, there is a strong resonance here with Kalekin-Fishman's writing. We may perceive teacher education to be more intimately intertwined with jurisdictional governments than we do legal education, but McGill also had to ensure that its legal education program met jurisdictional requirements and the expectations of graduates' future employers. Teacher education, like legal education, will have to meet jurisdictional requirements and employer expectations for the foreseeable future. The manner in which the McGill transformation both meets and transcends regulations and expectations may be instructive for teacher educators.

Historically, McGill University had offered two different and distinct legal education degrees: one for the English common law approach, and one for the French civil code approach. These two legal systems have distinct structures of thought, are based in different intellectual traditions, and reflect differing transcendent values and principles. The transformed program combines the study of these differing systems into a single, integrated program that provides all of the graduates with two legal education degrees: one in civil law (BCL) and one in common law (LLB). Each of the two degrees meets the respective regulatory requirements, but because of the manner in which the study of the two legal systems is integrated, using a comparative approach, the new program transcends the regulations and produces legal professionals who are much more cosmopolitan. It should be noted that the comparative approach taken is neither simplistic nor superficial. Because neither the underlying philosophical traditions, the basic ideas, nor the details of the two systems of law "map onto" or correspond with each other in any convenient way, superficial comparisons of the two systems cannot be made. The integration required a complete rethinking and redesign of courses with civil code professors and common law professors working together (and, in the beginning, teaching together), as well as the development of new teaching and learning materials. The complex comparisons of the different legal traditions and philosophies and the drawing of connections between the philosophies and the laws that result from them produce a far deeper and broader understanding of law and legal concepts than would otherwise be the case.

Jukier sees the comparative aspect of the trans-systemic legal education program as vital. What make the trans-systemic approach to comparative law different from conventional comparative law approaches are the integrated, rather than sequential, approach to the two traditions, and the focus on making the links between the legal traditions and philosophies and their resulting perspectives and practices (p. 176). She writes:

> What is needed is a program of study that can stimulate minds to become so agile and creative that they can think open-mindedly within alternate

> systems of thought, nimbly moving across and, as need be, transcending the boundaries of these systems … By working with different legal traditions having distinct historical and methodological underpinnings, students are exposed to a variety of perspectives and a contextual analysis of legal problems. The goal is to hone the students' skills of imaginative insight, all the while undermining the fallacious notion that there is one structure of reality. (p. 177)

The students use legislative, jurisprudential, and doctrinal materials from a number of countries, but trans-systemic law is much more than mere comparative law. It must go "beyond the confines of received conventional forms and link up with a philosophic inquiry into the justice of the relationships that are expressed within those legal forms" (p. 178, quoting Janda, 2005).

Thus, the third and fourth guiding principles seem to be the integration of both the study of comparative (or alternative) approaches to teaching and learning, and the philosophical traditions from which the different approaches arise. If I may adapt Jukier's words above, our teacher education programs must go beyond the confines of received forms of education and schooling, and link up with a philosophical inquiry into the justice of the relationships that are expressed within those educational forms. We must hone the teacher candidates' skills of imaginative insight, all the while undermining the fallacious notion that there is one best way to do schooling.[2]

The fifth guiding principle would be the incorporation of learning materials from other countries (p. 180). We might also incorporate the study of education systems in other countries and the philosophical bases upon which they are built and operated. We should incorporate as well the study of critiques of public education and the philosophical bases on which they are predicated.

The sixth thing we can learn from the McGill experience is that trans-nationalization of teacher education will take time, probably measured in years. It will be a process, not an event. At the time Jukier wrote her article, the McGill project was into its seventh year, though she summarizes a lengthy prehistory. "It is hard to pinpoint with any accuracy the precise moment this process of tough self-reflection began," she writes, "but in 1994, an integrated, comparative curriculum was the subject for discussion at an off-site Faculty retreat" (p. 182). Four and one-half years of ad hoc committees, discussions, and debates followed, until proposed changes were approved at the faculty and university governance levels. The integrated, comparative curriculum turned out to be the central feature of the new McGill program.

The seventh thing we can learn is that strong and indefatigable leadership will be required. In McGill's case, the leadership of the dean of the Faculty of Law kept the project moving (p. 183).

The eighth thing we can learn also arises from the prehistory of the McGill program, as well as the unique circumstances of the university. McGill University's unique legal education program arose in part from the fact that Montreal is located in the province of Quebec. For historical and cultural reasons, much of Quebec's legal system is based on concepts of civil law rooted in the French civil code system, which is quite different from the English common law approach in the rest of Canada, while Quebec's criminal law follows the English tradition. The point is that the McGill program developed as a result of the university's unique location, unique sociopolitical situation, the law faculty's unique set of professional programs, and the expertise profile of its faculty members. Our faculties of education likely do not share the same history, circumstances, or expertise. But we do have our own unique histories, circumstances, and profiles of expertise that we can use as starting points and resources for creating unique, challenging, transnationalized programs of teacher education. Who is to say that there is only one way or even "one best way" to transnationalize teacher education?

Jukier summarizes seven challenges to this kind of program transnationalization:

- *Language.* It is helpful if both professors and students can read in more than one language to increase access to foreign learning materials.
- *Faculty expertise.* Faculty members may have to develop additional expertise in order to implement such a program.
- *Teaching materials.* When the program was launched, there was a dearth of appropriately tailored learning materials. New materials had to be developed.
- *Course organization.* Existing course outlines tend to be rooted in the orthodox approach. Courses may have to be completely redesigned if not completely re-conceptualized.
- *Evaluation of student performance.* New and innovative courses may require the development of new and innovative ways of assessing student learning.

- *Internal and external "buy-in."* A major transformation requires much collegial discussion and planning. All stakeholder groups, including but not limited to students, alumni, and potential employers of the graduates must be kept informed and educated about the program changes.
- *Financial challenges.* There needs to be a conscious decision taken to devote resources to the new priorities. (see pp. 180–2)

"Teacher Dispositions for Effective Education in the Borderlands" (Cline & Necochea, 2006)

The Jukier case study reviewed above gives us some important insights into some likely themes and characteristics that would be important in a transnationalized teacher education program, and challenges that would be likely in conceptualizing, designing, and implementing transnationalized teacher education programs. Another article of a very different kind (Cline & Necochea, 2006) provides some significant insights as to what personal dispositions or characteristics teachers in the "borderlands" need to be effective when working with transnationalized children and their families. In the case of Cline and Necochea's article, "borderlands" means an area along both sides of the Mexico–United States border, but especially those areas in the United States where a large proportion of the population is Latino or Hispanic.[3] Though the article presents the results of an exploratory study, the findings are worthy of consideration and appear to be in keeping with the conclusions of other researchers. Again, I will not provide a detailed summary of the article here, as it is easy to access online. If we consider the personal dispositions identified in the study to be valid, then the admissions process for a transnationalized teacher education program either should seek to admit teacher candidates who already possess such dispositions to some degree, or we should seek to develop them during the program, or both.

The study involved twenty teachers from San Diego, California, and twenty from Tijuana, Mexico, who attended ten monthly sessions of the Border Pedagogy Biliteracy Institute during 2003–4. Extant data resulting from the participants' reflections, evaluations, feedback, and the instructional artefacts they produced were collected on a regular basis throughout the training sessions. The study used grounded-theory analytical procedures. Five themes relating to teacher dispositions needed for teaching in the borderlands emerged from the data. I will list the five themes, along with a short quote for each one to illustrate the nature of the findings:

- *Open-mindedness and flexibility.* "Borderland schools frequently must address the unexpected, e.g., the sudden arrival of Mixtecos from Oaxaca. Therefore, teachers must be open-minded and flexible regarding the students in their care and the curriculum they design and implement. Traditional structures and instructional practices often are ineffective with students who reside in the borderlands ... Therefore, teachers need to contemplate more effective schooling – at times without a blueprint to follow." (Cline & Necochea, 2006, p. 272)
- *Passion for borderland education.* "Effective teachers in the borderlands are passionate about the work they do, and do whatever it takes to help transnational students succeed. They have a positive attitude about working with border communities and seek instructional practices that are effective for students ... They meet the needs of students by familiarizing themselves with and understanding the students' families and community." (ibid., pp. 273–4)
- *Ongoing professional development.* "Professional development which focuses on understanding the transnational influences that impact students, families, and communities is especially important because it provides borderland educators with the knowledge and skills to design effective instructional practices." (p. 276)
- *Cultural sensitivity.* "The cultural sensitivity expressed by the study's participants went beyond teachers' superficial knowledge base of diverse cultures. The participants discussed a deep understanding of culture that included not only knowing the families, the communities, and the students in their classes, but also accepting and affirming their culture and ways of knowing and understanding the world. Participants valued those who are different and worked towards a greater unity of all cultures, socioeconomic groups, and classes." (pp. 277–8)
- *Pluralistic language orientation.* "Effective teachers foster the incorporation of multiple primary languages into the classroom and implement innovative instructional strategies to honor and value the mother tongue of each child ... They often use primary language support to ensure that students have access to the core curriculum and are able to master difficult concepts ... They do not see a second language as a liability or as something to be fixed, but as an incredible asset that needs to be nurtured and fostered – even to the point of learning the language themselves." (pp. 278–9)

Common Themes

The degree of commonality of themes arising from the transnationalization literature and the inclusion literature, as well as the Jukier and Cline and Necochea articles reviewed above, is striking. The main themes I perceive are as follows:

- the need to transcend boundaries, whether these are systemic and jurisdictional, or traditional forms and structures in school organizations, philosophies, curricula, and pedagogy;
- the need to be outward-looking, open-minded, more broadly aware of cross-cultural issues, and more accepting of other cultures, and to be able to think within alternative cultural and value systems without being judgmental;
- taking a comparative approach, examining philosophical bases for structural, curricular, and pedagogical differences;
- using language and cultural differences as resources to enhance learning, rather than viewing them as impediments or something to be fixed;
- the need for deep rather than superficial knowledge of students' cultures, traditions and values, communities, and families;
- the usefulness of the teacher understanding more than one language and valuing other languages in the classroom;
- a focus on continuous professional development, reflective practice, and the development of learning communities; and
- strong undercurrents of an orientation to social justice, broadly defined.

Themes of Transnationalization in One Ontario Pre-Service Teacher Education Program

We will now turn our attention to look at the test case pre-service teacher education program to determine which of the themes identified above are present. The program could not be considered as "transnationalized" yet, but, as noted earlier, transnationalization probably should be viewed as a process that may take place over an extended period of time rather than as a single event. As with the McGill Faculty of Law, the test case faculty of education has a prehistory and it is hard to determine just when in our collective past we began taking steps that could be construed as moving towards transnationalization of the pre-service teacher education program. It might have been during the 1980s when we began using "bio-data" (personal information) as a significant part of our admissions process in addition to the academic information provided by applicants' transcripts. It was also during the 1980s that we invited Donald Schön to visit our faculty on two occasions to talk about the reflective practitioner and reflective practice. Or it might have been in 1995 when, under a new dean, we did the first major (and radical, for Ontario, at the time) program revision in many years. Or it might have been in the early 2000s when another new dean, one who has written extensively on pluralization in education, led a process to rewrite our program's vision statement. On any of those occasions, we never talked about these steps as moving our program towards transnationalization, but in retrospect, all of them can be seen as having done so.

In the following, I will identify some of the more salient features of our pre-service program and discuss them in terms of the themes listed above. These features include the program's vision statement, admissions process, teacher candidates, focus on reflective practice, courses, practicum, alternate practicum, and the Teachers' Overseas Recruiting Fair.

Vision Statement

The vision statement for the pre-service teacher education program is infused with language that is consistent with the previously identified themes of transnational education (the complete statement can be found at the end of this chapter). The description of a critically reflective teacher as "one who asks questions that go beyond the immediate pressures of daily practice" certainly suggests the theme of transcending normal boundaries and forms. The ideas of "the teacher as an active agent in the development of a socially inclusive pedagogy aimed at social justice," "caring as a central value in the profession of teaching," and "inclusivity as a fundamental pedagogical principle" all speak to the teacher's disposition to be outward looking, open-minded, more broadly aware of cross-cultural issues, and more accepting of other cultures without being judgmental, as well as the disposition for deep rather than superficial knowledge of students' cultures, traditions, and values, and an orientation to social justice.

They also suggest the teacher as agent in the philosophical sense, rather than in the insurance sense. The idea that the program should integrate understanding of educational ends, purposes, and values and their philosophical and historical grounds also suggests the teacher's disposition for deep rather than superficial knowledge, as do the stated commitments to academic excellence and to learning how to learn, and the consideration that all teacher candidates should possess the literacy and critical skills associated with an educated person. The statements regarding learning how to learn, critical reflection, and collaboration and leadership all relate to the theme focus on continuous professional development, reflective practice, and the development of learning communities.

Though the vision for the pre-service program does not actually specify a vision for a transnationalized program, many of its ideas are consistent with common themes of transnational education and the dispositions of transnationalized teachers. None of its ideas appear to be contrary to the themes and dispositions of transnational teacher education. Unfortunately, while the wording is there, our program currently is more superficial than deep in those areas where the vision statement would support program depth, and where a truly transnationalized approach would require depth.

Admissions Process

The admissions process uses both academic data and "bio-data." The applicant's academic record is assessed through examination of previous transcripts in a fairly typical manner and helps us decide whether the applicant has a disposition towards academic excellence. A personal statement of experience written by the applicant helps us assess whether the applicant has dispositions towards social justice, caring, leadership and collaboration, and critical reflection, as well as literacy skills. In other words, we use the personal statement to try to determine which of the applicants most likely already have dispositions towards the qualities of a teacher identified in our vision statement. As the vision statement is consistent with the themes and dispositions of transnational education (as noted above), the admissions process is also consistent with the themes of transnationalization in education. On the negative side, it is a time-consuming and costly process, and has resulted in a complaint to the Ontario Human Rights Commission that took three years to resolve in a process that was very expensive in terms of time and legal consultation (no evidence of systemic discrimination was found). Some other Canadian faculties of education that previously used applicants' personal statements as part of their application process have abandoned the use of the personal statement because of the drain on resources, now basing their admissions solely on the academic record.

Teacher Candidates

As a generalization, the admissions process tends to produce teacher candidates who model, to varying degrees, certain of the personal dispositions of effective cosmopolitan, transnational teachers. In the thirty-five years I have been at the faculty, the visual composition of the pre-service class has changed remarkably. Then, the class was predominantly white. Now, a substantial proportion of the class is made up of visible minority students. Many of our teacher candidates come to us from Toronto, which has become a city of immigrants from all parts of the world. Our student body increasingly reflects this. Many of those admitted to our program are first- or second-generation immigrants, all of whom have facility in English, but many of whom speak other languages and have personal, deep experience with other cultures and education systems. In addition, many of the non-immigrant candidates have had significant experiences abroad, through study or work experiences abroad, living abroad with parents or relatives, or through extended travel including "backpacking." These factors could support the themes of broad and deep awareness of cross-cultural issues, acceptance of other cultures, ability to think within alternative cultural and value systems, taking a comparative approach, and using language and cultural differences that may exist in the classroom to enhance learning rather than viewing them as impediments. Our teacher candidates could well be one of our most potent resources in developing a powerful transnational teacher education program, but we tend to ignore the possibilities. We have not yet recognized nor learned how to take full advantage of this resource we have.

Focus on Reflective Practice

As noted in the vision statement, the program emphasizes reflective practice. Indeed, we talk about this so much that our teacher candidates have been known, on occasion, to complain that they are tired of reflecting. In addition to simple reflective writing exercises in some courses, the two major ways we incorporate the practice into the program are an action research assignment and a professional portfolio assignment which is presented to a panel of peers as a program consolidation exercise. All of these relate to the transnationalization focus on continuous professional development, reflective practice, and the development of learning communities.

Courses

In terms of the content of curriculum and instruction courses, the program focuses virtually exclusively on the curriculum guidelines produced by the Ontario Ministry of Education. There is little or no effort to bring in curriculum documents from other jurisdictions for comparative analysis, and to be frank, there would be little time for this given the very tight time constraints of our program. (The McGill law program accomplishes what it does in five years, rather than the traditional three years for Canadian law programs. At the time I write this, our main pre-service teacher education program in Ontario is an eight-month program after completion of a previous degree.) The Ontario documents provide learning outcomes that are to be accomplished but leave the teacher relatively free to select the specific learning materials and teaching methods to be used in assisting his/her students to achieve the expectations, though Ontario school boards choose textbooks from Ministry-approved lists. So, in essence, in Ontario, there is some limited flexibility to transcend boundaries in terms of learning materials and teaching methods, so far as the governmental jurisdiction is concerned. Because the government does not dictate materials and methods, we do have to teach well the concepts of lesson planning and presentation. We seem to do the latter reasonably well, as our graduates go to many different jurisdictions in Canada and abroad to teach and do so successfully.

Inclusivity and social justice are intended to be embedded themes throughout the pre-service courses, and to an extent this is happening in some of them. We have a few courses that relate directly to the identified themes of transnational teacher education. Three of them are "focus" electives: "Global Education through International Cooperation," "Educators Abroad," and "Teaching for Social Justice." The content of each of these courses is related to one or more of the transnationalization themes and has potential to make an important contribution to a transnationalized program, but with the exception of "Educators Abroad," they are rarely fully enrolled. We have two brief, required modules that deal with the historical, political, philosophical, and social contexts of education, but these are generally viewed with some disdain by many teacher candidates who do not see relevance in them given the short time they are allotted, and their seeming disconnection from the rest of the program curriculum. So, while we have a handful of courses that could contribute, our courses, in general, would benefit from serious reconceptualization or redesign and a higher degree of integration, if we wanted to pursue a transnationalized program more consciously. Much more critical consideration of alternative approaches to education and schooling, including comparative studies and their underlying philosophies, would need to be integrated with the curriculum and instruction courses.[4]

The Practicum

Our teacher candidates from the Toronto area usually wish to return there for their practicum placements. We try to accommodate them whenever possible. Many are placed in schools where the student population, and often the teacher and support staff population, are very diversified. In these cases, the learning that takes place during the practicum seems most directly related to the theme of being outward looking, open-minded, more broadly aware of cross-cultural issues, and more accepting of other cultures. In contrast, many of our teacher candidates are also assigned to practicum placements in smaller towns and cities, or rural areas, where the nature of the population is seemingly less diverse.

The Alternate Practicum

The alternate practicum is intended to give teacher candidates a self-selected experience in education that will provide a different perspective than that of a classroom teacher in an Ontario publicly funded school. They can teach in an Ontario private school, a public school in another province or country, or do many other things. The only limitations are safety concerns and the teacher candidate's ability to provide a reasonable rationale as to why and how the proposed experience will help him or her become a better teacher. Many candidates are both creative and resourceful in making their arrangements. Each year, approximately fifty to eighty candidates choose alternate practicum situations in other countries, including but not limited to developing countries. Often they teach in elite international schools where English is the language of instruction, but in recent years, small but increasing numbers have gone to indigenous schools in Africa and the Caribbean. Some have gone to inner-city schools in England. Typical locations also include South and East Asia, South and Central America, Europe, and the Middle East. A few select the far north of Canada. The faculty has some endowment money intended to support teacher candidates' travel to other countries and, with certain conditions, teacher candidates can apply for funding. Typically, up to about sixty candidates can receive partial financial support for their travel expenses each year. Others who select continuing projects do fundraising, and some finance their own expenses. Some describe their alternate practicum experience as "life-changing." Again, the learning that takes place during the alternate practicum seems most directly related to the theme of being outward looking, open-minded, more broadly aware of cross-cultural issues, and more accepting of other cultures, and to the theme of orientation towards issues of social justice.

Teachers' Overseas Recruiting Fair (TORF)

This is the one aspect of the pre-service program that is unique in Ontario, and probably in Canada. Each February for more than a quarter century, personnel in our Education Career Services Office have operated the Teachers' Overseas Recruiting Fair, considered the third largest in North America. Up to ninety recruiters come from international schools around the world, as well as around three hundred teachers hoping to secure international job placements. Most of the job-seekers are experienced teachers, including but not limited to our alumni, but a portion of the applicant positions are reserved for members of our graduating class. Though the Fair is not formally a part of the pre-service program, we believe that a graduate who teaches in another country will be a better teacher because of the experience when she or he returns to Canada and Ontario. Most of our graduates who gain their first teaching position through the fair return to Canada after an initial two-year appointment, but a few decide to make a career out of international teaching. Either outcome is consistent with the themes of transnational teacher education, particularly the theme of being more broadly aware of cross-cultural issues and more accepting of other cultures. The theme of transcending political and jurisdictional boundaries would also be germane here. A side benefit of operating the fair is that the staff in the Education Career Services Office has developed a network of reliable contacts in international schools and can assist teacher candidates in locating placements for the alternate practicum.

Factors Favouring Transnationalization

The pre-service teacher education program has a number of assets that provide a strong base for further development as a transnationalized program including the vision statement, the admissions process and the kinds of teacher candidates it supplies, the focus on reflective practice, and the alternate practicum. The practicum and the Teacher's Overseas Recruiting Fair can be considered as supporting factors at this point. I describe the practicum as supporting rather than as a strong factor only because not every candidate can have a placement in a transnationalized school or classroom.

Our geographical location, not *too* far from Toronto, is also a positive factor. We Canadians like to think of ourselves as a multicultural nation. But according to one online source, "Canada's multiculturalism is mostly in its major cities of Toronto, Montreal and Vancouver. For example, just over 50% of the people in Toronto weren't born in Canada. However, outside of a few major cities, Canada is a fairly Caucasian nation."[5] Our ability to attract teacher candidates from Toronto and provide practicum placements there is definitely an asset in terms of transnationalization. Clearly, smaller centres also have immigrant populations, and many of our graduates will go to serve those centres.

In terms of jurisdictional factors, the fact that, so long as we meet the basic curriculum and time constraints required by Ontario regulations governing pre-service teacher education programs, we are free to go beyond them if we wish, is a positive factor. Our vision statement implies our willingness to go beyond when it talks about dealing with questions that go beyond the immediate pressures of daily practice. Should the government decide to lengthen the program (which is under consideration as I write this), such a decision would be an additional positive factor in terms of providing time to engage in more integration of philosophical, political, social, and historical contexts into the program and to engage in more learning activities to help link underlying values and intellectual traditions to current, and to potential alternative, teaching practices.

Factors Impeding Transnationalization

Aside from the organizational problems of motivating faculty members to make decisions and take action to implement significant program changes, as well as any barriers caused by tight budgets, I see four main factors impeding the further transnationalization of our pre-service program. These are: the time constraints of the eight-month program; our failure to use our transnationalized cadre of teacher candidates as a powerful teaching and learning resource; the problem of how to help candidates clearly link underlying values and philosophical traditions to current and alternative teaching practices; and the problem of how to integrate comparative inquiry into all our courses to promote a deeper understanding of issues. As well, some "repurposing" of faculty members may be required.

Conclusions

This brief reflection has only scratched the surface of the topic at hand. I must admit that at the conclusion of this exercise, I am much more positive about the prospect of transnationalization of pre-service teacher education programs in Ontario than I was at the start. Frankly, I was quite surprised to learn how closely the current vision statement of the test case program coincides with the major themes of transnationalization in professional education, and that the test-case faculty already has a solid base in place on which to build a more transnationalized program. I was excited to see that we have in the teacher candidates a very significant resource that we could use to help transform our program, but dismayed that we are virtually ignoring it. I was also surprised by the realization that there are no real jurisdictional constraints in place, other than the short program time that the government of Ontario supports financially.[6] We could, with thought, planning, effort, and commitment, transform the program into a more fully transnationalized program and reap benefits for our teacher candidates and for their future students. In summary, the test case pre-service teacher education program could not yet be considered a transnationalized program, but it does reflect to some degree most, if not all, of the themes identified above as being reflective of transnationalized professional programs. There is potential and a solid base from which to proceed.

But the real point is this: I have been using my own faculty's program as a test case. I suspect that many other Ontario faculties could produce similar profiles, so if we have a basis on which to transform ourselves, other Ontario faculties probably do, too, though their bases may be different in their details than ours. In summary, based on this informal reflection, I conclude that transnationalization could be a viable paradigm for pre-service teacher education in Ontario. To some degree, given our increasingly diverse population, our increasingly diverse complement of teachers and teacher candidates, and our concern for and experience to date with inclusive classrooms, it is already. There is an argument to proceed with more formal studies of the proposition.

Appendix: Our Vision Statement

The vision statement for our pre-service teacher education program is as follows. It consists of a general statement of expectations in the first paragraph, followed by a bulleted listing of program characteristics. Like most vision statements, it provides a vision of a future state towards which we are working, rather than a documentary of a realized current reality:

Our vision of the graduate of Queen's University Faculty of Education is that of a critically reflective professional. Graduates are expected to integrate theoretical, practical, and experiential knowledge in the understanding and resolution of professional issues. We see the beginning teacher as an active agent in the development of a socially inclusive pedagogy aimed at social justice. In our vision, the critically reflective teacher is the one who asks questions that go beyond immediate pressures of daily practice, and who has a disposition to work in collaboration with other members of the profession and with all those involved in the education and development of all learners.

Characteristics of the Program

- The program sustains a commitment to academic excellence and to learning how to learn, and reflects teaching as both an intellectual and practical activity, according to Queen's principles.
- The program considers that all teacher candidates should possess the literacy and critical skills associated with an educated person.
- The program promotes caring as a central value in the profession of teaching, and inclusivity as a fundamental pedagogical principle.

- The program integrates the following domains: school context, curriculum, teaching and learning, assessment, evaluation and reporting, educational ends, purposes and values and their philosophical and historical grounds.
- The following themes are embedded in the program: inclusivity and social justice; collaboration and leadership; the use of information and communication technologies in teaching and learning.
- The program promotes the preparation of future educators who will address issues of sustainability in their classrooms by becoming environmentally aware, practicing resource conservation, and exploring new ways to minimize the impact of human beings on the environment.[7]

NOTES

1 An earlier, Spanish version of this chapter was published as an article in the 2012 issue of *Encounters on Education*. This English version has been revised and expanded.

2 My reference here is not only to Jukier's quote above, but to Raymond E. Callahan's 1962 *Education and the Cult of Efficiency: A Study of the Social Forces That Have Shaped the Administration of the Public Schools* (Chicago: University of Chicago Press), which demonstrates the extent to which early North American school administrators sought to model the school on the industrial factory and on the concepts of the early efficiency experts, whose motto was "one best way."

3 I was drawn to the article by the word "borderlands" in the title. Though the borderland to which it refers is a real place, the word is evocative and, in my view, can be seen as more expansive than the concept of transnationalism. While it certainly includes immigrant children and the children of immigrants and migrants, it might also include others living along metaphorical borders, such as First Nations, Métis, and Inuit children in Canada or native Americans in the United States, and even children with exceptionalities.

4 As I have often said to my colleagues, we need to offer a "Bachelor of Education" program, not a "Bachelor of Public School Teaching in Ontario" program.

5 Quoted from the wiki Answers.com. While the information is based on the 2006 census of Canada, the website is not a Census Canada official website.

6 There is the problem of the clause in the Ontario Education Act that requires (with the exception of additional language courses) that anglophone schools use English exclusively as the language of instruction, and that francophone schools use French exclusively. This may impede the use of children's primary languages to ensure immigrant children understand concepts being taught, as well as the use of other languages as a potent resource. This matter could be remedied by the provincial legislature.

7 Queen's University, Faculty of Education Calendar 2012–13, online at http://www.queensu.ca/calendars/education/. This statement was written by Dr Rosa Bruno-Jofré, dean of the Faculty of Education at Queen's from 2000–10, and was approved by various committees and the faculty board. Note that Bruno-Jofré is a historian of education, born in Argentina, and has extensive international experience.

7 Paradigmatic Changes in Teacher Education: The Perils, Pitfalls, and Unrealized Promise of the Reflective Practitioner

TOM RUSSELL

The major goal of this chapter is to problematize the virtually universal use of phrases such as *reflection, reflective practice,* and *becoming a reflective practitioner* in teacher education generally and in pre-service teacher education in particular. The introduction of these terms is widely and appropriately attributed to Donald Schön, who published three books on the topic. The first was *The Reflective Practitioner: How Professionals Think in Action,* published in 1983. It was followed in 1987 by the second, *Educating the Reflective Practitioner: Towards a New Design for Teaching and Learning in the Professions.* The third book is an edited collection titled *The Reflective Turn: Case Studies in and on Educational Practice* (1991). One of Schön's final contributions was a 1995 article entitled "The New Scholarship Requires a New Epistemology."

There are many features of Schön's three books that teacher educators appear either to have overlooked or to have interpreted loosely. Schön was not writing from a perspective of teacher education, but he did suggest that if one were looking for instances of *reflection-in-action,* then one of the last places one might find it would be a school. Perhaps the subtitle of his first book comes closest to indicating his focus: *how professionals think in action.* That first book includes a number of illustrative chapters from professions as diverse as architecture, psychotherapy, and urban planning; none of its chapters illustrates the work of a teacher, although in public lectures Schön did cite illustrations from teachers whose work was familiar to him.

The argument in this chapter can be summarized as follows: *Reflection* is an everyday word that can be interpreted in many ways. If we ignore its physical interpretations, most of the remaining interpretations of *reflection* refer to mental activities that may appear to be simple and straightforward because they often suggest a leisurely, relaxed activity. While Schön (1983, 1987) focused on what he termed *reflection-in-action* and its implications for professional learning, discussions and applications in the context of teacher education seem to pay little or no attention to Schön's focus on *reframing* and the associated implications for changes in professional *action*.

In this chapter, I review the arguments in a selection of publications on the topic of reflection in teacher education to illustrate this conclusion. I then develop a personal interpretation of the implications of Schön's work for teacher education and the opportunities for improving teacher education that seem to be missed by ignoring those implications. At this stage, it is useful to set out the three points that I believe are central to Schön's (1983) argument in the book that launched teacher education on its love affair with (critical) reflection. These points are a personal interpretation that grossly oversimplifies the argument:

1. The focus on putting theory into practice that is so deeply rooted in Western culture (summarized by the phrase *technical rationality*) is misleading and inappropriate when applied to situations of professional action and learning from experience.
2. We often focus on solving a problem without first focusing on whether we have identified the problem in the most appropriate way. Problems do not present themselves with labels; how we name a problem has a significant influence on how we attempt to solve it.
3. Alternative ways of framing a problem can arise spontaneously in any context of professional action, particularly in moments of uncertainty, puzzlement, or surprise. Listening to and conversing with the situation and the other individuals within it can stimulate new ways of interpreting (reframing) problems that suggest alternative courses of action. These may or may not prove to be more productive and thus need to be tested in action.

Personal Context

I began teaching in 1963 as an untrained volunteer teacher in Nigeria. In my first two years of teaching, I was working from my apprenticeship of observation (Lortie, 1975), acting as I had seen my own teachers act. I had not been taught how to teach in a formal, school-based way, but I did know (by extensive observation) how teachers behaved and what their basic strategies were in a classroom. I was certainly not a great teacher, but I was not a disaster, nor did that long period of uninformed teaching form habits that I could not change. Those experiences as an untrained teacher made me more than eager for the content of a pre-service teacher education program; the teaching that followed was both successful and memorable. After completing a PhD, I began teaching pre-service teacher education students in 1977; for the preceding three years, I had worked with experienced teachers in a variety of in-service teacher education contexts, and that work with experienced teachers shaped my expectations of pre-service teachers and how I should teach them. I was more interested in helping beginning teachers learn from their practicum experiences than I was in filling them with potentially unrealistic ideas about how teachers should work with their students.

I obtained a copy of *The Reflective Practitioner* shortly after it was published in 1983, as I was completing my sixth year of work as a pre-service teacher educator. Schön's discussion of reflection-in-action spoke directly to my concern that, when I visited schools to observe practicum lessons, I saw little evidence of the practices that I and others were suggesting in our teacher education classes. Theory-into-practice did not seem to be what teacher candidates were doing. A year's sabbatical leave provided an opportunity to explore the idea of reflection-in-action in the context of the program I was visiting. Fortuitously, a colleague invited Donald Schön to give three lectures at Queen's University in October 1984, shortly after my return to teaching. Those lectures were the most memorable I have ever attended, and they inspired and enabled me to take Schön's perspective more seriously than most teacher educators seem to have done.

By 1985, it was apparent that many other teacher educators were becoming interested in *reflection* as that term might be applied in the context of teacher education. Suddenly, the journals that teacher educators had been asking their students to keep were replaced by assignments that called explicitly for reflection. As I worked to explore the meaning of reflection-in-action through a series of research grants, I gradually realized that my personal interpretation of the term differed significantly from the interpretations that were appearing in the literature. In this chapter, I explore a small selection of the countless articles published on the topic, focusing on how the terms *reflection* and *reflection-in-action* have been interpreted in many different ways and for many different purposes. I also discuss the interpretation that I continue to find most productive in my own teacher education classroom.

Six Perspectives on Reflection and Teacher Education

Linda Valli: Cases and Critiques of Reflective Teacher Education

Valli's (1992) collection of seven case studies of teacher education programs focusing in various ways on reflection is accompanied by six critiques from a variety of perspectives. This book provides one of our best resources for understanding the complexity of what is involved in developing *reflection* in a meaningful way in a pre-service teacher education program. Although the case studies describe programs as they existed more than two decades ago, they illustrate clearly some of the many different ways in which reflection can be interpreted in teacher education programs. The cases describe various practicum structures from the perspective of fostering reflection.

Unfortunately, like most articles published about reflection and reflective practice in teacher education, there is little direct and specific reference to the pre-service practicum in the six critiques that offer various ways of interpreting the seven case studies. Calderhead's critique (1992) drew some valuable conclusions, but there is little evidence in the literature to indicate that his advice has been acted on:

> There are few well-established ground rules for teacher educators in this new area, and as a result tutors and supervising teachers are required constantly to examine what they are doing and where they are going. Teacher educators have set themselves some ambitious aims in reflective teaching and it is as yet uncertain what is actually achievable in the context of a pre-service training program. (p. 145)
>
> [Questions about what is possible] can only be answered through the experience of teacher educators, and the evaluation of that experience, in developing teacher education programs for reflective practice and in promoting our understanding of professional growth. In the process of developing reflective teaching as a goal of pre-service education, there is a need to develop our own knowledge about reflective teaching and how it is facilitated. (pp. 145–6)
>
> Before we can have reflective teachers, we need reflective schools and reflective teacher educators. (p. 146)

Calderhead's words help to sum up the contribution of cases and critiques such as those provided in Valli's book. *Teacher educators themselves need to make paradigmatic changes before expecting pre-service teachers to do the same.* Teacher educators need to explore how discussions of reflective practice, such as those by Dewey and Schön, apply to their own personal practices as professionals acting in the teacher education classrooms of our universities. We may well do more harm than good by adding the vocabulary of *reflection* to our mission statements and our assignments without also providing extensive support that includes modelling and explicit links to teacher candidates' practicum experiences.

Lynn Fendler: "Do Reflective Teachers Need the Assistance of Experts?"

By virtue of its widespread distribution in the journal *Educational Researcher*, Fendler's (2003) article, written from a historical perspective, is an essential piece of reading on the topic of reflection. Fendler opens the article with a simple quotation from Zeichner (1996, p. 207): "There is no such thing as an unreflective teacher." This statement is often quoted in misleading ways, because it is taken out of context when it omits the preceding and following sentences. A complete quotation reads as follows:

> First, one must recognize that all teachers are reflective in some sense. There is no such thing as an unreflective teacher. We need to move beyond the uncritical celebration of teacher reflection and teacher empowerment and focus our attention on what kind of reflection teachers are engaging in, what it is teachers are reflecting about, and how they are going about it. (p. 207)

Fendler's quotation appears to suggest that all teachers are reflective; the more complete quotation, with the critical words "in some sense," points to the importance of the content and processes of teachers' reflections.

Like many who wish to interpret Schön on the topic of reflection, Fendler goes back to Dewey, just as Schön himself did. Fendler quickly makes the link between teacher reflection and the improvement of teaching, which many assume to be the point of reflection. Thus, we see that reflection is not an end in itself but a means to the end of improvement, and most professionals are assumed to want to improve personal practices whenever possible. Fendler suggests that her article offers two contributions to the literature – a historical perspective and a perspective grounded in the work of Foucault and sociology.

In the conclusion of the article, while still suggesting that all teachers are reflective, Fendler poses a crucial question: "If educational researchers believe that all teachers think about what they do, then why is there so much talk about making teachers into reflective practitioners?" (p. 23). Fendler goes on to say:

> It is ironic that the rhetoric about reflective practitioners focuses on empowering teachers, but the requirements of learning to be reflective are based on the assumption that teachers are incapable of reflection without direction from expert authorities. The case of teacher reflection provides an example of the need for educational researchers to examine their assumptions about the relationship between research and teacher education. (p. 23)

While I agree that there are many assumptions to be examined, particularly with reference to teachers as reflective practitioners and the significance of reflective practice for teacher development, my focus is not on empowerment of teachers or on whether reflective practice requires training by experts. Analysing the tasks of teaching from Schön's perspective of *reflection-in-action* and the development of new practices based on reframing that is stimulated by interpreting students' action in new ways is not an approach taken by most teachers.

Ken Zeichner: Reflective Practice for the Advancement of Democracy

Zeichner is well known to most teacher educators, and his extensive writings include many discussions of reflective practice in the context of teacher education. In a 1996 book chapter, "Teachers as Reflective Practitioners and the Democratization of School Reform," Zeichner uses the terms *reflective practice* and *reflective teaching* interchangeably. He sees reflective practice as a "movement" (p. 200) and he uses phrases such as "reflection on one's own experience." Zeichner goes on to discuss "four ways the concept of reflection has been employed in preservice teacher education that undermine the expressed emancipatory intent of teacher educators" (p. 202). The four interpretations merit closer examination:

1. Replicating research practices.
2. Avoiding ethical and moral implications.

3. Avoiding social considerations.
4. Isolating individual teachers.

Zeichner sees viewing reflection as replicating research practices (pp. 202–3) as a strategy for encouraging teachers to replicate practices that empirical research by university researchers has shown to be effective. He correctly sees this as a persistence of theory-into-practice, or technical rationality. Under the heading of avoiding ethical and moral implications (pp. 203–4), Zeichner sees an interpretation of reflection that focuses on the means of teaching to the neglect of the ends of teaching (the ethical and moral implications). The next interpretation of reflection is critiqued as limiting reflection to the individual classroom, so that the social considerations that affect teachers' work are ignored. Finally, Zeichner critiques views of reflection that restrict it to individual teachers without interaction with other teachers: "All of these practices help create a situation in which there is merely the illusion of teacher development and teacher autonomy" (p. 206).

Having reached this conclusion, Zeichner then reveals the main purpose of his chapter: "Reflective teacher education that fosters genuine teacher development should be supported only, in my view, if it is connected to the struggle for greater social justice" (p. 206). In short, Zeichner appears to be using the idea of teachers as reflective practitioners as the basis for an argument that reflective practice should only be fostered in the context of reducing the social injustices that are so apparent in most societies. His purpose is not to set out a clear conception of reflective practice in the context of teaching and learning, yet it may be read that way by virtue of his high profile within the teacher education community.

Neville Hatton and David Smith: "Levels of Reflection Leading to Reflection-in-Action"

Hatton and Smith (1995) provide a detailed analysis of the concept of reflection in teacher education. Their discussion is an interesting mixture of grounded claims and personal assertions about various levels of reflection, including technical, descriptive, dialogic, and critical reflection (p. 45). They associate technical reflection with the idea of technical rationality much criticized by Schön (1983), while descriptive, dialogic, and critical reflection are associated with Schön's *reflection-on-action.*

They interpret Schön's *reflection-in-action* as the "contextualization of multiple viewpoints" drawing on the four types of reflection (p. 45). Their discussion of the place of reflection in teacher education is driven and supported by a small-scale project at the University of Sydney. They offer a statement that points in the direction of seeing that a paradigmatic change is required when incorporating *reflection* in a pre-service teacher education program:

> A critically reflective approach demands an ideology of teacher education different from that traditionally employed, which usually involves models of "best practice," emphasis on competences, and unrecognized conflicts between institutional ideals and workplace socialization. There need to be changes in emphasis and created opportunities which establish appropriate and supporting conditions for fostering in students different kinds of reflection. (p. 38)

The use of terms such as "unrecognized conflicts" and "changes in emphasis" could be a misleading attempt to minimize the significance of adopting a focus on reflection throughout a teacher education program – misleading because, as Schön (1995) suggests, a major shift in epistemology is required.

A significant contribution of this article appears in the authors' quest for evidence of reflection or reflective practice, and they offer lists of characteristics for descriptive writing, descriptive reflection, dialogic reflection, and critical reflection (pp. 40–1, 48–9). Their focus in the quest for evidence of reflection appears to be on what students have written about "the process of their curriculum planning, development, implementation, and evaluating" (p. 42). They acknowledge that this is *reflection-on-action*, but they hope that *reflection-in-action* was also present: "It is probable, however, that *reflection-in-action* occurred while the events were originally unfolding, so that students were thinking about reasons for what was going on as it happened" (p. 42, emphasis in original). They offer an additional comment about the tension between reflection and existing assumptions: "The traditional academic genre is characterised by features that are in many ways the antithesis of the personal, tentative, exploratory, and at times indecisive style of writing which would be identified as reflective" (p. 42).

My interpretation of the argument presented by Hatton and Smith acknowledges that they have recognized that *reflection-in-action* is a complex phenomenon that arises in the context of professional action. Their conclusion indicates that they are committed to seeing reflection as a process that develops through a hierarchy of levels from technical through descriptive to critical; only then is the practitioner who is acquiring experience ready for *reflection-in-action*. Their conclusion is informed by a study of pre-service teachers, but evidence is not provided to support the hierarchy of levels of reflection. They emphasize that their students need to develop metacognitive skills in order to move towards *reflection-in-action*, but they seem reluctant to admit that teachers in training might be able to experience moments of reframing while they are teaching real students in real classrooms.

Carol Rodgers: Returning to Dewey while Ignoring Schön

Rodgers (2002) makes a valuable contribution to our understanding of the concept of reflection by returning to the work of Dewey. Her purpose is worthwhile: "Over the past 15 years, reflection has suffered from a loss of meaning. In becoming everything to everybody, it has lost its ability to be seen" (p. 843). Her article appears to be an excellent introduction to Dewey's work on reflective thinking. Interestingly, despite Schön's role (1983) in taking our attention back to Dewey and the concept of reflection, she ignores the opportunity to interpret Schön's work in the light of that of Dewey.

Rodgers describes and discusses four criteria of reflection, drawn from Dewey's work: (1) a meaning-making process, (2) a rigorous way of thinking, (3) a process that happens in community, and (4) a set of four attitudes – whole-heartedness, directness, open-mindedness, and responsibility. "The four attitudes are the essential constituents of what Dewey calls readiness to engage in reflection" (p. 862). She summarizes her argument by saying that she has demonstrated that "reflection is not an end in itself but a tool or vehicle used in the transformation of raw experience into meaning-filled theory that is grounded in experience, informed by existing theory, and serves the larger purpose of the moral growth of the individual and society" (p. 863).

Rodgers's position that reflection is a means, not an end in itself, is an important signal to teacher educators. Her article includes descriptions of teachers' experiences, but she does not speak explicitly of the practicum experiences of those learning to teach. However, it is certainly important and appropriate to view the role of the pre-service practicum from the perspective of transforming experience into "theory that is grounded in experience" and "informed by existing theory" (p. 863).

Barbara Larrivee: Becoming a Critically Reflective Teacher

Larrivee's (2000) account of how one develops as a critically reflective practitioner adds little to a consideration of Schön's work, which she, like Rodgers, fails to mention. However, it is important to address this article here because it illustrates the extent to which "becoming a critically reflective teacher" has become a movement in its own right, quite independent of Schön's work, with individuals constructing quite different interpretations of reflection. Larrivee argues as follows:

> Critical reflection is the distinguishing attribute of reflective practitioners. The term critical reflection as developed here merges critical inquiry, the conscious consideration of the ethical implications and consequences of teaching practice, with self-reflection, deep examination of personal beliefs, and assumptions about human potential and learning. (p. 293)

Interestingly, she visits the work of Dewey (1933) on reflective thinking and that of Argyris (1990) on self-generated but untested beliefs in her efforts to raise critical reflection to the status of a defining characteristic of the teacher who is a reflective practitioner: "Reflective practitioners challenge assumptions and question existing practices, thereby continuously accessing new lens [*sic*] to view their practice and alter their perspectives" (p. 296). Three essential practices for becoming a reflective practitioner are "making time for solitary reflection," "becoming a perpetual problem-solver," and "questioning the status quo" (pp. 296–7). These are presented as processes that one must make time for, and thus they differ dramatically from Schön's account of reflection-in-action as a process involving spontaneous and intuitive, rather than deliberate and controlled, reframing. In further discussion, she seems to move quite close to Schön's work by speaking of framing and reframing. However, she then suggests that "by challenging themselves to create a new vantage point, teachers can assign new meaning to the classroom situations they confront" (p. 299). Here we see new ways of viewing professional situations portrayed as arising in isolation and long after action, rather than as arising from a "reflective conversation with the situation" (Schön, 1983, p. 167).

The many significant differences between Larrivee's and Schön's accounts of reflection become more apparent when one compares the following quotations. Schön presented an account of inquiry in the context of reflection-in-action in these terms:

> As the same time that the inquirer tries to shape the situation to his frame, he must hold himself open to the situation's back-talk. He must be willing to enter into new confusions and uncertainties. Hence, he must adopt a kind of double vision. He must act in accordance with the view he has adopted, but he must recognize that he can always break it open later, indeed, *must* break it open later in order to make new sense of his transaction with the situation ... As the risk of uncertainty increases, so does the temptation to treat the view as the reality. Nevertheless, if the inquirer maintains his double vision, even while deepening his commitment to a chosen frame, he increases his chances of arriving at a deeper and broader coherence of artifact and idea. (p. 164)

Schön's reference to "double vision" – entertaining old and new frames simultaneously while seeking evidence that one is more productive than the other – emphasizes his focus on the importance of professional action that is metacognitive, aware of the assumptions one is making while acting in a particular way. In contrast, Larrivee uses dramatic language to describe her view of the process of critical reflection as something approaching the heroic:

> If instead we are able to face the conflict, surrendering what is familiar, we allow ourselves to experience the uncertainty. This not knowing throws us into chaos. At this phase, if we "move into the eye of the storm," we "weather" the turmoil and a deeper understanding emerges, moving us to the reconciling phase. In this final stage, we have had a shift in our way of thinking and sensing. We are ... seeing things in a new light. We engage in new patterns of thinking and access new tools and strategies to respond more appropriately to classroom situations. (p. 305)

Although this account has some similarities to Schön's account of reflection-in-action many years before, Larrivee makes no reference whatsoever to Schön's work, nor does she offer evidence to support her interpretations. Schön's (1983) account is supported by a variety of case studies, and he emphasizes the importance of testing new ways of thinking, while Larrivee appears to assume that a new perspective will always be an improvement.

Reframing while Teaching and Learning to Teach: The Potential of Listening in Moments of Uncertainty and Surprise

Having examined but a small sample of the extensive literature concerning *reflection* in the context of teacher education, it is time to draw conclusions and be clear about what is and is not being claimed. I do not claim to be discussing *reflection* in the many different ways that that term can be interpreted. Three points are of particular interest to me:

1. Donald Schön's 1983 book is generally recognized as the source of the ubiquitous references within teacher education to the importance of reflection, critical reflection, and becoming a critically reflective practitioner. Schön did not use the word *critical*, which seems to have been added when the word *reflection* alone did not produce the desired results; adding this word and constructing levels of reflection is an interesting exercise, but again there is little evidence that it has changed how people learn to teach.
2. Schön's ideas have been discussed and critiqued extensively (Eraut, 1995, is one significant example), but there has been little effort to identify what Schön's work might contribute to the education of new professionals, including teachers.
3. My personal interpretation is that Schön was leading us to consider much more fully and carefully how new and experienced professionals *learn from their own experiences of professional action*. While there is extensive reference to reflection in the literature of teacher education, very little of that discussion relates to school practicum experiences where beginning teachers are able to learn from first-hand experience with the guidance of a mentor. Schön's (1987) second book focused on learning from experience in interaction with a mentor.

I would never suggest that Schön provides the last word on what might be involved in how a professional learns from experience. However, I have become increasingly concerned with the extent to which there is *little or no connection between university-based classes and school-based practicum experiences in pre-service teacher education*. I have worked in the same eight-month, postgraduate, university-based teacher education program for thirty-five years. For all but two of those thirty-five years, the program structure could best be described as traditional. The two years that were revolutionary proved to be far too revolutionary for most of my colleagues at the time. As I listen to the practicum experiences of those I teach, I hear one universal conclusion: *Practicum experiences are the single most important element of the pre-service program.* Increasingly, my students suggest that both course content and written assignments need to have more direct connections to their practicum experiences.

What might be achieved by more direct connections between the two very different learning contexts – courses and practicum – of most teacher education programs? While most experienced teachers have access to professional development resources (such as conferences, workshops, and professional learning communities within their schools), it will always be their classes and daily interactions with students that are their major opportunities for learning that improves professional practice. Perhaps the familiar gap between theory and practice is so pervasive because school classrooms rarely provide explicit attention to learning from experience. It is far more common to learn by reading and by listening to those (teachers) who are expected to know more than their students.

Whatever one makes of Schön's (1983) account of *reflection-in-action*, I suggest that we see little evidence of his ideas in discussions of reflection in teacher education *because we find it so difficult to construct direct links between education classes and practicum experiences.* University classes often seem perched on what Schön (1983, p. 42) referred to as the "high, hard ground," while practicum placements require would-be teachers to perform in "a swampy lowland where situations are confusing 'messes' incapable of technical solution." Those who teach university-based teacher education classes tend not to be the individuals who observe teacher candidates in their practicum experiences and thus tend not to be reminded regularly of how complex and unrealistic it is to speak of "putting theory into practice."

My own work with Schön's account of reflection-in-action leads me to suggest that we must help teacher candidates to learn how (better) to learn from classroom experiences. Doing so is certainly not easy (Russell, 2005a), for it can rarely be done by telling. Teaching how to learn from experience requires deliberate and explicit modelling by teacher educators. Understanding the importance of naming problems carefully before trying to solve them is one of Schön's contributions. Another involves the importance of a reflective conversation with the classroom situation. Professionals need to pay close attention to moments of uncertainty, surprise, and puzzlement that may stimulate reframing and generate new, possibly more productive ways of interpreting student behaviour, generating perspectives that may suggest new courses of action.

The Complexity of Paradigmatic Change: A Personal Example

In the introduction to this chapter, I indicated that I worked with experienced teachers for three years before beginning to teach pre-service teachers. In the last of those three years with experienced teachers, a colleague and I worked with five history teachers and their principal, first showing them how to identify patterns in transcripts of recorded lessons and then working with them to construct alternative patterns of teacher–student interaction that might be more productive (Ireland & Russell, 1978). The teachers arrived at two broad conclusions: (1) They had not realized how much they talk in every lesson they teach, and (2) they had no idea that it would be so hard to move away from that dominant pattern of teacher–student interaction in which teachers do most of the talking. I respected these teachers' willingness to open their teaching to the eyes of others and I respected their conclusions.

Four months later, I was standing in front of my first teacher education classes with a personal resolve that I would find ways to reduce the amount of talking (telling) that I would do. Like those history teachers, I had no idea how to replace talking with more productive alternatives. In retrospect, that first year as a teacher educator had many moments of what Schön would later term *reflection-in-action.* I struggled to develop new patterns of interaction, and the most productive proved to be patterns for listening to those I was teaching. I met with small groups to get to know individuals better, and I instituted a mid-course teaching evaluation in which I collected free responses under the headings of strengths, weaknesses, and suggestions. Returning the results to my classes prompted discussions in which I could begin to explain why I was trying to reduce the amount of time I spent talking to them. Unforgettably, one student expressed outrage by asking: "Why didn't you tell us you weren't going to tell us?"

As I complete thirty-five years of work in pre-service teacher education, I am acutely aware of the profound stability of teaching in general and teacher education in particular. I have been fortunate to do my research and writing in the context of teacher education itself. Over time, my teaching of pre-service teachers has changed dramatically as I listened to those I was teaching, as I studied my own teacher education practices (Schuck & Russell, 2005), and as I encountered innovative teaching ideas that I could adapt to teacher education and then work to make part of my professional practice.

The program in which I have worked has seen many changes over three decades, yet in many respects it has not changed at all. Practicum placements are now slightly longer. Thanks to the addition of *reflection* to the teacher education vocabulary, classes and assignments have changed in wording, yet there is little evidence to suggest profound changes in results. In 1997, a radical change in program structure placed extensive practicum experience (fourteen weeks) in schools ahead of most education coursework. Nine months later, faculty members voted to abandon that radical change. That experience generated a preliminary version of table 7.1, which illustrates some of the assumptions within two very different paradigms for framing how teachers learn.

Paradigmatic change in teaching takes time but, most importantly, it requires a willingness to take risks and a willingness to fail. Reflection-in-action, driven by "a reflective conversation with a situation" (Schön, 1983, p. 163), can inspire more productive ways of interpreting the complexity of what happens in our classrooms, but not every moment of reframing will generate a productive change. Similarly, when reframing inspires one to risk a new action, the new action itself will rarely be perfect the first time it is attempted and will require patient refinement and further conversation with the situation before it become a habit that is more productive than the one it replaces. In one of his last publications, Schön spoke of the need for a new scholarship:

> The epistemology appropriate to the new scholarship must make room for the practitioner's reflection in and on action. It must account for and legitimize not only the use of knowledge produced in the academy, but the practitioner's generation of actionable knowledge in the form of models or prototypes that can be carried over, by reflective transfer, to new practice situations. The new scholarship calls for an epistemology of reflective practice, which includes what Kurt Lewin described as action research. But in the modern research university and other institutions of higher education influenced by it, reflective practice in general, and action research in particular, are bound to be caught up in a battle with the prevailing epistemology of technical rationality. (Schön, 1995, p. 34)

Table 7.1 Comparing perspectives on teacher education design

Questions about learning to teach	Theory-into-practice perspective	Practice-and-theory perspective
What is the nature of teachers' knowledge?	The knowledge candidates' need to teach is propositional, and its meaning can be comprehended without teaching experience.	A teacher's practical knowledge involves images, feelings, values, and experiences as well as knowledge expressed in propositions. Theory cannot be fully understood without personal practicum experiences.
What do teacher candidates already know about teaching?	Candidates know little about teaching. They come to learn theory and other generalizations about teaching that they later express in practice-teaching placements.	Candidates have an extensive stock of images of teaching that guide their initial actions. They lack access to the thinking that accompanies teaching actions. Only during practicum experiences can candidates learn to link thought and action.
How strong are teacher candidates' educational values?	Candidates' values for improving teaching are fragile, weak, and easily eroded by exposure to undesirable practices in schools. Education classes should help them resist the inclination to adopt existing practices uncritically.	Candidates' pedagogical values are strong and grounded in images of their former teachers. They can and do apply these values to existing school practices, just as they apply them to analysis of how their education courses are taught.
How much experience does a new teacher require?	Short periods of experience (2 to 3 weeks) are adequate for practising the knowledge acquired in teacher education classes.	Extended experience supports and consolidates learning from experience and better prepares candidates for the first full year of teaching by building personal confidence.
Can candidates learn from their own experiences?	Candidates must be told how to think about theory and experience. Those with more experience should tell them how schools can be improved.	Candidates can and must think for themselves. They see value in learning from others' experiences as well. Significant others include associate teachers, faculty, and other candidates.
How does a new teacher improve as she or he gains experience?	Candidates improve with experience as their mentor teachers provide practical tips for them to accumulate. (Some associate teachers view what is taught in education courses as impractical or unrealistic.)	As associate teachers provide constructive criticism, candidates learn to critique their practices themselves. Candidates' improvements are also driven by their personal values and reasons for entering teaching.

Schön was not optimistic about the prospects for epistemological change within universities and schools. My goals in this chapter have included reminding readers that a *reflective practice* perspective is not easily achieved, either personally or institutionally. We must not expect our students to adopt new frames and change old habits when we who teach them have not done the same ourselves, so that we understand in deed rather than only in word just what it is we are asking our students to do.

Several Canadian colleagues and I recently developed table 7.1 for the purpose of contrasting the familiar or traditional theory-into-practice approach to pre-service teacher education with one that incorporates learning from experience *as well as* learning in university classrooms (Martin, Russell, Bullock, O'Connor, & Dillon, 2012). The practice-and-theory column illustrates how significantly assumptions and practices must change in a paradigm shift away from technical rationality or theory-into-practice.

Personal Actions Based on Reflection-in-Action

To continue this analysis of Schön's *reflection-in-action* and the general neglect of his specific contributions within the literature of research on teacher education, I present several examples of reflection-in-action that have made significant contributions to my personal practice as a teacher educator. I should remind readers that before publishing *The Reflective Practitioner*, Schön published several books with Argyris (Argyris & Schön, 1974) that focused on the organizational and interpersonal challenges associated with the fact that most individuals display significant gaps between their *espoused theories* (what they say they are doing) and their *theories-in-use* (theories inferred from their observed actions). This is a particularly important issue for pre-service and in-service teacher education, where what we do and what we say are *always* noticed and compared by our students. Those learning to teach quickly become frustrated when they are simply told that they should not lecture to students; being told not to do to students what one's teacher is doing is an obvious and frustrating contradiction.

I am not well qualified to address the broad question "What is learning?", yet I ask it here in the context of individuals who are learning to become teachers. Each individual who is learning to teach begins that task with a powerful apprenticeship of observation; she or he knows (by observation, not deliberate instruction) the *habits* of teachers and will enact those habits in a classroom, albeit awkwardly at first. Yet most beginning teachers seem to assume they know little about teaching. While they have acquired many habits of teaching during their careers as students, they know very little about the rationales for teaching – the perspectives on learning held by the teachers whose habits they have acquired indirectly and unintentionally. I like to use the term *frames* for these perspectives, because that term links well to Schön's idea of reframing. Notice that Schön's discussion suggests that it is when events are puzzling, surprising, or uncertain that we may, in a reflective conversation with the materials of the situation, be inspired to see things in new ways – to reframe the problem. Learning from experience is a complex process that is quite unlike learning from books or learning from others' experiences. When a teacher learns from experience, that learning has to be seen simultaneously from two perspectives – habits *and* frames. If we learn from experience, we act differently in the next similar experience and we think differently about how and why we are acting in a particular way in that context of action.

As every parent knows in some significant sense, a child's learning from experience also tends to be much more powerful than learning by reading or being told. Although I was not the first to think of this example, I always turn to the statement, "The stove is hot," to illustrate three types of learning. When we are *told* that the stove is hot, the stove probably looks no different than when it is cold; there does not appear to be any reason to act differently. When we *see* someone else touch a hot stove and jump back quickly, the stove may look no different, but the reaction of another person may send a message of caution that is easier to internalize. When we *touch* a hot stove ourselves, we jump back reflexively and we also realize that while the stove looked no different, it actually was quite different, and so we learn first-hand the lesson that we should be cautious when approaching a stove.

In my own thirty-five years of learning from experience as a teacher educator, change has come slowly at some times and more rapidly at others. Schön's 1983 book provided the first major instance of reframing of my experiences during the previous six years as a teacher educator. I was puzzled by the fact that when I visited my students in their practicum classrooms, I saw little evidence of behaviours that might have been inspired by their education classes. They were teaching as they had been taught. *Reflection-in-action* and the concept of reframing gave me a powerful way forward. As my own frames changed, my habits also changed, however gradually, as I found new resources and risked new patterns of interaction in my teacher education classroom.

The Perils, Pitfalls, and Unrealized Promise of the Reflective Practitioner

Schön's 1983 book set the profession of teacher education on the path of using the word *reflection* and trying to develop teachers as *reflective practitioners.* In the true spirit of technical rationality, the theory may have been promising, but putting it into practice has not achieved the required paradigmatic change. In the case of theory about reflection as set out by Schön, it appears that the theory was simultaneously ignored and also reinterpreted in a host of different ways to suit existing causes and purposes. Thus, I see a significant unrealized promise in the countless responses to the reflective path that teacher education has taken in response to Schön's title. Many perils and pitfalls arise when professionals change their vocabulary but not their actions. Teacher education programs rarely receive rave reviews from those learning to teach. Perhaps because the first years of teaching are so overwhelming and require so much personal learning from experience (Schuck, Aubusson, Buchanan, & Russell, 2012), experienced teachers may conclude that their pre-service program failed to prepare them adequately for the real work of teaching.

Like the practices of teaching in general (documented powerfully by Sarason, 1971), the practices of teacher education tend to be very stable. Only a paradigmatic change in the fundamental premises and practices of teacher education programs, accompanied at first by a new set of perils and pitfalls, seems likely to achieve meaningful links between what is presented as theory in teacher education classrooms and what is experienced in practicum placements. Schön suggested new perspectives and directions with respect to long-standing challenges of teacher education. We have yet to achieve the promise of the reflective practitioner perspective.

8 Ubiquitous Learning and the Future of Teaching

NICHOLAS C. BURBULES

1.

Teacher education in the future will need to address ubiquitous learning: the opportunity for anywhere/anytime access to information, interaction with knowledgeable peers and experts, and structured learning opportunities from a variety of sources. The gulf between formal and informal learning will disappear. Often this learning will be "just in time," anchored to the needs of an immediate question, problem, or situation. It will put control of when, where, how, and why one is learning more in the hands of the learner, and shift the motivational focus from "learn it now, use it later (maybe)" to "learn it now, use it now."

Of course, we have already entered this era: anyone who has pulled out a smart phone or portable computer to surf the web in answer to a question, or to call someone for information or advice, or to view a "how-to" video on YouTube in the midst of a crisis, has already become a ubiquitous learner. Because of the spread of handheld devices and wireless networks, which provide the means to learn something where and when it is needed, learning is being integrated into the flow of ordinary human activity.

Of course, learning in a variety of places and circumstances has always been part of human life, but the access to structured learning opportunities through technology makes the slogan "real life learning" a concrete reality to an unprecedented degree. And with the advent of "the cloud" and the possibilities of more or less continuous connectivity, the uploading and downloading of information of all sorts, interaction with others with the push of a button, wearable technology integrated into glasses, and so on, engagement with technology is being woven into the very fabric of ordinary experience. So-called augmented reality, for example, does this directly – using GPS and locational technologies to link information exactly to where you are, and using devices with cameras and screens (which may not look like computers anymore) to allow you to view your environment with supplemental data or images linked to that content.

Imagine your device automatically accessing the Wikipedia page about a famous building as you are viewing it through a view-finder, or accessing the Facebook page belonging to someone whose image you capture through a camera, or finding the nearest Italian restaurant to where you are in a new city, along with customer reviews and recommendations about the best items on the menu. Our very notions of "place" and what makes a place significant will need to be rethought (Burbules, 2005). The place is not just the physical location, but a hub or locus of supplementary information, including videos and so on.

There are many provisos to add here. The first is that access to this ubiquitous learning environment is hardly equal: people with certain economic means, people who inhabit certain parts of the world, people with better educations, people who live in cities, and so on, are already in this mode of living. Many others, clearly, are not (Burbules, Callister, & Taaffe, 2006). This is a serious equity concern. But it may be that as wireless connectivity becomes a free, truly ubiquitous utility provided to everyone, and as the size and cost of the devices through which one accesses the Internet decrease and the contents of the cloud continue to increase, more and more people will have access to them. People with better education and higher technology skills will still benefit more from them, but at least some basic level of access will be provided as a common threshold good. Nevertheless, this divide remains a major challenge for education.

There is also an important qualification: constant access will create its own problems (which is not hard for many of us to imagine), and the "off" or "not available" switch will become even more important in the future. We will not want a continuous flow of images, sounds, or data; we will not want to be in contact with others (or for them to be able to be in contact with us) at all times; we will sometimes prefer to experience life "in the raw" without captions, commentary, or supplemental information. This will be a matter of choice in the future, and different people will make this choice in different ways.

Finally, I need to make clear, ubiquitous learning is not all of learning, and not everything can be learned in this way. There will continue to be a place for teachers, and schools, and studying. Especially for younger learners, a deep foundation for learning needs to be in place before most of these other learning opportunities can have value or meaning: there continue to be knowledge and skills that need to be acquired in order for other learning to happen. Nevertheless, even these sorts of formal, structured learning opportunities are being changed by ubiquitous technologies and a culture of socially distributed, anywhere/anytime learning – for example, how and where students do homework. Schools need to be consciously connected to a range of other learning environments: learning from the school goes out into these other venues, and learning from these other venues comes back into the school.

Here, as throughout my discussion, technological changes need to be seen as interactively affecting and being affected by a host of other social and cultural changes – a culture of mobility, of collaboration, of "infotainment," of video games, of social networking and communication on a literally global scale. We cannot maintain the spatial and temporal boxes (if we ever could) that suit our convenience, or our assumptions about where and when learning happens. The larger sense of control we would like to maintain over the learning of our students now involves something much more like a partnership, in which our expectations need to adapt even more to their learning styles, preferences, and other options for access to learning – much of which is outside our control and may be beyond our ken. I will return to these ideas in my conclusion.

2.

What does teaching look like within a ubiquitous learning environment? I do not think that the teacher becomes superfluous; in certain ways, a teacher becomes even more important to the processes of learning. But the role, activities, and purposes of teaching, I believe, will need to change. And so teacher education will need to change. This is both a challenge and an opportunity: a challenge to rethink some things, a challenge to give up some traditional privileges and forms of authority that go with our ideas about "teaching" (and which may be part of what attracted us to teaching in the first place), and a challenge to change our relationships with our students as active learners, as well as with their parents and others. At the same time, the environment of ubiquitous learning creates a host of new opportunities for teachers.

(1) Universities often refer to "continuing education." The era of ubiquitous learning is one of potentially "continuous education," for learners of all ages from children to the elderly. Rather than learning sequences being structured in spatial and temporal units that serve institutional needs as much or more than they serve the needs, interests, or learning patterns of students, the substance of learning – and the disposition to learn – can be situated more within the flow of human activity. As I put it in an earlier paper: *To be is to learn* (Burbules, 2009).

The dispositional element is crucial here. Institutional education struggles constantly with the motivational economy that drives learning: grades, test performance, and teacher approval play central roles. But we also know that these factors are poor motivators for many students. Instead, we might think of ways to make the slogan "the learning society" into a concrete reality, where citizens and workers, adults and the very young, are brought up in a culture in which all sorts of activities and experiences, from work to entertainment to family life and beyond, are viewed as opportunities to discover and explore additional knowledge as a supplement to those activities and experiences. Taking pleasure in such supplemental learning can build upon the native human dispositions for curiosity and growing mastery of knowledge and skills. But these pleasures are grounded in the pleasures of the original activities and experiences themselves, not in something extraneous to them; this kind of learning is an enhancement to things people already care about.

The emerging reality of ubiquitous learning creates an opportunity for educators to open up a long-awaited conversation about the shared responsibility for creating and sustaining a learning society – not just as a duty of formal institutions – but also for fostering a disposition to learn as simply part of who we are as human beings. Rather than have educators struggle to motivate work and study among students who receive, in many cases, conflicting messages from other social influences, a society that understands the power and importance of ubiquitous learning will value learning in different ways. That would create a tremendous resource and support for the efforts of educators, but it also means, as previously mentioned, losing a certain control and direction over learning, as multiple influences and multiple purposes will motivate learning activities.

(2) Progressive educators and others of a social constructivist bent have long praised situated, contextual learning as richer, more complex, and more likely to be retained and used in the future. Ubiquitous

learning creates a resource for supporting situated learning as people seek out knowledge and skills they need for coping with real, immediate situations that confront them.

In a famous story from the January 2010 earthquake in Haiti, a man trapped in rubble used his cell phone to access information about how to stanch his bleeding injuries and buy time until he could be rescued, sixty hours later. While much more dramatically than in the usual learning situation, here someone faced an immediate problem and had an intrinsic – and very powerful – interest in learning what he needed to know. His lessons were of direct impact and he saw (and felt) their benefits. Would the same thing have happened if he had taken a first aid workshop two years previously? Perhaps. But so much of current learning is of this "learn it now, use it later" nature that it is impossible to tell in advance which pieces will be of life-changing significance, and which ones never used and forgotten.

There are two important points to make clear here. First, the Haiti case highlights a certain instrumental value that may not apply to other learning experiences which also contribute to a better life, but cannot be justified in terms of their direct usefulness or impact. Not all ubiquitous learning is about use value – sometimes it may just be about interest, curiosity, and enrichment. Learning as a supplement to human activity and experience may or may not have an instrumental impact down the road, but that does not mean it is not pleasurable and worthwhile. Second, there is a certain amount of learning that cannot simply be relegated to situated need and purpose: some learning really is preparatory to other learning and needs to be developed explicitly and systematically in order for other, more independent, learning to occur. I strongly suspect that this set is smaller than the set that schools currently preoccupy themselves with; it is certainly smaller for certain learners and their needs and interests. Hence, we must ask whether the compulsion to master certain material in school, for largely extraneous reasons, may not do more harm than good for many students, suppressing the disposition to learn that they bring with them to school, but then lose.

(3) Similarly, educators say that certain capacities for problem solving, critical thinking, creativity, and independent inquiry are themselves important educational goals, apart from specific content knowledge mastery. Where do these fit into the standard curriculum? We know that for many students they never do, and yet those capacities have more to do with future life prospects and success than content knowledge mastery alone.

Here again, ubiquitous learning creates a resource for teachers, an opportunity to relate learning goals to contexts and purposes beyond the classroom. Apart from dispositional factors and others I have already mentioned, a ubiquitous learning culture regards ordinary events as learning moments – whether one chooses to pursue it or not, people recognize that each activity and experience is surrounded by a penumbra or halo of additional information. Something more can always be said, and this changes the way the particular is viewed – no longer as an isolated "fact," but always as a node of interconnected facts and significations. If educators recognize this, and learn to navigate these networked relationships, they can help foster the kind of thinking that problem solving, critical thinking, creativity, and inquiry depend upon. Precisely because one cannot pursue all avenues, the process of choosing when and which avenues to pursue raises questions that in turn require second-order awareness and reflection on the interdependencies of knowledge. And, I would suggest, this understanding supports also a kind of metacognitive awareness of one's own understandings and assumptions – where they come from, where they begin, and where they end.

(4) Another aspect of ubiquitous learning – part of the larger "Web 2.0" trend – is the growth of collaborative learning communities. Here again, technological changes influence and are influenced by wider social and cultural changes. People increasingly see the Internet as a way of extending their social networks, and one way in which this happens is by co-creating and sharing text, video, and other products. Ordinary users seem less concerned with proprietary credit or ownership, and are more driven by what David Weinberger (2004) calls "an ethos of generosity." Similarly, Yochai Benkler (2002) proclaims the virtues of "commons-based peer-production." Crowdsourcing and similar distributed activities draw from and reinforce the identity of non-face-to-face community. People seem genuinely motivated by the idea that collective intelligence can do more than the achievement of individuals, and researchers like Benkler argue that such models are *more* productive than the personal credit-based incentive systems that predominate in a variety of workplaces. Elsewhere, I have written about "self-educating communities," in which people collectively take responsibility for learning together about matters that concern them (Burbules, 2006). In such communities there are no distinct teacher/learner roles: people learn from and with each other, being sometimes experts and teachers, at other times beneficiaries of the tutelage of others.

Teachers have long used group projects as one model of classroom work, and in a broader sense often promote the social value of "cooperation." But the reward systems and the broader accountability measures of schooling, at virtually all levels, still reward and incentivize individual achievement as the metric of success. As previously discussed, ubiquitous learning is less governed by such considerations and is related more to the needs and purposes of contextual circumstances. Under those conditions, collaboration is a plus. Indeed, for many purposes it is indispensable. The power of a ubiquitous resource often resides in the aggregated contributions made by many. Information about a place I am visiting comes from many visitors before; I often will trust the collective wisdom of many opinions more than those of an individual. But even when I am accessing advice or information from a single expert, this is also being shared as part of a distributed, collective good – something which I might then in turn share with others.

It would be fruitful, I am suggesting, for educators to regard this wider collaborative ethos as an educational resource and opportunity. One role for teachers in this context is to help foster and facilitate the creation of such distributed learning communities (in which they might be one of many participants, but perhaps no longer the central or essential one). It would certainly be beneficial to take advantage of the motivational and reward systems that drive learners to want to share and co-create work with each other. This will mean changing, perhaps, some institutional norms against "cheating" and "not sharing work." We might need to rethink what we mean by those strictures, and hence change, even abandon, certain traditional ways of evaluating and rewarding student work. But the simultaneous benefit would be a much more engaged and energetic motivational system to drive learning, one that should force educators to think about encouraging, fostering, and evaluating the strength of collaboration itself as a more important educational goal. As I have said, many of our students are there already, waiting for us.

(5) This changing approach to student motivation opens up other opportunities as well. In a context where student skills and familiarity with new technologies often outstrip the teacher's own (which is increasingly true as students get older), the teaching–learning relation can be made to look more like a partnership, one in which each party has things to offer the other. The teacher's role remains crucial, but changing: mentor, facilitator, role model, or tutor. In order to perform these roles well in a ubiquitous learning context, teachers will have to

become better informed and more engaged with what learners already know.

On one hand, this creates a resource for leveraging new learning that is related to the other contextual experiences and interests learners bring with them into the classroom. This idea is hardly new: John Dewey was saying it a hundred years ago (Dewey, 1915). These links are both matters of cognitive scaffolding and of motivation (Burbules & Linn, 1988). On the other hand, they make the cliché "Teachers learn from their students" into a concrete reality; in terms of both technical expertise and these contextual experiences and interests, students possess knowledge and skills teachers do not. This begins to introduce a theme I will address below: teachers need to become ubiquitous learners, too.

Another way in which the teacher's role remains indispensable is as an equalizer; for all the knowledge and expertise students bring to the classroom, outside-of-school resources, both technological and otherwise, remain profoundly unequal. Public education remains the one common resource that students from all kinds of backgrounds share, and the teacher is the focal point for recognizing and responding to those differences. Particularly in this realm, access to online learning opportunities is more than a matter of access to technology itself. It is not just a matter of a "digital divide" (Burbules, Callister, & Taaffe, 2006). It is a divide of all sorts of other opportunities as well – unequal chances to learn how to exploit the technological access people may already have, unequal support groups and social networks that help to foster technological skills and savvy, unequal contexts and time in which to play with and practise new technological resources, and so on. The most detrimental aspect of this kind of divide is that it is self-perpetuating and even accelerating; the more access to ubiquitous resources and learning opportunities one has, the more one is able to increase the distance from those who do not – better access to education, better access to job opportunities, better access to social networking, better access to citizen participation.

Each of these advantages allows the gap between haves and have-nots (or between quantitatively and qualitatively greater or lesser degrees of access) to grow over time. In short, the technologically rich get richer. Schools, and the educators in them, have a fundamental responsibility to try to counteract these tendencies; especially when overlaid on other dimensions of educational inequality, those who have ubiquitous access to technology and online networks live in substantially different worlds from those who do not.

(6) The dramatically new ways in which people now interact with technologies also provide an invaluable opportunity for teachers to rethink their work and their role. It is hardly news that much of the way in which people engage with new information, through the media or through online browsing, is based in multimedia – especially visual and video-based information. Much of the web is text, to be sure, but the ways in which information upload and download happens in ubiquitous contexts is often through image and sound. We increasingly want our technology – for example, GPS – to *show* us or *tell* us what we need to know. When it is being streamed through a simultaneous flow with other activities, it must be so, because we can't be reading extensive text while we are doing something else.

Here, again, the case of augmented reality is instructive: in some cases, it can be described as "the world with captions," but in more and more instances augmented reality takes the form of an additional layer of experience added to, and woven into, the flow of original experience itself. In the future, these layers may be increasingly indistinguishable from one another: much of life will be a multimedia experience. (Imagine walking through an art museum with running commentary, access to view artworks by the artists in other museums, and visual information about where and when artworks were created, for example. Think about being able to view a painting overlaid with the original sketches or the palimpsest of previous versions which were painted over and altered later.) Helping learners integrate formal learning, informal learning, and this new kind of situated, experiential learning provides, I am suggesting, a tremendously powerful educational opportunity and resource – one with truly unprecedented features and challenges. An even greater challenge is how to bring the learning styles and dispositions of a ubiquitous learning generation into the classroom.

(7) Fortunately, teachers are not alone in this new attention and learning ecosystem. Ubiquity also implies new potential partnerships – with parents, to be sure, but also with other participants in the different learning contexts where ubiquitous learning happens. Education itself needs to become a networked process, one in which the school and classroom may be central, but not isolated. Here again, long-standing educational slogans take on a new meaning and immediacy: parental involvement; lifelong, life-wide learning; learning by doing; a school without walls; learning for the real world; teachers

can't do it alone; and so on. Some of these other participants may be willing to interact directly with the classroom, as outside experts or as professional mentors. In such a world, even the distinction of formal and informal learning starts to break down, and new processes and new structures will need to break down the spatial and temporal boxes we have built to distinguish where and when certain kinds of learning need to occur.

That may seem overwhelming. But at the same time, the resources and support systems for learning are multiplying as well. Schools are not islands. The educational challenge involves linking and coordinating these systems, which is a different kind of challenge, but one involving familiar elements. We still need theories of learning and motivation, we still need educational aims and standards that tell us what is important to learn, we still need a commitment to equity and access to protect our democratic values, and we still need some formal structures and processes to regulate and evaluate the kinds of learning that are taking place. The point here is that each of these familiar elements of being an educator needs to be rethought in a ubiquitous learning world, and that this rethinking will need to engage others who become indispensable partners in this process of linking and coordinating a range of learning contexts.

(8) Finally, and perhaps most significantly, teachers are learners within a ubiquitous learning environment, too. All the resources described here are available to teachers: anywhere/anytime learning, mobile access, social networks of advice and support, multi-contextual learning, augmented reality, and so on. Teachers also are embedded in a flow of learning opportunities and experiences, and their growth and development can be continuous within that flow. Most of all, teachers can be refigured as members of their own distributed learning communities, not only in the ways in which professional networks have always worked, but as an immediate feature of daily life itself, potentially available for advice or support at any moment of their work lives. As I have said, teachers are not alone.

3.

How, then, do teachers take advantage of this continuous flow of access to information and to others as a potential resource and not as a "blooming, buzzing, confusion"? In what ways must learning to manage this flow become part of their professional training? What are the new skills teachers must master in becoming facilitators and coordinators of multiple learning sources and learning sites for their students?

Here is what they are not: they are not just the simple skills of teaching and explaining material to students; they are not just the mastery of content knowledge that teachers possess to "give" to students; they are not just the skills of classroom management and discipline; nor are they just learning to "use" technology as a resource in pedagogy. Of course these capabilities remain important, but professional training that is limited to these will not prepare teachers for a ubiquitous learning world.

The new skills and capabilities of teaching require a broader understanding of technology-based social networks and the range of learning resources available online, from YouTube to Khan Academy; they require a sociological and cultural understanding of varied learning environments and their characteristics; they require new learning theories that integrate formal learning, informal learning, and situated, experiential learning; they require skills in designing learning strategies that take advantage of, and interrelate, the learning that takes place in various diverse contexts; and they require the ability to work with a range of partners across those contexts. The teacher in a ubiquitous learning world is not just a pedagogue, but a planner, designer, and manager. This in turn suggests a certain breakdown in the categories of teacher and administrator, pedagogue and planner, practitioner and designer – and what they need to know and be able to do.

And, finally, these blurred boundaries pose an equally transformative challenge to schools of education, credentialing bodies, and professional associations to overturn their own categories and distinctions. Here, as described throughout this chapter, educators are going to have to re-examine their institutional stake and interest in perpetuating a certain way of doing things, and the attendant privileges they might seek to maintain – versus adapting to a rapidly changing teaching and learning environment that threatens to make those established ways of thinking about and doing things irrelevant.

FOCAL POINT 3

Aboriginal Education in a Globalizing Context

This focal point addresses Aboriginal education from three perspectives: philosophy of education, programmatic changes, and organizational dimensions of learning. Thus, the reader is led to a discussion of how the term indigenous is used and to suggestions for a reorientation, so that Indigenous education could become a bridge between cultures. Beeman argues for the notion of Indigenous education over Aboriginal education, emphasizing a mode of learning grounded in a different way of being in the world. Merino-Dickinson's case study of teacher education programs in central and southern Chile in areas with sizeable Aboriginal population examines the lack of integration of ancestral knowledge of the Chilean indigenous population. This is followed by an analysis by Robust of the inclusion of indigenous spaces, ancestral meeting houses, in university campuses and consequent infrastructural organizational changes. His chapter describes two examples of using traditional learning "institutions" in contemporary – in this case, culturally appropriate – spaces for learning: the ancestral meeting house at the University of Auckland and the Longhouse at the University of British Columbia.

9 Autochthonous Ed: Deep, Indigenous, Environmental Learning

CHRIS BEEMAN

This chapter is about two broad ideas. The first is a challenge to the way in which the term *Indigenous* is commonly used nowadays. I make this challenge because of the current popularity of the term *Indigenizing education* and my concern over its uncritical adoption. I suggest that its possibly too glib easiness needs to be questioned, and I propose a reorientation of Indigenous education so that it can be not merely a source of pride and a reconnection for many Aboriginal students, but also a bridge between cultures. The second broad idea is the suggestion that Indigenous education, properly construed and enacted, might be part of a solution for public education's increasing failure to reach all students, not just those considered to be marginal (though this solution would challenge the underpinnings of education as it is currently conceptualized in the West). Both ideas include the more-than-human world as part of Indigenous education.

While I want to acknowledge the importance of Aboriginal education, an area with which I have been involved for the past decade, the focus of this chapter is Indigenous education. I begin with the idea that the two are distinctly different projects with some admittedly overlapping areas. But by illustrating their distinctness, I hope to bring into relief another topic that I think needs more investigation: the sometimes unintentional confusion – and sometimes convenient conflation – of ethnicity and ontology. This will appear as a theme throughout this chapter.

While I will be addressing issues of relevance to Aboriginal learning, I will not be investigating Aboriginal education per se. Aboriginal education, in its more fully realized state, may be tentatively defined as education for Aboriginal and sometimes non-Aboriginal students, designed and delivered in ways that meet the particular needs of Aboriginal students, ideally taught by Aboriginal teachers, in recognition of the context of a long history of colonization and a longer pre-colonial past (Hampton, 1995), and with an appreciation of the likelihood that colonization in education, if left unchallenged, will continue (Smith, 1999). The social, spiritual, intellectual, epistemological, and political aspects of Aboriginal culture are its focus (Hampton, 1995), and service to the community to which the student belongs, rather than the welfare of the individual learner, is its end (Kiado Cruz, personal communication, 2008). In its enactment, as much attention needs to be paid to the mode in which learning and teaching occur as to its subject, because Aboriginal modes of teaching and learning are at times distinct from non-Aboriginal modes (Beeman, 2010; Cajete, 1994). The preceding definition contrasts with the form that Aboriginal education usually takes. While part of the project of Aboriginal education ought to be a recognition of the intrinsic merit and worth of the more-than-human world, Aboriginal education – as it currently appears in Canada – is more usually directed towards redressing some of the historical injustices to Aboriginal peoples and to providing conditions for the thriving of Aboriginal culture within, apart from, or in conjunction with existing political structures (Hampton, 1995). When current (non-ideal) practices of Aboriginal education occur with non-Aboriginal students, often this is part of basic, overlooked education about forgotten and marginalized histories.

For the purpose of this chapter, however, I want to set aside the evident and necessary work needed to fund, encourage, and support Aboriginal self-enactment through education and look instead towards what I think of as being a far more embracing project, one capable of addressing equally the explicit and implicit interests of both Aboriginal and non-Aboriginal students. This is the project of enacting a deeply *Indigenous* approach to learning. As soon as I use the term, however, there is a problem, because I mean to use the term here in a different way than it has come to be used. I hope to propose, without too much awkwardness, a new possible interpretation: instead of *Indigenous* referring some version of Aboriginal people, it may be interpreted as something like "those of any ethnicity enacting, in direct relationship with place and over the long term, practices that sustain them and their surroundings, in full consciousness thereof." To avoid confusion, in this chapter, except when quoting others, indicating special attention to be directed to the term, or referring to common usage, I will hereafter write the term *Indigenous* and its related derivatives in italics when referring to an ontological description, and without italics when referring to ethnicity.

The need for an exploration of this kind of *Indigenous* approach to learning derives from a simple claim, that what is of most benefit to both modern Western culture and Aboriginal people alike is that knowledge from this position be based on a different ontology – a different way of being in the world (Beeman, 2006; Burkhardt, 2004; Deloria, 2004). This different way of being is not ethnically determined, though in practice it is nowadays most often expressed by Aboriginal people. Instead, it is established through a particular kind of co-creation with place. Under this new interpretation of Indigenous that I propose, the difference between an *Indigenous* person and a non-*Indigenous* person would be conceived of in terms of a life being lived, rather than ethnicity. In other words, it would be largely based on ontology rather than ethnicity. This way of being is one of long-term, sustainable, eco-centric living, an enacted interdependence with place. Defined thus, the major, initially evident difference between Aboriginal and *Indigenous* education is that *Indigenous* education would *have to* account for the difference in knowing that is attributable to an eco-centric mode of living, while Aboriginal education only *may* do so.

Only if we permit the idea of *Indigenous* to be different from *Aboriginal* can *Indigenous* education become a bridge between cultures.[1] This is because, if Indigeneity is defined ontologically rather than ethnically, participation in the ontological condition of Indigeneity need not be limited to Aboriginal people. I mention this at the start of this chapter because unless this new aspect of the term *Indigenous* is immediately established, at least one intellectual risk looms large. This is the risk that conflating *Aboriginal* with *Indigenous* may render an "indigenized" education environmentally superficial. This is because, while many Aboriginal people still know – through lived experience and spiritual and cultural practice – the primacy of the more-than-human world as a determining factor of both existence and intellectual life, many more, thanks to the ontological colonization project that is modern Western culture, are out of touch with it. However, if the term *Indigenous* is not conflated with Aboriginal, then a particular niche is opened in which co-creation with the more-than-human may emerge.

Indigenizing and Decolonizing

In educational circles, much has recently been written about *Indigenizing* and *decolonizing* education. I have some concerns about the use of these terms, mostly because of their facile use, made most evident by the adoption of the verbal form of the ideas, which suggests that one might do something simple to an entrenched educational practice to effect its decolonization and indigenization.

Many interpreters will recognize a prima facie connection between the terms *Indigenizing* and *decolonizing.* This is perhaps because of the easy melding of ideas and evident historical relationships between various forms of the words *Aboriginal, Indigenous,* and *decolonize,* as they are commonly used, especially when applied to Canadian history. Some slurring of distinctions between related terms is natural in casual thought, but it might be an error when considering and designing future pedagogies. The body of this chapter begins with an examination of the terms at hand, and ends with a proposal for what Indigenous education might look like if it were to combine both Aboriginal and environmental roots.

Indigenize

Let me examine the terms *Indigenize* and *decolonize* separately, before bringing them together again. When I made several web and database searches recently (January 2012), the term *Indigenize,* as used in the field of education, appeared to refer most often to a relatively recent movement to include an Aboriginal perspective in standard pedagogy. The term *Indigenous,* when currently used by Canadian scholars, is normally employed to refer to Aboriginal people in other parts of the world. The term *Aboriginal* is normally employed for those in Canada (First Nations, Inuit, Métis) (Battiste & Henderson, 2000).

But in broader use, the term *Indigenous* does not only refer to this. Looking at the etymological origins of the word, "born in the land itself" or "beget within" are common definitions. So, when the term *Indigenous* is applied to people, both a literal and figurative connection to land is implied. And when we tug a little at the definition's roots and follow them from the main trunk of meaning, through the loose duff of lived language, the varyingly used term *Indigenize* could be conceived of as referring to all manner of pedagogies that re-establish human relationship with place, rather than those which simply introduce Aboriginal perspectives to a discussion. In addition to its application to people, the term *Indigenous* may also apply to plants, microscopic biota, and animals. The shared aspect of these uses seems to be the notion of originating from a place or being born there (*Oxford Dictionary of English*, 2010). In its current common usage in Canada, though, there is an exclusivity to the term; it might seem strange to use it to describe non-Aboriginal people, though the literal meaning of the term might extend to anyone born here. Perhaps it might be said that European-rooted people are indigenous to there, and displaced to here, while – because of a long history of living here (*ab originalis*, from the beginning, some would say) – only Aboriginal people are, in this sense of the term, Indigenous to here. In this sense, evidently, the "originating from" impulse ranks high.

On the other hand, Alistair McIntosh, recounting stories of his childhood in the Hebrides Islands in *Soil and Soul* (2001), comfortably refers to the long-term, non-Aboriginal inhabitants of the Hebrides Islands as indigenous. Were they the first and only human inhabitants? Or were they merely the latest generation of those to call themselves "the people"? This use of the term *Indigenous* illustrates another meaning of the term, and in so doing challenges its simple synonymy with Aboriginality. In this use, the word does not only apply to Aboriginal people, nor has it historically. Thus, a little flexing of meaning is made possible from a broader look at the word; applied to education, the term might be permitted to embrace both Aboriginal and non-Aboriginal learners. A subsequent possible question is: Given the hermeneutic space made possible through various interpretations of the term *Indigenous*, and knowing that *Indigenous* education might not necessarily be equivalent to Aboriginal education – that is, not simply equivalent to the inclusion of Aboriginal content and modes of learning – what would be the sufficient conditions for making education *Indigenous*?

Under this more encompassing definition of *Indigenous*, activities such as place-based and environmental learning might be considered "indigenizing," insofar as they deepen understanding and connection to a locale where students were born or consider themselves to be from. However, they would not, in and of themselves, be sufficient conditions, because the lived relationship with place would not necessarily be present. And this, of course, is the sticking point for most public schools, and why education that would at present qualify as *Indigenous* – if indeed any does – is also likely to be occurring in an Aboriginal context. I will explore some of these possibilities in detail in the section entitled "From Shallow to Deep Indigenous Learning."

In the section entitled "Deeply Indigenous Ecological Learning," I will attempt to articulate more thoroughly the ontological distinction between *Indigenous* and Aboriginal. In doing so, I hope to begin to lay foundations that may bridge lived experiences between non-Aboriginal and Aboriginal peoples.

Decolonize

The term *decolonizing* has similarly complex meanings. Especially in regard to Aboriginal peoples, *decolonizing* normally refers to the process by which Aboriginal peoples become more self-determining, self-governing, or self-enacting – the process by which the blanket of political, social, spiritual, and economic smothering is cast off (Smith, 1999). The term derives from post-colonial theorizing, in its various literary, political, epistemological, and other forms (Denzin, Lincoln, & Smith, 2008). *Decolonizing*, when used in the discipline of education, has been, until recently, rarely conceptualized as or linked to an explicitly environmental education per se, though there are exceptions (Norberg-Hodge, 1992; Shiva, 2005).

With these more nuanced explorations of the two terms at hand, it would be theoretically possible – employing the most distant meaning of each – to have an indigenous, yet colonizing education system, or a decolonizing and non-indigenous one. In the former case, for example, one might imagine a pedagogy premised on re-establishing human connection with place, perhaps ignoring earlier, Aboriginal relationships with the very place that holds the learning (Basso, 1996), all the while re-enforcing colonial relationships. In the latter case, one might imagine a politically, socially, and economically progressive pedagogy that, for example, addressed the needs of only urban Aboriginal people, was well informed by recent history, and yet ignored historical interdependence with the more-than-human world. While one might make the case that such practices would be quite mistaken – for example, many would claim that part of an Aboriginal identity is inherently connected with land – these examples illustrate the importance of carefully choosing descriptors and not taking meanings in common use for granted. I do not intend here to claim a precedence of dictionary-meaning over use-meaning, only that the terms are used in more complex ways than we generally admit.

I have taken apart the meanings to show that if we are to use these two words, *Indigenize* and *decolonize*, we need to do so in consciousness of their possible misuse and of their theoretical separateness. Yet, at a deeper level, I think it is reasonable to see that the two underlying concepts – and projects – are generally interconnected. The project of colonization, through its historical link with capitalism and by definition, has been an ecologically alienating one (Marx, 1964). Decolonization, if taken in a literal sense, cannot but include reference to the distance we now measure between ourselves and the world we inhabit, if this world is defined – awkwardly but necessarily imprecisely – as one that is "less intermediated by human interests." When we colonize, we usually take over places belonging to others, and we enact what is by definition a human-centred project that often takes attention away from the ecological. The act of decolonizing, viewed from this perspective, could be seen as one that facilitates human reconciliation with place by leaving space for an ecology to interact with people. Thus, the pedagogical project of *Indigenizing*, if defined in the sense of reconnecting people with the world, must at least contain an element of the decolonizing; it countervails one of colonization's most egregious wounds: the loss of connection of people with the more-than-human world (Marx, 1964).

On the Possibilities of Indigenizing Education

The possibly too-convenient new verb "to Indigenize" – itself derived from the more common adjectival form (Indigenous) – might be serving to cover a problem rather than to solve it. That is to say, "Indigenizing" might pretend the possibility of something which is impossible, but, by providing a word to go with it, gives the impression of its possibility. It might be that the phrase leaves open a possibility in imagination that cannot yet be met in reality and that to enact an indigenizing program, as it were, is antithetical to the possibilities of the concept of education in precisely the same way that to enact a colonizing project is consistent with it. One can colonize actively, but perhaps an education may only be *Indigenous* as a by-product of engagement with an *Indigenous* way of being in the world.

In addition, bringing an Indigenous component to education in a shallow sense might both hide systemic problems associated with educative practice, more broadly considered, that cannot be fixed by a cosmetic approach. Such an approach might serve to inoculate both students and teachers against perceiving the possibility of deep change, or of fully experiencing it when it is encountered. Of course, this may not be the intent of those proposing it in its shallow sense, but I will argue that for deeper *Indigeneity* to be enacted in educative practice, much will have to change in what is taken for granted in educational systems, and many of the hitherto accepted, simple premises of a shallow version might need to be challenged.

It is certainly questionable, and perhaps impossible, for the posited verbal form of Indigenize to apply to the broader field of education in much the same way that it may be impossible for the terms *education* and *environmental*, as they are normally used, to be accurately used together. In other words, it may not simply be a question of education being too broken – that much is evident; it may also be a problem that the two concepts of *Indigenous* and *education*, as education is comprehended by the modern West, are incompatible. I need hardly mention that this is not because an education that is *Indigenous* in a deeper sense would not be a vast improvement both to learning and possibly to the processes involved in thought, but because education, as currently broadly understood, might not allow itself to be so modified.

Or, perhaps, is the problem also that the verbal form of the concept is internally self-contradictory? A subject-verb-object form of sentence such as "We will indigenize education" both linguistically and figuratively expresses an objectifying relationship: to indigenize in this way is an act that may be performed *on* education, as if each element in the equation did not have reciprocal effect. It might be that environmental education cannot become *Indigenous* as the result of something done to it. It might be that this can only occur when something completely new is self-generated from within another ontology. As I will later show, the differentiation between self and place as it occurs in the global West leads to a possible incompatibility with the term *Indigenize*, one that would not be in play were the fuller notion of *Indigenous* that I propose operant.

From Shallow to Deep Indigenous Learning

In the preceding section I introduced, without defining them, the terms *shallow* and *deep indigeneity*, and *shallowly* and *deeply indigenous environmental education*. Perhaps, in ecological circles, the deep/shallow distinction has already been played out (Naess, 1989; Fox, 1990), but the parallels are evident here. An imagined shallow-to-deep continuum might be useful in seeing how the term *Indigenous* could apply to very different pedagogies. In this section, I imagine four positions within this continuum.

The continuum I imagine is a pool that I know. At the extreme surface of the pool, where the water striders stride and the raindrops tickle, I am using the term *shallowly Indigenous education* to refer to the project of maintaining a conventional pedagogy with an attempt to overlay some Aboriginal perspective. Terming this *shallow* is obviously not intended to be a comment on the value of Aboriginal components in learning, but rather a comment on the probable unwillingness of current visions of education to include more than a superficial account of such a perspective. Such a pedagogy would maintain a goal-oriented, transmission model of learning (Freire, 1970). It would use conventional assessment practices, whose purpose would be to establish and compare the relative worth of individual students according to external standards. It would deny the individual experiences, interests, and lives of those of marginalized communities. It would use an Aboriginal component for extrinsic reasons – in order to meet externally imposed standards, for example – or because it supposes that an Aboriginal component will make citizen-consumers more productive or profitable. Such a project would both misuse the term *Indigenous* and would not serve the interests of Aboriginal peoples. Another danger of this pedagogy is inoculation against the capacity to comprehend a deeper version. To teach shallow Indigenous environmental education may supplant deeper understandings and enactments.

A little deeper, just below the surface of the pool, where the minnows swim, is a much more thoroughly conceived and progressively intended version, still able to subsist within the current educational paradigm. But while such a pedagogy might be called "Indigenized" today, it still tends to refer to raising awareness of and about Aboriginal people and issues, with minimal importance given to the more-than-human. In it, elders and other informed people might come to school and speak about their views and the beliefs of their communities. A curriculum would be conceptualized from an Aboriginal perspective. Aboriginal culture, arts, stories, political views, and social understandings would be given fair representation. Aboriginal history and current political issues that relate to Aboriginal people would be addressed. Such a project might serve to raise awareness, understanding, and support for Aboriginal people to the extent that Aboriginality can be conceived of within a Western ontology; however, as described, it fails to honour adequately the ecological aspect inherent in the root meaning of the term *Indigenous*. So, while *Indigenous* might be currently applied to such a model, I suggest that this would still be living where the minnows do: at the shallow surface of an indigenous environmental education spectrum. This model sometimes occurs within the most progressive programs currently available.

A little deeper still in the continuum-pool, where bass, pickerel, and perch swim in early summer, the project of education itself begins to change. Its purpose, for example, goes through a shift. It tends to move from individual gain to community benefit (Sylvio Beltran, personal communication, 2008; Kiado Cruz, personal communication, 2008; Gustavo Esteva, personal communication, 2008). And *community* includes the more-than-human. Through story, history, legend, ceremony, and the arts, the significance of the more-than-human is remembered, honoured, and enacted. The natural world is involved intimately and deeply in all parts of education, not simply theoretically but in practice. Aboriginal culture, spirituality, and history are given significance. Aboriginal modes of learning are enacted. Academically recognized learning often occurs outside the classroom. Relationships with the more-than-human are valued and seen as necessary in learning. Individual aptitudes are honoured and encouraged. Gregory Cajete's (1994) thoughtful work supports such a pedagogy, and there begins to be – in Māori, Hawaiian, and some Canadian contexts – evidence of such practices.

Deeply Indigenous Ecological Learning

At the deepest levels, where the lake trout live, *deeply Indigenous learning* honours everyone's actual interdependence with the more-than-human. This kind of learning is comprised not of "knowledge" but the re-establishment of a particular kind of lived relationship with place, from which position derives the thoughtful consideration and intellectual sharing of that lived experience.[2] *Deeply Indigenous learning* knows, honours, and lives the intrinsic value of the world. Learning occurs within the context of a particular kind of living that is sustainable, eco-centric, and conscious of this enacted relationship of interdependence. Certain contemporary Aboriginal people and, historically, most Aboriginal people, as well as some who would not identify as Aboriginal, are the most knowledgeable about this way of being in the world. These lives of ecological interdependence are, for the most part, invisible to the interests and attention of the global West. Deeply *Indigenous* learning is not about the knowledge of these people. At this depth in the continuum-pool, what is learned is about *human interaction with the more-than-human, as living needs are directly met through interactions with an ecosystem*. In this kind of learning, how we understand the institution of school must change, because, by definition, almost no school does this. Learning is entirely for the benefit of the widest possible definition of community, including all beings, known and unknown. And in this pedagogy, the form of being-in-the-world becomes the locus of learning. This learning includes and encompasses all that lies above it in the pool.

Such statements as those I make above have been critiqued for being too romanticized. Yet for those who have lived this kind of knowledge, such as several elders I have known, this kind of knowledge is not merely cerebral. It is understood through emotions, body, spirit, and mind, and is both generated by and expressed through their lived life-in-the-world. Such knowledge touches the learner differently. These phrasings perhaps appear awkward to the reader from the global West, but I use them intentionally: there is no other way but in awkward expression that what is uncomfortable and awkward to the global West can be expressed while using its language.

Here I have to invoke an experience with an elder who taught me a great deal. He spoke of listening to the world for guidance. And of course, as a (mostly) non-Aboriginal scholar, I assumed he was telling me a metaphorical tale, that he was romanticizing his way of knowing (Beeman & Blenkinsop, 2008). I later realized that he was, in fact, speaking in a most literal way. He was telling me exactly what steps to follow in a particular circumstance. It was the fault of my previous limitations in knowing that prevented me from hearing accurately. But I had to have the experience myself while in a similar lived relationship with place – undergoing, in other words, my own ontological shift – before I was able to understand him as I think he intended.

There is always the danger of privileging certain kinds of knowledge, which I do not wish to do. But if there are different ways of knowing such as the ones I describe, I am speaking of understanding ideas and concepts utterly differently, not because of just any shift in perspective, but because of a lived relationship with place such that the "rightness," "wrongness," accuracy, depth, force, and interconnectivity of understanding are comprehended by one's whole being – the being that directly interacts with the place one lives. But more significantly, ideas are also comprehended by something that appears to extend beyond the self as it is currently construed in the modern West: this is a self-place form of knowledge – in other words, a way of knowing in which "knowledge" appears not to be in the possession of the person, but rather a shared co-creation between person and place. The "I" and "mind," which normally owns and contains knowledge as viewed from a Cartesian perspective, cease to function with such capacity for differentiation between mind and nature. This is not a "romanticization" except when seen from the perspective of those who can only know intellectually; it is a much more complete form of knowing that is normally acknowledged in the global West. Many Aboriginal students are ill served by a Western-designed system of education because it does not recognize this way of knowing; many non-Aboriginal students are likewise ill served. "Whereof we cannot speak," began Wittgenstein; and perhaps it is at this point that I must remain silent.

Deeply Indigenous ecological education can be viewed as merely one aspect of a different ontological state. This is because for an *Indigenous* perspective to be understood, it needs to be actually lived. If the project of learning in a deeply *Indigenous* way is to be undertaken, then it will entail bringing an *Indigenous way of being* to education. By this I mean approaching issues, ideas, information, and interpretations from the ontological stance of *Indigeneity*. And by this I mean roughly what I have characterized by the term *attentive receptivity* (Beeman, 2006; Beeman & Blenkinsop, 2008), a term describing the ontological position of a person living in close interconnection with the more-than-human, in moment-by-moment consciousness of this state. What occurs outside this state is usually within a realm of thought and being that is characteristic of what occurs in the culture of the global modern West, and what lies therein is antithetical to the state of attentive receptivity.

I know that if the preceding claims are true, then an attempt to bring *Indigeneity* to a conventional school in any modern culture is precluded. Phenomenologically, what is "learned" in attentive receptivity feels far less like the acquisition of knowledge or skills or even values, and much more like growing in a loving relationship with the world. Spinoza's third way of knowing is uncannily resonant with certain Anishinaabe understandings, for instance (Alex Mathias in Beeman, 2006, for example). The "god" in this relationship is not distant, not heavenly, not personified. It, as world, is proximate, earthly, and more-than-human. In Spinoza's phrasing, it is Nature.

The concept of school and standard Western pedagogy flashes as a category error when applied to this more nuanced appraisal of *Indigenous*. It is not within the purview of love to be green, just as it is not within the purview of *Indigeneity* to be schooled. By definition, the two are not just different but opposed. Schools, as currently construed by globally powerful centres, tend to be about behaving oneself *into* a fairly limited view of citizenry, and using the power that accrues for personal, and sometimes broader, advance. With rare examples, even thorough ecological studies are undertaken for merits extrinsic to themselves. But *Indigeneity* is the state of being conducive to conversation with the world such that paths which may not appear initially to be of benefit to humans are exposed. For those daring to risk it, the paths are followed. Sometimes they lead to utterly unexpected beneficial circumstances. Sometimes the world demands what is not of benefit to people. For those who have experienced attentive receptivity, it is evident that the kind of learning that occurs therein, and the kind of learning that occurs in school, are two different things. If we are attempting to bring one to the other, it behoves us to recognize their difference and, possibly, their final incompatibility.

So, we appear to be left with a choice of either narrowing what *Indigenous* could mean by continuing to use it in a sense limited to Aboriginal, or adopting the term and accepting its incompatibility with schools, even relatively progressive ones. If this is the case, resultant questions that I find much more engaging are, first, "Is it *conceivable* that a place of learning could be somehow compatible with *Indigeneity*?" and, second, "If it is, is it *likely* that this could someday be enacted in practice – and, if so, what might it look like?"

Elders with Me

As I write this, some elders are with me. Predictably, they are entertained. I hear them saying, "Why don't you get down to it? What is it you want to say?" Perhaps it is fair to give them the next-to-last word – the elders I know are expert at getting to the heart of things. Let me take one tiny example of how an idea could be misinterpreted by a perspective purporting to be *Indigenous*, but actually acting against the full understanding of the concept.

I interviewed Michael Paul in 2004. One thing he said was:

you wake up
and you have no game plan

and you just go out

maybe you want to paddle
down the lake today

or go up the river
go down the river

but no matter how you feel
it's you

this land is telling you
what to do

Many interpreters would see this as an Indigenous perspective primarily because a First Nations elder is speaking. Most interpreters that I know would understand this statement only figuratively, at least in some sense of the term. That is, that "listening" stands for an inner stillness, or perhaps that the land stands for a deeper sense of the self, that the "I" that Michael represents must be disconnected, in some way, from the world he seems to be hearing.

But I think there is another way of listening to Michael Paul with far more disturbing consequences. And by *disturbing* I mean to the ontological position characteristic of the global West – *homo mobilis.* In this, as in other conversations with elders, it appears that Michael really is listening not to "'nature" as the modern West construes it, as an always-humanized and thus never intrinsically valuable entity (Cronon, 1995). It is quite the opposite. Michael is listening to a powerful, independent, functioning other. If his words are taken literally, *the land* is capable of intent and instruction. It will tell him what to do if only he will listen.

I know this feeling from my own work in small-scale farming and my own travels in wilder places. When one travels with or works long and solo with land, and the relatively louder sounds of the human world are temporarily subdued, the world is freer to speak, or, rather, to be heard. It becomes apparent that this world may be in constant communication with us – or, rather, in constant attempts to communicate with us humans. It is offering what could be thought of as ideas, and these ideas all have to do with how we may dance with the world, with relatively little of our own control or intent. We have to be willing to not will an outcome.

In educational contexts, I call this non-human-directed learning *meanderstanding*. It is the epistemic concomitant of the ontological state *attentive receptivity*, and a kind of learning that occurs in the absence of set goals. It is thus utterly incompatible with the mechanistic world view of knowing that predominates in current goal-oriented schools of the global West. If you listen to a famous child of A.A. Milne's creation, Christopher Robin, you can hear it; if you listen to the wind in the willows, you can hear it there, too. Learning occurs here, just not the learning that was expected. Perhaps one of the things so appealing in these works of imagination is that they permit moments of uncontrolled time and uncontrolled direction in ways that instrumental thought cannot. They permit openness to the possibility of the unexpected and they bring what cannot be imagined. The implications for educational practice are clear. *Indigeneity* might be incompatible not only with the relatively obvious case of end-directed learning, but perhaps even with the learning of facts or methods – that is, what constitutes most of what the global West calls learning.

There is so much, in the way of what our culture posits as ideas, that other cultures, and I think the world itself, consider instead to be the residue of interaction with the more-than-human world: truly other forces, forces that would baffle the mind's attempt at rational explanation. The flick of a grass stem may lead to the knowledge in a leg that it should turn to the right; it does, and the world's events are forever shifted. This interactive kind of knowing, one that is interdependent with non-human forces, is generally ignored in the modern West.

A Track Well Hidden

And here is the hidden track – well, two legs of a track, which seem to bring more, rather than less, complexity to the discussion. Tracks come in all varieties. Suppose the kind I speak of here is not of the virtual variety secreted in electronic media, but a path long disused and now covered with forest debris. The first leg of this track consists of a simple declaration that I have experienced the more-than-human in the way I describe here. As, I suppose, have many who have read this far. On whatever journey we are making here, some may consider this evidence for my claim; others, proof of the opposite. Yet, we are stuck between worlds of experience and expression. There are certain factors that may predispose us to these kinds of knowing, and if we are to speak about educative practice, these need to be explored. I have experienced the more-than-human in periods of long-term immersion, almost always in the absence of other people. In pragmatic terms, these interactions comprised both the continuation of my life and the continued health of the ecosystem. In a truly *Indigenous* educational system, these interactions, the buildings of a relationship, might be called *learning*.

The second leg of the track is more unexpected. I have written about these ideas in the voice that I learned – that of being a member of the global West, of coming from a family whose roots were European, and from living, with minor variations, a pretty standard life in the culture to which I belonged. It was these origins that, when I had experiences of the world in the way described by *attentive receptivity*, required me to assume that these experiences, if they could be accessed by me, must be accessible to everyone. Hence, my insistence on considering them as ontologically dependent, rather than genetically or ethnically influenced.

It was something of an intellectual inconvenience, then – though a pleasant one – to discover through family stories recently told to me, that at least some branches of my family – and probably the branch upon which I leaf – had Aboriginal ancestors who were Wendat. I begin to question the fragments of material that I carry in my body that might, perhaps, contribute to my experiencing attentive receptivity. Though I ask the question, on balance I believe otherwise. Even the "non-Aboriginal" parts of me come "from the beginning" of somewhere.

Perhaps those parts of me are more displaced than those parts which came from Turtle Island. But my strong sense is that, as all our ancestors were *Indigenous* to some place, most of us have not irretrievably lost the possibility of experiencing the deep interconnection with the more-than-human. The essence of this interconnection is that it occurs in actions *in* the world, as opposed to the wishful thinking *about* the world that characterizes and accompanies most academic theorizing and most school planning – perhaps, especially, the school planning that purports to represent the interests of Aboriginal peoples.

Autochthonous Ed

I close with a recognition that in exploring more complex meanings for the term *Indigenous*, I might inadvertently contribute to a process that takes something away from what has been a progressive education phase. My desire is the opposite. In fact, what partly motivates me is the hope that a deeper understanding of *Indigeneity* will lead to an appreciation of the depth of difference of possible alternative to the ways of being acknowledged and practised by the global West. I hope this chapter has begun the process of showing some distinctions between

Aboriginal education per se, environmental education that includes Aboriginal content, and a deeply *Indigenous* education that points to a very different way of dwelling in the world.

If my argument holds, there remains something unnamed that is different from either Aboriginal education or Indigenous education, as the terms are currently broadly understood. So, let me propose a term that will be the subject of a future paper: *Autochthony.* The word, derived from Greek, with a cognate in French, combines the meanings of self and soil. If education were autochthonous, it would "spring, itself, from the soil." Despite my earlier efforts in this chapter to change bring nuance to the term *Indigenous,* as it is commonly used, it is at its root a people-centred and territorial term. It rests on where one comes from – *beget within* – for membership. *Autochthony* links the concepts of self and earth to point to something like a human-earth co-creation. From an etymological stance, autochthony recognizes the deep interconnection between the earth and people and points, at its roots, to learning that takes place in another way of being in the world.

NOTES

1 This is in contrast to the use of "Indigenous" proposed by Marie Battiste and Youngblood Henderson in 2000. In their use, the term "Aboriginal" is used for First Nations, Inuit, and Métis peoples. The term "Indigenous" is used for Aboriginal peoples elsewhere as a global term, in the absence of particular names of peoples. However, I understand this distinction to have been made necessary in the context of Canada and North America, and primarily for clarity. As I later address the issue, the idea of Indigenous is far more complex than this.

2 Certain helpful commentators have expressed concern over devaluing the intellectual. Education is commonly conceived of as an intellectual endeavour, especially by people like me who write and read papers such as this one. When it is not so considered – when, for example, in designing public education policy, the depth of the divides I allude to here are brought into relief – it becomes problematic for this view. Yet the intellectual is part of the kind of learning described here; it is just not the only aspect of such learning. And to not speak so expressly would obscure the degree of difference that characterizes a deeply *Indigenous* learning from intellectual learning.

10 Exploring Teacher Education Programs and Policies in Chilean Universities and Their Commitment to Intercultural Acknowledgment

MARÍA EUGENIA MERINO-DICKINSON

This chapter studies the degree of incorporation of indigenous cultural knowledge in the curricula of nursery and elementary teacher education programs in Chile. It describes a case study focused on three universities located in the regions of Tarapacá in the north, Valparaiso in the centre, and Araucanía in the south of the country. Curricula, course programs, and professional profiles were analysed together with the voices of the students in these programs. Main findings show that the curricula do not incorporate ancestral knowledge of Chilean indigenous groups (Aymara, Quechua, Pascuense, and Mapuche) that inhabit the regions mentioned above. Furthermore, they neither prepare students to interact and act pedagogically in intercultural class contexts, nor do they consider indigenous knowledge as an intercultural option to enrich teacher education programs and policies.

Introduction

In the past forty years, the world has witnessed a revolution in the relation between states and ethnocultural minorities. Older assimilationist and homogenizing nation states are being challenged every day by multicultural models of citizenship and state. This is reflected in a wider acceptance and tolerance of diverse cultural and religious world views brought by immigrant groups, together with the acceptance of territorial autonomy, language rights for national minorities, and the recognition of land claims and self-government rights for indigenous peoples (Kymlicka, 2009). This change has often been the outcome of domestic political processes after a period of conflict, debate, and negotiation in response to intense mobilization of particular minorities, as is the case of Mapuche indigenous people's demands for recognition in Chilean society.

Consequently, a considerable number of countries coincide in the view that old state–minority group relation models are not appropriate, given their specific demographic and historical circumstances. These new processes are more evident in European countries, as well as in Canada, Australia, and New Zealand. In Latin America, however, recognition of indigenous minorities' autonomy has taken a much slower pace, with Paraguay, Mexico, and Brazil being outstanding exceptions. For example, a 2000 UNESCO report highlighted the successful development of intercultural bilingual (Spanish-Guarani) education in Paraguay and the country's policies on indigenous languages. In Mexico, the Teachers' Union for a New Education in Mexico (UNEM) and independent teachers from Chiapas have set forward alternative educational proposals that emphasize social valorization of the aboriginal cultures as the starting point for intercultural articulation with other cultural groups (Sartorelli, 2009). Furthermore, bilingual intercultural education in Brazil has contributed to the development of literacy in indigenous languages, triggering better learning outcomes for indigenous students, which has meant linguistic revitalization and socio-economic mobilization (Hornberger, 2003).

Chile's history as a nation has shown that since its beginnings, indigenous minorities have been the object of unfair treatment, and have been subjected to strong policies of assimilation, discriminatory practices, and exclusion, mainly with the aim of preserving the belief that Chile is a culturally homogeneous country (Merino & Mellor, 2009). Only in the late twentieth century did Chilean governments start to transition from assimilationist policies to more tolerant and intercultural views. This has mainly been stimulated by the launching of the Indigenous and Tribal Peoples Convention by the International Labour Organization (1989), which recognized the right of every indigenous group to keep its culture and language and have access to territorial autonomy. At present, there is a growing commitment on the part of democratic governments to repair this historic injustice through various legal instruments like the National Corporation for Indigenous Development (CONADI) and the recent anti-discrimination law which regulates societal respect for indigenous cultures and other minority groups, such as sexual or religious minorities and those with physical or cognitive disabilities. These regulations have set the foundations for the development of a new consciousness within the Chilean population with regard to minorities and aboriginal groups and their legitimate rights to keep and practise their own culture and language.

Although the ministries of education of recent democratic governments have made various attempts at implementing intercultural education in rural schools with Mapuche student populations, the outcomes have not been successful, mainly due to an erroneous conception of interculturality.[1] The ongoing intercultural programs in rural schools in the Araucanía region, in the south of the country, have mainly aimed at teaching Mapuche children knowledge of their own culture and language, but have made no connection with the non-Mapuche students who are also part of the class. Since its beginnings, Mapuche children's education in Chilean schools has been based on Western patterns, disregarding the logic of the Mapuche culture; this has generated sociocultural conflicts in children's identity construction.[2] This monocultural view of education has meant teaching aspects of the Mapuche culture to children who have already learned them at home, and at the same time providing non-Mapuche students with culturally de-contextualized and meaningless content.

At the level of secondary education, there are a small number of technical and agricultural high schools – mainly in rural areas of the south, where the largest Mapuche population resides – that aim at intercultural education. These schools are incorporating Mapuche content into their curricula to offer indigenous and non-indigenous students the necessary knowledge on the Mapuche culture, so that the students' future professional activities become more culturally pertinent. However, a monocultural perspective still underlies the programs because, although they may provide non-Mapuche students with indigenous knowledge, they do not offer Mapuche students the social, cultural, and linguistic tools of the Chilean culture to allow them to interact professionally and efficiently with mainstream society.

In tertiary education, the intercultural situation is even more deficient. At present, teacher education policies do not consider, neither do they demand of university curricula, the incorporation of indigenous knowledge, even though there are a number of regional universities located in areas with large indigenous populations.

This situation has motivated the case study presented here, which aims to examine the degree to which intercultural world views and aboriginal knowledge are included in teacher education programs at universities. We will focus on three regions of Chile where there are large indigenous populations: Tarapacá in the north, with Aymara and Quechua populations; Valparaiso in the centre, where Pascuense youth from Easter Island come to work and study; and Araucanía in the south, where the largest Mapuche population resides.

Through this study, we hope to contribute useful knowledge that may stimulate the formulation of innovative proposals for policymaking and teacher education curricula with a more intercultural emphasis, which may in turn improve Chilean education.

This chapter is divided into three parts. We first define the epistemological perspective that supports our study and define the core issues for teacher education curricula. Second, we analyse and describe a case study of teacher education programs in three Chilean universities. Finally, we draw conclusions, including one innovative proposal for improving teacher education from an intercultural perspective.

Inter/Multiculturalism, Education, and Social Justice

At the present time, education around the globe is being conceptualized within a global economy framework, which has compelled the governments of many countries to maximize their spending on education, though with an emphasis on efficiency and the pursuit of economic, rather than social and cultural, goals (Keanne & Villanueva, 2009). The result has been what Robertson (2000) calls the "commodification" of education, which aims to prepare students to act in a global economy and help maintain the economy's structure and ideological influence, to the neglect of education as a tool for reconstructing society and making it more fair and egalitarian (Butt, 2000). However, within this global regime, a genuine preoccupation with local cultures and a new perspective of the "other" has emerged, focusing on what is common between cultures, the normality of being different, and the need for negotiating the self and the other in terms of commonality. For example, in the past two decades the European Commission has implemented policies to generate a common language in terms of educational standards and democratic and civic values across Europe (Keanne & Villanueva, 2009).

The concept of multiculturalism promoted by international organizations is a morally progressive extension of existing human rights, as regulated by the United Nations' declaration on minority rights, which focuses on human rights and fundamental freedoms.

In a similar way, UNESCO's declaration has emphasized the practice of respect for cultural diversity, while the International Labour Organization convention has promoted the right of indigenous peoples to maintain their cultural practices (Kymlicka, 2009). From this perspective, the notion of interculturalism reflects the historical, social, and geographic realities of the peoples and cultures juridically incorporated into diverse states across the globe. Interculturalism involves a kind of co-inhabiting relationship of different cultures, regardless of the level of knowledge each culture may hold of the other groups. For example, although in Chile the mainstream society and aboriginal peoples co-inhabit the same territory, the non-indigenous population shows very little interest in knowing about and learning from the indigenous cultures.

From a historical and contextual perspective, the main structural forms of global cultures developed from specific exchanges between them. Demorgon (2000) states that these societies, generally characterized by violent relations and also by alliances, constituted the base for the transition from royal and imperial societies towards today's society of information. It is interesting to reflect in this regard on how education has accommodated itself to these new multicultural scenarios, adapting to each nation's sociocultural characteristics. For example, in Canada the key to building its national identity has been the recognition of diversity, as well as the redefinition of the concept of welfare. This helped societal integration and facilitated the re-accommodation of French and aboriginal peoples to make up a federal state. In this respect, Bruno-Jofré and Henley (2001) argue that, due to education being the responsibility of each province, policies and multicultural education took diverse shapes and emphases over different time periods.[3] However, in the late twentieth century multiculturalism developed as the practical articulating principle that "offered an avenue to deal with issues of identity, allegiances, and with the place of Canada in the world" (p. 54).

In Chile, multiculturalism does not form part of the cultural and political ideology that sustains governmental education, and the concept is given a more ample and general meaning.[4] However, in 1993 the Ministry of Education adopted a bilingual intercultural education approach for rural schools located in regions with indigenous populations, a decision motivated by two key issues. The Indigenous Law, particularly articles 28 and 32,[5] and the Constitutional Law for Education no. 18.944, launched in 1990,[6] became fundamental juridical instruments that have oriented Chilean educational policies towards an intercultural perspective on education in indigenous contexts.

It is within this new context of human interaction and understanding that we place our conceptualization of what teacher education in a transnational world is to be. Educating teachers for the present and the future is largely a question of social justice, a position that educators, policymakers, and governments should take up as an urgent issue. According to Cochran-Smith (2009a), teacher education for social justice in the United States can be put into practice if four premises are followed. First, teacher education is not merely a question of methods, but a coherent, intellectual approach to prepare teachers that acknowledges the social and political contexts in which teaching, learning, and ideas about justice have been located historically, together with the tensions that operate between competing goals. The second premise states that teaching and teacher education cannot be neutral activities, but necessarily involve political and ideological ideals, power, and access to learning opportunities. Third, teacher education is a key interval in the process of learning to teach, with the potential to become a site for educational change. This means that teacher preparation interacts with the particular conditions of school cultures and the larger socio-cultural contexts in which they are embedded. The final premise establishes that teaching for justice is for all students, regardless of their socio-economic conditions, whether they are advantaged or disadvantaged, minorities or from mainstream societies. This point is essential, since it allows students to become active participants in a diverse democratic nation.

Particularly interesting for our understanding of intercultural teacher education in Chile is King's (2008) proposal for a "blues epistemology," which draws on the recognition and incorporation of knowledge traditions and lived experiences of marginalized and oppressed groups, challenging the hegemony of ideologically-based knowledge held in teacher education. King argues that the crisis of academic and school knowledge in teacher education research and practice in the United States is due to the absence of the epistemologies of African Americans and other marginalized groups as a foundation for teacher learning. In sum, what is needed is more autonomy and civic participation for all members of society, including those in marginalized groups, and a revision of curriculum and educational goals that enhances students' capacities for deliberation, disagreement, and interpretation.

Defining a More Inclusive Curriculum for Teacher Education

One influential contribution to the improvement of teacher education in recent times is that of Darling-Hammond and Baratz-Snowden (2005), who define the professional and academic profile for a good teacher. They propose a knowledge-based framework for understanding teaching and learning based on three interrelated domains that conceptualize teaching as an "action profession," similar to the medical profession, that is mainly built on practice. The first domain is focused on the knowledge learners should acquire and their development in social contexts, which implies that the student-teacher understands how students learn, how they develop, and how they acquire language skills. The second domain concerns the knowledge of subject matter, or content knowledge, and the aims of the curriculum – in other words, how the discipline becomes connected with the schools' curricula, the learning objectives, and students' own needs. The knowledge of teaching constitutes the third domain and focuses on how to develop content-specific pedagogies, how to teach diverse learners, and how to manage class activities. One critique that the model has received is that it is mainly based on a prescriptive view – what student-teachers "should" learn – neglecting the knowledge of how student-teachers "actually" learn today. This is an important issue that teachers and policymakers need to consider before embarking on curriculum revision and modification.

From our perspective, a more integral view of what should constitute teacher-education curricula is proposed by Cochran-Smith (2009b). She states that the knowledge to be acquired should become a referent, since it normally reflects the traditional canon of school knowledge, and it also should be used as part of an interpretive frame of understanding reality. In order for educational practice to be consistent with the aims of social justice, Cochran-Smith proposes that the commingling of knowledge, experience, beliefs, and values set up clear interpretive frames which allow teachers' decisions and filtering of what and what not to include in the curriculum and programs. This perspective is based on the linguistic, cultural, and experiential capital students bring along from their own social contexts. This, in turn, would allow the understanding that all persons have multiple identities and life histories structured by class, race, culture, and the other aspects of the societal system they belong to. Furthermore, this view allows teachers to turn their class practice into a research activity developed through critical questioning of assumptions (of one's self and others) and the establishment of research problems. In this way, curricula, tests, and other assessment activities become descriptive or generative tools rather than prescriptive ones, where the role of the teaching practice influences society's current distribution of resources and current respect/disrespect for social groups.

In order to put this new perspective into practice, Cochran-Smith (2009b) argues, teaching practice for social justice should be not only a matter of knowing and applying specific techniques, but rather one of "guiding principles" that play out in a given context through a variety of methods and strategies, depending on particular circumstances, students, content, and communities. Within these orienting principles, the author highlights the need for developing caring relationships with students, providing relevant opportunities for all students (including those with special needs, students labelled "at risk," and students with low test scores), challenging the hegemony of the canon by providing social supports and scaffolding for the learning of new skills and materials, and, lastly, making issues of equity/inequity and respect/disrespect for individuals and social groups explicit in the curriculum and in the classroom. The latter approach supports cross-cultural discussion and the development of interpretive capacities in all students, which are essential values in democratic societies and in an interdependent global community.

Finally, Cochran-Smith (2009b) points at four key issues to be considered for good teacher preparation: "who should teach," which is directly related to selection and recruitment; "what teachers learn," which deals with the curriculum and pedagogy; "how and from whom teachers learn," which has to do with the intellectual, social, and organizational contexts and structures that support candidates' learning; and how the outcomes of preparation are measured and assessed. The core idea underlying these issues is that teacher preparation for social justice is transformative and collaborative, but also challenges the status quo and prepares students to be critical of what has been normalized by the prevailing socio-economic system.

Education and Teacher Education in Chile

In the past ten years, Chile has experienced an important expansion in the number of students who have access to university studies. Today, one out of three persons eighteen to twenty-four years old is engaged in tertiary education, with 70 per cent of these being first-generation university students. According to a report of the United Nations Development Programme (2005), university students' enrolment in undergraduate programs increased by 322 per cent between 1990 and 2004. In addition, within the same period state expenditures on tertiary education increased 80 per cent. This means that the percentage of the Chilean PIB (an economic indicator that measures the country's financial state, similar to GDP) allotted to education increased from 2.4 to 4.3 per cent. This indicator, together with private expenditures in tertiary education, which have increased from 1.6 to 3.3 per cent, make up 7.6 per cent of the country's PIB invested in tertiary education. This latter figure is among the lowest compared with other Latin American countries' investments on education.

The educational system in Chile is currently undergoing a crisis of social dissatisfaction due to two main factors. First, low standards and students' poor results on standardized measurements in elementary and secondary education have endured over time, with little improvement from 1998 to 2001, as shown by the results of the 2001 SIMCE (Measuring System of Education Quality, Ministry of Education) test. The SIMCE measured the level of reading and mathematics abilities in students in the fourth and eighth levels of elementary education, in both state and private schools in Chile.[7] Results for students in the fourth level of elementary education show that only 31 per cent of them can read at a basic level, 27% can read at an intermediate level, and 42% are able to read at an advanced level. In mathematics, 31% manage a basic level, 39% an intermediate level, and 30% an advanced level. Of students in the eighth level of primary education, 35% can read at a basic level, 38% at an intermediate level, and 27% at an advanced level. In mathematics, 65% of students manage skills at a basic level, 24% at an intermediate level, and 11% at an advanced one. These figures reveal that students in the fourth and eighth levels of elementary education in Chile exhibit an extremely poor competence at reading, while in mathematics skills the situation is not much different.[8]

Along with children's poor abilities in these essential skills, Chilean society has been affected by teachers' low level of preparation at university, whose results have been made public through the INICIA test (Ministry of Education of Chile, 2011). This test measures the knowledge and management of content and teaching strategies of recently graduated teachers in preschool and elementary education in Chile.

Results reveal that 31 per cent of them manage[9] a basic knowledge of content and the teaching strategies, while 69 per cent attained unsatisfactory levels in Spanish language, science, mathematics, and social sciences, and are therefore not prepared to teach classes. This test also revealed that out of twenty-five universities assessed, twenty-one have more than 50 per cent of their graduates displaying an insufficient level of pedagogical mastery, and only four universities are preparing their teachers at a satisfactory or intermediate level. These figures explain, to a large extent, how the poor educational levels that children exhibit are intimately related to the quality of teacher education programs that Chilean universities are offering.

Hence, it becomes clear that there are considerable structural failures in Chilean education. For example, a consistent epistemological guiding framework is lacking, leading to the poor educational policies emanating from the Ministry of Education, as can be observed in the national curriculum and plans for teacher education programs. Furthermore, in the area of multicultural and intercultural education in Chile, inefficient policies impede the incorporation of indigenous cultures' knowledge into the programs and curricula of nursery, primary, and secondary education. For instance, the LEGE 2007 (General Law of State Education) makes only superficial reference to the issues of diversity, interculturality, and linguistic and education rights for indigenous peoples. In undergraduate programs at university, only a few programs in disciplines such as social sciences, humanities, anthropology, sociology, and education deal with interculturality. Intercultural studies are visible at only a few university research centres and in postgraduate studies, in spite of the fact that Indigenous Regulation no. 19.253 demands in one of its articles the need to establish chairs of history, culture, and indigenous languages at all levels of education.

The above situation can be explained to some extent by the general belief that Chile is a "homogeneous" country, hence concepts like interculturality and multiculturalism are not yet part of the collective imaginary of Chilean society and its institutions. This in spite of the fact that the country has an important number of European immigrant groups (Germans, English, Swiss, and Italians) that arrived in the late nineteenth and early twentieth centuries. In later times, larger groups of Arabian and Asian immigrants settled in too; and recently Latin Americans – Peruvians, Colombians, and Cubans – have also arrived in the country.

However, at present one can observe a more open-minded society that is becoming more conscious of the need for respect, tolerance, and legal recognition of the rights of minorities for equal status, treatment, and opportunity. For example, one initiative put forward by the Ministry of Education in 1990 is the PEIB (Intercultural Bilingual Education Program), which focuses mainly on rural elementary education in regions with large indigenous populations; however, the program still exhibits poor outcomes.

In sum, the state of Chilean education, as described here, is far below the minimum international standards required today in terms of quality, efficacy, and social justice. As for intercultural educational programs, it can be said that interculturality is still moving towards adulthood, whereas that multicultural education will likely have to keep waiting for a future with more open-minded social conditions. This is an ethical and moral issue for the government, its institutions, and Chilean society as a whole.

Teacher Education in Three Chilean Universities: A Case Study

We now present the results of a case study, conducted in 2012, designed to examine the degree of inclusion of aboriginal knowledge and world views in teacher education programs at universities in three regions of Chile where four indigenous populations live. In the Tarapacá region in the north, we find the Aymara and Quechua population; in the Valparaiso region in the centre of Chile, a large population of Pascuenses from Easter Island come to study and work; and in the Araucanía region in the south is found the largest Mapuche population. Out of the total indigenous population in Chile (5% of the country's overall population), 88% are Mapuche, 7% Aymara, 3% Quechua, and 0.7% Pascuense (Instituto Nacional de Estadística, 2009).

The study's methodological approach was qualitative and descriptive, and included teacher education programs and curriculum analysis, in addition to semi-structured interviews given to indigenous and non-indigenous students of two teacher education programs at Universidad de Tarapacá (henceforth, UTA) in the north, Universidad de Valparaiso (UV) in the centre of the country, and Universidad Católica de Temuco (UCT) in the south. The two first universities are state institutions and the latter one is private, though it belongs to the CRUCH (Council of Chilean University Presidents), an organization recognized and consulted by the Ministry of Education.

Program description and curricular data was collected online and through personal contacts with teachers at the selected universities. The interviews were administered to three indigenous and three non-indigenous students at each university, for a total of eighteen students interviewed. These students were selected from those registered for two teacher education programs: Preschool (Nursery) Education and Elementary Education. We selected these two programs for the impact they have on laying the foundations of children's education. The participants were contacted through personal emails and the selection criteria for indigenous students required that they have at least one indigenous family name and that they should self-recognize as being indigenous.

The interviews were structured as conversations and were conducted through Skype communication and tape-recorded. The interviews to indigenous students focused on three key questions:

- Does your teacher education program incorporate cultural knowledge from Chilean indigenous groups in any of the course plans?
- Do your teachers incorporate indigenous knowledge from your culture in class texts and/or teaching strategies?
- Do you consider that indigenous culture knowledge should be made more visible in your teacher education program, and if so why?

The interviews to non-indigenous students focused on the following key questions:

- Does your teacher education program incorporate cultural knowledge from the indigenous group of this or other regions of the country in any of the course programs?
- Do your teachers incorporate indigenous knowledge from such culture/s in their class texts and/or teaching strategies?
- Do you consider that the knowledge of the indigenous group of this region or other regions of the country should be made more visible in your teacher education program, and if so why?

We used a discursive approach for analysis, revealing, on one hand, the voices of the curriculum-makers to determine how the program is structured, what courses are being taught, and the professional profile stated; on the other hand, the students' perspectives were analysed to understand their views about the curriculum, the courses offered, and how the curriculum can be improved to incorporate more knowledge about the indigenous cultures in Chile, leading to better and more contextualized teacher preparation. The results of the selected teacher education programs are discussed below.

Nursery Teacher Education Program

At UTA, the program is offered with two intermediate diplomas: "Paradocente" (teacher assistant of two-year preparation), "Nursery Teacher" (four-year preparation), and "Psychopedagogy" (five-year preparation). These three programs share the same curriculum, which is built according to discipline and specialization order. The curriculum incorporates the course "Education and Interculturality," offered in the second semester, which has a course plan declaring that it "prepare[s] students with a historical view of indigenous groups in Chile to enhance preschool children's knowledge of the existence of other cultural groups." The professional profile for the three diplomas is brief and rather vague, following the Ministry of Education general guidelines for the program. For example, the "Paradocente" profile declares that the student will develop "initiative to lead and manage activities to improve his educative unit," while the Nursery teacher profile states that the teacher will be prepared for "designing and applying innovative and stimulating methodological strategies for the children"; finally, the profile for Psychopedagogy declares that this professional will be prepared to "diagnose educative problems and provide adequate psycho-pedagogic treatment to children in need." As can be observed, none of the above profiles make reference to any intercultural contexts nursery teachers are likely to encounter with the Aymara or Quechua student populations that inhabit the Tarapacá region.

On the other hand, a student at the UTA Nursery Teacher program declared that "we do not feel prepared to incorporate indigenous knowledge in our lessons, neither do we feel prepared to integrate indigenous students in our future classes." The indigenous students of the program were more critical about the objectives of the course, with one stating that "it is too general and it does not prepare us to teach intercultural classes and incorporate indigenous knowledge in our classes." However, in general terms, students valued the fact that there is at least one course that aims at interculturality, although they highlighted the need to improve the curriculum with more courses of the kind.

At UV, the Nursery Teacher Education curriculum offers the course "Caring for Diversity and Interculturality" in the program's sixth semester. This course prepares future teachers to "deal with children with various physical and cognitive disabilities, and also with indigenous groups." It calls to our attention that the same course gathers two different issues as part of the same objective, and seems to place indigenous groups in contact with Chilean society as "a problem to be solved" more than as an advantage that may enrich teacher preparation programs. The professional profile declares that "the graduate will be able to construct knowledge in the dimensions of 'being,' 'knowing,' 'knowing how to,' and 'interacting.'" In addition, it portrays the future nursery teacher as "an agent of change, knowledge generator and promoter of a healthy lifestyle." In a similar way to the UTA program, the UV profile makes no reference to the intercultural characteristics of the region, nor does it promise to provide a future nursery teacher with effective intercultural tools.

A student at UV declared that "the only course related to intercultural issues becomes confusing for us and our teacher preparation because students' disabilities and learning incapacities are not related in any way with having indigenous student population at school; these are two totally different things and should be treated separately in separate courses." An indigenous student of the program added that "for us as Pascuense descendants it becomes an offence that the university and its academics seem to hold the prejudice that because students are indigenous they may be disabled in some way." Moreover, "this course, as it is built, reflects an ethnocentric perspective and the ignorance of Chilean society about the indigenous cultures of the country."

Nursery Teacher education at UCT offers two programs: "Intercultural Education" and "Pedagogy, Family and Community Connections." The curriculum is shared by both programs and includes two courses that deal with intercultural issues: "Programs and Pedagogic Experiences in Infancy and Interculturality," offered in the fifth semester, and "Competence Development in Intercultural Contexts," in the sixth semester. The first course aims at "studying the programs for Nursery teaching from the Ministry of Education, and also learning from experiences in intercultural schools and indigenous communities from the Araucanía region." The second course "develops intercultural competences to teach in Mapuche school contexts." Apart from these two courses, the curriculum incorporates ten pedagogic workshops or progressive internships whose objective is to "articulate theory and practice in urban and rural schools and communities, particularly in Mapuche contexts." The professional profile makes a subtle allusion to the "cultural scenarios of the future teacher" by declaring that the future nursery teacher will be able to "design and implement innovative strategies, establish relations with the school community and contribute to the diverse social and cultural scenarios." However, this last statement does not make it explicit that such "contributions" involve a commitment to intercultural education in Mapuche contexts.

A student from the UCT Nursery program expressed that, although they value the presence of the two courses and the ten internship workshops, "these are not enough for supporting a good preparation, especially for some of us who have chosen the 'Intercultural education' specialization; many of us find this specialization very attractive since most of us come from the Araucanía region and other southern regions, so we are most likely to get a teaching post in this region where the Mapuche student population is very high." Furthermore, the student added that "the preparation we receive in the courses and internships is too basic, so we do not feel prepared to face an intercultural class." Moreover, Mapuche students of the program criticize the "monocultural" perspective of the two courses, with one arguing that "these courses provide basic knowledge on the Mapuche culture which is useful to non-Mapuche students for interacting in Mapuche contexts because they have already mastered the Chilean culture. However we, as Mapuche students, are not prepared to engage in real intercultural teaching with Mapuche students because we do know how to bridge both cultures; we feel this is essential for intercultural communication, and so most of us prefer to work in the cities and develop only the national curriculum."

Nursery and Elementary Teacher Education Programs

At UTA, Elementary Teacher education follows the same structure as Nursery Teacher education, offering two intermediate diplomas, "Paradocente" (teacher assistant of two-year preparation) and "Preschool Teacher" (two more years), and a final program, "Psychopedagogy" (one more year). These programs share the same curriculum, which offers the same course, "Education and Interculturality," offered to nursery teachers. Therefore, the curriculum assumes that there is no difference in competence building and pedagogic strategies between teaching kindergarten children and elementary school students. With respect to the professional profile of Elementary Teacher education, it declares that "the future teacher will develop the general competences demanded by the national curriculum," but again does not refer to any eventual intercultural abilities among its graduates. On the other hand, a student at the UTA Elementary Teacher education program held the perspective that "we do not feel prepared to deal with interculturality in our future classes because we do not have the tools and strategies, nor the knowledge of indigenous cultures, to teach an intercultural lesson."

At UV in Valparaiso, the Elementary Teacher education program is not offered. When we inquired about the reasons, we were told that their policy is not to compete with the Elementary Teacher education program offered by the University of Playa Ancha, located in the same city. We inquired about the curriculum of this latter program and realized that it is offered with a specialization in "Rural Education and Development." Although this program was not part of the original data, we studied the curriculum and found that there was no reference to interculturality and that this program's concept of "rural" education does not aim at indigenous students nor at intercultural educational contexts, but only at rural development.

At UCT, the curriculum for Elementary Teacher education offers four diplomas: Language and Communication, Mathematics, Natural Sciences, History and Geography, and Social Sciences. The curriculum is common and does not offer any course relating to intercultural issues, only ten progressive internships, the objectives of which are to "articulate theory with practice in Mapuche contexts and communities, so students are situated in Mapuche realities of indigenous education within the family and the indigenous community and build a more coherent pedagogic knowledge among disciplinary content, sociocultural Mapuche knowledge, and professional practice." However, the professional profile of this program makes no explicit reference to any intercultural aspects and adheres to the national curriculum for the program by stating that the future teacher will "manage the disciplinary content of his specialization and didactic competences to design, implement and assess learning situations according to the requirements of the National Curriculum Framework for Elementary Teacher Education."

A student of this UCT program declared that "we see a disjunction between the curricula of Nursery Teacher Education and that of Elementary School Teacher; we feel this because the former offers two intercultural courses in the curriculum while our program does not have any course in interculturality." The student added that "this is an important flaw in the curriculum because the Elementary School level is the continuation of Nursery level in terms of the national educational curriculum." However, students valued the ongoing pedagogic internships they would have over their careers, with one stating: "This is the only instance we have to operate in intercultural contexts, particularly if we get a post in schools in the Araucanía region after we graduate, which is a fact for most of us." In addition, Mapuche student teachers concurred with their peers from the Nursery Teacher program in criticizing the "monocultural" perspective of the pedagogic workshops, with one interviewee stating that these "increase the knowledge of non-indigenous student teachers about the Mapuche culture, which is good because they are Chilean and will know the two cultures. But nobody teaches us to deal with interculturality in indigenous school contexts, [and so] we do not know how to make the connection between the Chilean and the Mapuche cultures and their different world views."

In addition, UCT offers the program "Intercultural Elementary Teacher Education," an undergraduate degree originally oriented towards Mapuche students (1992–2003) and financed by the Bilingual Intercultural Education Program (PEIB) of the Ministry of Education, but since 2003 opened to non-indigenous students. The curriculum focuses on the teaching of Mapuche language throughout four semesters of "Mapudungun workshops," seven semesters of "intercultural pedagogic internships," plus courses on history, science, and natural resources from an intercultural perspective. The curriculum is complemented by native speakers of the language who conduct weekly conversation workshops with students to foster oral practice of the language. The professional profile is explicit in declaring that "the graduate will be prepared to revive sociocultural Mapuche values and generate intercultural curricula proposals in schools and the community with active participation of Mapuche families and the indigenous communities."

In the interviews, students declared that they were satisfied with the courses offered in the curriculum; however, as one student recognized, "the problem is that only students who enrol in the program already proficient in the Mapuche language, at least in oral comprehension, are able to advance to an intermediate or advanced level of Mapudungun," and emphasized that "these are the minority, because most of us are urban Mapuches and have not had much contact with our indigenous families in the communities; so when we start the program we neither understand the language nor speak it." The student added that "this situation makes it very hard for us to acquire the [necessary] linguistic skills, so the majority of us end up our program managing only a poor or only satisfactory level of Mapudungun." A student criticized the fact that, "if mastery of the Mapuche language is a key issue in the program, all courses of the curriculum should be taught in Mapudungun, meaning that teachers should focus on the teaching of Mapudungun as a foreign language, as is the case with the English Teacher Education program offered in the Faculty, where students finish their programs and are able to speak, read and write fluently in English." A student also referred to a serious problem that graduates have: "We avoid engaging in rural schools where the majority of Mapuche communities are and prefer to look for work opportunities in the city of Temuco or other surrounding cities." In students' opinions, there are two main reasons: the poor and undervalued wages that rural schools offer, and their poor mastery of Mapudungun. The final outcome, according to one student, is that they "prefer working as cultural advisers in diverse public and private institutions and organizations in the city of Temuco or in the surrounding villages."

Still, in general terms, it seems that students in this program were optimistic about it because it is the only one of its kind offered in Chile. They declared that if the approach to teaching Mapudungun were improved, this program could become a national example for intercultural teacher education.

Conclusions

In this study, we examined the degree to which teacher education programs in Chile incorporate knowledge about indigenous cultures and their world views in their curricula. To this end, we conducted a case study at three regional universities by analysing the "voices" of the curricula and professional profiles, as well as those of the students enrolled in such programs.

Findings indicate that the majority of Nursery Teacher and Elementary Teacher education programs analysed do not incorporate indigenous cultures' knowledge, nor do they consider interculturality as an option to teacher preparation, regardless of the important indigenous population presence in the country that is culturally and linguistically active. Only vague attempts were observed in some curricula, such as isolated courses that lacked coherence with any disciplinary area.

It was also observed that there is a generalized conceptual misunderstanding of the relation between "diversity" and "interculturality" in education. While the former aims at children's cognitive or physical disability and the latter points at aboriginal cultures, they are taught in one course, which causes confusion and promotes ethnic prejudice. Furthermore, professional profiles made no reference to eventual intercultural knowledge formation in the future teacher, nor do they allude to the intercultural characteristics of the regions where the universities of the sample are located.

Students' voices were clear about the above deficiencies, emphasizing that this will limit their future pedagogic action in classes and schools because they do not have the necessary intercultural tools to efficiently integrate indigenous children into a culturally diverse class. The only exception found in the sample was the Intercultural Elementary Teacher education program at UCT, which offers a curriculum that explicitly incorporates courses and ongoing internships at schools within Mapuche communities, and also prepares students in the Mapuche language and culture.

When comparing students' voices with the voices of the professional profiles, it becomes clear there is a disconnect between what national and university teacher education policies prescribe and what students feel they need. Their perspectives run along different roads and there is no dialogue about the topic. In sum, future educators' needs, expectations, and approaches on education and interculturality are not being adequately addressed.

If we contrast the above case-study findings with Cochran-Smith's premises for education for social justice and King's "blues epistemology," we can infer that teacher education in the Chilean programs does not constitute an efficient bridge to a better education that is in harmony with the new multicultural world order of citizenship and state. Neither do these programs prepare teachers to become agents of social justice for the equality of the marginalized and indigenous groups of the country, since the voices of those historically marginalized are still not heard.

We believe that Chilean teacher preparation for modern times should be based on the concept of education for social justice, which incorporates indigenous and other minority groups' epistemologies. This would up bring about a critical thinking pedagogy based on research and reflection on teaching practice, with a teacher education curriculum that incorporates the knowledge of aboriginal as well as other ethnic groups that co-inhabit the same territories.

In sum, there is still much to do for Chilean educational authorities, faculties of education, and academics to change current teacher education policies and practices; only when this happens might our education be able to reach the required international standards and contribute to a more egalitarian and integrated democracy. We then appeal to Chilean universities and their academics, young teachers, school board representatives, indigenous and other ethnic group organizations, together with the Ministry of Education, to open a social and multi-institutional dialogue with a genuine attitude of "hearing the other's voice" that may allow the building of an inclusive educational model for teacher education in the country.

NOTES

1 We understand interculturality as the dynamic process of encounter between two or more different cultures based on the following aspects. Cultures and interculturalism are defined on the basis of social institutions in interrelation with the ongoing historical process; additionally, the future of cultures and their interrelations depend on the orientations and strategies of the actors involved. The two preceding aspects generate a new social dynamic aspect which allows the functioning of culture interrelation and of its actors. [Author's translation from Demorgon (2000).]

2 The impact of such monocultural programs in school curricula can be observed in the distance between the rationale of educative knowledge and teachers' pedagogic view on how to teach and make use of Mapuche cultural heritage in class. [Author's translation from Quintriqueo & McGinity (2009).]

3 These authors state that the Quebec government developed its "interculturalism" educational policy on the basis of ethnocultural groups,which implied the recognition of the French language as a general language, respect for liberal democratic values, and respect for pluralism. In 1987, the liberal and culturalist-based approach to education in Canada was reformed around a more critical pedagogy incorporating problems of exploitation and oppression in schools, as well as racial discrimination and prejudice that persisted within the educational system.

4 According to Recasens (2001), multiculturalism may mean different things when used in rural and urban contexts. In rural schools, it is relativized by various factors external to the classroom setting such as parental relations, village history, beliefs, encounters in markets, and religious celebrations.

Students' parents generally are small-scale fishermen, farmers, commerce dealers, and state and county-hall workers. By contrast, the meanings attached to multiculturalism in urban settings vary depending on the different social stratum of students' parents, which becomes an invisible but assumed wall segregating one student from another.

5 By means of this law, the state recognizes the existence of eight ethnic groups in Chile: Mapuche, Aymara, Rapa-nui or Pascuense, Likay Antai, Quechua, Colla, Kawashkar or Alacalufe, and Yagan. The two articles referenced above declare that it is the responsibility of mainstream society, particularly the state, to ensure that its institutions respect, protect, and promote indigenous development – their cultures, families, and communities – by means of appropriate policies and regulations. Two examples of this are the establishment of the National Corporation of Indigenous Development (CONADI) and the launching of the program of bilingual intercultural education.

6 This is the first legislation that allows educational institutions to design and implement their own plans and programs regarding the specific sociocultural needs of their neighbouring milieux, on the condition that they follow the ministry's fundamental objectives and obligatory curricular contents.

7 In Chile there are three types of educational institutions: state schools administered by each local county hall, schools that are subsidized by the state but administered by private corporations, and private schools financed and administered by private groups. These latter schools' fees are extremely high, so only a minority of the Chilean student population can afford them.

8 These results principally reflect the outcomes of state and subsidized schools. This is mainly because education and wealth distribution in Chile are highly socially stratified and are therefore unfairly distributed; hence, SIMCE results from private schools exhibit a totally different reality, with outcomes ranking at international standards.

9 It must be clarified that this is a newly implemented test and is only at a pilot stage, taken optionally by recently graduated teachers who agreed to participate. The number of teachers assessed represents 19% of all teachers who graduated from universities in 2011.

11 Indigenous Spaces in Contemporary Learning Institutions: Theoretical and Methodological Frameworks in Approaching Māori Education

TE TUHI ROBUST

In this chapter, I discuss the theoretical and methodological issues involved in undertaking a comparative case study of two institutions in two distinct cultural and national contexts – the ancestral meeting houses at the University of Auckland, and the Longhouse at the University of British Columbia (Robust, 2013). As the case study has been undertaken, I will discuss findings in regards to issues of knowledge and methodology in the context of understanding these indigenous spaces. The inclusion of *marae* (Māori ancestral houses) on university campuses in New Zealand has been a significant development since the mid-1980s. This initiative provided indigenous space for Māori to meet, teach, and study in a culturally appropriate environment, and has since been added in other schools and educational entities. The University of Auckland ancestral meeting house, Tane-Nui-A-Rangi, and the ancestral Longhouse at the University of British Columbia, Sty-Wet-Tan, are examples of indigenous infrastructure and space development within university settings. The development of indigenous "space" is examined here within the context of *kaupapa Māori* (Māori principles and philosophies).

A Model of *Kaupapa Māori* Educational Intervention

A theoretical framework for considering how the *wānanga* (traditional learning institution) model might be used in a contemporary institution provides a foundation for the examination of culturally appropriate space within university settings. *Kaupapa Māori* theory and practice are used as a framework for an intervention designed to bring about increased Māori participation in a tertiary institution.

Graham Smith (1997) described *kaupapa Māori* theory and praxis as being the response by Māori to the *Pākehā* (state)-dominated interests within a cycle of conscientization, resistance, and transformative action.

The concept of conscientization can be illustrated in events leading up to widespread efforts aimed at the retention of Māori language in New Zealand. The conscientization was the realization by Māori, based on Benton's 1971 survey, that Māori language was in danger of becoming extinct. There was also a growing awareness that its infrastructure did not meet the perceived needs for prospective Māori students considering tertiary study options. This concern centred on the institutions being able to cater for the needs of all Māori students, including applicants from total immersion schools such as *kura kaupapa Māori* and *whare kura* (secondary or high schools).

In the case of the development of *kohanga reo* (Māori language nests) and *kura kaupapa Māori* (schools characterized by total language immersion), the concept of educational resistance focuses on how significant members of the Māori community did not accept inequalities in the achievement of Māori students that has been typical in the mainstream school system. It was also a resistance to the effects on language. Resistance can also be applied to the process of Māori not seeking to enrol in mainstream tertiary institutions that were not catering for their needs in tertiary study.

For Māori schooling, the transformation initiative developed in part as a result of the surveys and research undertaken by the Māori Unit of the New Zealand Council for Education Research, led by Dr Richard Benton. In the 1970s, he found that urgent action was required if Māori language was to survive (Waitangi Tribunal, 1989). Benton and others also presented submissions to the Waitangi Tribunal in 1989 that considered a claim on the acknowledgment of *te reo Māori* as an official language of New Zealand, signalling the research undertaken and that the revival of *te reo Māori* had begun through the establishment of *kohanga reo* (Māori language nests). It was noted that in 1913, 90 per cent of Māori school children could speak Māori, and by 1953, the percentage had dropped to 26 per cent. In 1975, it was less than 5 per cent. Benton told the Waitangi Tribunal:

> There are many reasons why the language has declined so rapidly over the last two or three decades but the major causes stem from the fact that language is first and foremost a social phenomenon. Languages do not

> flourish in a social vacuum and they are learned and established most effectively through use in a wide variety of contexts. Social changes in recent New Zealand history have greatly reduced the contexts in which Māori speaking people can use their language; urbanisation, improved communications, industrialisation, consolidation of rural schools and internal migration have all taken their toll. For children especially, the massive influence of English at school, and in the neighbourhood through radio, television and the movies has had the same effect where the Māori language is concerned as pollutants have on the health of oysters in an oyster bed; when the environment becomes polluted beyond a critical point neither the oysters nor their linguistic counterpart can survive. (Waitangi Tribunal, 1989)

The specific aim of *kōhanga reo* was to bring about the revitalization of *te reo Māori*. The first *kōhanga reo* was opened in 1982 near Wellington, New Zealand, and by 1994 there were over 750 centres serving over 14,000 children, aged 0–5 years. Initially, the schools were funded by parents. However, in 1990 the administration of the movement was transferred to the Ministry of Education because of the way in which government funding was released to organizations from treasury sources on the regular budget cycle. This meant that all *kohanga reo* were subject to a regulatory and compliance environment within the early childhood sector of the Ministry of Education. Nevertheless the uniqueness and "coherence" of the philosophy of the *kōhanga reo* movement remains the same. It continues to deliver education programs in *te reo Māori*.

The Recursive Cycle

The theoretical elements presented in the *kaupapa Māori* model can also be used to explain the process of intervention, including analysing the effectiveness of the intervention. As with the *kōhanga reo* movement, the transformation which took place to meet the needs of *te reo Māori* graduates at the University of Auckland occurred in a wider context, which saw the university repositioning its infrastructure to present itself as one of the pre-eminent research-led universities in the world. This repositioning saw it presenting itself to prospective applicants as a leading tertiary institution with credentials or qualifications that are recognized around the world. But the transformation process for Māori occurred within this construct and can be likened to the traditional *wānanga* (tribal university). The presence of leaders, chiefs, and *tōhunga* (high priests) can be aligned with the contemporary institution as the vice-chancellor or chief executive.

Significant events and related activities confirm experiences at the University of British Columbia that parallel those at the University of Auckland. Further analysis of this model as applied to the case studies suggests the necessity to consider other external forces which affect the student dynamic in an increasing climate of competitiveness in the tertiary sector. Key to the *kaupapa Māori* model is that any person can participate, but in this case the initial impetus within the University of Auckland is to build an infrastructure responsive to Māori students. The model examined by Smith (1997) predicts setbacks that may occur in any developments of this nature, but it is inevitable and part of the conscientization, resistance, and transformation processes. The *kaupapa Māori* intervention involves a strategy applied from a Māori perspective. The model responds to structural impediments; any model must be flexible enough to take all the "ups" and "downs" of struggle, similar to the description of an "incremental victory" referred to by Habermas (ibid.). This suggests that any change that takes place will have an impact on people, the organization, and other factors in different ways, producing a history of ebbs and flows. This is an integral part of a process of change.

The characteristics of participation in the process depend on the specific settings that include the people involved in the reshaping of institutions. An important element of the model is that for effective transformation to occur, a collective vision and philosophy of the institution, people, and community needs to be developed and maintained. Smith (1997) refers to this concept as being a dynamic part of the development of *kaupapa Māori*. It is a process that is continually evolving as each party contributes depending what they have to offer.

It might be assumed that this type of configuration for *kaupapa Māori* is a linear type of exercise in decision making. Figure 11.1 suggests that the process of change in Western research methodology happens in a particular series of events one after another. This is seen to be appropriate to some institutions. However, it implies that the process is inflexible in its present form, and that one stage cannot happen until another stage takes place or reaches completion. This is not what Habermas predicts and certainly not what the *kohanga reo* (Māori language nests) and *kura kaupapa Māori* (Māori state schools) processes indicate.

Figure 11.1 Linear change model

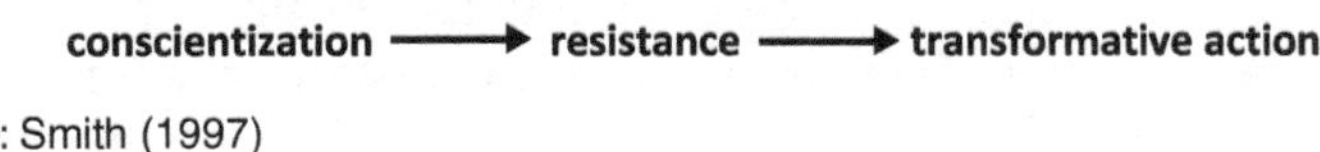

Source: Smith (1997)

Figure 11.2 Circular change model

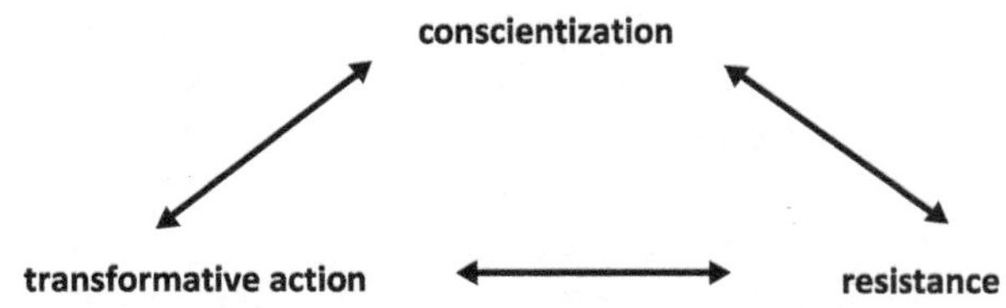

Source: Smith (1997)

A different perspective to Western research processes is presented in the circular model of Smith (1997) as shown in figure 11.2. This model assumes movement by dynamic shifts, including recursive change and cycles depending on the individual(s) and their respective situations in implementing change or forms of reposition. A key element in this type of model is the flexibility of movement by all parties to enter into the circle at their discretion or at any point in time.

There are closely related theoretical frameworks. The concept of critical theory (Smith, 1997) sees people working towards crisis intervention to support Māori and to gain more control over their lives. Freeing themselves from various layers and formations of oppression, exploitation, and containment is a result of self-critical examination. Another element is that within critical theory, the linear model is often *voiced* as being the only way in which to address intervention of this nature. However, within the components of *kaupapa Māori*, there is the element of flexibility to change, the need to move depending on what variables are required to make things happen. Smith considers that this flexibility is related to the need for critical interventions to be done for the good of the collective group.

The term "empowerment" in this instance is understood within the framework of dominant and subordinate power relations. To "empower" someone is to immediately structure the "power giver" into a dominant position. As discussed in the University of Auckland intervention model, endeavours to diversify this power occurred through the creation of positions within senior management for Māori, with the specific aim of encouraging individual faculties to model the same approach within their respective areas of responsibility. Critical to this approach is the infrastructural change within the organization of university committees (Robust, 2013). The University of Auckland created a *runanga* (tribal council) or advisory group consisting also of senior Māori staff from across the university. The University of British Columbia put in place a similar group, as well as an elders' group.

The flexibility of the model in figure 11.2 allows organizations and people to be able to appraise their situation(s) and then enter at a point that suits them. For example, the decision of some Māori parents to take their children out of the state schooling system and educate them in *kōhanga reo* (Māori language nests) occurred before 1987, when such initiatives first received state funding. Parents of these children then moved back into the state system and continue to participate in different levels and forms of immersion education. New Zealand legislation has also been developed to cater for the different types of Māori medium education programs now offered to all children in state schools and in particular those of Māori descent.

The Smith model provides some understanding in examining why Māori parents took this action and how they came to move back into the state system once legislation had been approved, therefore ensuring that their children were being given access to educational options not previously enjoyed. The model also presents a perspective that education is lifelong, and confirms ancient teachings of Māori society in which parents and *whānau* (family) are responsible for the child from birth to the grave. However, in critiquing this model, it is suggested that it should be seen as a base only, from which researchers can build discussion on future developments or models that will be able to cater for more diversity instead of just Māori people. The model could be used to enable other indigenous researchers to critique their respective situations in seeking to create indigenous space or infrastructure within tertiary institutions.

The University of Auckland case study is an educational intervention that can be understood using *kaupapa Māori* theory (Robust, 2013). Notwithstanding the internal reconstruction at the University of Auckland, the development of this educational intervention emerged as a response to the failure of state schools to solve the underachievement of Māori students. The goal of *kaupapa Māori* theory is to explain and predict positive educational outcomes for Māori. It is premised on a definition of a Māori perspective on thought and on action, which feels culturally appropriate and seriously takes into account Māori aspiration. For example, Graham Smith (1997) suggests Māori forms of education initiated in the 1980s by Māori are a means of understanding the potential of *kaupapa Māori* approaches in intervening in Māori educational crises.

The notion of theory as discussed above provides a basis for discussing how traditional forms of *wānanga* (tribal university) for Māori can be used to validate and inform contemporary schooling and educational practices within a tertiary institution. The development at the University of Auckland in identifying barriers that had to be overcome, in moving to implement a model for intervention across the university, illustrates the theoretical significance. Historical events at the university since its establishment in 1883 also need to be considered a part of the process. The resulting intervention in its structure was a model of organization and management unique to the University of Auckland. A key focus for the development was the aim to build a critical mass of Māori credentialed academic and general staff across the university.

Smith's argument provides a framework for exploring how indigenous "space" can be created within an educational initiative. It can be argued that the patterns of change have added significant pressure to develop more effective schooling opportunities for Māori. The use of elements such as information technology within the process of transformative action and within an indigenous pedagogy is essential in supporting these new developments. The case studies can be seen as educational initiatives that took the form of "transformative praxis." These initiatives have placed considerable pressure on government and other agencies to provide resource support that is appropriate to cater for educational crises.

Notions of Worthwhile Knowledge

Kaupapa Māori theory does not suggest an approach that is wholly opposed to accepted Western forms of research theory as educational interventions. Western research theory can be seen as being socially constructed, therefore likely to be serving "cultural" or "social" interests (Smith, 1997), as is the case for *kaupapa Māori*. Therefore, critical questions need to be considered, such as what counts as knowledge; how is knowledge produced; do different interest groups value different knowledge, and if so, are these fairly employed in promulgating knowledge; who has access to existing knowledge and how is this access controlled; whose interests does knowledge serve; how does prevailing knowledge legitimize existing methodologies; and what ideological appeals (hegemonies) justify and legitimate knowledge?

In the case of *kaupapa Māori*, it is argued that traditional Māori epistemology can still be significant in shaping and influencing Māori people's thinking and knowledge. However, in the pursuit of knowledge at tertiary institutions, it can be expected that prospective Māori students would, among other factors, consider the learning environment. With a key consideration concerning *whānau* (family) connections, then, the institution providing a supportive learning environment encompassing particularly appropriate Māori elements would obviously be more attractive as a "home away from home." This argument can be considered alongside Bourdieu's (1992) argument of cultural reproduction, which is that cultural elements of an institution create a disconnection within a "home culture." This is further enhanced with the argument that there are forms of culture in the home that are different from what is in the tertiary institution, and their mismatch has an impact on how or why a person acts and feels as they do. The consequence is that if they can create greater epistemological matches, then traditionally peripheral participants will be enabled to become central participants.

Māori incorporate cultural perspectives through core initiatives and practices. The *marae* (a common meeting place for family and extended members or tribe) is an institution both of life and of practices. It is also a significant learning institution. Māori epistemology that is encapsulated on the *marae* has a role within Māori society that influences *Māori* individually and as a social group. This suggests that traditional parts of Māori society specific to an issue – such as methodologies of appraisal and expertise discussed earlier (Best, 1986) – can be used to inform Western theory to embrace values, knowledge, and culture that many Māori accept as a natural part of their way of life or society. One example of this is the implementation of Māori pedagogy and curriculum through *te kohanga reo* (Māori language nests), *whare kura* (secondary or high schools), and more recently *wānanga* (tribal universities). The elements of this pedagogy have been described by critics such as Pere, Nepe, and Smith as *kaupapa Māori*; they represent Māori philosophies and practices (Smith, 2002).

Michael Apple (2001) argues that with the act of repositioning, institutions such as those described in the case studies of the University of Auckland and the University of British Columbia encounter the significance of power and the control of knowledge – and in these cases, the notion of the curriculum as brokered at the institutions. This suggests that the institution controls what counts as "official knowledge." This chapter further discusses the importance of this knowledge being taught through a prescribed process of learning. However, integral to the process is the need to ascertain the types of knowledge to be taught and the legitimization of that same knowledge. As with the traditional institution, the type of knowledge was taken as being the "official" information that the student was taught, and therefore seen as the truth. This approach is affirmed within the contemporary tertiary institution where the subject matter taught is seen as the legitimate form of knowledge for students.

Apple (2001) argues that, in some cases, the legitimization of knowledge by non-indigenous peoples and some Māori traditional forms of appraisal do not "fit" within a contemporary context where the outcomes of research are mainly driven by the economy. However, in traditional Māori society, the control of the knowledge was kept by the *tōhunga* (high priests) and seen as intellectual property. It was legitimated through the selection of Māori by birth or status, as part of selection for enrolling in the *whare wānanga* (tribal university). The knowledge was linked to the ongoing survival of the group or individual. Māori travelled from region to region presenting their knowledge. This allowed for forms of critique and participating in benchmarking with other like-minded people on the same area of interest. The similarities between the acquisition of legitimate knowledge in the traditional and contemporary environments are close. What is important from an indigenous perspective is the need to harness and create indigenous "space" for Māori students, as well as for Māori researchers to proceed to tell and write their stories within a supportive tertiary learning environment.

The University of Auckland case study contains reference to Māori education having been characterized by a history of failure (Robust, 2013). Numerous reports give voice to this negative view, such as the traditional *Wānanga* Treaty Claim 718 (Waitangi Tribunal, 1999). This claim sought to have the three state-funded *wānanga*[1] or tribal universities allocated funding resources equivalent to those of other non-Māori tertiary institutions. Previous institutional responses to this failure had not used critical elements of the model discussed here and had not ameliorated the history. This was despite the more general argument that, in combination with employment and income support policies, education and training could provide a way of assisting those without the relevant skills and experience to take advantage of continued job growth (Lange, 1988). It is through this approach to the mobilizing of the workforce that government policies sought to address the need for increased access, recruitment, retention, participation, and success for Māori people. This paradigm brings the need for credentials in entering any part of the workforce, but that is dependent on the function of the institution.

The increased focus on resource allocation to cater for identified student learning needs in schools – equity funding for schools, tertiary institutions, and parental income testing for student allowances – signals a shift of the type of management now required in education administration. Targeting has the potential for "space" within which new tools (new ways or new media for understanding and acting) can be developed. But the *kaupapa Māori* theory predicts that, in creating the space, this would fall naturally to other developments evident in any society with the building of a critical mass of skilled people in different fields of knowledge. The tertiary institution would play a critical part in these developments. The University of Auckland, as a tertiary institution, has responded to the current crisis by developing an infrastructure that has traditional elements and is innovative and positive in seeking to meet the challenges for students, staff, and community. The *kaupapa Māori* educational intervention is a theoretical test and the institution will participate in the conscientization, resistance, and transformative praxis in different configurations.

Methodology

Methodology as a Tool

The specific research question for this study concerns the process of developing an educational intervention which draws on features of traditional *wānanga* (tribal university). Can a model based on traditional *wānanga* provide a framework for tertiary institutions to be responsive in creating indigenous infrastructure to support Māori participation and contribute to Māori development today, in a tertiary setting? And can the development of traditional *wānanga* be explained using *kaupapa Māori* theory concepts?

A distinction between methodology and method is often drawn in any discussion on research methodology (Smith, 1999). A research method is a technique for gathering evidence. Analysis of methodology is important because methodological concepts frame the questions being asked, determine the set of instruments or tools and methods to be employed, and shape the analyses of evidence. Within an indigenous framework, methodological debates are concerned with the broader politics and strategic goals for indigenous knowledge. It is at this level that researchers need to clarify and justify their intentions. Indigenous methodologies are often a mix of research methods and indigenous practices. The mix reflects the training of indigenous researchers, which continues to be within the parameters of the academy, and their commitment to have common-sense understandings which govern how indigenous communities and researchers define priorities and outcomes for research.

The research question provides an opportunity to consider a model of intervention within the University of Auckland as a tertiary institution aimed at meeting the needs of Māori, which draws on critical features of *kaupapa Māori* as an educational intervention. A collaborative case-study-based approach was used to gain the information needed to answer the research question. The approach enabled an account to be developed from people who provided knowledge both about institutional phenomena and about the elements of *wānanga* (Robust, 2013).

Comparative Case Study Research

A comparison of case studies is the most suitable approach for the research question and its location within the *kaupapa Māori* framework outlined earlier in this chapter. It was crucial that each of the informants on *wānanga* (tribal universities) were acknowledged keepers of histories handed down from their elders, and were nurtured by these same elders, who supported them and their families in pursuing their goal of gaining educational qualifications and work experience, with the underlying expectation that they would in time contribute back to the community. The University of Auckland intervention model is conceived within the *kaupapa Māori* theory development outlined previously. In retrospect, the model can be seen as an attempt to re-represent a traditional concept within a contemporary situation. The concern is to find a way to integrate the development of indigenous structures and space without detracting from the overall integrity of the work of many Māori and other indigenous peoples.

A comparative component adds to the model used at the University of Auckland. Similar developments at the University of British

Columbia, Canada, provide an opportunity to consider two models of "best" practice. The prime concern is to examine the University of Auckland model using *kaupapa Māori* theory. However, this chapter is aimed at providing a foundation from which further analysis of indigenous models can take place in the future. The similarities in development between both institutions have therefore been considered, as there were common goals and events. The common goal was to create a framework that promoted access, participation, and success for indigenous peoples. Moreover, they are similar institutions. Both have positioned themselves as excellent universities with international profiles. Both these situations appeared more suited to case-study methodology through observation, reconstruction, and analysis, incorporating views of "actors" or active participants and their experiences that form the basis of their respective stories of development within the tertiary institution.

Both institutions have a traditional meeting house located on the main campus of their respective universities. Events leading to conscientization, in the case of the University of British Columbia, came in the form of a review of native Indian programs. The University of Auckland also has its traditional meeting house – *Tane Nui A Rangi* – as the focus of all Māori development. It resulted from a conscientization process. Reports for both institutions before and after the construction of the traditional meetings houses have led to ongoing development of the cultural elements that such traditional structures bring to each organization.

The usefulness of analysing the situations of both universities as contrastive case studies is supported by Robert Yin's arguments for case studies (1984, 1989a, 1989b, 1993, 1994). As long as the parameters for comparison are clearly defined and applied to each case undertaken to maintain consistency in the model, then the evidence for conclusions is able to be used. Yin (1989a) points out that a case study requires a methodology that has rigour and contains three core elements of study: describing, understanding, and explaining. The same author also identified at least six sources of evidence in case studies. These include documents, archival records, interviews, direct observation, participant observation, and physical artefacts (Yin, 1994). In the case studies developed here, each of these sources of the information was critical. This approach to the research in collating the data links with *kaupapa Māori* theory. In this case, the focus is on people being able to provide their collective and institutional knowledge.

Shared Knowledge in the Case Studies

In seeking to gain the trust of key people, it was important to involve them in the process of the research from the beginning to the end. The transparency of the format was a key element of the way in which information has been processed in this chapter. The primary question is whether the creation of indigenous "space" within a tertiary institution can promote better outcomes for Māori in having access, participation, and success in education at the tertiary level. Because of this, the position of a Māori researcher within the framework of *kaupapa Māori* research is an important consideration in the methodology.

The methods adopted were based on those of Jo-Ann Archibald and Madeleine McIvor (personal communication, 2003), who argue for the significance of hearing indigenous stories. Sharing of stories underpins the basis of this research in describing, understanding, and explaining indigenous knowledge from a *kaupapa Māori* theory perspective. Hilda Halkyard-Harawira (personal communication, 1999) echoes this point, stating that "what Māori need to do is to 'seek and find ways to tell their stories in their own way.'" Her statement is more than a reference to the way in which Māori or indigenous peoples approach research. Māori seek to tell their own stories without the fear of being marginalized, dissected, and criticized in forums outside of their cultural contexts, but at the same time their stories can be subject to rigorous analysis.

It is important to state that this research continues to be informed by the processes based on a *kaupapa Māori* model and how it relates to the methodology used to bring about the discussion of transformation in the case studies. In using *kaupapa Māori* theory as a "tool," Linda Smith (1999) argues that the idea of appropriating and exploring "tools" is not foreign for Māori society (Belich, 1986). In Māori society, it is expected that elders or peers will continue to seek knowledge in creating the freedom to make appropriate choices for the group. Given certain collective responsibilities, opportunity is allowed for an individual to make their own choices in their own time in seeking to gain knowledge. In a global context, this means that the collective experience can align itself to new technologies. In *kaupapa Māori* theory, this means using methods appropriate to whatever needs to be ascertained within the model itself. The technologies that are employed may constrain one's understanding and activity in other areas. For example, literacy can be used as a "tool" for colonization (Jenkins, 1991). However, Cummins (1995) argues that "literacy can be explicitly focused on issues of power as seen in the work of Friere who highlights the potential of written language as a 'tool' that encourages people to analyse the division of power and resources in their society and work toward transforming discriminatory structures."

Yet, the impact for Māori in not having access to "tools" such as literacy or education or effective methodology has been wide-reaching. The definition of a "tool" offered by Vygotsky (1978) is elaborated in his exploring of the concept of human labour and "tool" use as the means by which man changes nature and, in so doing, transforms himself (p. 7). This introduces a rationale for the utilization and development of a variety of methodologies such as *kaupapa Māori.*

A second component in the "tools" for the methodological process is collaboration. *Kanohi kitea* or the "seen face" is how Linda Smith conveys the meaning that being seen by the people confirms your membership to the people. For example, when you attend special events within the community, your credibility in research and the community is developed and maintained. Within First Nations and Native American communities, as in the Māori community, strict protocols exist governing this accreditation, which include the need to be respectful and reciprocation in kind – behaviours that are to be maintained at all times. The behaviours lead to becoming accepted within the community, but only at the invitation of the community. In Hawai'i, Kanaka Maoli (native) researchers indicated that the extended family also needed to be consulted prior to the giving of information to the researcher. The First Nations people of Australia discuss within this context different levels of entry to be negotiated when researchers seek information (Smith, 1999, p. 15).

The idea of collaboration is needed to gain confidence and information that is regarded in this instance as the "intellectual property" of the interviewee. They own it and they are offering to share it with the researcher. Linda Smith (1999) represents an indigenous perspective on the history of research that reaches back to the times where indigenous people and their experiences were being continually dissected by European or Western researchers. The struggle for survival as indigenous people was consolidated, and significant barriers imposed by the various institutions and parties associated with imperialism. Research has been integral to the formation and maintenance of barriers.

Linda Smith (1999) illustrates the use of methodology as an approach to address the control and colonization of space from where stories can be told or shared:

> Western classifications of space include such notions as architectural space, physical space, psychological space, theoretical space and so forth. Foucault's metaphor of the cultural space archive is an architectural image. The archive not only contains artifacts of culture, but also is itself an artifact and construct of culture. For the relationship between people and the landscape, of culture as an object of study, have meant that, not only has the indigenous world been represented in particular ways back to the west, but the indigenous world-view, the land and the people, have been radically transformed in the spatial view of the west, in other words indigenous space has been colonized. (Smith, 1999, p. 158)

Imperialism, now seemingly reinvented as globalization, has had an impact on indigenous research for centuries. However, the understanding of the impact of globalization is an important aspect of indigenous cultural politics and forms the base for indigenous language critiques and the development of research methodologies. Smith (1999) discusses this aspect within two strands of knowledge. The first strand is the notion of authenticity of a time before colonization, in which we were intact as indigenous peoples and therefore had complete control of our lives. The second strand confirms that Māori have an analysis of how we were colonized, of what is meant in terms of our immediate past, and what it means for the present and future. The strands intersect and form the solutions of the time before colonization and the time after. Decolonization encapsulates both sets of ideas. The indigenous research challenge to accept European forms of good quality research has been presented by Graham Smith (1997), who argues that

> Māori philosophy and practices were the initial approach by Māori of "freeing" themselves from multiple oppression(s) and exploitation. In particular "Kaupapa Māori"/ Māori philosophy and practices as an intervention strategy, in the western theoretical sense, critiques and re-constitutes the resistance notions of conscientization, resistance and transformative praxis in different configurations. In particular this work rejects the notion that each of these concepts stands individually, nor are they interpreted in this analysis as being a lineal progression from conscientization, to resistance, to praxis. (Smith, 1999, p. 66)

Linda Smith (1999) has taken this argument further by highlighting the work of researchers within an indigenous context. Creating "space" for indigenous research means it has its own dynamic, as have any other accepted research methodologies. In addition to the components of narrative and collaboration, there is the concept of *whānau* (family), which contains both values (cultural aspirations) and social processes (cultural practices) which are fundamental to a *kaupapa Māori* approach. Central to the concept of *whānau* is the role of the leader. This idea can be applied to the question of who assumes the role of leadership in the research undertaken by a group of indigenous researchers. Russell Bishop (1996) argues that the "true leader" is one who takes a lower role in the decision-making process while participating in the research, therefore not taking a lead role in the process. This suggests that in trying to ascertain who the leader is, it is important to consider the person who has taken on a lower or different role in the decision-making process within Māori society. In the research described here, a contribution is made by all participants in the research process as a natural part of the intervention.

Validity of Indigenous Research

Linda Smith (1999) argues that the assumption of Western researchers that they had the "right" stories challenges them from an indigenous perspective to validate indigenous views and input. This validation needs to utilize an indigenous context so that an understanding of the social world is presented from an indigenous perspective. Furthermore, the development of practices linked to the past still influence the struggle for the conscientization of indigenous peoples' claim to their intellectual property, existence, and being able to determine their own destiny in their fight for survival as a people. This struggle requires the protection of the above factors and the language and other forms of knowledge they have as a right. The forms of knowledge belong to them due to *whakapapa* (genealogy) handed down by their ancestors. It is the struggle for conscientization that is the key to this type of research. The fight for survival as conscientization occurs within circles of a *Pākehā* (European-dominated society) will only be successful if it is within the criteria Māori have set in place and protected over the many years. But there is still the need to validate research in the wider context of a community of researchers. How would it be achieved?

This is an important tension to resolve. On one hand, comparisons between *kaupapa Māori* (Māori philosophy and practices), research aspirations, and international models need to be treated cautiously (Bishop, 1996). The practice for researchers is to make sense of results in research undertaken by referring to criteria outside of the experiences and context of the researchers. This tension has been recognized by Linda Smith (1999). Her approach is to create space for indigenous researchers by taking indigenous researchers into international forums, allowing first-hand experience in the presentation of papers and ideas to other indigenous researchers. This is of benefit to the indigenous researcher and confirms a notion of collaboration from an indigenous perspective. But the process has roots in the indigenous context and is referenced back to that context.

The framework presented by Smith (1999) implies that the results of research are of little use to people if they themselves are the subjects of research and have not been involved in it from the beginning. The way in which research is made available and therefore its ongoing use is also an issue. If the results are couched in such a way that participants cannot understand them, then the control of results is again with the person undertaking the research. In debating the issue of being able to control research, Margaret Mutu (1998) signalled several issues that need to be taken into account by the indigenous researcher in New Zealand. The "defence" by Māori of their respective rights is seen to be guaranteed under the Treaty of Waitangi (i.e., the relationship stated in the treaty document signed in 1840). This leads to an ongoing need for good quality information and researchers trained in both Māori and *Pākehā* (non-Māori) *tikanga* or cultural practices, with the understanding that they avoid the abuse of power and failings of researchers who had in the past a hidden agenda which accompanied the acquisition of knowledge.

The validity of research undertaken by the indigenous researcher is probably the most difficult challenge that one has to encounter. Things taken for granted such as oral or inherited rights to *whakapapa* (genealogy), and in other cases *tapu* (sacred elements) for *whānau* (family), take on another shape or form. In this context, the researcher will have to seek the appropriate guidance in accessing these elements. It might involve a different agenda that would take time and particular scrutiny, and would not be evident to others due to the respective culture or *whakapapa* (genealogy) of the people involved. In the case of the present study, the formative use of historical records and interviews from Canadian institutions supports the experience at the University of Auckland, offering both a local and a global presence.

Justification in the use of case studies to describe the process within each of the universities involved in creating indigenous "space" is crucial to this discussion. Recalling of events is central to both case studies.

An event, such as the rugby match that took place between both countries in 1927, combined with similar initiatives embarked upon by indigenous leaders from both tertiary communities to create a physical presence for First Nations and Māori, who are key elements in the case studies.

Cultural connection and a style of operation that is inclusive can enact, in part, the values raised by Madeleine McIvor: respect, reciprocity, relevance, and responsibility. The factors all converge. The collaboration undertaken over long distances and periods of time has made possible the creation of a record of these stories for both institutions that can be added to in the future.

NOTE

1 Te Wānanga o Raukawa, Te Wānanga o Aotearoa, and Te Whare Wānanga o Awanuiarangi.

FOCAL POINT 4

The European Setting: Erasmus, Bologna, and the European Higher Education Area

This focal point addresses the various transformations of education in light of the Bologna Process and other controversial policies current in Europe. Mobility is a key concern here, and all the chapters in this focal point touch on this. Mobility is examined historically in Toporkoff's chapter, and critically in Martínez Valle's. While mobility is historically connected to the development of citizenship in Europe, it has more recently been implicated in the nationalism of (particularly) German universities. The standards-driven model common to the Bologna Process and other international accords described by Kutsyuruba has resulted in the loss of a common concern: wisdom. Jover and Gonzaléz Geraldo argue for a reclamation of this wisdom in the face of increasing standardization and corporatization of education in Europe. Finally, from the prospect of increasingly dismal economic performance on the part of European nations, smaller economies of scale – using a model based in the older tradition of the *métiers nobles* – would benefit from apprenticeship training across nations, as well as provide opportunities for trained individuals to take up jobs in an increasingly tight employment market. Higher education should play a leading role in this transformation to a more "guild-like" model of apprenticeship education; this is the thesis elaborated by Robinson.

12 The European Program Erasmus on Mobility and Its Impact on the European Dimension of Higher Education

SYLVIANE TOPORKOFF

From the Genesis of Mobility to Its Institutionalization: The Intellectual Wandering and Evolution of Universities

From antiquity among the Greeks, masters of rhetoric and philosophy or sophists moved from town to town to dispense their teaching. The origin of the university dates back to the Middle Ages, an era during which higher education would flourish in the great European institutions, each organizing itself around a group of professors and students. The rise of cities coincided with these architects of the mind who organized themselves into corporations. The latter finally gave birth to the university. The universities then attracted thousands of students from all countries of Europe and exchanged masters: Thomas Aquinas, to Paris, Rome, Naples; Albert the Great to Cologne; and so on.

The highways of Europe were travelled by a crowd of intellectuals and students seeking what they deemed necessary for their instruction, and formed an intellectual and cultural intermingling. In fact, the structures of higher education were already assuming an international character even before the foundation of universities. This allowed Jacques Le Goff (1985a) to talk about intellectual wandering as illustrated by the Goliards,[1] a name given to a foreign group of intellectuals from the twelfth and thirteenth centuries who had escaped from the constricting order of medieval society and who criticized the establishment, especially the Church, by their lifestyle: "Those goliardic scholars or wanderers are called vagabonds … are presented as gypsies, pseudo-students, and are looked at sometimes with emotion and sometimes with fear or disgust." In fact, they were the forerunners of international mobility: "These poor students of no fixed address live the intellectual adventure following the master they like, going after the renowned one, gleaning from city to city the teachings given there, and forming the body of this academic wandering that characterized the 12th century."

Numerous universities – intellectual and cultural centres – were born in Europe as early as the twelfth century and into the thirteenth. After Bologna in 1119, others were created, including those of Valencia in 1209, Oxford in 1214, the Sorbonne in 1215, Krakow in 1347, and then Budapest, Naples, Padua, Cambridge, Prague, and Heidelberg. Without excluding a few specificities of each university, they represent in the Middle Ages a surprising unity – different, on the juridical level, only by their organization according to the *Parisian mode* or the *Bolognan mode*. Thus, according to Verrier (2004), the universities are the result of the students' and teachers' need to regroup into university corporations. The students often attended several universities – the use of Latin as sole cultural language facilitating exchanges – carrying their own books, ideas, knowledge, and a common way of envisioning the world, thus participating in the intellectual movement in all of Europe (Verger, 1999).

Are the European dimensions of the Middle Ages and of today finally comparable, in terms of mobility of teachers and students? During the Middle Ages, the exchanges were also facilitated by the absence of boundaries, and the *peregrinatio academica* (academic pilgrimage) was an integral part of student life. Moreover, Verrier (2004) draws a parallel between the medieval and the contemporary eras, and advances the hypothesis that the sense of belonging to a European body of higher education which motivates all the actors would actually only indicate an awakening after a prolonged slumber.

In their "grand tour," the teacher and student of the Middle Ages moved from one university town to another. For the teachers and students away from their country and family, the university is the *alma mater*, the foster mother who must fulfil these needs in the crucible of personal intellectual and physical adventures. By integrating the journey, university formation becomes formation through experience, a rite of initiation and of passage. The journey is therefore not only a moving through space and time, but also a discovery of knowledge that is broader, more universal, and personal – a true *peregrinatio academica*.

Universities lost their international character during the fourteenth and fifteenth centuries because numerous new universities were founded with recruitment operating at the national and even regional level. The states closed their frontiers; the fifteenth century is often associated with the decline of universal powers. New universities were also created – not by kings, emperors, and popes, but more often by regional governors, religious orders, or urban districts, a process that accelerated the supranational character of universities (Brizzi, 1999, p. 27). The *peregrinatio academica* was in decline.

Later on, in the sixteenth century, the learned humanists with their universal curiosity – without ignoring the methodological value of science and the effort of thinking to explain reality – recommended direct experience of life, as Rabelais pointed out. Montaigne would go even further in advising the experience of life, human knowledge, and travel. Remember that he spent one and a half years pilgrimaging across Germany, Switzerland, and the Tyrol: "I know very well what I am fleeing from, but not what I am looking for. Running away from the day to day, the humdrum of a country rustic … a France that is sinking in the wars of religion … Because of this: the company of men, and the visit of foreign countries, but mainly to bring back the tempers of these nations, their ways, and to rub our brains against the brains of others." As well, in his chapter on "the institution of children," Montaigne (1595) declares: "I wish we would begin touring him from his early childhood, and first, to kill two birds with one stone, touring him through neighbouring nations where the tongue is further away from ours and where unless you train it early, the tongue cannot adapt to."

The honourable sixteenth-century man must "practise exchanging with men through travels and become familiar with the world." It seems obvious that as early as the Middle Ages, voyage – understood as mobility – was a source of development not only of knowledge but also of the mind, for the honourable man encountering different ways of living, of thinking, and different kinds of cultures: "This tendency to hunger for new and hitherto unknown things helps to nourish in me the desire to travel" (Montaigne, 1595). Through the centuries, academic peregrinations, as any trip would be, were accompanied by discovery of landscapes, cities, and the sociability of the Other European (Verrier, 2004). Voyage and mobility are connected with experience and trial. St Bernard, speaking to teachers and students said: "Flee from the Babylon milieu" – the big city was then synonymous with perdition – "flee and save your soul. You will find in forests much more than in books. The woods and the stones will teach you much more than any teacher" (Le Goff, 1985b). Bernard Fernandez (2001) defines the intellectual voyage as an element of reflection and a quest for knowledge. Voyage, he argues, could be an indispensable element in the ideal formation of people, operating in them an unheard of and unbelievable transformation.

Creating the European Space for Higher Education

The post–Second World War period was marked with a strong growth of international communities of researchers, and mobility increased in a significant way; this contributed to expanding the field of higher education. The second half of the twentieth century shows an economic explosion that engendered, among other phenomena, a growth of migratory flux and the implementing of globalization.

Article 128 of the Treaty of Rome (1957) did not address education per se. Professional training alone was the aim, in order to "promote a harmonious development of national economies and the Common Market." In 1969, the Council of Europe began reflecting the goal of creating a greater mobility of students, who were perceived as too set in the national system. In 1976, the European Commission revisited the idea of developing the notion of European citizenship by banking on the youth.

It was only at the beginning of the 1980s that the notion of "studying in foreign countries" within the framework of programs of studies emerged in Europe, with the onset of a European educational policy. This policy of exchanges prevailed during the 1980s and 1990s. The universities and high schools progressively availed themselves of a department of international relations, dedicated first and foremost to managing student mobility. Its services, often initiated for the head office only, have expanded and become a strategic entity for the whole establishment.

The Erasmus Programme

Created in 1987, the EuRopean Community Action Scheme for the Mobility of University Students (Erasmus) Programme is part of the European Commission's lifelong educational and training program. Erasmus is an acronym, but the name also evokes the humanist monk and theologian Erasmus (1465–1536), who travelled many years across Europe to enrich himself from the different cultures and develop his Christian humanism, the basic action of which was to attempt to conciliate the religious conflicts opposing Catholics and Protestants. The quintessence of the humanistic thought based on moderation and prudence sought to conciliate the study of Classics and the teachings of the Gospel.

The creation of the Erasmus Programme was motivated by the following acknowledgment of fact: in 1985, there were in Europe approximately six million students attending more than 3600 universities, but only one in a hundred was studying in another country's university. In 1998, the signing of the Declaration of the Sorbonne opened a vast work site centred on the economy of knowledge and harnessing member countries of the European Union to give birth to a European space of higher education. From this followed the Declarations[2] of Bologna[3] (1999), Lisbon (2000), Prague[4] (2001), Barcelona (2002), Berlin (2003), Bergen (2005), London (2007), and Louvain (2009). Among the main ideas of these declarations, the following is noteworthy:

> A Europe of Knowledge is now widely recognised as an irreplaceable factor for social and human growth and as an indispensable component to consolidate and enrich the European citizenship, capable of giving its citizens the required competences to face the challenges of the new millennium, together with an awareness of shared values and of belonging to a common social and cultural space. (European Ministers of Education, 1999)

Europe does not have the unique vocation of creating an economic space, but has the foundation of the Europe of Knowledge, the will to be competitive on the educational markets of the world, the development of human resources, and the growth of mobility and employability in Europe – the two latter objectives being major objectives of the Declaration of Bologna.

Today, thirty-three countries from the European Economic Space (the twenty-seven member states of the European Union plus Ireland, Lichtenstein, Norway, Sweden, Croatia, and Turkey) are involved in the program. Erasmus has become a formidable vector of student mobility and is now integrated in the EFTLV program,[5] the emblematic educational and training program of the European Union, which allows 200,000 students each year to study and spend a training period in a foreign country. Erasmus is not only for students but also for professors who wish to teach abroad, as well as university personnel and employees of businesses desiring to benefit from training in a foreign country. More than 2.5 million students have participated since its inception in 1987 (European Commission, 2011a), as well as 270,000 professors and other members of the higher education personnel since 1997. The program also finances cooperation between higher education establishments in all of Europe.

The Erasmus Programme is endowed with a budget close to 7 billion euros for the period 2007–13. Its sector-based program, which aims to contribute to creating a European space for higher education and to foster innovation throughout Europe, completed its twenty-fifth year in 2012. The annual budget of the sector-based program (decentralized actions) surpasses 415.25 million euros and benefits the participation of 2982 higher education establishments (European Commission, 2011a) in thirty-three countries.

Student Mobility

Mobility is treated as a means to reinforce European cohesion. It promotes the sense of belonging to Europe and the emergence of a European citizenship. Erasmus aims to strengthen the European dimension of higher education by encouraging transnational cooperation among the establishments. In 1985, 3000 students participated in European pilot projects. The Erasmus Programme was officially launched on 15 June 1987. Since then, more than 1.5 million students have been able to benefit from a mobility lasting between three and twelve months. Mobility is now recognized in the degree courses, thanks to the European System of Transfer of Credits (ECTS). Erasmus students are mainly enrolled in management (30%), languages (16%), and engineering (13%), but all disciplines are represented. The number of students in Erasmus mobility reached 3 million in 2013. Mobility of students can occur in the guise of mobility of studies, but also of mobility of work experience, the two being able to combine.

Sonia Dubourg Lavroff, who directed the Agence Europe Education Formation France (AEEFF) for six years until June 2009, notes a turning point for the Erasmus Programme, which we must rather see as a change in the utilization of this program: "Henceforth, with the possibility of having periods of work experience, students have an even greater tendency to apply for this type of mobility." The quality and value added by Erasmus sojourn periods must then become a priority; Erasmus is no longer *"l'Auberge espagnole* (The Spanish Inn)," confirms J. Bertsch, director of AEEFF. For participation to be successful, young people need to understand the world of enterprise and new forms of mobility will need to emerge. Indeed, student mobility remains the best known activity of the program, but other activities are developing such as teacher mobility, university and business personnel mobility, and even institution mobility.

Teacher Mobility

Many agents are involved in the organization of student Erasmus mobilities. Teachers in particular have a determinant role – they are the ones who develop partnerships between their university and other European universities, but they also set up exchange agreements and are therefore very much upstream in the process of student mobility. More downstream, they also act as coordinators. Within this framework, they select from among the candidates students who will effectively benefit from a mobility scholarship. Before the students' departure, teachers determine the courses they will take, and they control which knowledge they will have to go through in the host university, as well as what modules will be validated upon returning, according to the principle of ECTS.

The teachers themselves also have the possibility to teach abroad within the framework of the Erasmus Programme. They may leave for from one to eight weeks, while their foreign homologue has in turn to come at a convenient time, since the program involves reciprocity. The teachers may also make a preparatory visit to make contacts for the following year or to see their students abroad during their Erasmus stay. However, this type of mobility poses problems as the teacher is not replaced while absent, which means they must go during their breaks.

The role of teachers in the Erasmus Programme is essential. Participating in a mobility program is, for a teacher, an opportunity to acquire and pass on knowledge and also to establish new partnerships with member countries of Erasmus. Teacher mobility has a positive impact on the teacher, as well as on students. It allows teachers to share teaching practices and facilitates university exchanges, as well as training experience abroad for students. Contacts made with the receiving establishment help to better promote partnership while they facilitate and improve the organization of student mobility. Teacher mobility helps institutions to become mutually better acquainted with their partner institutions. This is necessary in order to advise student candidates concerning Erasmus mobility, to create and maintain relations of trust that are fundamental for lasting cooperation, and to establish work habits and collaborations that are useful in managing efficient exchanges.

It is interesting to note that student mobility and teacher mobility are correlated. This link helps promote and use the teachers' departure as a lever for student mobility. The correlation between the two has been tested and confirmed at a threshold of significance of 5 per cent, by using three different statistical tests: Kendall, Pearson, and Spearman. With each of these tests, the coefficient of correlation is 97, 98, and 99 per cent respectively.

This mobility is offered to any personnel of an institution of higher education, so includes not only teaching personnel but also administrative and technical employees. It allows them to complete a training mobility within one to six weeks in an institution of higher education, a business, or a training organization in another European country.

Towards a "Europeaneity" of Teaching

According to Ján Figel, commissioner for Education, Culture and Youth (as quoted in European Communities, 2008), "students participating in Erasmus acquired an extremely concrete experience of Europeaneity. We now talk about the Erasmus generation, 80% of whom had never stayed in a foreign country before. Therefore, this shows that experiencing the program has the power to transform the students' lives. Several studies show that one of the substantial advantages of the program resides in improving job prospects, developing communication skills and sensitivity to the 'cultural factor.'"

Higher education is internationalizing more and more. Universities and faculties around the world compete among themselves to obtain the best partnerships, to attract the best students and professors, and to innovate in international programs offered to their students. Benita Ferrero-Waldner, European commissioner for External Relations and European Neighbourhood Politics from 2004 to 2009, stressed the importance of modernizing the higher education system of Europe: "In our present global economy and our society based more and more on knowledge, reinforcing international co-operation and mobility among higher education institutions of the European Union and other countries can only bring advantages and contribute to mutual enrichment of nations and to a better understanding among peoples, while promoting economic and social development" (Commission Européenne, 2007).

Through its decision dated 18 December 2006, the European Parliament ruled that 2008 would be the European Year of Intercultural Dialogue. It was part of the first European agenda of culture in the era of globalization. One of the objectives was to assign to education the essential role it deserves in teaching respect for diversity and understanding of other cultures. Finally, during the Conference of European Ministers in charge of higher education held in London on 17–18 May 2007, it was stipulated once more that the European space of higher education ought to take up the challenges of globalization and that promotion of student and personnel mobility should remain a priority for 2009. The year 2010 recorded the transfer of the process of Bologna to the European Space of Higher Education (EEES); all the ministers reaffirmed their commitment to higher education. This constitutes a key element towards helping our societies continue to develop and to perform.

Erasmus's Impact on Europeaneity and the Program's Quality, Openness, and Internationalization

The European Commission published a 2009 study on the impact of Erasmus since its creation in 1987. It relied on an inquiry conducted at the European level, with approximately 750 directors of institutions and more than 1800 Erasmus coordinators simultaneously in the international offices and faculties. The main conclusions referred to the effects of the program on two levels: political and institutional.

According to 30 per cent of the institutions surveyed, an unexpected result was the positive impact recorded in the area of the reinforcement of cooperation between the universities and businesses. According to close to 90 per cent of central Erasmus coordinators, their institutions had progressively acquired a more international profile, and close to half of them reported that the Erasmus Programme had a great – even very great – influence in raising the degree of professionalism in the management of higher education institutions. The majority of the staff of these institutions (92%) admitted that participation in the Erasmus Programme had helped to modernize their institution and to bring about favourable changes. Seventy per cent insisted on the need to continue and improve with regard to the European objectives and the activities within the institution.

The recognition of qualifications across the European System of Credit Transfer (ECTS) allows the Europeanization of teaching and is recognized by businesses. The Erasmus Policy Statement (EPS) plays an important role. In fact, the Declaration in Matters of Strategy Erasmus (DMSE) must be formulated by each institution to be accepted by the European Commission. The declaration determines the whole strategy of the institution and will form the basis of all its projects of Erasmus cooperation. It must describe in summary form the strategy of the establishment and the objectives and priorities of Erasmus activities, such as individual mobility, multilateral projects, and network projects. Also, the dispositions taken within the framework of the politics of non-discrimination must be included, such as projects relating to equality of the sexes, integration of personnel and students with disabilities, and the fight against racism and xenophobia.

The EPS makes it possible to prepare students for the international labour market, employability, and the recognition and harmonization of diplomas, and for institutions to become attractive and to enjoy a wide popularity. Many institutions state that they changed their EPS because of the Declaration of Bologna. Most institutions acknowledge that having to submit an EPS has contributed to raising their awareness and improving European cooperation. Moreover, half (53%) affirm that the EPS has led to the creation or improvement of administrative services dealing with international relations. It has, however, provided less encouragement for students to go to a foreign country or to stimulate institutions to cooperate with other regions of the world. The European programs in support of education have certainly directly and profoundly influenced the French institutions of higher education by obliging them to truly take into account the international dimension.

Evaluation of the New Mobilities

In the first semester of 2009, the office of Project Europe requested that a study be undertaken to determine the impact of the Erasmus Programme, to evaluate whether the new types of mobilities introduced in 2007 to its integrated educational and lifelong training program had an impact on the quality of the relationships between universities and businesses. This study, "Impact of the Erasmus Programme (IMERA)," took place after only one year of experimenting with these new mobilities; this fact probably influenced the results and analyses. The Erasmus mobility work and training experiences are increasing rapidly, especially the mobilities of personnel training that the institutions are beginning to use.

The main conclusions of the IMERA study give an interesting insight into the Erasmus Programme and the impact of these new mobilities on university and business relationships. From the study's results, it seems obvious that these relationships still need to develop: these training periods are not often perceived as a major test of the relevance and appropriateness of training for the needs of the business establishments. They are seen by the institutions as beneficial to the students only; it would seem from that point of view that the receiving institutions and enterprises might not have yet explored all the benefits such a plan can bring to the sending and receiving structures.

It is surprising to observe that the answers from the establishments on the impact of mobilities on the business enterprises sometimes contradict the answers of the enterprises themselves (which include enhanced value of the networks and increased impact due to the increased length of training periods). This confirms a certain lack of knowledge of these two worlds. The establishments and the receiving structures are otherwise in agreement on the fact that a better follow-up would improve the impact of mobilities (including training periods and mobility periods), and agree on the relevance of interface structures to improve the quality of these new Erasmus mobilities. The preparation for and follow-up to the training periods are very dissimilar or ill matched, according to the establishments; the smaller ones offer many more tools and good practices, while the bigger ones seem to take on a management responsibility that leaves them no more time.

The functioning of transnational mobility also seems to vary considerably from one establishment to another. Sometimes a service or an individual is dedicated to its management, while it also happens that the teachers (of language, most often) take up this role during their spare time.

All the participants in the inquiry agree on one point: interface structures in charge of coordinating and following up on the organization of transnational mobilities (mobility or training periods) would improve their impact and quality.

It seems strange that, from this point of view, consortiums do not seem to be used to the fullest for the benefits that could be derived from them. Up until now, the establishments have seen them as devices for mutualization of the administration and financial management of the Erasmus training periods.

With regard to the results of the IMERA study, it seems that the establishments have not yet exploited all the opportunities offered by the Erasmus Programme. It also appeared clearly, according to the students' answers, that the training period is not only an occasion to put in practice what they learned, but it allows them to acquire new theoretical knowledge. The period therefore brings new theoretical knowledge supplementing what was obtained through training.

Concerning, more particularly, mobilities for the training of personnel, this new opportunity of the Erasmus Programme is still underexploited by the establishments: only one-third of respondents had planned to organize one or more personnel training mobilities during 2007–8. These mobilities are mainly organized by larger establishments, where they are more easily implemented, whereas in a smaller structure, the lack of a salaried coordinator would make it more difficult.

In the area of personnel-training mobilities, as in the area of student training periods, the respondents are convinced that interface structures for the purpose of moderating and managing these projects would improve their impact and quality.

The Role of Erasmus in the Europeanization of the Labour Market

Finally, the responses from the various institutions confirm the role of the Erasmus Programme in the Europeanization of the labour market, since more than 50 per cent of the youth that participated in an Erasmus training period hope to find employment in a foreign country, especially in the one where they trained. Linguistic training was often cited (68 per cent) as an essential factor of success in the exchanges and as an added value for diplomas on the labour market.

Numerous studies conducted by the European Commission indicate that a period spent abroad enriches the life of students not only on the academic and professional level, but also on the level of language learning, of acquisition of intellectual competencies, and of growth in autonomy and self-awareness. The students' experience allows them to understand better what it means to be a European citizen. Moreover, many employers give much importance to these sojourns abroad, which increase student employment and future chances of employment. Exchanges of personnel present similar beneficial effects, as much for participants as for establishments from either countries of origin or host countries.

Other European Programs

The Erasmus Programme is undoubtedly the best known, but there exist other programs within the program for education and lifelong training of the European Commission. The name of the Comenius program refers to Jan Amos Comenius (1592–1670), a Czech theologian and philosopher who directed a school that proposed to adapt the transmission of knowledge to each student. The program promotes exchanges and cooperation between school establishments in Europe, from kindergarten to high school. In Europe every year the Comenius program links 11,000 schools and allows 850,000 students and teachers to get involved in a European project. It also allows 7000 teachers to take part in an ongoing training activity in Europe.

The Leonardo da Vinci program for teaching and professional training allows mobility aimed at acquiring professional experience. It is for trainees after their initial professional training and for others already qualified, as well as for professional teachers and trainers and members of organizations active in this area. The program allows organizations in the professional teaching area to work with partners from all of Europe, to exchange good practices, and to improve their employees' skills and expertise. The program aims to increase attraction to professional teaching for young people and stimulate the global competitiveness of the European labour market by helping individuals to acquire competences, knowledge, and new qualifications. The innovation projects are essential to the program. They aim to improve the quality of training systems by creating and transferring policies, courses, teaching methods, procedures, and innovative material. Leonardo da Vinci aimed to have 80,000 individuals complete business training by the end of 2013.

The Grundtvig program for adult education deals with ongoing training and aims to strengthen the European dimension of adult education. The program expected to support mobility for 7000 individuals involved in adult education annually by 2013.

Tempus supports modernization of higher education and creates a space for cooperation in the EU's neighbouring countries. This program, set up in 1990, now covers twenty-seven countries, from the West Balkan and Eastern European regions, as well as from Central Asia, North Africa, and the Middle East.

Erasmus Mundus is a program that aims to improve the quality of higher education and promote intercultural understanding. The program encourages and supports personnel mobility and cooperation between European and non-European establishments. Its objective is to promote the European Union as a space of academic excellence on a worldwide scale, to contribute to the sustainable development of higher education in developing countries, and to offer students the best career prospects. The program has a budget of 950 million euros for the 2009–13 period.

Another example is the specific program of "co-operation" of the Seventh Cadre program. This program supports all types of research activities carried out by research organizations in transnational cooperation. It is divided into ten themes that reflect the most important matters of knowledge and technology, in response to European challenges in the social, economic, public health, environmental, and industrial areas. Four measures are proposed: collaborative research (European excellence), coordination of national research programs, technological initiative, and technological platforms.

Conclusions

The Erasmus Programme has enabled Europe to integrate politics with matters of higher education. The accords have permitted the reinforcement of academic collaboration among institutions. However, it is obvious that to set up an accord of cooperation, it is essential that the two parties have a common interest and the will to develop exchanges for students, doctoral students, and teachers in the long term and even to carry out research projects together.

However, Erasmus is not open to all students. First of all, only those students fulfilling certain criteria for admission can participate. This privilege is given only to students enrolled in a superior establishment (universities, institutes, schools, conservatories, and secondary schools for degree courses of BTS, a post-secondary technical certificate) who have completed their first year of university studies. The student must be a citizen of one of the eligible countries or have permanent residence, be a stateless person, or have political refugee status. Other criteria are also necessary regarding the capacity to adapt: one must be able to cope with the courses and the language, which requires a certain level of proficiency, and also be able to adapt to the country's rhythm.

All the necessary preparatory steps – such as gathering the required papers to assemble an application – take a long time, therefore one must start early. However, there are many bursaries from different national ministries of education and mobility bursaries, as well as regional assistance, to cover all kinds of costs (such as lodging, travelling, food, furniture, and other expenses) in order to help students undertake Erasmus. Therefore, more improvements need to be carried out in order to make Erasmus more efficient and accessible.

We may aptly conclude this paper with the following quotation from Giovanni Giacomo Casanova: "The man who wants to educate himself must travel to rectify what he has learned."

NOTES

1 *Le Petit Robert* (dictionary).
2 Note the symbolic choice of the oldest university cities.
3 Twenty-nine states adhere to the process of harmonization by introducing the European Credit Transfer System (ECTS), judged adequate for the promotion of mobility.
4 The Declaration of Prague set the pace toward the Europe of the Universities.
5 EFTLV: *L'Europe de l'Éducation et de la Formation Tout au Long de la Vie* (Long-Life Education and Training in Europe)

13 Harmonizing the Disparate? Bologna's Implementation in Secondary Teachers' Education in Germany and Spain

CARLOS MARTÍNEZ VALLE

The Bologna Process aimed from its inception at creating a European Higher Education Area – that is, at harmonizing superior education and fostering the mobility of students and the labour force within Europe. It could be construed as a perfect example of the Stanford neo-institutional conception of globalization. This paradigm maintains the existence of a world-level educational culture and ideology that supports the diffusion or globalization of models or rationalized myths, leading to educational isomorphism across the world. However, multilayered decision instances, new governance, and vagueness or contradictions in the objectives cast doubt upon the achievement of the desired homogenization. The maintenance of heteromorphism is evident in one of the arguably central objectives of the reform, secondary school teacher training (SSTT). As the historic-comparative analysis of the German and Spanish cases shows, different political constellations, regional and national academic culture, and institutional inertia reproduced the differences in SSTT between both countries and within the German states. In practice, the SSTT reforms implemented under the aegis of Bologna, more than the diffusion of a global model, could be understood as local-idiosyncratic answers to the reforms of secondary school that took place in both countries during the previous decades.

Introduction

The early debates about Bologna's two-tier system in Spain encountered a first problem: names. The Spanish form of the word bachelor, *bachillerato*, already designated Secondary II degrees. Furthermore, academia began to ask if the reform would change the established and respected *licenciaturas* into something like the myriad devalued, non-regulated "Masters." Obviously, the financial situation of Spanish universities made it quite difficult for them to achieve the level of the top MBA programs. Neither did universities appreciate being compared with informal schools offering expensive but low quality certificates. The difficulty persists because the denomination "Master" is not restricted to university courses, and universities still offer old Masters (Nebot, 2009). This is only one example of the difficulties in harmonizing Spanish tertiary education with the Anglo-Saxon model proposed by the European Higher Education Area (EHEA).

"Harmonization of the architecture of the European higher education system" – that is, convergence towards a model – has been the explicit objective of the measures known as the "Bologna Process" since its inception in the Declaration of the Sorbonne (1998). For understanding processes of structural and curricular harmonization across the world or processes of "globalization," the neo-institutional strand of the Sociology School of Stanford University developed its paradigm. Central for this paradigm – as a basis enabling the adoption of models, structures, ideas, and so forth – is the sharing across the world of general educational values and ideas, of a world-level educational culture. Therefore, Bologna could be construed as a perfect example of Stanford's neo-institutionalism paradigm of globalization, as one of the most successful (Crosier, Purser, & Smidt, 2007)[1] processes of "diffusion" of "imagined models" (Voegtle, Knill, & Dobbins, 2011) leading to isomorphism across the world (Schriewer, 2007). As part of this culture, the "rationalized myth" of a purported Anglo-Saxon elite university model, transmitted by communication and imitation and by international (EU) and national top-down policy, would have changed the structures of the most venerable European institution – the university.[2] Furthermore, consistent with Stanford's paradigm, the model, transposed into policy measures, would have expanded beyond the borders of the ratifying states, becoming a new worldwide policy standard (Beneitone et al., 2007).

In contrast with the globalization narrative sketched above, the purpose of this chapter is to exemplify the resistance of educational systems to harmonization through the analysis of one of the arguably prior objectives of the reform, secondary school teacher training. If elsewhere the author has discussed the Stanford neo-institutional paradigm through the analysis of educational discourse – a non-formalized standardized indicator (Schriewer & Martínez Valle, 2004, 2007) – this chapter will focus on indicators often used by the Stanford group: formal institutional structure and curriculum. However, other than the typical comparison designs used by the Stanford group, including countries of a wide array of cultures and socio-economic and political characteristics, the present analysis compares two EU members and Bologna-ratifying states: Germany and Spain.

For explaining the maintenance of the heteromorphism within and between German and Spanish SSTT, the analysis focuses on cultural and value heterogeneity within every culture, in this case within a purported world-level educational culture shared by Spanish and German educational agents. Even sharing an eventual general educational culture or ideology, the *Wertkonkurrenz* – that is, the need to give precedence to some values – means that different agents, with different precedence of values and interests, will adopt different stances and options. In short, our analysis introduces politics within policies of diffusion.

This chapter proposes an alternative reading of the Bologna Process as a belatedly systemic adjustment to the changes in secondary schools, the most reformed educational level in the 1990s (Esteve, 2003; Eurydice, 1997; Pedró, 1996; Schulte, 2005). It is no wonder that (secondary) school teacher training was "considered across Europe as critical" (Keuffer & Oelkers, 2001; McKenzie et al., 2005). Furthermore, the Lisbon Strategy of 2000 set the achievement of Secondary II degrees for 85 per cent of all twenty-two-year-old students as a goal for all European education systems. For coping with this situation, criticisms, and demands, SSTT had to change and Bologna was a good instrument to force reform, resorting to foreign models and competition. This interpretation acknowledges systemic socio-economic similarities throughout clusters of countries, but stresses at one side the different institutional and structural inertias, and at the other the role of political interests and cultural differences in understanding and in answering similar challenges.

The chapter analyses the transformations introduced by Bologna in secondary school teacher training, which arguably was among the most disparate curricular and structural arrangements in Europe. After a historical sketch of SSTT in Germany and Spain, and the reasons for the adoption of Bologna, in particular those related to SSTT, the chapter moves towards the images of the EHEA envisioned by different actors in both countries. It explores the inertias of the German and Spanish educational systems and their resistance to these proposals, and in particular, the role of extra-systemic conditionings unmodified by the agreements. Later, it focuses on the manifestations of internal and cross-system differentiation, which contrast with the agreements' declared intention of achieving a higher degree of homogeneity and transferability. Finally, it points out some of the problems introduced by the new structures.

Problems and General Considerations in the Study of SSTT

School teacher training or *Lehramt* studies were followed in Germany in the 2010/11 winter semester by 216,192 *Lehramtsstudenten* (Statistisches Bundesamt, 2001, p. 47), while in Spain, SSTT was offered in 2009–10 by 45 universities and followed by 10,800 Masters students. This data is assorted, as there is a great degree of differentiation between the concepts *Lehramtsstudenten* and "secondary school teacher" in the countries under study. In Spain, the term includes the teachers who will develop their work at vocational education (*Formación Profesional*) centres, as well as teachers at secondary education I (compulsory) and II (non-compulsory) levels. In Germany, meaningfully, the main statistics about students don't disaggregate into primary or secondary school teachers. Furthermore, the concept "secondary school teacher" designates different studies and careers, at different institutions, and with different names across Germany – those who will work at the different kinds of secondary schools: the Haupt, Real, Regional, and Gesamtschulen; the Gymnasium; and vocational studies (*Fachlehramt, Lehrer/in für Fachpraxis im beruflichen Schulwesen*). Not all of these studies are pursued at university (in Baden Württemberg, for example, all teachers except gymnasium and vocational teachers study at universities of education or *Pädagogischen Hochschulen*). The difficulty in examining SSTT increases owing to university autonomy and the federal-autonomic administrative structures of Germany and Spain (Eurydice, 2001, p. 8; Hübner, 1994; KMK, 2003, p. 77; Ministerium für Bildung, 2000).

Both members of the European Union, Germany and Spain apparently share some common features. Both countries left behind old authoritarian traditions, adopting democratic federal or semi-federal political systems. This process was related to the extension and democratization of the educational system and the granting of autonomy to the universities, which took place in different times and to different degrees in both countries. However, education and science in Germany are under the sovereignty of the different federal states (*Länder*) that regulate studies through *Studienordnungen und Prüfungsordnungen*. The loose coordination of the *Hochschulrahmengesetz* (derogated in the recent federal reform) and of the Council of Educational Ministers (Kultusminister Konferenz) was too weak for constituting common educational policies and structures (Fischer et al., 2004; Hübner, 1994; Schulte, 2005).[3] In addition, policies favouring the autonomy of universities and "Institute-Universities" (departments in which a chair determines autonomously the lectures' contents, uniting, in the "Humboldt" spirit, teaching with research – that is, adapting teaching to the research agenda) led to organizational and curricular diversity within German universities (Kiuppis & Waldow, 2008). This freedom and the lack of a rigidly structured curriculum allowed German students to have a high degree of choice and self-organization. They used this freedom for working, travelling, and studying at home or abroad, which explained the long duration of individual studies. These loose structures allowed a great degree of interdisciplinary work and specialized research, and created mature and experienced students.

In contrast, policies, structures, and curriculums in Spain – even if diversified by the increasing power of the regional governments (*Regiones Autónomas*) – maintain a substantial degree of similarity. The central government regulates education through general "frame" laws (*Leyes Orgánicas*), and "minimum curricular content decrees" (*decretos de contenidos mínimos*). The basic power units in Spanish universities are the departments. The central, top-down definition of university curriculums resulted in similar distribution of work areas and departments across Spanish universities, even in interdisciplinary departments. As students are socialized in an environment with a strict division of knowledge (there are no majors and minors), they tend to reproduce these same structures in their later careers. Therefore, academic departments, central agents in the negotiation and implementation of new curriculums, tend to maintain isomorphism throughout Spain.

In both countries, pedagogy as an academic field is traditionally theory-focused. In Germany it is based in hermeneutics, while in Spain it relied on a corpus of philosophical-normative doctrines derived from "Catholic humanism." These academic cultures weren't prone to the development of didactics. However, the hermeneutic methods, the specialization fostered by the organizational principles of the Institute-University that led to research, the modernization of academia, and the influence of vocational studies and of *Pädagogischen Hochschulen* changed the field in the German system, which nowadays pays substantially more attention to the praxis and practica than its Spanish counterpart (Colom

Cañellas & Rincón i Verdera, 2004; Keiner & Schriewer, 2007; Schriewer, 1998; Schriewer & Martínez Valle, 2004, 2007).

Secondary School Teacher Training in Spain and Germany: Historical Background

In Germany, the gymnasium teacher's initial "formation" ("training" has connotations proper to Anglo-Saxon conceptions) followed until the mid-1960s the old two-consecutive-phase model, with the first phase devoted to university studies on subjects like mathematics, history, and geography, and the second on educational and practical (professional) formation in *Studienseminare* and schools (Berg et al., 2004; Keuffer & Oelkers, 2001).[4] By contrast, the *Realschule* and primary school teachers were trained mainly in the *Pädagogischen Hochschulen*, combining studies on the teaching subject matters with professional formation until students were ready to take the second exam for entering the civil service (Arnold & Reh, 2005; Bölling, 1983).

Despite the situation of educational expansion, the corporative opposition of educational agents hindered – from the mid-1960s until the early 1970s – the hiring of teachers without educational formation (Horn, 2002, p. 254). This oppositional pressure achieved the union of (most parts of) the *Pädagogischen Hochschulen* (and therefore of other parts of SSTT) in the universities, the creation of educational majors, and, therefore, university schools of education. Furthermore, the short pedagogy course (one *Semesterwochenstundenzahl*) that dealt with some ethical and psychology problems during the university studies was extended to one lecture and a practical class in 1965 (four *Semesterwochenstundenzahl*) (Berg et al., 2004), or several courses (16–20 *Semesterwochenstundenzahl*) in the 1980s. These transformations gave form to a model of SSTT characterized by the simultaneity or "integration" of the two specialization or teaching disciplines (except for art, religion, and special education, which could be studied alone) with general educational and specific didactic subjects in the *Lehramt* courses. Professional corporations also argued for more practica and a closer coordination of studies and practica, always a desideratum, until the most recent reforms (Keuffer & Oelkers, 2001, p. 19; Merzyn, 2004). State exams between the two phases and after the second practicum (*Refendariat*) complete the above-mentioned model. Doubtless, the tradition of combining diverse studies (different majors and majors-minors) eased the establishment of an integrated (not consecutive) initial training.

Although teaching trainees were an important student contingent in all university schools, they were considered in some ways inferior or not belonging fully to their area of specialization; for example, they were considered pedagogy students and not mathematics or history students. However, the lower prestige of educational studies and school teacher training meant that students themselves identified with their specialization as historians or mathematicians, more than as history or mathematics teachers (Bölling, 1983).

The parsimony in and paucity of the implementation of the early 1970s reforms – Merzyn (2004) affirms that the reform debate died around 1975, even if most of the reforms weren't put in practice – resulted in very different implementations of the proposals across Germany, in particular on curriculum and contents, proportions of times devoted to the didactics, and educational and the teaching subjects.

However, the expansion and integration of educational studies was opposed by traditional corporative or political interest groups like the Society of Natural Scientists and Medical Doctors (Verein Deutscher Naturforscher und Ärzte) or the Scientific Council of the Government and the Parliament (Wissenschaftrat), constituted by researchers, politicians, and civil servants. The former defended the academic discipline knowledge, the research, and the high standards of the university – that is, their jobs; the latter promoted a shorter and sequential study more adapted to the changing demands of the teaching market. The opposition to an integrated school teacher training manifested again during the absorption of the East German states, when the German Society for Education issued the Declaration of Dresden (Berg et al., 2004), contrary again to the Wissenschaftsrat's proposals (Wissenschaftsrat, 1992).

The educationalists' and educational civil servants' diagnosis of the problems of German school teacher training from the late 1960s until the reform proposal in Hamburg, or the Kultusminister Konferenz commission "Perspectives on the Teacher Training in Germany" in the 2000s and beyond, point recurrently to similar problems: the need for a more stringent and professionally defined curriculum and therefore more coordination and internal relation between practica, teaching or specialization subjects, specific didactics, and general educational contents. This new curriculum implied necessarily a clear determination of core and priority contents and their distribution among the faculty, which ran against the teaching and research freedom traditional at the Institute-University. Recent proposals also included the need to learn from students' experiences and assessments, and to introduce standards based on clear agreements about the objectives and requirements. Proponents stressed, disregarding feasibility, that these reforms should not change the main contribution of academia, the Humboldtian habitus of learning through research (Beckmann, 1968; Keuffer & Oelkers, 2001; Merzyn, 2004; Schubarth, 2007; Tenorth, 2012; Terhart, 2000; 2001, p. 165; Wiebke et al., 2011).

Although defending different interests, Wissenschaftsrat and Verein Deutscher Naturforscher und Ärzte adopted similar stances. On the other side, not all educationalists agreed with the scientization of the studies derived from academization of educational science, and criticized it both as a threat to educational science and as a change that could dehumanize studies (Tenorth, 2012; Terhart, 1996, p. 450; 2005). Furthermore, those both for and against integrated studies used the same argument – the mythical Humboldtian conception of the university as an institution combining research and teaching and rejecting the narrowing focus on professional praxis – to plead their case (Merzyn, 2004; Schmoldt, 1989).[5] The concurrence of the values conveyed by the mythical Humboldtian model of the university and the need to fix a precedence among these values is demonstrated in the different importance given by the different actors to the different parts of student teacher training: praxis, formal knowledge of teaching matters, general education, or specific didactics.

Until the early 1970s, secondary education was an elitist phase in the Spanish educational system. Conceived as a preparation for the entry exam to the university (*Reválida*) and having a propaedeutic character, the *Bachillerato* shared the features of the university: academicism, disciplinary definition of the curriculum, and disdain for didactics. The law that ratified the incipient opening up of the educational system (Ley General de Educación, passed in 1970) called attention to the formation of teachers who had to teach students with a wider range of socio-economic and cultural backgrounds and, therefore, needed more didactic and psycho-pedagogic resources.[6] However, the resistance of political elites and of the educational system – in particular the old Institute chairs – diluted the reforms. The importance given to academic contents over pedagogical and didactic training reduced SSTT to a poorly financed *Curso de Aptitud Pedagógica* (CAP) that took place consecutively after the *licenciatura* on the respective specialization or teaching matter. The half-hearted reform was manifested in the consecutive organization of the courses and their restricted duration: 150 hours of theory and 150 of practicum for secondary school teachers, and 100 hours of theory and 80 hours of practicum for vocational education teachers. The theory dealt with "systems of educational innovation" and "principles, objectives and problems of education in a historical, psychological and sociological perspective." The biggest block of the theory hours was assigned to the specific didactics of the teaching subjects. However, these hours were typically used to repeat the content already studied during the *licenciatura*. This distribution showed up in the differing powers of departments and university schools.

The courses were not administratively attached to the faculties of pedagogy or teachers colleges, but to newly founded institutes of educational sciences (ICEs), which would also provide the initial training of university professors (Castillejo Brull, 1982). This institutional arrangement followed the established civil service hierarchy, consolidating the administrative status of school teacher training in a way closer to that of university professors than of primary school teachers.

The overcrowded ICEs did not have the necessary resources for hiring good professors, creating structural links with the schools, arranging and supervising the students' practica, or rewarding the work of the practica's tutors (Castillejo Brull, 1982; Catalán & Forteza, 2011). As the practica were not really supervised, they were skipped by many students, who got them approved by friend teachers. As private schools were allowed to hire teaching staff without a CAP, it became a prerequisite merely for the civil service entrance exams. Furthermore, the courses became the place for a clash of cultures, where modern, young, scientific-oriented academics encountered badly paid beginners or old professors of the teacher colleges, heirs of a normative-conservative pedagogical tradition directed mainly at primary education. The poor reputation of the courses was unavoidable and lasted until the end of the model in 2009, even if the efforts of the ICEs led to many improvements.[7]

The 1990 reform increased the compulsory schooling age to 16 years, and brought more socio-economic and cultural diversity into secondary school.[8] However, none of the belated SSTT reform proposals (TED, CCP) were implemented. The reform brought in under the Bologna aegis could be understood primarily as a systemic answer to this new situation under the disguise of a European Reform (Catalán & Forteza, 2011).

The Reasons for Bologna and SSTT Reform

The diagnosis of German higher education that led Minister Jürgen Rüttgers to sign the Sorbonne Joint Declaration of 1998, which preceded the EHEA agreements, pointed to four issues: (1) the heterogeneity of university studies across Germany; (2) the expense, length, and high drop-out ratio of German university studies (Lewin, 1999; Minks & Schaeper, 2002; Reissert & Marziszewski, 1987);[9] which was related to (3) the necessity of increasing the competitiveness of German industry in a globalized market through the production of qualified workers; and (4) attracting better students from abroad, increasing the appeal of German universities (Winter, 2009).[10]

So, for instance, in 1952 the Kultusminister Konferenz suggested for school teacher training a study of two or three majors/minors of specialization – for instance, Philosophy and German and Greek Philology, or History paired with Geography – for eight semesters. However, in 1966 more than 50 per cent of the students needed more than thirteen semesters for finishing (Bölling, 1983; Kath, Oehler, & Reichwein, 1966, p. 142).

Although the ratios of gymnasium and university students have increased steadily from the 1960s, the 2012 report of the Federal Ministry of Education and Science (BMBW) shows that the total percentage of students enrolled in German universities, including foreign students, is still under the OECD average of around 50 per cent (Autorengruppe Bildungsberichterstattung, 2012, p. 124; Bundesministerium, 1992). This enrolment rate doesn't meet the current job market's need for academics, and several reports point to the fact that between 2020 and 2024, the demand will grow to 1,360,000 academics. The teacher market is facing a similar deficit. Germany has one of Europe's lowest percentages of Primary and Secondary I teachers under thirty years old, and one of the highest percentages of those over fifty years old. In the 2003–4 academic year, the average age of German school teachers was forty-seven years. In 2011, around 44–55 per cent of teachers, depending on the kind of secondary school, were sixty or older. The Council of the Education Ministers of the Länder (KMK) estimates that by 2015, only 296,000 students will have concluded their pre-service practicum (*Refendariat*); however, 371,000 teachers will be needed, leaving a negative balance of 75,000 vacant positions (Autorengruppe Bildungsberichterstattung, 2012, p. 265; KMK, 2003, p. 77; Meetz & Sprütten, 2004). Reducing the average time needed for finishing studies was, in Germany, a central objective of the Bologna implementation (Breyer, 2007; Winter, 2007).

Therefore, new programs had to be shorter, more structured, homogeneous, competitive, and should foster excellence, although all these objectives do not harmonize necessarily among them. As previously remarked for the SSTT, both the diagnosis and solutions adopted through Bologna were old. The Dahrendorf-Plan (1967) or diverse reports of the Scientific Council (Wissenschaftsrat) had already criticized the lack of practical, job-related content in most programs and suggested shorter courses of study. In Winter's words, the Bologna reform was implementing forty-year-old reform programs (Bartz, 2007; Winter, 2009).

For the Spanish educational administration and some academics, Bologna promised the improvement of educational quality in higher education. Bologna was seen as a chance or a mere excuse for advancing towards more professional, practice-oriented curriculum and for active learning under more personalized supervision, all of them old desiderata in academia. These promises were to be achieved by (1) a new system of accreditation and quality assurance for both programs and professors, (2) a substantial reduction of the student/teacher ratios that would allow for (3) a change in educational methods intended to foster a transition from knowledge-focused to competence-based formation in order to increase employability (Miguel Díaz, 2006; Pérez Álvarez, 2011; Rodríguez Fuentes, Caurcel Cara, & Ramos García, 2008; Sotelo, 2009; Viñao Frago, 2009). Since the educational reforms of the 1970s, which had the Bachelor-Master as model, the university studies were divided into a three-year *diplomatura* and two-year *licenciatura* for Humanities, Social Sciences, and Medicine, and four and five years respectively for the *ingeniería técnica* and the *ingeniería superior*. However, instead of maintaining the 3+2 or the 4–5 structure (which was perfectly in accord with Bologna's model), Spanish politicians decided to change the entire structure, fusing *diplomaturas* and *licenciaturas* and creating huge debates and fights among departments for the definition of subjects and the distribution of staff capacities (Carabaña, 2009). As stocktaking reports show, the Spanish educational system was eager to implement accreditation systems (Veiga & Amaral, 2006). Accreditation was expected to stop the disorderly growing supply of studies in the new regional universities and campuses, and to prevent departments from promoting new subjects just to assure jobs for their members. More important, accreditation was expected to impede traditional nepotism, acting as a filter for assuring minimum quality standards for all professors and researchers (Programs PEP, Academia, and Docentia). As an idealized image of Anglo-Saxon elite universities, Bologna implementation would increase resources or liberate them (with the reduction of the standard duration of the course of study) for ending overcrowding. The "practical" classes were expected to serve as a way of reforming traditional teacher-centred classes.

The Debates: Stances against Bologna

The discussion around the implementation of Bologna was very different in both countries. Although the reasons were those mentioned above, in Germany the whole discussion about Bologna was tainted by the mediocre results of the Programme for International Student Assessment (PISA, 2002), a shock which called into question the nation's self-perceptions of excellence and aroused the public opinion that educational problems were the origin and solution of the country's economic crisis (Halász, 2004; Lütgert, 2008, p. 38; Schaeper, 2008; Schratz, 2011). Therefore, even if there was an intense public discussion and some academic publications wrote about Bologna as a threat to the mythical Humboldtian university, there was no great political, social, or even academic opposition to it (Essbach, 2004; Hörisch, 2006; Nida-Rümelin, 2008; Schmoll, 2004, p. 10; Schultheis, Cousin, & Roca i Escoda, 2008).

The two-tier structure was extremely problematic for the German educational and economic systems. Legally, the right to a place of study after finishing the Bachelor should be protected. Structurally, Bologna implied the transformation of the prestigious *Diplom* and *Magister* into the Bachelor and Master titles, which were uncertain in terms of quality and professional demand. Furthermore, in Germany there were already technical universities that offered short job and and praxis-oriented courses of study, and the shortening of all university courses raised questions about differentiation among different tertiary institutions.[11]

It was also problematic for SSTT, since, for instance, a Bachelor's degree in education met no demand and wasn't recognized by the state as an accreditation leading to a defined position in the civil service. The reduction of the course of studies' standard duration put into question the traditional system of studying two different disciplines as teaching subjects, which in turn implied the reduction of versatility and employability of future teachers (Arnold & Reh, 2005; Schaeper, 2008; Winter, 2007).

The teacher training reform debates and plans were triggered by Germany's PISA results, and not by Bologna. However, Bologna became a vehicle for old reform proposals. On the other side, student teacher training became central in Bologna as reform could be used to force changes in all those courses of study related to it, such as specialization or teaching matters (Tenorth, 2007, p. 35; Thierack, 2007, p. 47). Given the two-tier structure, university schools and Wissenschaftsrat awakened again the idea of a consecutive teacher training with all the educational contents placed in a specific Master of Education, which would have been the easiest structure. The opposition of professionals and educational civil servants forced a refinement of this position, the so-called "Y model." This model – implemented by some institutions, including Ruhr-Universität Bochum, one of the largest universities in Germany – basically put the bulk of the educational contents in the Master's program, but integrated in the Bachelor some polyvalent competences useful for both future teachers and professionals in the studied fields, such as the presentation and communication of contents. Proponents of theY model stressed its flexibility, and the way it provided undecided students with opportunities to change studies and offered a quicker solution for job market fluctuations (Schaeper, 2008).[12]

However, the coalition between educational civil servants, who pushed for the reform of teacher training, and the politicians who wanted the establishment of the Bachelor-Master, defined new structures of teacher training that would serve as a model for the reform of all university studies (Winter, 2007). The two forces produced an agreement: a Bachelor-Master structure, but with an integrative model with more relevance of educational – didactic – parts. The pressure of educationalists and educational civil servants achieved a resolution of the Conference of Educational Ministers of the Länder in Quedlimburg in 2005. The agreement was possible also because the university schools realized that they needed the teacher students to maintain their staff capacity. The increased time for tutorials proposed by the Bologna plans seemed to support these hopes (Thierack, 2002; Weegen, 2004; Winter, 2007; Wissenschaftsrat, 2008).

Spanish students and professors criticized Bologna because of the risks of commercialization (privatization, pragmatism, and economization) and the consistent obliteration of humanities and social sciences the plan induced. They feared bureaucratization, the burden of the accreditation process, and the imposition of new teaching methodologies based on a "stupid psycho-pedagogic jabberwocky." They also questioned the imposition of class attendance, which by the existing scholarship system amounted to an economic segregation of those students working to pay their fees, and predicted a quality decrease as result of the time reduction (Viñao Frago, 2009, p. 103).

However, the bigger resistances had to do precisely with the Master of Secondary Education. At the onset of the negotiations about the implementation of the two-tier Bologna structure, a debate came out in Spanish newspapers and journals about the need for pedagogic (educational) knowledge among future secondary school teachers and the focus on competences instead of on the (now endangered) content (Gimeno, 2008). Diverse corporations aired their frustrations about the CAP. The reduction of the five-year *licenciatura* to four-year Bachelor (*grado*, in the Spanish nomenclature) put many jobs at risk in different university departments, in particular those of the humanities and social sciences, where faculty members did not have clear professional prospects other than secondary school teaching. These criticisms joined a pre-existing conservative discourse which attacked the comprehensive educational reforms of the 1990s that made secondary education compulsory until sixteen years of age. Conservative critics and university departments blamed in particular the introduction of constructivist pedagogical principles (which never happened) and the new curricular focus on competences, and "pedagogization" in general, for the reduction of knowledge and discipline among secondary school students. They also warned about the repetition of the phenomenon at the universities. These criticisms were also answers to progressive movements' desire to eliminate the old privileged status of the Instituto (secondary school) chair and replace it with a new unified administrative category for all primary and secondary teachers. In fact, the anti-comprehensive policies discourse was decisively driven by the old Instituto chairs (secondary school professors), who were against the relegation implicit in their administrative union with other school teachers.

Although in Germany the need for educational science at the universities is still questioned by some authors, the debates never became as aggressive as in Spain. There, newspaper articles denounced the uselessness of, or even the damage caused by, "pedagogy" for secondary school teaching (Berg et al., 2004, p. 160).[13] These articles proposed an on-site didactic-educational SSTT that would take place during a practicum similar to that of medical students, which would have meant a total and expensive restructuring of the SSTT system (Vilches & Gil-Pérez, 2010). The educational budget met the new "Bologna" needs with no new funds. The campaign was successful and the humanities and social sciences schools took control of the future school teacher training Master. The negotiation was led at the national level by the Conference of Rectors, the Conference of Deans and Directors of University Schools, national and regional educational and research civil servants (Instituto Superior de Formación del Profesorado), and the National Accreditation Agency (ANECA). General professional associations (not teachers associations but, for instance, the Consejo General de Colegios de Doctores y Licenciados en Filosofía y Letras y Ciencias) and labour unions took only ancillary roles in the negotiations (Tribó i Traveria, 2006).[14] The second round of negotiations took place at the level of the Autonomous Regions and within the universities; the Schools of Education did not have representation (Catalán & Forteza, 2011).

Although there is no official European agreement about the duration and credits of the Masters, the Spanish consultative bodies adopted implicitly a structure of 300 ECTS, 240 for the Bachelor and 60 for the Master (4+1 years).[15] Criticisms of this conception, even from the accreditation agency, did not modify the scheme (Haug, 2009). In fact, the transformation of the SSTT Master into an integrated system could have been easy, introducing the educational and didactic contents as free credits or optional subjects. However, such a degree of interdisciplinarity would have been completely new for Spanish universities. Structural inertia, the poor reputation of educational studies, and the opposition of university schools that defended their disciplines and their role as producers of specialized researchers explain the paucity of the mentions of integrated models in the debate.

Exogenous Determinants: Civil Service Entrance Exams

A restrictive definition of educational policy as affecting only training and education systems leads necessarily to partial reforms (Luzzatto & Moscati, 2005). Consideration of environmental factors or the *Umwelt* is necessary for implementing effective reforms, as is consideration of the job selection and hiring processes graduates will face. In both countries, the recruiting of teachers for the civil service (in the case of Germany, the immense majority of the job market) is completely different. Although falling under the Länder governments' authority, the *Staatsexamen* required for passing to the second phase of a teacher training program and entrance into the civil service were closely linked within the process of teacher formation. Therefore, in Germany, the adoption of the two-tier structure created a problem for achieving the qualifications and means for entering the civil service. The eventual elimination of the *Staatsexam* would have transferred to the universities of a bulk of the administrative work and responsibility for civil service recruitment. It would have also required increased control over the students (such as measuring attendance), which runs against the traditional habitus for managing individual learning of German university students. It is not surprising that the relation of the Bachelor-Master studies to the *Staatsexam* was one of the most problematic and debated issues of the reform. The complexity of the coordination between the new phases, the definition of a more stringent curriculum (*Modularisierung*), and the *Staatsexam* delayed the introduction of the Bachelor-Master in the courses of study that culminated with a *Staatsexam* (Arnold & Reh, 2005; Thierack, 2007, p. 57).

The training reforms haven't affected the Spanish system of access to national secondary school service through an *oposición*, an exam on pre-established themes that must be memorized and recited in front of a jury. Traditionally, the CAP was fully disentangled from the *oposición* and the places for preparing for these exams were private schools, not the universities. However, this separation heavily affects the initial training, maintaining the inertia of the system. The *oposición* reinforces the habits of rote learning and the traditional lecture-centred teaching styles. It postpones the students' work and interest from the Master program to a remote future, moulding the students' expectancies and transforming the Master into a mere formality to overcome. It also deprives professors and practica tutors of selection responsibility, allowing them to lower their requirements and standards for the students and themselves. This would be much in line with the Bologna process, as one of its values is the viability or efficacy of the studies, which implies adapting the contents to permit an average student to finish the studies in the pre-established time (Viñao and Frago, 2009, p. 111).

Furthermore, in the Bachelor-Master, an integrated selection process would imply *numerus clausus* and a decrease in the enrolment numbers adequate to meet the demands of the market. This would mean a decrease of income for the universities and of the required work-hours for the university departments involved. For sure, the *oposición* is one of the elements that run against reform and a feature that will continue conferring on the Spanish system its singular character (Catalán & Forteza, 2011). Its survival bears witness to the difficulties of reforming single subsystems or even of vast reforms that imply transformations in curriculum or a system's structure and power relations (Luzzatto & Moscati, 2005).

New Divergences: Structures

The implementation of Bologna in Germany caused a continuous stream of changes in teacher training in recent years. The federal constitution, university autonomy, and Institute-University structures have resulted in diversity and hybrid structural arrangements for the training of teachers. As examples, three different states – from north and south, west and east, Protestant and Catholic – show striking differences.

Hamburg established the Bachelor and M.Ed. (3+2 years) for all teachers in the winter-semester of 2007/8. The Bachelor comprises two specialization disciplines and educational science, plus two practica. The Master's degrees offered from the winter-semester of 2011/12 are specialized in the different kind of schools. One semester of the Master's is devoted to a practicum tutored by the university and the *Landesinstitut für Lehrerbildung und Schulentwicklung*. The Master's exam is followed by eighteen months of pre-service practicum (*Refendariat*). Entering the civil service requires passing a *Staatsexam* after the *Refendariat*. The Landesinstitut offers diverse aids throughout the initial phase of service and promotes compulsory continuous education.

Rostock and Greifswald Universities from Mecklenburg-Western Pomerania ceased implementation of the Bachelor and Master after they defined a binding and articulate curriculum or "modularization." Their teacher training program lasts ten semesters. All school teacher trainees study two teaching matters, worth 105 ECTS (European Credit Transfer and Accumulation System points) each for Gymnasium teachers and 90 ECTS each for the future teachers at *Regionalschulen*. All trainees study specific didactics (15 ECTS) and educational science (30 ECTS), plus one social practicum (60 ECTS) and two school practica (15 ECTS each), and must complete a final research project (15 ECTS). The study finishes with the *Staatsexam*. The second *Staatsexam* follows a two-year practicum (*Refendariat*) (Ministerium, 2000).

Bavaria has adopted an in-between structure that combines Bachelor and Master with the *Staastexam*, except for the formation of vocational teachers, which follows a Bachelor-Master structure (as also found in Hessen or Baden). The future *Hauptschullehrer* has to study educational science, specific didactics, and one discipline for teaching subjects, while future gymnasium and *Realschule* teachers need to learn a given combination of two disciplines as future teaching subjects, such as mathematics paired with physics. Some of the practica need to be done even before the beginning of studies. The Bachelor exam and the first *Staatsexam* (*esrten Lehramtprüfung*) allow access to the Master.

The new differentiation among SSTT structures at different federal states is one of the most salient outcomes of the implementation of the EHEA agreements in Germany. A detailed study of every case seems impossible.[16]

In Spain, the idea of Bologna as a plan that will shorten university studies (and therefore the five-year limit) and the pressure on the universities to maintain the bulk of studies in the Bachelor resulted in a general adoption of a strong four-year Bachelor (240 ECTS) plus a one-year weak Master structure (60 ECTS). The traditional tendency for uniformity and a reaction to the previous deregulated Masters degrees is apparent in the general establishment of a one-year Master, irrespective of the objectives and subjects of the program. The semi-professional M.Ed. was designed with the same length as a continuing education or specialization Master. In fact, the Helsinki Agreement (2003) considered 60 ECTS as an option only for those Masters that continued directly after a Bachelor, not for an M.Ed. with educational and didactical contents. The M.Ed. can be likened to pouring the old wine of the CAPs into the new bottle of an MA (Nebot, 2009).

New governance, but also the refusal to ascribe all SSTT Masters to the Schools of Education, has created administrative diversity among the Masters depending on whether they are housed within education schools, the old Institutos de Ciencias de la Educación, or ad hoc public or private centres, such as the Centro de Formación Avanzada e Innovación Educativa in León.

Curriculum

The Minimal Content Decree requires that SSTT Masters in Spain offer 60 ECTS divided into three blocks: 12 credits for general educational contents,[17] a specific didactic module of 24 credits,[18] and the practicum of 60 credits which includes the completion of a final research project (Escudero Muñoz, 2009b). The decrees regulating the minimal contents in Spanish universities created a great degree of formal curriculum isomorphism throughout Spanish universities. However, the decrees permit an eventual extension of contents and of credits, and some autonomous regions have authorized Postgraduate Official Programs without a previous evaluation or accreditation from regional or national agencies. These facts open the possibility for differentiation among Spanish SSTT Masters (Haug, 2009, p. 14).

The above-mentioned structural differences of the teacher training courses across Germany, which impeded mobility and were unequal in their exigencies, forced the Council of the Education Ministers of the Länder to agree in 2004 to "Educational Science Standards for Teacher Training" (Standards für die Lehrerbildung: Bildungswissenschaften) and in 2008 to "The Contents of the Teaching Matters and the Specific Didactics to Be Required in All Länder" (Ländergemeinsame inhaltliche Anforderungen für die Fachwissenschaften und Fachdidaktiken in der Lehrerinnen und Lehrerbildung). The force of these regulations is increased, as certain "frame conditions" must be met for the accreditation of the teacher training programs (KMK, 2008a, 2008b, 2010). Empirical studies have found a high degree of diversity in the implementations and effects of the reforms, although studies on other disciplines cast doubt upon the impact of reforms in curricula (Winter, 2011, p. 22).

However, in Germany, the main curricular standardization process – the "modularization" – coincided with, but was not related to, Bologna and the introduction of a two-tier structure. Bologna acted as a sort of subterfuge or smokescreen to allow educational civil servants to impose upon the universities a stringent and clear curriculum determined by professional, scientific, and didactic priorities. Bologna's implementation became a homogenizing or standardization process as it ran against the traditional "Humboldtian" freedom of the Institute-University chairs in defining the curriculum in line with their research agenda (Winter, 2007). However, it is doubtful that these institutions have changed their procedures overnight for the sake of complying with exogenous norms.

At any rate, as the structures of programs remain very different among German Länder, the requirements and contents also remain necessarily diverse. It is not surprising that the professional association Verband Bildung und Erziehung argued in January 2011 for greater standardization and homogenization, claiming that "federalism and Bologna had transformed teacher training into chaos" (Auding, 2011).

The harmonization of competences offered by Spanish and German universities is made difficult by structural differences in the countries' university systems. In Spain, the system is dominated by *departamentos* with disciplinarian conceptions of knowledge, whereas in Germany, in a system led by chairs, a research-based curriculum prevails; this makes difficult the understanding, definition, distribution, and assignment of competences in a transferable way. It is uncertain if teaching staff in both countries are prepared and willing to adapt their habits to a focus on competences, which require more time to teach and assess (Nebot, 2009; Paricio, 2007).

The disciplinarian character of Spanish academic culture and the short duration of the M.Ed. makes implausible the transformation of methodologies and adoption of an active role by secondary school teacher trainees envisaged by Escudero Muñoz (2009a). The top-down substitution of contents with competences as the main educational objectives does not necessarily lead to a change in students' and professors' habits (Mora & Vidal, 2005; VIII Foro ANECA, 2007). Whatever the degree of homogenization or standardization within each country might be, a cursory comparison of Rostock's curriculum with the one established by the Spanish Minimum Contents Decree makes it appear likely that the curricular differences between Germany and Spain will be upheld (Universität Rostock, 2012).

The Practicum

Perhaps the main differences between both systems are the number, duration, and meaning of practica. Under the CAP system, the practicum was the weakest link in Spanish initial SSTT. The economic, administrative, and intellectual conditions of the implementation of the Master explain its ongoing problems, with the poor organization of the practicum being one of the most commonly cited issues (Catalán & Forteza, 2011). In fact, the establishment of Bologna without budget changes can be linked to the failure of the organization of the practicum, as they are generally coordinated by professors who do not receive adequate compensation. It is not surprising that, in particular, the lack of coordination between academic and practicum supervisors or tutors and program content has been criticized. The neglect of the practica was a logical consequence of the traditional disregard for praxis found in the system's academic culture. In the practicum of pedagogy, which we can use as a proxy here, the students still reject, in a very high proportion, the assessment and marking of the workshops intended to reflect on the practicum. Leniency on the practicum's assessments, which was normal in the old CAP system, persists in the new Master and shows the lack of regard for practical matters (Armengol Asparó et al., 2011, p. 96; González Riaño & Hevia Artime, 2011, pp. 214, 223).

In Germany, differences in the number and duration of the practica have been a matter of concern for researchers, students, and professional associations. The increase in the number of practica in the Bachelor program is derided in some German media as "the pretention of practica." For example, in the first practicum, the third-semester trainees aren't significantly older than secondary school students, and trainees can't teach classes, only attend and observe them. The increasing number of practica in the Bachelor and Master has heightened the pressure placed on practica schools and tutors, which may be expected to handle many students during one course. As in Spain, in Germany one of the more criticized aspects is the lack of organizational and curricular coordination between universities and schools (and in Germany also, a lack of coordination with the *Studienseminare*) (Auding, 2011; Breyer, 2007; Schaeper, 2008, p. 31; Schubarth, 2007, p. 23).

Problems

The analysis of the changes introduced by Bologna in both countries should close with an overview on some of the problems that will force a new reform. As the problems in each country remain different, it is likely that the solutions will remain different.

In both countries, students complain about the shortcomings of the didactic-educational content, the redundant coverage of specialization knowledge or teaching matters, and the general lack of curricular and organizational connections between their initial training and educational praxis (González Sanmamed & Fuentes Abeledo, 2011, p. 57). German *Lehramt* students argue for more attention and respect, and for a fairer distribution of time among the different subjects (Arnold & Reh, 2005).

Socio-Economic Segregation and Numerus Clausus

The compression of program content into a shorter period of time and its effects on obtaining scholarships, the profusion of exams, and the exigency of attendance could lead to increased socio-economic and cultural segregation, strengthening the socio-economic bias found in universities. These developments threaten principles of meritocracy and the right to education, and run counter to Bologna's objective of increasing the numbers of well-trained academics for the job market. There is no agreement about the future socio-economic consequences of the establishment of the two-tier structure in Germany. Kiuppis and Waldow (2008) do not perceive a risk that the break between Bachelor and Master could result in a socio-economic discrimination – the Bachelor being the frontier between mass and elite education – because "open access to higher education for all holders of an academic secondary school certificate (*Abitur*)" is a central myth of the German educational system (Ash, 2006; Witte et al., 2004). However, these fears are being realized in Spain, as the conservative ministry – citing the financial crisis – increased the Masters fees geometrically for the 2012–13 academic year.[19] In Germany, the restrictions have another character; the increased demand, the success in reducing the duration of programs, and the economic problems led some universities and Länder to establish phoniatric or psychological tests as prerequisites for entry (Dietz, 2008; Kassel, 2008; Kühne, 2012).

'Schoolization' of Higher Education

In Germany, the "Modularisierung" of programs has deprived students of much responsibility and freedom in choosing and designing personalized courses of study, and has imposed upon them study rhythms that were foreign to German universities. Even if the total workload and time devoted to study have not substantially increased as a result of the reform, the new structures and assessment culture emphasized in both Germany and Spain have led to a greater number of assessments and different subjects in every semester. German students, particularly those in Bachelor programs, have to face now – as is traditional in Spain – at least five or six exams or essays every semester, a workload that doesn't allow for individual reflection and critical thinking. All these changes have modified the students' approach to knowledge, learning styles, and intellectual habitus, producing a *Verschulung* or "schoolization" of university (Bargel, 2011; Multrus, Ramm, & Bargel, 2010; Winter, 2011, p. 28). Learning for the exam and considering studies as an obstacle to be overcome – and not as a space for acquiring competences or knowledge, achieving personal growth, and developing critical thinking skills – are in Germany, as is already the case in Spain, some of the signs of this "schoolization." As in many German federal states, the Bachelor marks can be crucial for entering the Master, so another effect of these reforms is that the new structure is fostering a culture of competition instead of the cooperative spirit needed for professional life.[20]

In the Spanish case, time pressure increases because – although secondary school and Bachelor programs do not provide preparation for any scientific work, and the Master is the students' first exposure to pedagogical knowledge and problems – they are asked to work on a short research project on educational issues, to be presented directly after the second semester of the Master's program.

In Germany, the professional qualification earned in the Bachelor's program did not meet any demand, as there was neither a civil service category for it nor the political will to create one. However, even if its status is questioned, the Bachelor in Education creates a new devaluated professional category (teachers' assistants) that could open the way to a diversification of professional hierarchies and the de-professionalization of teaching (Arnold & Reh, 2005).

In Spain, the reform has missed the opportunity to achieve a closer link between the studies, the practica, and the professional life.[21] Different voices have suggested the necessity to include in the Master experienced secondary school teachers with general and specific didactic knowledge (Vilches & Gil-Pérez, 2010). A solution would be to contract part-time *Asociados* professors with the required profile. The Master for SSTT preserves the different civil-service hierarchies, a division that has made the professionalization difficult.

Mobility

The original idea that triggered the Bologna process was the need to achieve more homogeneous and standardized curricula and structures in higher education to increase the "transferability" and mobility of students, professors, and workforces within Europe. The literature, however, has warned about the increasing difficulties for students, who now must pursue a more stringent course of study if transferring universities (Witte, 2004). The statistical data is inconclusive and shows a differentiated panorama, as the increasing numbers of German students abroad have more to do with *numerus clausus* in German universities or are related with studies that have a strong international character such as philology, law, or economics. On the other side, if the number of foreign students who matriculated in Germany in 2010 doubled the figure of 2006, this increase took place mostly at the *Fachhochschulen* (polytechnics), while the biggest contingent of foreign students are from China and Eastern Europe (Bundesministerium, 2010). Student teacher trainees were always reluctant to study abroad and with good reason, as teaching is so culturally and linguistically determined that the market is necessarily fragmented.

The problem of lack of transferability remains in Germany. The Ministers of Education Council (KMK) had to issue a rule for the mutual recognition of Bachelor and Master programs among German states. However, the ongoing criticisms from professional associations show that the problems persist (KMK, 2005).

Conclusion

The implementation of the measures proposed to shape the European Higher Education Area, rather than increasing the homogeneity or isomorphism of the German and Spanish SSTT, has maintained the differences across both countries. Furthermore, in the case of Germany, it has led to "immense diversity" in the educational structures and therefore the requirements and contents between the different Länder (Schaeper, 2008, p. 34). In both countries, the resultant SSTT systems represent not an adaptation of Anglo-Saxon or European models, but a proper creation of the German and Spanish agents. In their political interplay, these agents use the argument of common or shared educational culture and ideology to defend and advance different positions. Examples of this include the rhetorical use of the myths of Europe and the requirements for its construction, of elite Humboldt and Anglo-Saxon universities, or of common educational values (Haug, 2009). Structural, socio-economic, and cultural differences between both countries – that is, different forms of understanding and answering similar challenges – explain the maintenance of the heterogeneity of the German and Spanish SSTT systems. These results were foreseeable, as the open method of coordination, the multilayered decision and implementation instances, and the multiplicity, vagueness, and even contradiction of the objectives met in each country divergent structural-institutional starting points, inertias, and cultures, which introduced much contingency in the process (Cerych & Sabatier, 1986, p. 14; Veiga & Amaral, 2006).

The implementation of Bologna has brought, directly or indirectly, some undesired effects. Contrary to the Bologna promises of fostering the mobility of students and workers within Europe, the mobility of school teacher trainees and teachers remains or has become more difficult within Germany. The compression of the standard duration of school teacher training and its modularization are, plausibly, changing the study and intellectual habits of German students, producing what has been called the "schoolization" of the German university. Athough planned to increase the number of university-trained people as an economic indicator, the division into Bachelor and Master may actually lead to a reduction in enrolments and research, increasing socioeconomic segregation in Spain.

NOTES

1 For a contrasting vision, see A. Veiga, Amaral, A., & Mendes, A., Implementing Bologna in Southern European Countries: Comparative Analysis of Some Research Findings, *Education for Chemical Engineers, 3* (2008), 47–56.
2 For discussion of the role of the states in top-down policy imposition, see G. Krücken, The Europeanization of Higher Education and the Bachelor/Master Reform: Some Lessons from the German Case, *Management Revue – The International Review of Management Studies,* 18 (2) (2007), 187–203. For the myths of Humboldt and Anglo-Saxon Elite Universities, see Ash (2006).
3 Hübner (1994) maintains that "in particular, for teacher training," there was no agreement in the KMK (p. 153).
4 The university formation of SST (*Gymnasiallehrer*) is perhaps the only idea in this history that really originated in Humboldt. See F. K. Ringer, *The Decline of the German Mandarins* (Cambridge, MA: Harvard University Press, 1969).
5 For a critical vision of the process, see G. Geißler, *Eingliederung der Lehrerbildung an der Universität* (Weinheim, Germany: Beltz, 1973).
6 *Ley General de Educación de 1970. Orden Ministerial de 8 de julio de 1971. Orden Ministerial de 25 mayo de 1972.*
7 The assessments of the students were devastating; see J. L. García et al., La Profesión Docente, in J. L García (Ed.), *Elementos para un Diagnóstico del Sistema Educativo Español 1997. Informe Global* (Madrid: MEC-INCE, 1998); J. Esteve, *La Formación Inicial de los Profesores de Secundaria* (Barcelona, Spain: Arie, 1997), 109–123; I. González Gallego, Una Formación "Invertebrada" la de ser Profesor, in F. de Vicente (Ed.), *El*

Profesorado y los Retos del Sistema Educativo Actual (Madrid: Instituto Superior de Formación del Profesorado, 2005), 205–260; Castillejo Brull (1982).

8 Real Decreto 1692/1995.

9 See H. Griesbach et al., *Studienabbruch* (Hanover, Germany: HIS, 1992). Griesbach et al. maintain that until 1992, it grew up to 27%.

10 See also: DGfE, *Bericht und Empfehlungen der Kommission zur Einführung neuer Studiengänge und Abschlüsse – Bachelor of Arts, Master of Arts (BA, MA) – im Fach Erziehungswissenschaft*. http://www.dgfe.de/fileadmin/OrdnerRedakteure/Stellungnahmen/1999_10_BAMASTR.pdf

11 Some interpret in this sense article 12 of the German constitution (*Grundgesetz*). https://www.btg-bestellservice.de/pdf/10060000.pdf. Kiuppis & Waldow (2008). In Germany, the students don't conceive the Bachelor as a final study and most continue with the Master. Winter (2011).

12 The OECD also proposed a consecutive model: OECD (2005).

13 Some examples: J. L. Pardo, La Descomposición de la Universidad, *El País*, 10 November 2008; Facultad de Filosofía de la UCM, Facultad de Filosofía de la UCM contra el Master, *El País*, 3 November 2008; R. Moreno, Algunos Males del Sistema Educativo, *El País*, 4 December 2008; F. Carreras, Plastilina en la Universidad, *La Vanguardia*, 29 May 2008; A. Pérez Reverte, Subvenciones, Maestros y Psicopedagilipollas, *XL Semanal*, 8 March 2008, 1.064.

14 For the negotiation of the Bachelor, see Viñao Frago (2009).

15 Real Decreto 1393/2007, 29 October, and Orden ECI/3858/2007, 27 December.

16 A general overview can be found at Kultusministerien, Deutscher Bildungsserver, http://www.bildungsserver.de/Kultusministerien-580.html

17 Which includes the following subjects: learning and personality development; educational processes and contexts; and society, family, and school.

18 Including: complements to disciplinary formation, learning and teaching the subject matter, and teaching innovation and introduction to educational research. It deals, among other things, with the history of the disciplines or of the educational system.

19 Real Decreto-Ley 14/2012

20 Some diagnoses and solutions: B. Fleckenstein, Aspekte der Lehr-Lern-Beziehung im modularisierten Studiensystem, in G. Bechthold and P. S. Helferich (Eds.), *Generation Bologna: Neue Herausforderungen am Übergang*

Schule – Hochschule (Bielefeld, Germany: Bertelsmann, 2008), 37–46; B. Caputa-Wiessner, Die Erfahrungen der Reform, ibid., 59–63; M. Ebert, Lernen, Beurteilen und Prüfen, in Hochschulrektorenkonferenz (Ed.), *Von Bologna nach Quedlinburg – Die Reform des Lehramtsstudiums in Deutschland* (Bonn, Germany: Hochschulrektorenkonferenz, 2007), 142–145.

21 The need of continuously remembering Schulman, for instance, is an indicator for this problem. See González Sanmamed, M., & Fuentes Abeledo, E. (2011), p. 52.

14 The Bologna Process and Teacher Education Reforms in Eastern Europe: The Changing Policy Terrain in Ukraine

BENJAMIN KUTSYURUBA

The launch of the Bologna Process marked a new era in higher education reforms in Europe. The reorganization, sometimes called "the most profound revolution in European higher education" (McMurtrie, 2006, p. A39), is well under way with the commitment of forty-seven signatory countries across the European continent to create an integrated European Higher Education Area (EHEA). However, there is no uniform pace for countries to implement the proposed changes; while countries with established systems of higher education, such as Italy, Spain, and Germany, are taking a longer time, most of the former Eastern Bloc countries have enthusiastically embraced reforms (Charbonneau, 2009). In Börzel's (2003) terms, there exist Bologna leaders and laggards. Although Ukraine had joined the Bologna Process only in 2005, it quickly became one of the leaders in this movement among Eastern European countries.

As in other Eastern European countries, the education system in Ukraine has been caught in an era of rapid transformation over the last two decades. Since the collapse of the former USSR, the system of education has undergone significant changes, wherein "the vector of changes focused on transition from the 'Soviet school' model to the democratic European one" (Ministry of Education of Ukraine, 1999, p. 3). The system of education was one of the first social spheres that underwent rapid and radical transformations after the country gained independence. Education, like the Ukrainian society in general, was caught amidst a transition from totalitarian Marxist-Leninist ideology to democracy and pluralism. The new realities required profound educational reforms, including the structural organization of secondary schools, universities, curricula, and teacher and educational administrator training programs at all levels (Koshmanova & Ravchyna, 2008). The Bologna

Process became embraced by the Ukrainian government as one of the mechanisms to achieve this goal. As officially reported to the UNESCO European Centre for Higher Education, the top priorities of education policy in Ukraine have been further development of the national education system, its adjustment to a new economy, and its integration into the European and global community (Kremen & Nikolajenko, 2006).

Since the announcement about Ukraine's intention to sign the protocol to join the Bologna Declaration in 2005, European and Ukrainian educators became concerned about the impact of the Bologna Process on the country's higher education system and its integration with EHEA (Artyomenko, 2005; Kotmalyova, 2006). This marked the start of the major reforms in higher education in Ukraine and its commitment to an international effort to harmonize higher education by redesigning the curriculum, switching to a three-cycle degree structure, and submitting to cross-national mechanisms of quality assurance (Clement, McAlpine, & Waeytens, 2004; Kremen & Nikolajenko, 2006).

As Ukraine seems to be one of the most active participants in the implementation of Bologna Process provisions, of special interest is the transition to the democratic European system and the impact of the Bologna Accord on the policy framework related to teacher education. Uniquely positioned at the crossroads between the higher education and primary and secondary education systems, teacher education is significantly affected by transformations and reforms pertaining to both areas. Therefore, the focus of this chapter is twofold: (1) to examine the history, objectives, achievements, and challenges of the Bologna Process implementation in Ukraine; and (2) to examine the impact of the process on policy frameworks guiding teacher education. Through the analysis of the extant literature consisting of academic research, evaluations, conceptual reviews, government policies and statutes, and official reports on the impact of the Bologna Process on the education system in Ukraine, this chapter outlines the achievements and challenges of educational reforms and posits that greater attention to the *actual* versus *stated* outcomes of Bologna-initiated policies and reforms in teacher education is needed.

Context of the Bologna Process

The frameworks of globalization and internationalization have had an impact on academic programs, institutions, innovations, and practices around the world. In regard to Europe, Altbach and Knight (2007) argued that the trend of European regional integration was a catalyst for the harmonization developments which underlie the Bologna Process. Echoing this sentiment, Prado Yepes (2007) argued that the process was created under a framework of a "new regionalism" paradigm, a multi-dimensional form of integration (pp. 83–92). Furthermore, the common development of higher education required member nations to commit to a common frame of reference aimed at improving external recognition and facilitating student mobility and employability. Overall, the Bologna Process is viewed as a platform for transnational communication (Voegtle, Knill, & Dobbins, 2011) and an unprecedented forum for countries to learn from each other and make their systems more comparable and compatible in a voluntary way (Zgaga, 2009). The breadth of higher education activity that the Bologna Process covers is great, spanning, among other things, the architecture of qualifications through to the doctorate level (thus incorporating qualifications frameworks, credits, and learning outcomes) as well as notions of institutional autonomy, student involvement, higher education as a public good, and lifelong learning (Birtwistle, 2009).

Focusing on the implications of this international agreement, Floud (2006) noted that the aims of the Bologna Process are to expand access to higher education to more of the European population, to better prepare students for the labour market, to promote lifelong learning, to attract increasing numbers of non-European students, and to provide a fundamental underpinning to European democracy. Furthermore, establishing and implementing the Bologna Accord was a way to give European universities more autonomy from their governments. The arguments that permeate the process stress the importance of strong, diverse, adequately funded, autonomous, and accountable institutions that continuously adapt to changing needs, society's demands, and advances in scientific knowledge (Zgaga, 2009).

Implementation of the Bologna Process

A number of analyses have documented educational reforms prompted by the Bologna Process and the ways its principles have been adopted by and implemented in the various signatory countries (Curaj et al., 2012). The variability in implementation mainly exists due to the fact that the Bologna Process is not endowed with legal obligations. In other words, the signatory countries are not bound by any conditionalities or legal requirements and are encouraged to implement the Bologna policies for the sake of the benefits of cooperation and the future benefits of the expected EHEA outcome (Luchinskaya & Ovchynnikova, 2011). Furthermore, the "colourful rainbow" of varieties among European higher education systems constitutes segments which can become barriers to faster and more efficient implementation of new higher education philosophy proposed by Bologna (Zgaga, 2009, p. 98).

Lažetić (2010) argued that the voluntary nature of the Bologna Process leads to uneven implementation. Specifically, the Bologna Process seeks consensus about policy formation at the European level, but leaves the implementation to nation states and institutions, which are only indirectly involved in policy formation. He concluded that a key challenge of the process is keeping up the political momentum and interest of political leadership and policy entrepreneurs for the reform process, while preventing it from becoming overly bureaucratic. Scholars noted evidence of convergence of higher education policies, especially in terms of the "architecture" of higher education systems (e.g., degree structures) and the use of specific policy instruments (such as national quality assurance and accreditation schemes) (Elken et al., 2010). However, the Bologna Process independent assessment (Westerheijden et al., 2010), the *Trends* reports by the European University Association, Bologna stocktaking reports, and Eurydice reports indicate the persisting diversity in higher education systems (Elken et al., 2010). This diversity exists due to a convergence-diversity nexus and the differences in the national historical and cultural contexts, goal ambiguity, and bottom-heaviness of higher education institutions (Huisman, 2009). Heinze and Knill (2008) argued about the impact of cultural, institutional, and socio-economic factors on higher education systems and adoption of the Bologna Process. Examining how country-specific factors affect the harmonization of national policies over time, they concluded that the more dissimilar the cultural, institutional, and socio-economic characteristics of countries, the less convergence between them in adopting and implementing the Bologna Process. Using the *Trends V* report, which analysed the nature and extent of implementation of the Bologna reforms, Birtwistle (2009) noted a shift in focus away from governmental actions to implementation within institutions.

Blass (2012) voiced concerns in his analysis of the sustainability of the Bologna Process, particularly within the context of the current global financial crisis. He found that issues such as the upholding of academic freedom, institutional autonomy, and regional academic values are resulting in uneven implementation and could jeopardize the future of the Bologna Process. In addition, he noted, the global financial crisis, which resulted in EU members being bailed out of bankruptcy and reducing their spending on education, has jeopardized the successful implementation of the Bologna Process, and concluded that its overall impact on institutions of higher education has been weak. Similar sentiments about the constraints of financing higher education in times of financial crisis were mentioned in the most recent Eurydice network implementation report of the Bologna Process (EACEA, 2012a). According to this report, the implementation process has been uneven due to the different contexts, orientations, funding schemes, and demographics of each signatory nation. A major recommendation is that the implementation process be streamlined and enhanced, particularly because the goal of providing equal chances for all students has not yet been achieved. As implementation structures, approaches, accomplishments, and challenges tend to be context-specific for different signatory countries, we will now turn to the discussion of the impact of the Bologna Process in Ukraine.

Bologna Process Policy Implementation in Ukraine

According to the then-minister of education, Nikolayenko, the implementation of Bologna underpinnings in Ukraine revolved around the following basic aspects of the program: quality assurance (QA), a three-cycle system of education, and the qualifications framework (QF) in the EHEA. Important steps in implementing the regulations of the Bologna Process have been undertaken in the higher education system of Ukraine; there was also an action plan prepared for their implementation up to 2010 (Nikolayenko, 2007). Namely, the Ukrainian government established the Bologna Follow-Up Interdepartmental Commission, which reports to the Ministry of Education. With the support of the government structures, the work of the National Team of Bologna Promoters and the Ministry of Education and Science was directed at the formation and implementation of the National Qualifications Framework (NQF) and alignment of its constituents with the QF in the EHEA.

According to the 2009 *Bologna National Report Ukraine,* 2009 *Bologna Stocktaking Report* (BSR), and 2010 European Neighbourhood Policy implementation report (European Commission, 2011c), other key developments in Ukraine since 2005 have included the following: (a) amendments to the law on higher education encompassed key aspects of the Bologna Process, including implementing the three-cycle system, enhancing university autonomy, and facilitating student involvement in university governance, as well as providing a legal basis for external assessments; (b) Ukraine has become a governmental member of the European Quality Assurance Register (EQAR); (c) a system of ranking Ukrainian higher education institutions (HEIs) of Ukraine was introduced; (d) the Ukrainian Association of Student Self-government (UASS) gained membership in the European Student's Union; (e) the cabinet of ministers issued an order on diploma supplements to university degrees to better facilitate degree recognition and student mobility; and (f) most HEIs achieved the Bologna Process goals of implementing a two-cycle system, quality assurance measures, the European Credit Transfer System (ECTS), and recognition of diplomas. Other reports indicated that the benefits of implementation were evident in increased student mobility and employability and the development of autonomous learners (Kovtun & Stick, 2009).

Luchinskaya and Ovchynnikova (2011) examined the national and stocktaking reports to trace the Bologna Process policy implementation in Ukraine. According to their analysis, Ukraine had been active in some aspects of implementation and sluggish in others. For instance, the *Bologna Process Stocktaking Report* rated Ukraine's progress in the recognition of foreign degrees and implementing the ECTS as "very good" and "excellent" in 2007 and 2009 (Rauhvargers, Deane, & Pauwels, 2009). Ukraine was among the eight countries that have reached a high degree of implementation, with ECTS being applied in more than 75 per cent of their programs and higher education institutions, for the purpose of both credit transfer and accumulation, and credit points being based on both learning outcomes and student workload (EACEA, April 2012). As for the achievements in the adoption of the new degree system (two-cycle), the ratings for Ukraine, compared to other Bologna priorities, have been the highest in the 2007 and 2009 *BSR*s. The implementation of quality assurance had mixed ratings for Ukraine, as only some HEIs produce a strategy for the continuous enhancement of quality, have made arrangements for the internal approval of programs and awards, and describe their programs in terms of learning outcomes. No Ukrainian HEIs design student assessments of HEIs to measure the achievements of the learning outcomes, but all of them publish up-to-date information on the programs they offer. Ukraine also received high ratings for student involvement in quality assurance (*Bologna National Report Ukraine*, 2009).

Kwiek noted that it may seem relatively easy to change laws on higher education, especially if arguments of catching up with the West are used for promotional purposes, but changing laws is not enough to reach the objectives of the Bologna Process, although the effort may be understood in this way by many government officials (Kwiek, 2004). Therefore, it is not surprising that Ukraine has faced significant challenges with regard to the implementation of the process (Zaspa, 2008). Major challenges for Ukraine, as outlined in the 2009 *BSR* include: developing a NQF compatible with the EHEA overarching framework; introducing the innovative institutional structure, three-cycle system, and joint degrees; establishing programs for foreign students; aligning university programs with the Bologna structure; developing the national qualifications framework for lifelong learning; creating mechanisms for recognition of prior learning; implementing the Diploma Supplement in the EU/CoE/UNESCO format; creating the national quality assurance agency in compliance with European Standards and Guidelines (ESG) with the aim of European Association for Quality Assurance in Higher Education (ENQA) membership and inclusion in the EQAR; increasing outward and inward mobility; assuring portability of student grants and loans; providing equal access to higher education; adapting curricula to labour market needs; and promoting cultural values and democratic ideals.

Given the different tradition in higher education and the political and cultural context, the process of introducing the new model of tertiary education promoted by the EU partners remains challenging in the Eastern Partnership countries (GHK, 2011). The main factors affecting the implementation were the transition period and difference in the organization and structure of higher education from Western and many Eastern European countries (Zgaga, 2009). The system of higher education was centrally planned and administered under the Soviet system, had strong links with the labour market and an emphasis on science and technology, and underwent substantial reform during the post-Soviet transition (Luchinskaya & Ovchynnikova, 2011). As recent studies have shown, the results remain patchy, and implementation efforts have been complicated by significant differences in the organizational path dependence of Ukrainian universities as compared to their Western counterparts (Shaw, Chapman, & Rumyantseva, 2011, 2013).

Other analyses on Ukraine's adoption of the Bologna Process have addressed specific challenges with regard to the implementation process, and have focused on both positive and negative outcomes. In his discussion of higher education reform under the Bologna Process, Nikolayenko (2007) noted that the adoption of the process has led to increased training, creation of more scholarships, improvement in accessibility, and increased inter-university mobility within Ukraine. However, a number of problems still existed, including the need to create a system of quality assurance, the lack of provision of international mobility for students and staff, and the lack of communication between universities and employers and public associations. Similarly, weighing the pros and cons of the Bologna Process for the system of higher education in Ukraine, Goodman (2010) pointed out that participation in the Bologna Process had the potential to strengthen Ukraine's standing in Europe, promote linguistic diversity, and facilitate the goals of European integration. As for the potential negative consequences of the process, Goodman focused specifically on the dominance of English under the Bologna Process and the negative effects this may have on the Ukrainian language. Zaspa (2008) reported issues surrounding the funding of higher education institutions to implement the process, the influence of markets and privatization on the quality of professional education, and the impacts on the amount and quality of research produced by universities undergoing the transformation process.

In a recent case study on the perceptions of education practitioners and administrators of the implementation of the Bologna Process at a selected higher education institution, Kovtun and Stick (2009) highlighted the implementation shortcomings and disadvantages. These included excessive centralization of the administration, insufficient training and resources, participants' attachment to the old system, decreased quality of education, and loss of tradition. They concluded that the Bologna Process appeared to benefit the students more than the professors, through the increased mobility and employability for students and the development of autonomous learners. Lytvyn (2009), by contrast, emphasized the negative consequences of the Bologna Process on students. In particular, she discussed how many students felt that the way Ukraine was implementing the Bologna Process was disruptive to their education. Lytvyn suggested that rather than adapting the Bologna Process to fit Ukrainian standards, the Ukraine should adopt the European standards outlined in the process. Furthermore, institutions of higher education should focus on the tools of the Bologna Process instead of using existing structures to achieve its goals. She concluded that these recommendations would solve problems such as inconsistency in grading, degree recognition, and course requirements.

In the study of Ukrainian professors' perceptions of the Bologna Process, Telpukhovska (2006) found that, while many reforms were welcomed as useful and necessary, their implementation was complicated by the current economic and social conditions of the country. In their analysis of the transformation process that Ukraine was undertaking to adhere to the Bologna Process, Makogon and Orekhova (2007) argued that the adoption of the Bologna Process was an example of the corporatization of international education that was ultimately resulting in the commodification of education in Ukraine. They concluded that the fact that academic institutes have been transformed into "businesses" would have a profound effect on individual states, globalization, and the internationalization of education. This negative outlook complements Goodman's (2010) conclusion that the Bologna Process is a mechanism of bureaucratic control over the education system of its members and a form of political hegemony over members who are not in the EU.

Education Reforms and Teacher Education in Ukraine

Ukraine has a complex history regarding teacher education and related reforms. As the country made a transition from a totalitarian Marxist-Leninist ideology to democracy and pluralism, changes that occurred at the societal level greatly affected education (Zhulynsky, 1997). The declaration of Ukraine's intention to transform into a democratic state with a regulated market economy gave birth to strategic plans to reform education as part of a nationwide transformation. Thanks to the capacity and potential of education to articulate and instil new norms of social and cultural behaviour in the newly formed country, the system of education was one of the first spheres to be subjected to the reforming process (Wanner, 1998). Reform of the teacher education sector was stated as the main goal of state policy in the sphere of education (Ministry of Education of Ukraine, 1994, p. 53). This policy encompassed the formation and strengthening of the potential of primary and secondary school teachers and comprehensive financial and material support for pedagogical cadres and their social protection. However, significant economic, political, and social factors negatively affected the implementation of those policy guidelines (Kutsyuruba, 2011). As reported by the World Bank (2011), the economic collapse of the 1990s had substantial long-term adverse effects on Ukraine's education system, which, together with the implications of the economic reforms, had created new challenges to reforming the education sector. Furthermore, the nature of educational reforms in Ukraine was fragmentary and yielded only a partial transition to the new paradigm of education set by the Ministry of Education policies.

Three major directions of initial education reforms in Ukraine were identified by Fimyar (2008): (1) change of the language of instruction in schools from mostly Russian to Ukrainian, (2) adjusting secondary education to a twelve-year basic education cycle in line with European standards, and (3) assessment policy reform. According to the 2010 European Neighbourhood Policy implementation report (European Commission, 2011c), particular attention in recent years was given to all levels of education, with new reform plans to accelerate convergence with the developments in the EU. Reform objectives included strengthening educational governance, improving educational quality and accessibility, and ensuring the continuity of education levels and financing. The government identified pre-school education as a new reform priority and adopted a concept for a state program of pre-school education development to 2017, with objectives and benchmarks closely aligned with those of the EU's Education and Training 2020 targets. The Ministry of Education and Science initiated secondary curriculum reform with the adoption of two state programs from 2010 to 2015 to improve information and communications technology (ICT) as well as science and mathematics education, and to enhance teaching skills. Furthermore, secondary education was reduced from twelve to eleven years in 2010, a reversal of the reform of 2001. Subsequently, these reforms were instrumental in changing the policy terrain guiding the country's teacher education programs.

According to a comprehensive study on teacher education in the Eastern Partnership countries initiated by the European Commission (GHK, 2011), the major teacher education reforms achieved to date in Ukraine are introduction of specialized education in secondary school, a competence-based approach to learning, the revision of the content of national education, and implementation of programs and projects at national and regional level related to the modern technology of education. As for the problematic areas, one of the major impediments in teacher education reforms was the erosion of the teaching profession's status after the collapse of the Soviet Union; this has resulted in a large number of low-performing students entering pre-service teacher education institutions. Highlighted also were the difficulties the education sector had collaborating with the private sector to develop innovations in schools. Other limitations included stereotypical thinking among teachers, the fear of publicly violating the state standards for educational training for teachers, reluctance of some teachers and school managers to innovate, insufficient financial support for schools, low-quality teaching practice, and the country's overall difficult social and economic situation.

The Bologna Process and Teacher Education

The results of the European Commission study indicated that some of the Bologna targets have already been executed to varying degrees in the area of teacher education. These included progress in adjusting the multilevel degree system to meet the European three-level system of academic degrees, as well as approving the qualification levels with regard to curriculum at the Bachelor of Education level and working towards establishing a permanent system for Master of Education programs. In addition, Ukraine was complimented for undertaking a complex system of quality assurance of teachers and providing professional development, whereby Ukrainian teachers are mandated by law to advance their qualifications at least once every five years in the post-graduate teacher training institutes. Of high significance also were support systems, known as *banks*, which have been put in place to disseminate innovations in information and communication technologies to aid in enhancing teaching strategies among teachers. Finally, the report noted the importance of the draft law on higher education for prospects in the field of teacher education. In addition to successes and achievements in the implementation of the Bologna Process, this report also highlighted struggling areas, such as upgrading the threshold of qualifications to enter the teaching profession, increasing teachers' salaries, updating the curriculum, improving classroom practice, modernizing in-service teacher education to respond to teachers preferences and the demands of the labour market, creating incentives for teachers to remain in the profession, and developing a continuous support system throughout the professional lives of teachers.

In summary, the European Commission report concluded that, in terms of ensuring convergence with EU standards and implementation of the Bologna Process principles, the needs for developments in the area of teacher education closely aligned with the overall directions of higher education reform in Ukraine. Some of the recommendations as to how the Ukrainian teacher education system can continue to modernize and meet the goals of the Bologna Process included increasing the use of modern teaching strategies in regard to information and telecommunication technologies, ensuring that the content of teacher education is in line with the demands of schools, encouraging collaboration between schools and university teachers, implementing education monitoring by research groups and organizations, increasing the popularity of professional development programs, and adopting valid regulations governing innovative educational activities.

Several studies assessed the impact of the Bologna Process on teacher education. The prevalent belief among scholars is that educational reforms in Ukraine had thus far resulted only in external transformations of the teacher education curriculum and the introduction of some innovative-methods courses, whereas more changes are needed to ensure the successful implementation of the Bologna Process in the system of teacher education (Koshmanova & Ravchyna, 2008). Pukhovska and Sacilotto-Vasylenko (2010) claimed that, while the Ukrainian government has adopted programs that support the integration of Ukrainian higher education into the Bologna Process, this has not been achieved with regard to teacher training programs. They attributed this to insufficient funding and issues surrounding implementation, such as a limited capacity to plan, manage, monitor, and evaluate these programs. As a result, they argued, teachers have not been prepared to assimilate the methods and approaches that adhere to the Bologna Process; these principles are based on Western pedagogical theories and many teachers had difficulty finding ways to incorporate them into their practice.

The calls to further reform teacher education have come from a number of scholars. Writing around the time Ukraine was preparing to sign the Bologna Accord, Shestavina (2004) argued for the need to modernize the Ukrainian education system and expressed hope that adherence to the Bologna Process would facilitate this. She gave special mention to the teacher training programs used by various institutions of higher education in Ukraine and the necessity to get these programs up to European standards. Scholars emphasized that the traditional pedagogic models used to train teachers, established under the Soviet system, were no longer suitable for students, and teacher training institutions in Ukraine needed to search for effective ways to adapt the national traditions of teacher training to the demands made by the process of integration with European standards and globalization (Baynazarova, 2005; Marchenko, 2010). Furthermore, arguing that

Ukraine should considerably reform its education system, Koshmanova (2006, 2007) found that tolerant attitudes and behaviours were not fully accepted by Ukrainian educators and that most educational policies and practices were still monocultural and ethnocentric. Koshmanova and Ravchyna (2008) posited that, successfully managing and implementing such a large change aside, many educators believe that the main difficulty of implementing the Bologna educational reforms in Ukraine stemmed from the authoritarian style of relationships teachers have with students. These relationships seemed to be grounded in "banking education" models and behaviourist educational psychology and served to contribute to the problem of perpetuating totalitarianism in classrooms. They concluded that these beliefs may generate obstacles for Ukraine's integration with Europe.

Studies examining teacher education reform in Ukraine have also taken a comparative approach, using other European nations as models that Ukraine can look towards. Sacilotto-Vasylenko (2008) used the goal of lifelong learning to analyse the evolution of teacher training within the context of the Bologna Process in France and Ukraine. In regard to Ukraine, the examples of recent educational changes that could be interpreted as lifelong learning strategies included short teacher training modules called "thematic courses," school-based training and consultancy, external professional development programs and projects, and distance in-service training. Despite these developments, the author criticized the teacher training policies, as they do not integrate the idea of teacher empowerment, which she considered to be the main condition for positive educational change, and concluded that the educational system in both countries, where teacher professional development depends mostly on administrative decisions, remains rigid and bureaucratic. Rolyak and Ohiyenko's (2008) study also explored lifelong learning as a key goal that teacher training institutes in Ukraine should work towards. Comparing the Ukrainian teacher education system with those of Scandinavian counties, they claimed that their successes and progress may help with addressing the challenges in the teacher training system in Ukraine, particularly in the areas of candidate selection into teacher education programs and the low status teacher education has in universities. Other scholars were more specific in that they held teacher education programs in Finland (Khustochka, 2009) and Germany (Folvarochnyi, 2011) as models for Ukraine to emulate in order to ensure successful implementation of the Bologna Process.

Teacher Education Reforms: Stated versus Actual Outcomes

To sum up the discussions in this chapter, there is no "one size fits all" answer to the question on the role of the Bologna Process for the so-called transition countries (Zgaga, 2009); local national realities and circumstances always need to be taken into account to understand the implementation of this process in individual countries of EHEA. Or, in the words of Kvit (2012), "to understand the way things work in Ukraine, one must remember that it is a post-Soviet state with its own features that cannot be compared to any other system in the world." Designed to meet the needs of a centrally planned economy, the Soviet Ukraine's education system had been characterized by high funding for education, high literacy levels, a majority of graduates with solid basic knowledge, a large core of skilled workers available for the industrial sector, and cultural and scientific achievements. However, the post-Soviet systemic problems remained characterized by declining quality of education and low efficiency (World Bank, 2011).

As mentioned before, teacher education in Ukraine is uniquely positioned at the intersection between the higher education and primary/secondary education systems, and thus is significantly affected by reforms pertaining to both areas. As for the Bologna Process's impact, official government reports and Bologna reports have indicated a number of positive changes in the system of higher education in Ukraine. For example, the *Bologna National Report Ukraine* and *Bologna Process Stocktaking Report* highlighted significant steps at the national policy level to accelerate convergence with the developments in the EU. Similarly, the report by the European Commission on primary and secondary education in Eastern Partnership countries noted the progress Ukraine has made in terms of aligning its teacher education programs with the standards set out by the Bologna Process. However, as posited by Kovtun and Stick (2009), though some accomplishments are notable, certain Bologna provisions might still be "on paper" alone, which emphasizes the presence of a number of implementation challenges in Ukraine.

The implementation of the Bologna Process in Ukraine in general, and in teacher education in particular, has not been a smooth undertaking and some reforms have not taken root in the education system for a number of reasons. First, although the Bologna Process was indeed an external push to strengthen the national reform process, educational reforms during the transitional period have been characterized by a struggle between forces of progress towards innovation and forces of a reactionary past (Kononenko & Holowinsky, 2001). Therefore, reform endeavours have been more bureaucratic than substantive (Nikitin, 2008, p. 1) and have lacked a unity of direction and solid foundation (Kutsyuruba, 2008).

Second, one of the most destabilizing factors in Ukraine during its independence period has been a frequent change of governments (Lunyachek, 2011). Accordingly, the change of ministers of education, whose personalities influence the development of education, and shifts in the political orientations of office holders have had a dramatic impact on reforms in Ukraine. A vivid example was the introduction in 2001, and reversing in 2010, of the twelve-year secondary education reform, which undoubtedly exerted uncertainty and turmoil in teacher education programs. Frequent changes of governments led to chaotic administration of the policy process, based on a "fire-fighting" approach, with the focus of government on immediate problems rather than sustained policymaking (Fimyar, 2008; Krawchenko, 1997).

Related to the above, the third reason for slow progress was the need for more time to implement innovations outlined by reforms in the educational sphere. Many of the reforms were perceived to be introduced haphazardly and without proper preparation, as an attempt to destroy and discard the existing base without a clear idea of how to create the foundation for future development (Kutsyuruba, 2008). Implementation difficulties encountered in the Ukrainian education and teacher training system can be attributed to the gap between political decisions and local realities; in other words, the reforms occurred more quickly than educators could accommodate themselves to the new demands (Pukhovska & Sacilotto-Vasylenko, 2010). Moreover, the changes pushed by state policy directives were often not straightforward and reflected the complexities, contradictions, and ambivalences of the post-Communist era (Wanner, 1998).

Fourth, the formal structural aspects of Soviet education were easier to reform than the practices instilled by the values of the Soviet system (Wanner, 1998). Dyczok argued that the pace of change and reforms in Ukraine was affected by the fact that many educators and administrators were products of the previous education system and not familiar with alternative models. The practices and institutional culture of post-Communism in education remained fairly unchanged since the Soviet times, thus creating greater disparity between education policy declarations and actual practical changes (Wolczuk, 2004).

Fifth, the economic uncertainty of the post-Soviet era, characterized by significant cuts in educational budgets and lack of resources for educators, negatively affected the progress of reforms. Analysing the post-Soviet transition of Ukraine with regard to its educational system, Holowinsky (1995) stressed the inadequate funding for educational reform. Similarly, the European Commission report on teacher education in Ukraine outlined the difficult social and economic situation of the country as one of the main limitations for innovations in teacher education. Consequently, the status of the teaching profession has degraded, leading to the departure of skilled teachers from schools in search of more lucrative careers (Kutsyuruba, 2008) and an increased intake of low-performing students into pre-service teacher education institutions.

Finally, one of the main problems of higher education in Ukraine is its quality, as indicated by the fact that the country's most prestigious higher education institutions have low indices in the world university ratings (Lunyachek, 2011). Lunyachek argues that the reason is not only imperfect licensing and accreditation, but also the lack of impartial external assessment of students' knowledge by independent institutions, the low academic motivation of students, an outdated resource base of the majority of higher education institutions, corruption and bribery, and insufficient individualization of education. As a result, graduates of Ukrainian higher education institutions may be unable to take full advantage of the benefits provided by the Bologna Process.

Helpful in understanding the changing policy terrain and teacher education reforms in Ukraine is the distinction between *policy as stated* and *policy in use* (Sergiovanni et al., 2009). As opposed to policy that is created and mandated by policymakers, policy in use refers to policy that is created as guidelines are interpreted, mandated characteristics are weighed, differential priorities are assigned, action theories are applied, and ideas come to life in the form of implementing decisions and professional practice. The discrepancies in the Bologna Process's policy implementation progress, as stated in official reports (macro level) and actual outcomes of the policy in use in higher education institutions and primary and secondary schools (meso and micro levels), vividly display how policy statements are interpreted and felt by stakeholders that are directly affected by them.

Moreover, the policy effect tends to lose its strength as policy guidelines move deeper into the institutional structures. Thus, institutional factors, contextualized by local national realities and circumstances, have the ability to not only hinder coherent implementation of reforms but also contribute to the purely formal or bureaucratic implementation of reforms. Therefore, greater attention to the *actual* versus *stated* outcomes of Bologna-initiated policies and reforms in teacher education is needed through detailed analyses of how specific policies affect institutional adherence to and implementation of the Bologna Process. Further research into implementation accomplishments and challenges at the level of higher education institutions charged with preparation of future teachers and the subsequent effects of that new teacher force on the school level would illuminate the actual outcomes of the changing policy terrain in teacher education in Ukraine.

15 Transnationalization of Higher Education Teaching and Learning at European Universities: Rethinking the Way to Wisdom

GONZALO JOVER AND JOSÉ LUIS GONZÁLEZ GERALDO

The university is the meeting place of all sciences. In so far as these remain an aggregate, the university resembles an intellectual warehouse; but in so far as they strive towards unity of knowledge, it resembles a never-finished temple.

K. Jaspers, *Way to Wisdom*

For over a decade, European universities have found themselves immersed in a transnational process of adapting their structures to create the European Higher Education Area (EHEA), also known as the "Bologna Process" because the agreement was formally adopted in Bologna, Italy. It is transnational because it permeates the different national systems, although it is not imposed upon them by any higher authority, nor is it strictly binding (Clement, McAlpine, & Waeytens, 2004). And yet, it has become perhaps the greatest change to European universities since they first appeared, with the creation of the *studium generale* and *ius ubique docenti* (Hunt, 2010), to the point of stretching beyond the borders of Europe and taking on a decidedly global character (Carter, 2007).

The implementation process formally ended in 2010 (Budapest-Vienna Communiqué, 2010; Leuven Communiqué, 2009), and although meetings are still being held periodically to estimate its effects and effectiveness (Bucharest Communiqué, 2012), the interest it initially piqued has long since subsided. Still, a university is a living, historical institution; there will be other processes and other cities to bear their names. What new changes are in store? As Nóvoa (2009) points out: "Thinking of the future is a risky and often futile business, and yet it is hard to resist the temptation of imagining what is to come, as a way to try to reach a destination that so often escapes us" (p. 181).

We will take that risk here. First, the future cannot be imagined without initially thinking of it from the present and the past, so they too must be considered. For the time being, it suffices to remember that when talking of the origins of the modern university, especially in reference to European universities, the discussion usually refers to the ones that arose in Italy and France in the eleventh century, particularly the universities in Salerno, Bologna, and Paris, each of which was specifically related to a profession: medicine, justice, and theology, respectively. With this background in mind, the Scottish philosopher and pedagogue Simon Somerville Laurie (1891) stated: "We may say, then, that it was the improvement of the professions of medicine, law and theology which led to the inception and organization of the first great schools" (p. 148).

Moreover, when academics discuss the origins of the university, seldom is any reference made to the times of the ancient city of Alexandria and the institution created by one of Alexander the Great's generals: the museum or "temple of the muses." It is there, thanks to the great library that would later be built around it, that we find the seed of the university. Once again quoting Laurie (1891): "In connection with this library, Ptolemy founded a college, or rather what might be called a Studium Generale, and endowed its professors" (p. 44).

It is interesting to note that the famous library at Alexandria may be considered a sine qua non requirement for setting the university bases (Latorre Gaete, 1984, p. 36) and yet, at the same time, not be a sufficient requirement:

> As might be expected in a university so carefully organized and endowed, the teaching was of a far more definite and practical character than at Athens. And this practical character, arising largely out of the pursuit of medicine, mathematics, and grammar, gave Alexandria pre-eminence and power after the leadership had passed away from the mother city in Attica. (Laurie, 1891, p. 45)

Regardless of which origin is chosen, an emphasis is detectable in both cases that goes beyond mere information and becomes successful because of the practical applicability of knowledge. Thus, we see how the university owes its origins to the ability to turn information into action. This aspect arises again in a new form in the genes of the EHEA and its insistence on adapting secondary education to fit the needs of the job market within the context of a competitive global economy, in which being the winner requires taking first place in the race for knowledge.

On the other hand, the Internet has transformed not only the ecology of our classrooms but also the very functions and aims of educational institutions themselves. We may even say that it has become a revolution, more than an innovation or mere evolution. The education system, which until now was the custodian and transmitter of information, has been replaced by wikis and blogs. It is no longer enough to just *have* information; one needs to know how to *manage* it and turn it into knowledge. Furthermore, students must construct that knowledge actively, since what the student does is much more important than what the teacher did, does, or will do (Shuell, 1986; Tyler, 1949).

While information and its transmission have always been one of the main objectives of education systems since they first appeared in the nineteenth century, the competence-based education of today once again stresses the need to take what is learned and put it into practice. The present belongs to the "knowledge society," the logical evolution of the previous "information society" and an attempt at making up for its shortcomings.

However, by emphasizing the shift from pure *knowledge* to *know-how*, we may lose sight of the no less important objective of *knowing how to be* (Delors, 1996a, pp. 91–103). This third way of knowing identifies a new social model to be addressed by education in the twenty-first century: rather than the information society and the knowledge society, it is the wisdom society, based on the classical scale of understanding (Savater, 1999). As Esteve (2010) points out, knowledge becomes wisdom when it is put to use in the search for being in the world (pp. 117–18). In other words, wisdom has a fundamentally moral meaning.

The aim of this chapter is twofold: (1) to analyse the potential and the obstacles presented by the Bologna Process from a pedagogic point of view, and (2) to debate what direction to take once that process is settled, and the consequences that direction will have in training university professors.

To do so, we will structure the chapter into three sections representing an encounter, a falling out, and a re-encounter – respectively, a look at the past, the present, and the future. In the first section, we will look at the coming together intended by the Bologna Process in the wider context of educational policy in the European Union. In the second, we will examine the falling out that occurred after its application. In the third section, we will argue in favour of a re-encounter as the knowledge society underlying the EHEA passes to a wisdom society that at present is still only a hope.

This endeavour poses a particularly compelling and complex challenge for education. In his classic work *Learning to Be*, Faure (1973) stressed the need to prepare human beings not only for the present but also, and perhaps especially, to live in societies that have not yet been created, but that they themselves will contribute to making (p. 62). This in turn places great importance on how to train future university professors.

Encounters: The European Higher Education Area in the Framework of Education Policy in the European Union

The EHEA got its start in the Sorbonne Declaration signed on 9 May 1998. With it, the ministers of education from France, Germany, Italy, and the United Kingdom agreed "to engage in the endeavour to create a European area of higher education, where national identities and common interests can interact and strengthen each other for the benefit of Europe, of its students, and more generally of its citizens" (Sorbonne Communiqué, 1998).

One year later, the initiative set into motion in Paris was formally taken on by the ministers of education from more than thirty European countries who were meeting in Bologna mainly to make their systems of higher education more compatible and comparable, thereby fostering mobility within Europe and competitiveness on an international scale. Thus, the Bologna Process was born. It also set the following objectives, which would be carried out in subsequent biennial agreements: (a) adopting a system of readily comparable and understandable diplomas; (b) implementing a structure of studies based on two cycles (later, the doctorate was separated from this initial structure and made into a third cycle); (c) establishing a credit system along the lines of the European Credit Transfer System (ECTS); (d) developing mobility for students, teachers, researchers, and administrators; (e) fostering European cooperation in matters of quality assurance by means of developing comparable criteria and methods; and (f) promoting the European dimension in higher education.

Although the EHEA is not, strictly speaking, the result of a European Union policy, at the Council of Europe in Lisbon in March 2002, the EU pledged "to become the most competitive and dynamic knowledge-based economy in the world capable of sustainable economic growth with more and better jobs and greater social cohesion" (European Council, 2000). The EU had come a long way to reach this point.

For many years the original economic orientation of what is now the European Union kept education and the regulation of education systems, long deemed instruments for generating national identity, out of the sphere of EU policy. Except for a few preliminary initiatives in vocational training, the EU made its first incursions into education matters in the 1970s, and it initiated a number of subsequent programs for cooperation and mobility in the 1980s as a methodology for Europeanizing the education systems. The discussion and approval of these programs soon bore witness to the conflict between creating a vision of education based on the promotion of shared values, on one hand, and an instrumental vision for purposes of economic growth, on the other (Neave, 1987).

A decisive step towards an EU-wide policy on education was made twenty years later, in February 1992, in the treaty that instituted the European Union. The older Constitutive Treaty of the European Economic Community was modified to provide a firmer legal base for the actions that were being carried out, as well as to set the basic principles of cooperation:

> The Community shall contribute to the development of quality education by encouraging cooperation between Member States and, if necessary, by supporting and supplementing their action, while fully respecting the responsibility of the Member States for the content of teaching and the organisation of education systems and their cultural and linguistic diversity. (European Community Treaty, Maastricht consolidated version, art. 126.1)

The quoted statement confirmed the basis for European education policy to be what we can call principles of respect for cultural diversity and subsidiarity, in keeping with the views that European politicians had been expressing from the late 1980s. Both principles are susceptible to rather contradictory interpretations, which reflect the ambivalent feelings to the union-building process. The principle of respect for cultural diversity suggests a liberal reading based on notions such as those of autonomy, neutrality, and non-interference. This has been referred to in different Union documents. As one report by the European Commission from the late 1980s stated:

> It is vital to preserve and respect the rich diversity of educational traditions in the Community, and to draw the best from this common heritage in promoting higher standards for the future. Blanket harmonization or standardization of the educational systems is entirely undesirable; it is not the Commission's objective in this field. The effort of all Member States and the Commission should be designed to improve the overall quality of educational provision by bringing the different systems into a long-term process of contact, cooperation and concertation and avoiding unnecessary divergences which would otherwise impede the free movement of persons and ideas. (European Commission, 1989, p. 5)

Much greater attention in the Union has been given to the principle of subsidiarity. In the European Union, the appeal to subsidiarity – whose early precedents go back to the 1970s – was encouraged primarily by the Christian Democratic tendency in the European Parliament, committed to the goal of a future federal Europe. In the absence of such a goal in the Union Treaty, the principle came to carry out, above all, the political function of a guarantee against the fear of an excessive concentration of powers in the institutions of the Union. The treaty alluded to it on several occasions, mainly in article 3B of the founding Treaty of the European Community, according to which:

> The Community shall act within the limits of the powers conferred upon it by this Treaty and of the objectives assigned to it therein.
>
> In areas which do not fall within its exclusive competence, the Community shall take action, in accordance with the principle of subsidiarity, only if and insofar as the objectives of the proposed action cannot be sufficiently achieved by the Member States and can therefore, by reason of the scale or effects of the proposed action, be better achieved by the Community.
>
> Any action by the Community shall not go beyond what is necessary to achieve the objectives of this Treaty. (European Community Treaty, Maastricht consolidated version, art. 3b)

Various commentators at the time of the Maastricht Treaty's approval pointed out the legal ambiguities of this article. But the ambiguities were premeditated, intended to foster different readings. This strategy turned the principle of subsidiarity into a wild card in which everyone could be reflected, even if from extremely differing stances. However, after years of becoming worn down by the different uses everyone made of it, subsidiarity lost much of its political strength. In the less favourable climate towards speeding up integration in which the treaty reforms took place, in the middle of the 1990s and in the early twenty-first century, it is understandable that European Union institutions and most of the member states were reluctant to reopen the debate on subsidiarity. Political discussion on the formulation of the principle was left behind more formal questions regarding its application (Jover, 2002).

These principles are the bases of the political background of the academic convergence underlying the EHEA. The Bologna Process is not about standardization but about standards (Carter, Fazey, González Geraldo, & Trevitt, 2010). The main issue is about fostering quality through harmonization rather than standardization. But how should quality be understood and fostered? Here is where the *falling out* comes into play.

Falling Out: The Discussion on Instrumental Orientation in Higher Education

One of the consequences for education policy caused by the lack of political debate in a European Union that had increased in size was the predominance of instrumental objectives focused on economic competitiveness, relegating any objectives involving construction of a sense of belonging and togetherness to mere words. Recently, for example, the *2012 Joint Report of the Council and the Commission on the Implementation of the Strategic Framework for European Cooperation in Education and Training (ET 2020)* set the priorities by pointing out: "Education and training systems have to be modernized to reinforce their efficiency and quality and to equip people with the skills and competencies they need to succeed on the labour market. This will boost people's confidence to be able to stand up to current and future challenges. It will help to improve Europe's competitiveness and generate growth and jobs" (European Union, 2012, p. 9). These priorities nourish the EHEA, as revealed by some of its main pillars, such as adopting the ECTS credit-based system and orienting education towards achievement in professional competences.

The European Credit Transfer System (ECTS) was adopted in 1989, as part of the Erasmus Program framework, as an instrument for transferring course credits – that is, as a mechanism to facilitate recognition of periods of study done in other countries, based on the work the student does at the host institution. The convergence process towards the

EHEA adopted the ECTS as the system not only for transferring credits but for accumulating them as well, for use in recognizing the activity performed on all levels – institutional, regional, national, or European – and for integrating training processes in formal, non-formal, and informal areas (European Commission, 2002, 2003).[1]

Because of an odd conversion, at Spanish universities the ECTS changed from having a merely administrative meaning to becoming a pedagogic principle that seemed to promise education as a panacea for every context and circumstance. Just as happened to the idea of subsidiarity, the ECTS has also become a wild card, in this case to justify a change in instructional methodology that focuses more on learning, on the student, and on the student's activity than on the teaching. This transmutation is making it necessary to review and revise the structures of university-level work.

In addition, the ECTS is reinforcing the paradoxical nature of the concept of the student underlying the EHEA process, as referred to by Bienefeld and Almqvist (2004). On one hand, students are actors and participants in their learning, a suitable consequence of considering students as a subject of their education. On the other hand, the ECTS may also foster a client-patron vision of the student as a consumer who earns, transfers, and invests in credits as per the demands of the job market and an instrumental conception of knowledge, whose only value is the one set by the marketplace.

This potential derivation aligns the ECTS with certain tendencies occurring on the international scene, trends that are producing a change in core values of academic culture – such as excellence, academic freedom, or the idea of public service – all of which often clash with objectives aimed at immediate economic profit. Thus:

> Many students deploy new linguistic habits with the following meanings, such as the unstated notion of the student as a client and the instructor as the purveyor of the requested service. This image betrays the traditional notion of student-centered learning, since it emphasizes enabling the individual in terms of competences and great skill, and no longer in the academic terms of a critical and reflexive intelligence. (Bruno-Jofré & Jover, 2008, p. 413)

The enabling of students in terms of competences linked to professional profiles is also one of the requirements in adapting teaching to the EHEA. As in the case of the ECTS changing into a methodological criterion, here too we find an unexpected departure from the original intentions of the process, although consistent with the philosophy focused on the achievement of economic goals.

Emanating from the area of vocational training and professional management, the concept of competence has in recent years made the leap to education in general. In Spain, this idea has found some advocates and an even larger group of fierce detractors, especially in the field of higher education (Gimeno, 2008). The detractors consider that an education that aims to prepare students exclusively in the mastery of competences, defined on the basis of the needs of the job market, does not address the requirements of a truly integral and humanizing education (Jover, 2008). Consequently, the discourse takes on a confrontational nature between a lofty, sublime conception and a lowly, worldly view of education, which is also detectable in other European contexts (Tenorth, 2008) and which obliges us to wonder what the "higher" is in higher education (González Geraldo, 2014).

Even today, in this irreducible duality of conceptions, the old debate continues between advocates of a liberal orientation of university education and advocates of a more practical orientation. The debate reached a culminating moment in the controversy in the 1930s between Robert M. Hutchins, then president of the University of Chicago, and the pragmatist John Dewey – a controversy we seem intent on reproducing today.

Hutchins (1936) harshly criticized the infiltration of pragmatism (or instrumentalism, as Dewey preferred to call it) into the university, and its glorifying of the professionalizing function and of scientific research, which deprive "the university of its only excuse for existence, which is to provide a haven where the search for truth may go on unhampered by utility or pressure for 'results'" (p. 43). In contrast to that situation, Hutchins advocated an initial general education centred on cultivating the intellectual virtues by means of *permanent studies* and contact with the great books of the tradition, after which time the university would then take care of the higher forms of knowledge, especially metaphysics, which are the ones that give a unifying view above the chaos caused by pragmatism.

For Dewey, however, Hutchins's proposal was predicated on two erroneous premises: (1) the belief in the existence of fixed, eternal principles and truths, and (2) the need to distance higher education as far as possible from contemporary social life. Dewey (1937) even called this conception authoritarian and easy prey for fascist positions:

> Any scheme based on the existence of ultimate first principles, with their dependent hierarchy of subsidiary principles, does not escape authoritarianism by calling the principles "truths." I would not intimate that the author has any sympathy with fascism. But basically his idea as to the proper course to be taken is akin to the distrust of freedom and the consequent appeal to some fixed authority that is now overrunning the world. There is implicit in every assertion of fixed and eternal first truths the necessity for some human authority to decide, in this world of conflicts, just what these truths are and how they shall be taught. This problem is conveniently ignored. Doubtless much may be said for selecting Aristotle and St. Thomas as competent promulgators of first truths. But it took the authority of a powerful ecclesiastic organization to secure their wide recognition. Others may prefer Hegel, or Karl Marx, or even Mussolini as the seers of first truths; and there are those who prefer Nazism. As far as I can see, President Hutchins has completely evaded the problem of who is to determine the definite truths that constitute the hierarchy. (p. 104)

In a recent review of the debate, Johnston (2011) points out that it comes as no surprise that the debate was never satisfactorily settled (p. 13). Perhaps what was missing was another point of view: seeing the university as a space not only for functional continuity with the world, as Dewey meant, nor only for liberal discontinuity, as Hutchins would have it. As Pestalozzi (1898) would say in unifying fashion, a university must be capable of understanding education as an imbrication of hand and head, and both with the heart: "Great ideas for improving the world, which rose out of elevated views of our subject, and which soon became exaggerated, filled our heads, confused our hearts and made our hands careless of the needs of the Institute that lay before our eyes" (p. 21).

Today, there is less doubt than ever that the modernization of higher education must make use of its huge potential for growth and job creation, as the European Commission stated recently in the framework of the *Europe 2020* initiative (European Commission, 2011c). No one can deny that the university must set its sights above and beyond the current circumstances, and towards the society of the future, with firm commitment. That commitment requires educating and training people who are informed and competent, but also creative and ethical, who have the ability not only to adjust, but to be critical and transformative. It is at this point that we find the proposals involved in the Bologna Process and competence-based learning to be insufficient.

The change triggered by Bologna should only be considered as a step in our search for university excellence, to advance from the information society and the knowledge society to the wisdom society. In the following section, we will sketch out the implications of this ideal for the work of the university and the training and preparation of its teachers, as if it were arranging a re-encounter between competences and wisdom.

Re-encounter: From the Information Society to the Wisdom Society

Until recently, it was commonly said that we lived in the *information society* as a result of the development and spread of Information and Communications Technology (ICT). However, nowadays we accept that this society, left over from the last century (Bell, 1973), is rather behind the times, and that the leitmotif that drove it – "information is power" – needs some clarification. Information alone will be power only if we manage to turn it into knowledge. Therefore, it has been suggested to consider the term knowledge as a perfectible and dynamic concept[2] that, unlike information, gives meaning to the mere structured accumulation of data: "Information is data that has been given structure and knowledge is information that has been given meaning. In essence, knowledge is information that has been interpreted by individuals and given a context" (Ward & Peppard, 2006, p. 503).

In the knowledge society, *knowing* (information) is achieved by acting in a particular context – that is, it turns the essence of the competence-based learning postulated by the EHEA into *know-how* (knowledge):

> In the so-called knowledge society, the individual is overwhelmed by the tremendous amount of information ... Our job as university teachers is to focus not on the capacity for reception of information that is soon to become obsolete, but on the mastery of strategies for searching, selecting and understanding that information. In other words, we must help students learn to transform information into knowledge. (Mérida, 2006, p. 8)

Underlying competence-based education is an attempt to address not only the acquisition of information (knowing), but also how to put it into practice (know-how). However, it may be that insufficient attention has been paid to the necessary attitudes (knowing and know-how) for information and knowledge to be useful for individual and social development. Thus, we should not be surprised that such basic aspects as emotional intelligence are deeply defended, while few professors concern themselves over whether their students are assertive, empathetic, altruistic, or supportive of good causes. These are politically correct aspects that find their place in the legislative framework, but still have no effective reflection in daily teaching practices at the university.

Using Paulo Freire's (1992) ideas, we could say that our state of consciousness in this regard addresses *transitive* premises in which there is a desire for change, but change does not, in fact, come about, in pure Lampedusian manner. For this change to take place, we need to take one more step, and progress from a knowledge society to a wisdom society, as several different voices have been proposing in recent years (Barnett & Maxwell, 2008; Blasi, 2006; Marga, Berchem, & Sadlak, 2008; Maxwell, 2007).

It may seem anachronistic to turn to the old notion of wisdom as a future horizon of the type of society universities should inspire, but it is not. The notion of wisdom is not hermetic. As existentialist philosopher Karl Jaspers (2003) noted, knowledge is achieved, whereas wisdom is sought after and longed for, so those who cultivate it have rightly been called philosophers, lovers of wisdom (p. 12). Wisdom consists more of an attitude of seeking than of a finished state.

In terms of the quest, wisdom is most in accordance with the style of university as "a never-finished temple" (Jaspers, 2003, p. 164). However, this sense of university – based on the oneness of scientific and philosophical knowledge, like a work in progress, and which was still evident in the nineteenth century, Jaspers adds – no longer exists: "The situation has changed. The sciences have become fragmented by specialization. It has come to be believed that scientific cognition, marked by the neatness of universally valid particular knowledge, could break away from philosophy." The university seems set on what another existentialist, Gabriel Marcel (1954), called *le déclin de la sagesse*. Therefore, the question is: can we go back to this ideal, but under new conditions?

In the debate we saw above, Hutchins (1936) blamed instrumentalism and empiricism for the *déclin* that, in his eyes, had plunged the university into chaos:

> The tremendous strides of science and technology seemed to be the result of the accumulation of data. The more information, the more discoveries, the more inventions, the more progress. The way to promote progress was therefore to get more information. The sciences one by one broke off from philosophy and then from one another, and that process is still going

> on. At last the whole structure of the university collapsed and the final victory of empiricism was won when the social sciences, law, and even philosophy and theology themselves became empirical and experimental and progressive. (pp. 25–6)

Dewey himself, being a master at giving new meanings to old concepts, appealed to the ideal of wisdom on several occasions. In the "ethics" conference he gave at Columbia University[3] in 1908, he looked to ancient Greece in search of its meaning, noting that Plato's shrewdness in observing the wealth of the social world around him led him to consider that "morals and philosophy are one: namely, a love of that wisdom which is the source of secure and social good" (Dewey, 2003, p. 33). Wisdom appears here as an object of desire. But, adds Dewey, looking to the past in search of this ideal, which is intellectual as well as moral, cannot remain there, prey to its limitations and blinded by the intention to attain an unconditional *summum bonum* to the current problems and aspirations and the tried-and-true solutions throughout the ages:

> Morals, philosophy, returns to its first love; love of the wisdom that is nurse, as nature is mother, of good. But it returns to the Socratic principle equipped with a multitude of special methods of inquiry and testing; with an organized mass of knowledge, and with control of the arrangements by which industry, law and education may concentrate upon the problem of the participation by all men and women, up to their capacity of absorption, in all attained values. (p. 47)

As a moral rather than only intellectual capacity, wisdom cannot be centred on an allegedly disinterested search for truth. Its best part concerns interest, with the practical function of achieving a better life and human environment. Its model can no longer be that *beatus* one who is separated from business, by Horace (Epodos, 2.1), nor the life of ease of he who flees from mundane noise, as per Fray Luis de León (Oda, 1), nor the *esjouissance constante* that is like that of things above the moon, by Montaigne (*Les Essais*, 1: 25), all echoes of forms of society that no longer exist. Nor can its image be the *cosmocentrisme* of which Gabriel Marcel (1954) spoke, in which "the true aim of knowledge and of life is to be integrated in the universal order, and not at all to transform the world by bringing it into subjection to human will, to man's needs and desires" (p. 42). This may be a valid stance if it means conscience as a feeling of universal belonging that, as Hansen (2011) says of cosmopolitanism, makes us learn "to balance reflexive openness to the new with reflective loyalty to the known" (p. 1). But that stance can no longer act as a model of wisdom as long as it is interpreted as turning one's back on the human needs persisting in this world, forgetting that "the world is what human beings make of it, subject to conditions of their mortality, vulnerability, and fallibility" (p. 6).

Wisdom must address the aspirations and circumstances of its time in order to be able to see beyond them to something desired in a world that, even though it does not exist, depends on human will and the actions deriving from it, "for our cleverness has not only enabled us to adjust means to ends, it has enabled us to imagine new ends, to dream up new ideals" (Rorty, 2011, p. 13). No longer can wisdom remain enclosed in a purely contemplative attitude, nor in a mere function of technical and scientific adjustment to the given, as if no other options were possible. One thing our time period has taught us is to be wary of the promises of a progress in which, as Jaspers's follower Hannah Arendt (1994) criticized Dewey, "science, and not man, takes the lead in the argument" (p. 195). If we mean to recover the ideal of wisdom as a moral guideline, the focus cannot only be on the past, or only in faith in scientific progress in and of itself. The emphasis must go elsewhere: on the discovery and attention to the other as a real subject.

Here is where suitable preparation of teachers becomes especially important. It must address a simple yet complex task. Simple, because "the aim of teaching is simple: it is to make student learning possible" (Ramsden, 2002, p. 7); complex, because each and every student is as unique and unrepeatable as his or her dreams and potential. The wisdom-based society updates the old idea that deep knowledge is not transferable, it must be achieved on one's own, but that does not mean denying the presence of the teacher, whose value is still undeniable. Competences can still be acquired by mechanical procedures. Wisdom must be seen as work embodied in someone's life.

In the early 1800s, Joseph Jacotot (1841) proposed his method of universal teaching, valid for teaching anything without having to appeal to a special knowledge, under the assumption that "tous les hommes ont une intelligence égale" (p. 11). To Rancière (2010), Jacotot's ideas open the way to intellectual and political emancipation in a *pedagogized* society, which takes the initial inequality between teacher and student as its source of justification. However, in an alternative reading, the attempt at a universal method of teaching, valid for any type of content, opens the way to more formal *pedagogization* of the teacher–student relationship. The "democratic" ideal of annulling the authority of the teacher for the formal rationality of the method involves frequently denounced contradictions in the modernization process. Impelled by the Bologna Process, those contradictions reappear today in some derivations undergone by the notion of the student as the centre of education. We refer to the derivations that combine this centrality of the student with high levels of planning that remove the capacity for action from the teacher and learner alike. As Payne (1881) said of Jacotot, "Much may be effected by this method in the hands of a skillful teacher, but a charlatan might make it an excuse for ignorance and neglect" (p. 62).

Many universities have started programs for training the teaching faculty, inspired by the Bologna Process. But it becomes clearer day by day that this is not enough. As Rubem Alves (1996) points out, the more we progress in improving the formal system of education, the more clearly its shortcomings appear. The university needs a type of training that prevents the wrong interpretations of the keystones of the Bologna Process to which we referred in the previous section, and helps us rethink aspects such as the centrality of the student and the preparation of professionals.

For *student centrism* to not fall into patron-clientism, it must be compensated for with an ability to place oneself in a world outside one's own. We may refer here to Ortega y Gasset's (1982) proposal in *The Mission of the University* (1930). In Ortega's opinion, the need to start from the student originates in the principle of economy of teaching – of teaching only what the student can and should learn, which means not only trimming back the contents, but also changing the orientation:

> The principle of economy not only implies that it is necessary to economize in the subject matter to be offered. It has a further implication: that the organization of higher education, the construction of the university, must be based upon the student, and not upon the professor or upon knowledge. The university must be the projection of the student to the scale of an institution. And his two dimensions are: first, what he is – a being of limited learning capacity – and second, what he needs to know in order to live his life. (Ortega y Gasset, 1982, p. 49)

However, Ortega's perspective was different from the one often used in putting the student in the centre in the Bologna Process.

Economy of teaching does not justify disdaining any knowledge that does not have immediate usefulness, something Ortega would find inconceivable. Rather, there is the need to join preparation of professionals with a broader general training that will ready them for the times in which they live, and from there let them carry out the social responsibility of the universities. To do so, Ortega proposed creating faculties of culture, which for him was a set of ideas that help human beings find their place in the world. That is the driving knowledge of life that, according to Ortega, is needed by the prototypical or average European citizen of his or her time, embodied by the figure of the professional "more learned than before, but at the same time more uncultured" (p. 37).

Ortega's words were originally presented to the students of the Federación Universitaria Española at a turbulent time in Spanish history. But in today's terms, they suggest that – beyond some narrow interpretations of the student-centred principle – the training of university teachers must also include the ability to place their field of specialization on a horizon of broader human meaning. From that point, university teachers must work towards the decentralization of the future professionals and help them overcome the tendency towards nihilism that, according to Charles Taylor (1992), especially grabs hold of young university students (pp. 60–1).

A society that aspires to wisdom does not need most of its members to have advanced, erudite knowledge of mathematics and literature; it needs more people able to read the newspaper differently than how they read it the day before. In a society of wisdom, education is not given over exclusively to fulfilling instrumental goals, but to enabling each student to bring out the best she or he has inside, to find her or his *element* (Robinson, 2009), and thus, by means of self-realization, find the best and most sincere way to help for the good of all. The society of wisdom does not require bombarding students with more knowledge, but must change the way they see themselves and the surrounding world.

As a result, there is a need to correct the pre-eminence that competence-based learning has taken on in the Bologna Process with more holistic perspectives, such as Amartya Sen and Martha Nussbaum's capability approach, in which values such as human rights, democracy, and sustainability constitute objectives in their own right, and not just by-products of instrumental learning (Lozano, Boni, Peris, & Hueso, 2012; Walker, 2012). For Nussbaum (2010), democracy as both an ethical as well as a political aspiration does not require so much an education based on economic profit as one that helps one discover the other and oneself with the depth found in poetry and art:

> We do not automatically see another human being as spacious and deep, having thoughts, spiritual longings, and emotions. It is all too easy to see another person as just a body – which we might then think we can use for our ends, bad or good. It is an achievement to see a soul in that body, and this achievement is supported by poetry and the arts, which ask us to wonder about the inner world of that shape we see – and, too, to wonder about ourselves and our own depths. (p. 102)

According to Nussbaum, the actions of the groups of belonging, the family and peer groups, are as fundamental to developing one's capabilities as what is taught at education institutions, schools and universities, and the pedagogic methods used therein (pp. 44–6). Teachers should use their teaching and employ the most suitable pedagogical methods to help students become not only competent professionals capable of transforming information into knowledge, but also, most importantly, critical and committed thinkers willing to collaborate, each from his or her field, on creating a world where – to use Kant's formula – others are seen as ends and not just as means.

Thus, teacher training cannot only focus on how to teach or, in Bologna Process terms, on how to stimulate students to acquire a set of useful competences for their future professional career. That is necessary, but not enough. Being a good teacher involves something more. As Hansen (2011) puts it: "Good teachers tap into the ever-rushing life within students and provide occasion after occasion for them to experience why curriculum is itself a vivid, ever-changing response to life" (p. 124). A good teacher's curriculum shows a "quest for meaning," Hansen adds, a search for answers on the problems of life that are never conclusive and involve deep ethical and political aspects. The good teacher induces a questioning attitude towards life, a life that is not a solitary biography but one that commits everyone to each other as inhabitants of a common human environment. The university professor, whose work consists of dealing with the daily challenge of knowledge and knowing, is in a privileged position to foster that attitude, whether she or he works in the humanities or the arts, or in the sciences or technical fields. Either way, pedagogical resources are needed to stimulate students' curiosity, interest, and willingness to see their future career not only as the application of a set of useful skills, but also as a socially responsible practice that involves judgment and moral deliberation in a shared setting for living.

It has been said that "something is profoundly wrong with the way we live today" (Judt, 2010), and that we have come to the point where more is not necessarily better (Albom, 2005). Education requires thinking of the future as a world where everyone feels acknowledged. Therefore, university teacher training needs the heart – the aspiration to achieve this world – to be as important as the head and the hands. Recent research such as that by Wilkinson and Pickett (2009) shows that "almost all problems which are more common at the bottom of the social ladder are more common in more unequal societies" (p. 42). In other words, problems such as a lack of trust, mental illness, lower life expectancy, obesity, school dropout rates, unwanted teenage pregnancies, and committing crimes occur more often in countries that have great inequality among their citizens. We may think these countries are rich, but that is far from the truth, because these problems affect the quality of everyone's life. More is not always better. This line of reasoning provides some justification for our proposal for university teacher training without having to appeal to ethical criteria: to help these teachers prepare competent professionals who first and foremost are people who work to make a more just society, and not only for their own benefit and that of those closest to them. In the long run, such a society is a benefit to all.

The society of wisdom is eminently utopian, as any ideal of the future must be. Although it represents a lofty ideal, this society must still be pursued through educational action, even at the university level. We must not fall into what Sir Ken Robinson (2010) calls the tyranny of common sense and refers to as the unattractive attitude of thinking "That's just how it is, and there's nothing I can do about it." If it were true that nothing can change, education itself would be pointless; each teacher, with his or her students, in their classrooms, day by day, can do much to make a difference in those who will soon be business leaders, governors, workers, and artists in tomorrow's society. They will be professionals trained to integrate their competent work into a human project for making a better present and future.

Perhaps the most important realization we might have in finding our way towards that society is to understand that in order to be good teachers, teachers must be good people.

NOTES

1 This is why some countries now call it the ECTAS (European Credit Transfer and Accumulation System), to denote its accumulative nature as well.
2 Some authors (see Ward & Peppard, 2006, p. 504) defend the use of the word *knowing* instead of *knowledge*. Similarly, in places where the word *skill* is preferred over *competences*, it would be preferable to speak of *skilfulness* so as not to disregard the dynamism required in the teaching-learning process (Chris Trevitt, personal communication, 2008).
3 The lecture was published in 1910 in *The Influence of Darwin on Philosophy* with the title "Intelligence and Morals."

16 Guilded Youth? The Returns of Practical Education

ANDREW ROBINSON

The Fall of Icarus: A Lesson for Today

In Breughel's painting "The Fall of Icarus," Icarus is seen falling to earth, having flown too near the sun; but the ploughman below him, almost oblivious, continues his work, his efforts focused on preparing patiently for the harvest to come. Icarus was flying high, transgressing borders, from Earth and the heavens, and failed. The foresight, ambition, and skills he invested in his invention – his wings – proved fatally inadequate for the perils ahead. The humble ploughman, however, sticks with his trade and progresses, providing for himself, his family, and his community. Only one Icarus dared (and died), while the symbolic ploughman represents the vast majority of society, work, and community.

For more than twenty years up to 2007, the solar eruption of apparent growth – based in many countries on financial speculation, deregulation, privatization, and debt – had eclipsed the true role of the financial sector to develop and fund the real economy. Like Icarus, this ascent of money, in reality of the downbeat of debt, was not sustainable. But unlike Icarus, its fall has affected millions, and also weakened trust and confidence in that form of market capitalism in much of the developed world.

But the financial burnout since has not only revealed the inherent, and reckless, weaknesses of that period, but also uncovered the value and purpose of systems of more permanent societal value. Financial capitalism's instability is forcing a reassessment of the needs of the real economy, re-industrialized not de-industrialized, and with a skills agenda meeting the needs of the many not just the few. The mantra of the knowledge economy has been shown to be insufficient by itself, when over-focused on an unregulated financial service sector, to build, and now rebuild Western economies in the face of a multipolar world. Before this flaw in what was once dubbed the "New Economy" leads to a wider rejection, the adaptive learning cultures and instruments of both manufacture and capufacture (practical skills and intelligence combined) will need to be harnessed in domestic markets so that they can compete and collaborate in cross-border regional and international arenas. Not just the "Old Economy," but a much "Older Economy" – where guilds shaped skills, community values, and border-free networks of journeymen – offers legacies, evidence, and lessons for policymakers today.

Better Futures: Entry Restricted?

It is widely assumed that we are living through a major shift of global influence, with the supposed benefits of globalization creating signs of increasing disruption to national and regional economies and societies. This is in part because trade liberalization has not been accompanied by any international legal framework to control many of its prime advocates and accelerators, such as banks and multinationals. Many of the "First World" countries have seen elsewhere in the world state-directed capitalism (or communist capitalism in the case of China) create stronger firewalls against contagion following the 2007–8 financial crisis. The elites in many parts of the West are facing a crisis or re-examination of the types of higher and further education adapted to this collapsed but still functioning taxpayer-funded economic model. This is now creating major social tensions as elites continue to prosper on the basis of a flawed economic and social construct, denying to many young people less fortunate the pathways to even a working wage, unencumbered by major debt. The promise of embourgeoisement of the majority is being replaced by the reality of a gradual reduction in the wealth of the middle classes, intensifying the divide between super-rich and the rest.

Massive hikes in university tuition fees and the burden of their repayment are already causing concern for both families and also lending authorities in the United States, a pattern which may be seen in the United Kingdom soon also, with increased fees introduced in 2012. With stagnant or recession-hit economies in those countries that led the deregulation crusade over the last three decades now blighting growth, jobs, security, and youth employment, attention will turn to those models in Western countries which still offer hope, competitiveness, growth, and social justice. These models are often not national, but regional or even local, and have better chances to stabilize the inherently fragile or even chaotic nature of a rule-free, interconnected, but not interdependent, financial economy. It may be that it is precisely the local, modest, citizen-centric approach to growing the skills base which gives the best chance, to citizens in front-line countries exposed to the 2008 crash, of securing benefits from the real economy in a globalizing world. However, this localism will have to balance the integrity and solidarity to be derived from a cluster-based approach with an active engagement to work with other communities of practice, in both the private and public sectors, beyond the domestic market.

Meisters: The New Masters of the Universe?

If Western elite universities continue to provide the high-level skills, networks, social poise, and confidence to manage an increasingly multipolar market that is neither coherently global nor tidily local, other channels will need to provide more accessible and fairer opportunities to the majority of less-advantaged young people. One example of this process is the German dual system of apprenticeship training, blending on-site experience in local companies with classroom experience each week. The results are impressive: in Germany (and also Austria), apprenticeship take-up is high and youth unemployment is low. Furthermore, though neither country had an extensive, durable colonial presence, their share of global exports and understanding of the world market for their goods and services has grown impressively. Even the German language, not spoken widely outside Europe, has been no bar; rather the opposite, as young Germans increasingly master a key element for global trade, namely, the English language. This model is the bedrock of the German *Mittelstand*: companies in niche technology sectors, supported by local banks deeply networked within their area, family-owned, with local skilled workers, operating within the dispersed economic framework of Germany, and in many cases expanding their exports in world markets.

However, the confidence in evidence today is the managed reaction to shocks in the recent past. Some ten years ago, Germany was stung by the OECD's PISA report into its educational attainment levels, which showed that they were not as good as the Germans thought, and were slipping compared to those of other competitor states. That report spurred Germany at the federal and Land levels to embark upon a thorough overhaul of its training system, including teacher training. The result is a workforce, and therefore companies, more able to compete internationally. At the same time as this jolt to the national consciousness, there was the following ten-year austerity plan, the permanence of a well-established dual-system training scheme for apprentices, new flexibility in employment laws, and a robust manufacturing sector exporting with a competitive euro.

Maybe it is because Germany has remained essentially a Continental – and recently created and recreated – power, without the legacy, baggage, and external resentments of imperialism, that it is able to more clearly prepare for international commercial advantage in a world which remains stubbornly but understandably differentiated by culture, history, language, and traditions. Those countries with a direct imperial memory such as the United Kingdom have been paradoxically disadvantaged by their past, especially where it lives on in the imagination of its elites. They find it more difficult to adjust to what is not, in fact, a globalized economy, but a connected set of very different economies and societies. However, this is a much wider problem, as 95 per cent of small and medium-sized enterprises (SMEs) in the European Union have no sales outside their own region, and most have no idea that there are national budgets to support the entry of SMEs into exporting. It is not surprising, then, that the local educational and training schemes, meeting the limited ambitions of domestic SMEs, remain narrowly focused.

This static attitude reinforces and reflects evidence of moves calling for de-globalization, where regions feel that they are the victims, not the beneficiaries, of open markets. The global recession has also led some heavily indebted companies and banks to retreat from cross-border activity, compounding populist political sentiment. In the boom years, companies and especially banks could claim to be "global." But in the recession years, the debts of banks and of countries revert to being a national concern. This is the very test the member states of the EU are now facing, as the tensions between new federal responses come up against traditional beliefs in economic sovereignty. However, given the increasing power of Continental power blocs – and the human capital needed for the future – the smaller economies must not retreat to narrow, technical, and provincial specialisms, only meeting domestic demands. They must blend a new local resilience with active strategies to utilize the resources from wider labour pools and ecosystems.

Reviving the Noble Skills – the *Métiers Nobles*

There are signs that a manageable, accessible, and socially inclusive approach to economic and learning leadership and growth is finding converts and emulators elsewhere in Europe, and beyond. Some European countries are now drawing on their own pre-imperial traditions. In France (as in England and throughout Europe at the time) the medieval guilds produced cohorts of journeymen-apprentices, building the cathedrals, towns, and infrastructures, in testimony to their skills, companionship, and faith.

Industrialization swept away much of that tradition of mobility and companionship – the *métiers nobles* – but it did not disappear altogether. In the middle of the twentieth century, the tradition was revived in France in the form of the Compagnons du Devoir, an organization which trains thousands of young apprentices for both traditional and new craft and industrial skills, and with a requirement today that each Compagnon spend at least a year in another country, preferably within the EU. It is this element of mobility, of a wider experience of both the itinerant and the host company, which gives confidence, resilience, and wider opportunities. The motto of the system is "Savoir, Savoir Faire, Savoir Être," to which might now be added informally "Savoir Voyager." Compagnons are to be found in companies as far afield as Japan, the United States, and South America.

But the increasing emphasis on having a wider European experience foreshadows what the EU has only developed in a modest manner to date: a mobility scheme for apprentices. The Leonardo scheme exists, and will be expanded further after 2014. This will help reduce the barriers to the cross-border mobility, experience, and confidence of what may become a new elite – namely, local young people, living outside the mega-cities, unburdened by university fees and debt, and embarking on a route to sustainable work using practical intelligence. As the perception of university debt is already persuading many young English people, for example, not to go to university (rates were down 9 per cent in 2012), the apprenticeship route is increasingly attractive. Add to that route a cross-border dimension, whereby students are encouraged to work not just with SMEs but with major global corporations, and there may an emergence of a new kind of European elite, or rather an elite-lite: modest, confident, able, and work-ready.

In the United Kingdom, the influence of the Compagnons has already influenced change, demonstrating the value of cross-border and cross-cultural exchanges. The manager for work placements in the UK and Irish Republic of the Compagnons relocated in 2010 from London to Newcastle in the north of England. The result was lower operating costs, closer supportive and influential networks locally, access to influencers, easier transport and connectivity, and, not least, a sense of belonging to a local area. But there was a further benefit: the Compagnons system so impressed local groups in the north-east of England that it decided to pilot a new initiative called TIBI – Trades Incorporation for Britain and Ireland. Inspired by the Compagnons, it was launched in 2012 in an article reported in the *Financial Times*. It is now recruiting colleges, companies, and organizations that see how a supposedly low-level route can aim high if it restores prestige to manual skills and practical intelligence, and if it can link young apprentices to the skills and technologies of tomorrow. The global challenge and mindset are as much needed in this sector as in the well-publicized area of global financial trading, exemplified by the cities of London and New York. A website designer trainee in Belgium or the UK is as likely to be competing for a job as online candidates from Singapore or Hong Kong, who might well offer to do the job at a distance, and more cheaply.

This is exemplified by the close interest shown in the TIBI and Compagnon scheme by large UK further-education colleges such as Gateshead College, the major training provider for Nissan, the UK's largest automotive plant, just six miles away from the Gateshead campus, and a leader with Renault in zero-carbon mobility. Here, then, is the beginning of how a Europe-wide medieval tradition of mobility and skills, revived in one country (France), is transmitted to another European country, and forms the basis for a new tradition which will benefit both local young people and their communities, as well as the ambitions of a giant multinational.

This model – drawing on a medieval, pre-nation-state tradition – may sit better with the challenges of internationalized economies than the statist, national approach. There is little doubt that the success of the German economic and social model exerts an influence across borders because it works, and not just in countries like France and Germany. Turkey and countries in Eastern Europe are also shaping, or reinforcing aspects of their training systems, on the German model, whose legacy is by now already known. The bigger challenge now is for the EU to grasp the opportunity of a wider Leonardo system of Apprentices For All, as a counterweight to the Erasmus system for university students. TIBI, the Compagnons, and the recent steps to create a Compagnonnage for the Mediterranean region are forerunners which can inform and inspire the EU as, of necessity, it tackles the challenge of high youth unemployment and confidence in its economic and social model.

Teaching the Guilded Entrepreneur

With evidence of the revival of interest in and adoption of the journeyman-apprentice as a mobile, smart actor in the labour market – moving often alone between companies and countries, and managing individualized networks of opportunity and capabilities – the question arises of how this rediscovered pathway can be introduced within the existing further- and higher-education provision system.

The guild system held together clusters of expertise of highly skilled individuals within a community of shared practice and values, a closed environment which acquired and retained the prestige of practical intelligence, some exclusivity, and a sense of shared values. Paradoxically, within the citadels of global finance such as the city of London, such guilds still exert power and influence in the form of the various livery companies. This tight-knit, elite, and internationally focused cluster – apparently anachronistic – survives today, reflected also in the collegiate system of some prestigious universities which provide the knowledge workers for the financial sector. However, instead of serving primarily the traditional crafts of the draper, carpenter, or silversmith, today the guilds advance the cause of global financial trading behind the historic form of a medieval network of power.

If that link between ancient knowledge clusters, epitomized by the guild system, and cross-border financial trade has been preserved, it must be because it is valuable and serves a purpose today. The question arises as to whether the real economy of practical intelligence (as compared to finance) needs to be supported by some reordering of priorities within the learning structures that underpin it. For while the university has traditionally been the preserve of cross-border mobility, with research and science being intrinsically international, the level below of further education has usually been very localized, reflective of industrial models of focused skills provision and the needs of major local employers, and leading supposedly to a long-term, well-defined job. That industrial model is now rapidly changing – for large companies and for SMEs – with the requirements of employers being less for defined skills in the workforce than for qualities such as flexibility, teamworking, adaptability to changing markets and technologies, and comfortableness with an international dimension.

What is emerging is the need for people trained for an entrepreneurial economic model that encourages them to embrace and acquire (and also discard) several sets of changing skills, aptitudes, and capabilities – professional as well as personal – as they move mentally, culturally, and geographically through their own working environment. This model is not confined to small firms. Even in large, successful automotive plants, employers nurture and adopt the changes, often small but significant, which an individual employee, encouraged to think and act smartly, can bring to large-scale productivity, efficiency, and technical issues. And sometimes the successful adoption of individualized creativity has its origin in an older industrial environment, as with automotive workers from a mining tradition whose ethos was imbued with a strong sense of teamwork, innovation, safety, and survival.

This can be an entrepreneurial dimension of both large and small enterprises, but one linked to the artisanal world of the apprentice, because some of the hallmarks of the apprentice, linked to a guild, are similar. These include working mainly in small groups and associations; using transformative, smart skills to solve practical problems; and seeing that work is learning, and vice versa. To embed this reality of the workplace within the teaching environment will require changes in how skills, attitudes, and capabilities are taught and championed. Often the Cinderellas of the education system in countries like the UK and France, the further-education system – training millions of people at considerable cost – now faces major challenges. They will be increasingly required to adapt their ethos, curricula, and benchmarks of success to the nurturing of students as smart, self-managing learners, ready to widen their portfolio of skills regularly, and open to the benefits from international experience and practice.

Although this model is informed by openness, mobility, and flexibility, its counterpart is community, proximity, and security. It is precisely because a specialized niche *Mittelstand* company in Bavaria has highly developed technical products and a future-facing, internationally attuned skill set in its workforce, that it can achieve its ambitions in exports while remaining with its core team in its native area. Just like the guilds clustering within a medieval city – surviving, today, in the city of London to support international financial trading – in the real economy at the local and regional level, there should be a debate and engagement within colleges, schools, businesses, and local authorities to help shape the process of change required. This process involves revisiting and reviving the value and prestige of guilds and apprenticeships to achieve a sense of community in and through work, anchored in places of often natal attachment, where people wish to live in trustful relationships and yet are able to prosper in a multipolar world.

E Pluribus Maximum? The Skills Trilemma in Europe

The European Union demonstrates a clear and urgent need to try to match something of the mobility of workers in the United States if it is to remain competitive, smart, and agile as it defines itself as a region with national cultural, social, and linguistic diversity; manages the pull of integrationary, federal forces; as well as handles the external pressure from non-EU industrial and industrializing societies. This is the skills and attitudinal trilemma for the EU today.

A recent report (2012) entitled "Turning the Tide" by the Accenture consulting group, based on a wide-ranging survey of five hundred European business leaders, highlighted starkly the impediments to a better-functioning European labour market. It showed that in the economic slowdown, most companies were freezing both recruitment and investment in training. Only 18 per cent of those surveyed were investing more in human capital for the future. This bodes badly for the longer-term outlook for the skills Europe will need to come out of the current crisis and sustain economic growth over time. The report flagged three areas for action:

- Activating untapped labour pools, at the domestic but also at the cross-border level.
- Improving mobility and the transportability of skills, again with a strong transnational dimension.
- Strengthening the skills ecosystem, focusing on greater links between business and educational establishments, and between businesses themselves across the range of sizes and sectors within a region.

Some of the tools to do this already exist, supported by funded programs of the EU, such as the Leonardo program mentioned above, the European Employment Service (EURES) scheme for jobseekers in other member states, the European Credit Transfer System (ECTS), as well as myriad pilot projects into cross-border skills enhancement and partnership schemes. But they often fail to make an impact, are not widely known, and thus have limited take-up. However, some countries do make more use of them than others. For example, Germany has developed an extensive EURES, far ahead of that found in the UK. This German deployment of the EURES scheme will now complement the benefits of its ten-year Harz program of structural reform, resulting in reduced unemployment and the need to boost its workforce through attracting skilled labour from other parts of the EU, especially the peripheral areas on its southern rim. Unless these cross-border measures are boosted, and understood by employers, they may either continue to freeze any upgrade in their skill sets, poach from other local firms, or go to the global market outside the EU for the skills they need. A labour market which operates only on national lines – within an integrating, federalizing economic Europe – will be a recipe for rising unemployment, among not just those with low skills, but also those with transferable capabilities in other countries. Europe will need evidence that an integrationist labour market works, and will meet demand. The few large European companies which are truly cross-border in their structure and products, such as the Airbus Group, will be the standard bearers for this drive for greater interoperability of the battle for skills across the Single Market.

The emergence of the Single European Market, the eurozone, and the likely further moves towards deeper integration following the crisis affecting in particular some peripheral states of the EU will focus attention on competitiveness and structural reforms throughout the region. Business Europe is probably twenty years ahead of both Citizen's Europe and Education Europe. A company can operate and secure new contracts cross-border, but evidence shows that for citizens and the future labour force in most EU states, there remain practical barriers to mobility, mutual recognition of qualifications and education curricula, and teachers' awareness of employers' needs. Even more worrying is the fact that Europe will, in all likelihood, be embarking on a major set of new *grands projets* to stimulate growth, affecting sectors such as renewables, electric vehicles, nuclear power, and physical infrastructure, which will be Europe-wide in their remit and impact. In the United States, Russia, China, and many of the emerging economies, a national strategy is planned to advance these game-changing sectors, embracing a full-spectrum engagement of education and training. They are doing new things with new tools. The challenge for the EU is to tackle these new challenges with new tools as well. Education, training, and teacher education at national and local levels in Europe must be aligned with some determinants of these futures, creating at the very least an active understanding of how the distinct, almost unique nature of European diversity and integration can be harnessed to prepare a cadre of people for rebuilding the European economic model around the real economy, the real European economy.

But how prepared is teacher education for this challenge? Teachers are trained by national governments for national purposes. But what is the wider national purpose today? In the days of empire, in state schools and perhaps more often in the private sector, that dimension had some regard for training the representatives of the European colonial powers in far-flung parts of the world, such as India. The emphasis was, of course, not on intercultural and multi-linguistic education, but on the transfer or imposition of the language, curriculum, and value system of the home country. Today, the EU faces the paradox of the nationalism of its teacher training systems, a steep rise in youth unemployment, and the headwind of competition from highly trained workforces in emerging – often, in fact, emerged – countries. Moreover, education is definitely not a competence of the EU, being under the sovereign competence of member states, although a number of programs such as Leonardo and some strands within the European Social Fund (within its cross-border dimension) help to address opportunities for cross-border partnerships for apprenticeships and similar training area developments.

Looking ahead, will the need to encourage this emerging dimension come from the EU with impact and conviction, or will national or regional demand force the pace of change, or will it be a mixture of both? Will the public sector step up to the plate, or will it be left to the private sector to fill the gap? With further economic integration planned for the Eurozone – which includes the highly successful dual-system training practices of both Germany and Austria, with high apprenticeship participation rates and low unemployment – will that process of integration also lead to emulation of such models across the zone? And what of the non-Eurozone members like the UK, with its sharp divisions of private- and public-sector secondary education, high fee levels now in universities, and reliance on devaluation of its currency to boost exports for economic recovery? Not to mention a Euro-scepticism at odds with its trading and financial reliance on the rest of the EU, and the Eurozone within it. Would the City of London view with equanimity its financial reach being weakened by a Eurozone now determined to use all its powers to protect itself from any further instability, social disruption, and industrial dislocation? If one day the UK were to adopt the euro, there is no doubt that its educational priorities would also have to be adapted to a world view rather different from one that believed in an almost effortless entitlement to global reach and influence – but which has not matched, for example, Germany's hard-won skills and manufacturing reputation, economic performance, and international competitiveness.

Can Cross-Border Partnerships Be a Spur?

What is the role and value of cross-border initiatives in fostering a local, accessible pathway to education and training in preparation for a workplace increasingly integrated by immigration and challenged by outsourcing to cheaper labour markets and footloose Internet-enabled services? While the teaching profession for the many remains often narrowly national – with a smaller, wealthier cohort being trained to have a global mindset and the promise of global employment chances (and salaries to go with them) – there are lessons to be learned from projects which show how learning cross-border can stimulate smart thinking, teaching, and learning, allied to an active sense of social justice and the widening of participation.

National Educational Organizations Working Cross-Border in Africa

The Open University's OpenAfrica program is building learning bridges between the British pioneer in open and distance learning and communities in Africa. The pioneering IFADEM project led by the Agence Universitaire de France and the Francophonie Agency, mainly in sub-Saharan Africa, is addressing the pressing need to teach skills for teachers in basic subjects such as the French language and mathematics. A special link has recently been made between both projects with the prospect of harnessing the results and opportunities from both schemes so that the impact, value, and support for their work can be increased at many levels, including greater appeal to multinational funding agencies.

Bilateral Projects

The year 2013 marked the fiftieth anniversary of the Franco-German Treaty – the Élysée Treaty – marking not just historical reconciliation, but core work on nurturing cross-border understanding and opportunities between French and German young people. This work is reflected in initiatives such as the Franco-German University and the long-standing Franco-German Youth Exchange Office. There were intensified efforts in 2013 to deepen and widen these programs, reflecting the urgent need for countries in the eurozone to address the challenges thrown up by the moves towards closer political integration – a process intensified by the instability of monetary union without the vital pillars of economic, social, and educational convergence.

Another example is provided by the ECSEL project (Entente Cordiale Science and Engineering Leadership), led by the regional development agency in north-east England in 2008–10. This project aims to strengthen bilateral working focused on key technological sectors, underpinned by current and potential collaborative programs with the theme *Faire Mieux Ensemble*, doing things better together. Here, it is the university sector, especially clusters in renewable energy and automotive technology, as well as research organizations which have propelled the project, one anchored in transnational exchanges and – most important – trustful alliances and personal networks.

Interregional Schemes

A new scheme, recently launched and supported by the European Commission (EC), involves several regional players, such as Corsica, the Highlands and Islands of Scotland, the Learn Direct organization in the UK, and the University of Newcastle. The project, called eSape ("e-learning" in Corsican), aims to spread the benefits of e-learning to the many scattered communities in Corsica, which leads the project. The examples from Scotland's northerly areas, developed by the University of the Highlands and Islands, have direct relevance to Corsica with its similar terrain – once a bar to access to learning and jobs, but an island which can now be opened up to all via e-learning. Allied to the project is a cross-border element to help develop a new marine biotechnology research centre at Stella Mare in Corsica, drawing on the expertise of the well-established marine centre at Newcastle University in the UK. In this way, a cross-cutting small-scale project around e-learning for all also helps nurture the social understanding of a technology-orientated specialism, whose aim is to embed advanced marine research in Corsica but, crucially, is linked to the real requirements of local fishermen, and the future job and training opportunities for local people.

Moving Forward at Scale

If these projects can show how success can grow from cross-border working and sharing, the challenge for Europe is to scale up the programs, to achieve wider impact and sustainable tangible value. It will still require bottom-up pressure from committed colleges, universities, and industries to force the pace and produce innovative projects with enduring results. It may also require some new instruments, inter-program alliances, and links to other EC funds such as Horizon 2020 (the EU's new research program) to achieve real awareness, impact, and sustainability.

The Ivy League Accessed from Your Mobile?

Bridging the gap between social divides and geographical divides can, of course, be helped today by harnessing the power of mobile technology. Every country has both public and private providers, offering up-skilling, training, and educational courses across a wide spectrum. Top-rated courses from the UK's Open University are accessible internationally, and many major physical universities are now offering online courses, or even reinventing themselves as hybrids with both physical and virtual learning opportunities. Examples in the Anglo-Saxon world include elite providers like MIT and Stanford University, and new niche entrants like Udacity, OpenLearn, and TED-ed. This trend is spreading from continent to continent, as exemplified by the OpenAfrica program mentioned earlier. This outreach using web-based courses is not confined to English-language providers, with the entry of e-learning suppliers in most advanced countries offering learning opportunities cross-border, though the bulk of their students remain in the domestic market. One e-learning expert, Sebastian Thrun from Stanford, expects in fifty years' time that there will be only ten institutions delivering higher education (and he predicts that Udacity will be one of them). Whatever the final outcome, there is strong pressure to create learning for all via the Internet, accessible at home or on the move from your mobile, reducing barriers imposed traditionally by poverty, geography, and lack of aspiration – and today by social inequality and the debt burden of university fees.

Looking Ahead

Belief in globalization – heralded as the miracle process of ubiquitous prosperity flowing across states and continents, aided by the gurus and practitioners of trade liberalization, privatization, and indebtedness – is now at a tipping point. If parents believe that the future for their children will be worse than it was for them, then the model will have to change. This model cannot long survive if it is served and sustained only by a top-jobs education accessible to 1 per cent of the population. The crisis of market capitalism is forcing a major reappraisal of the function, place, and role of finance in society. It is clear that when the engine of globalization falters, the economic agenda ceases to be easily cross-border but defensively national. Banks with balance sheets several times larger than their domestic market, spread across continents, are not bailed out by those distant countries in which they operate, but by their own national government, and by their domestic taxpayers.

States will be states, as de Gaulle once declared. But states now operate in increasingly federalistic paradigms, with the European Union a prime example of a unique process of both national diversity and cross-border sharing of some sovereignties. This move is also calling for new models of integration of education and training which draw on older forms of training and fellowship such as apprenticeships, often inspired by medieval practices, and also by transnational efforts to stimulate a more efficient labour market than the one operating only behind national boundaries. Regional and local experiments are demonstrating some of the solutions to strengthen the skills base, often informed by exchanges and ideas from beyond the domestic arena. E-learning is a further accelerator of this process, offering ubiquitous learning opportunities and tutor–student exchanges. The Internet revolution had already started to adjust perceptions of social and educational access before the financial crash of 2007–8. The enduring economic contraction thereafter has put into stark relief the need to harness both the technological opportunities of e-learning together with the structural changes needed in local, national, and international educational provision and attitudes. This urgent need to widen access will help ensure that any contraction of the economy does not entail a further retreat to educational exclusivity and elitism, but rather a re-engagement with the concept and reality of excellence in education as a social good for all that, fortunately, has been enjoyed by sufficient numbers of beneficiaries who will live to see it resume its place in civilized society.

FOCAL POINT 5

Transnationalization and State Policies

This focal point uses two case studies to call attention to the role of the state, in light of changes in the nature of education policy in a transnational and globalizing context. In the case of Chile, neoliberalism made the market a regulating force, and from 2008 there has been a move on the part of the state and within the context of international influences to increase accountability. As described by Cox, Meckes, and Bascopé, the policymaking process took its own characteristics from the negotiation of different ideologies and perspectives, including the advocacy groups linked to a market-oriented view of teacher education. The second case, as elaborated by Snowdon, refers to Canada and specifically to the province of Ontario, emphasizing the government's role in the public policy arena and its impact on international enrolment in higher education.

17 Teacher Education Policies in Chile: From Invitation to Prescription[1]

CRISTIÁN COX, LORENA MECKES, AND MARTÍN BASCOPÉ

Teacher education in Chile is under a dual pressure to change. As in the rest of the world, institutions and programs are faced with educating prospective teachers who will be capable of responding to the complex demands of the knowledge society and globalization (McKenzie et al., 2005). At the national level, since the mid-1990s, teacher education programs have been struggling to meet the requirements for preparing teachers who will be able to implement the new national curriculum, with its increasingly ambitious learning objectives, and to deliver a quality education to all students in order to advance equity in education (Cox, 2007).

Assessments of newly graduated teachers in both national and international tests have shown that teacher preparation programs in Chile are far from meeting these challenges. The performance of Chilean teachers in the international Teacher Education and Development Study in Mathematics (TEDS-M) showed very low levels of subject and pedagogical knowledge (Tatto et al., 2012). Scores on the country's university exit exams have mirrored these poor international results. In 2011, 42 per cent of newly graduated teachers did not reach the standard on the pedagogic knowledge test, and 69 per cent failed the subject knowledge test (Ministerio de Educación, 2012). These results have been a source of concern among policymakers and in the debates in the public arena regarding educational quality.

The dramatic increase of enrolment in teacher preparation programs over the past decade is in sharp contrast with this growing public concern about and distrust in the quality and value of teacher education programs. It is quite clear that currently these programs must respond to contradictory pressures. In the policymaking arena, the quality of their work is being scrutinized and even condemned. At the same time, given the drastic expansion of the social groups whose sons and daughters are in a position to apply to higher education institutions for the first time, these institutions face a strong demand to increase their number of vacancies.

In what follows, we will characterize the evolution of teacher education in Chile through an analysis of the forces that are working to shape it. These forces include, on one hand, the market and the dynamics of supply and demand and, on the other, changes in educational policies. The latter, in turn, have been shaped by different ideological perspectives, as well as by the growing body of international comparisons regarding national policies on the teaching force in different countries. We will argue that the particularly mixed nature of the regulations that have been adopted is the result of a compromise between these different pressures, which are, in turn, the result of different "advocacy coalitions" at work in the policy process.[2] At the same time, we shall argue that a structural shift has taken place in which the aforementioned compromises have been reached *within* a framework that accepts the need for an effective external regulatory framework in the teacher education field. This was politically impossible in the previous three decades, and it is indicative of policymaking in this area being a particularly visible learning process in which international influences play an important role.

Social Mobility and Market Forces: Drastic Expansion of Enrolment in Teacher Education Programs

The rate of increase in enrolment in teacher preparation programs in Chile since 2002 has been much more pronounced than the growth in enrolment in other areas of tertiary education. It also shows a weak correlation with the number of teachers actually required by the school system. Figure 17.1 presents the evolution of enrolment in teacher preparation programs over the past four decades. Between 1970 and 1999, enrolment figures in teacher preparation programs fluctuated between 20,000 and 40,000 students, regardless of the different political regimes, the diversity of policies for higher education, and, more notably, regardless of the number of pupils in the school system. For example, after 1973, enrolment in teacher preparation programs dropped, but there was no decline in school enrolment during the same period. Therefore, it can be said that there has been a "loose coupling" between the evolution of the

Figure 17.1 Total enrolment in teacher education programs

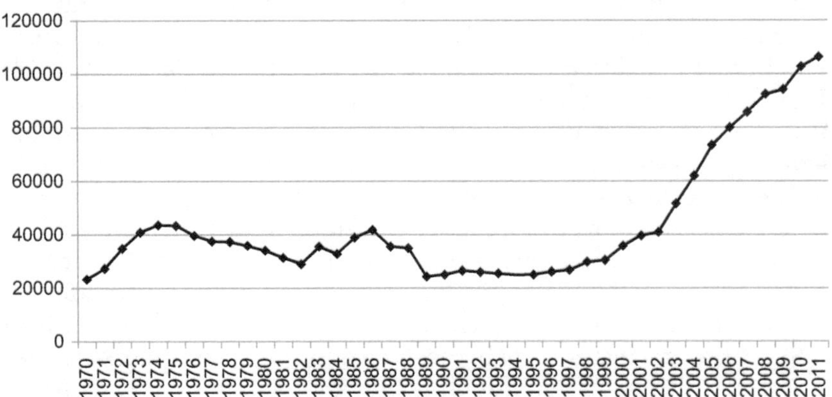

Source: Authors' elaboration retrieved from "Chilean Economic and Social Indicators" of the Central Bank and INDICES database from the National Education Council (CNED)

number of students being prepared to become teachers and the actual needs of the school system. However, since 2002 the growth rate in this sector changed drastically, with total enrolment tripling in one decade, thereby making this dynamic completely autonomous from the needs of the school system, whose enrolment started to drop in 2006 as a result of demographic changes.

This dramatic growth can be better explained by new generations of high school graduates demanding higher education and favouring teaching as a privileged route into the world of professional careers and, hence, as their pathway to social mobility. During the same period, tertiary enrolment as a whole experienced a very marked growth; however, enrolment in teacher preparation programs is even more salient. In fact, while the overall number of students in tertiary education doubled, enrolment in teacher preparation programs was 2.6 times greater (Cox, Meckes, & Bascopé, 2010).

The choice of teaching as the favoured route to higher education among these new generations from the lower-income socio-economic quintiles is not new. This was, in fact, the strategy for social mobility through the *écoles normales* in Chile, and this was also the case in England by the end of the nineteenth and beginning of the twentieth centuries (Floud & Scott, 1962; Núñez, Weinstein, & Muñoz, 2010). From a broader perspective, this can also be explained by the impact of the habitus of families and students with lower economic and cultural capital, and their expectations and choices when entering the world of professions and higher education (Bourdieu, 1984; Bourdieu & Passeron, 1964). From an economic point of view, studying even in the less selective programs of tertiary education in Chile is much more convenient than entering the labour force straight out of high school (Meller, 2010).

The sharp increase in enrolment in teacher training programs was possible in the context of a higher education system that was able to respond quickly to the increased demand for its services. During the 1980s, educational policies in Chile encouraged private institutions to participate in tertiary education. Thus, a large number of new private universities and institutes of higher education joined traditional universities. In Chile, higher education is financed mainly by private funds, and currently more than 85 per cent of higher education spending comes from students and their families. From early 2000 onward, most private institutions gained "autonomous" status and were authorized to offer new programs that did not require approval from the Higher Education Council, a public regulatory agency. Consequently, opening new programs for teacher preparation became popular, since these were inexpensive and easy to establish. In this way, the increased demand for positions in higher education coupled harmoniously with the increased capacity of the university private sector especially, but also some state universities, to offer new programs to absorb this demand.

Table 17.1 shows that while the number of programs in private universities grew by 678 per cent and in professional institutes by 410 per cent between 2000 and 2011, programs in traditional universities only grew by 35 per cent. The situation is similar to the total enrolment, which is led mainly by private institutions.

This stark growth has been at the expense of academic selectivity in the choice of applicants. Every year, universities administer a national university admission exam. However, it is not mandatory to use the scores from this test as a requirement for admission, nor is there a common cut-off score in teacher preparation programs for applicant selection. During these years, the expansion of non-selective institutions (those that do not even require entrance exams and those that admit students from the lower 70 per cent of high school graduates) has been much more prominent than growth in selective programs and institutions (those able to select applicants from the top 30 per cent). For instance, in 2000, 41 per cent of primary teacher graduates came from

Table 17.1 Growth in programs and enrolment in teacher education, 2000–2011

	Programs			Total enrolment		
	2000	2011	Variation (%)	2000	2011	Variation (%)
Traditional universities	164	221	35	23,591	38,147	62
Private universities	60	467	678	8,011	50,699	533
Professional institutes	41	209	410	4,312	17,661	310
Total	265	897	238	35,914	106,507	197

Source: Drawn from the Consejo Nacional de Educación's databases on higher education in Chile

selective universities, whereas in 2008, only 23 per cent of graduates had studied in a selective program (Meckes & Bascopé, 2012). This is confirmed by the data gathered through questionnaires administered to newly graduated teachers when they took their exit exams. Close to 70 per cent of graduates from teacher education programs are the first generation in their families to attend higher education (Brunner, 2009). According to Castillo and Cabezas, such applicants' scores on admission exams tend to be lower than those of students whose parents have higher-education degrees (Castillo & Cabezas, 2010).

To summarize, in Chile, teacher education rose sharply during the first decade of the new century as a result of a combination of social mobility dynamics and market forces in higher education. On one hand, there is the drastically increased demand for higher education in social groups whose children are the first generation applying for this level in the educational system and who opt for teaching as their career. On the other hand, the institutional features of higher education allowed private institutions to rapidly expand their supply of new placements in teacher preparation programs.

Landmarks in the Evolution of Policies Related to Initial Teacher Education in Chile

Parallel to the situation described above, policies implemented by the Ministry of Education regarding initial teacher preparation evolved slowly, from support strategies and incentives for the improvement of the quality provided in the late 1990s, to policies that combine support, incentives, pressure, and high-stakes accountability since 2007. The first initiative – the Improvement of Initial Teacher Training Programs (FFID) – was a state program that cost a total of 30 million dollars between 1998 and 2002, and consisted of projects for teacher education institutions to design and implement to improve the quality of their services. The requirements established by the Ministry of Education to select the universities and projects involved in the program were flexible and very few. For example, the project presented had to constitute an increase in the time devoted to the practicum in the teacher education program, but it could focus on a variety of purposes, from strengthening research capacities to improving bonds with a disciplinary faculty within the university. Each participating institution received on average a total of 1.7 million dollars over five years.

The second program, implemented between 2004 and 2007 and sponsored by the Ministry of Education (MECE-SUP), was slightly more structured in terms of its requirements for the institutions. It directed teacher preparation institutions to implement changes that focused on a problem that had been prioritized by the ministry: the scarcity of specialized programs to prepare teachers who would be able to teach specific subjects between the fifth and eighth grades. Thus, the Ministry of Education provided financial support to the institutions if they presented projects to prepare primary teachers for these grades in any of the following subjects: math, language, science, and social studies. Fifteen universities participated and received small grants to implement these changes. The results, however, were negligible. While in 2003 a third of teacher education programs in the country offered subject-based training for primary education teachers, this figure dropped to 6.1 per cent by 2005 and to 5 per cent by 2008 (Cox, Meckes, & Bascopé, 2010).

The next milestone in the development of policies related to teacher education was the approval of a law in 2006 that determined that the teacher preparation program accreditation was mandatory (as was the major in medicine). The accreditation reviews' procedures include examination of the institution's curriculum and its consistency with the purposes of the program, the qualifications of the faculty and academic staff, and the infrastructure and resources available to students. This law can be regarded as a move towards limited regulation and soft accountability, as the accreditation bodies did not have the power to close down the programs that were not accredited, and programs that fail accreditation can continue to function and undergo the process again after two years. In fact, only 4 per cent of teacher training programs have failed accreditation in Chile, while 63 per cent have been accredited for three or fewer years and 7 per cent for six or seven years (Dominguez et al., 2012a).

The international study on mathematics-teacher-education institutions, regulations, and the knowledge of recently graduated teachers in different countries (TEDS-M) produced a differentiated picture of quality assurance policies in place in the participating countries. The study classified countries according to the strength of the quality assurance policies of their teacher force. Countries with strong quality assurance typically showed arrangements to ensure (1) high quality of the entrants in teacher education programs; (2) high quality of teacher-education provision through supervision or accreditation, with severe consequences for those who do not meet the quality criteria; and (3) high quality in the qualifications that graduates of teacher education programs must have in order to enter the profession. The report portrays the situations in participating countries until 2008 (Tatto et al., 2012). Chile was one of the countries with the two weakest quality assurance mechanisms (together with Georgia), because until 2008 there was no control over the supply of teacher education students, no common selection standards for choosing candidates entering teacher education, and very limited procedures for promoting teaching as an attractive career. To these characteristics, there should also be added the low-stakes accreditation of teacher education programs and, finally, the lack of any barriers to or need for certification of their readiness to teach (other than the certification provided by the university where they had studied) before they entered the teaching profession.

Since 2008, the Ministry of Education has adopted a much more active role in the implementation of teacher-education-related policies. A comprehensive agenda for the transformation of teacher preparation was implemented, and it included three components: (1) national standards for teacher education programs; (2) a national exam for graduates, which would be progressively aligned with these standards; and (3) financial support for teacher education institutions so that they can improve their academic staff, adjust or change their curricula, and organize the student teachers' practicum according to the newly established standards. The condition for providing this financial support is that the projects presented must show alignment with the standards, and the institutions must demonstrate improvement in their performance indicators to renew their contracts with the Ministry of Education. The exam, the first of the three components to be implemented, has been in place since 2008. The drawing up of national standards for recently graduated teachers was commissioned in 2008, but these were launched only in 2011 and 2012. In the following sections, we will discuss the possible reasons for this delay and the conflicting positions in the political arena regarding standards for graduating teachers.

The national testing program assesses subject matter knowledge and pedagogical knowledge, as well as basic writing, and information and communication technologies skills (Manzi, 2010). Although the test was voluntary during the first four years of implementation, the participation rate has been high among both institutions and students. Between thirty-eight and forty-three institutions have participated in the exam each year since 2008, representing between 75 and 80 per cent of teacher education institutions in Chile. The Ministry of Education started publishing institutional results and rankings in 2011, which raised the stakes of the exam for all participating institutions.

Since 2011, the government has provided full tuition grants to candidates with high university entrance test scores who apply to teacher education. The condition for receiving this scholarship is that the beneficiary must work for three years in the subsidized school sector (including both public and private schools). Furthermore, since 2010 the Chilean government has presented to parliament two laws that have focused on teacher education. The first establishes a higher salary for novice teachers who perform in the upper 30 per cent on their exit exams if they work in the state-subsidized sector, while the second mandates that novice teachers pass the national exit exam if they wish to be hired in any state-subsidized school (which, in Chile, represents 93 per cent of school enrolment). These laws are still being discussed in parliament, and it is unclear if the mandatory status of the final exam will be accepted in the end.

Summing up, in the last decade Chilean teacher-education-related policies have gradually moved from a situation of very weak public regulation to one of increased accountability, incentives, pressure for results, and public availability of these results. Figure 17.2 illustrates this evolution from 1998 to 2012, a five-step journey, beginning from a program that offered support to schools of education that were invited to embark on projects for change but without much framing by the government (Avalos, 2002). It goes through intermediate phases of focused support for improvement projects, mandatory accreditations, and voluntary examinations upon leaving preparation programs to, finally, a public regulatory framework that includes standards and mandatory examinations.

Figure 17.2 From invitation to prescription: Evolution of policies in initial teacher training (ITT), 1998–2012

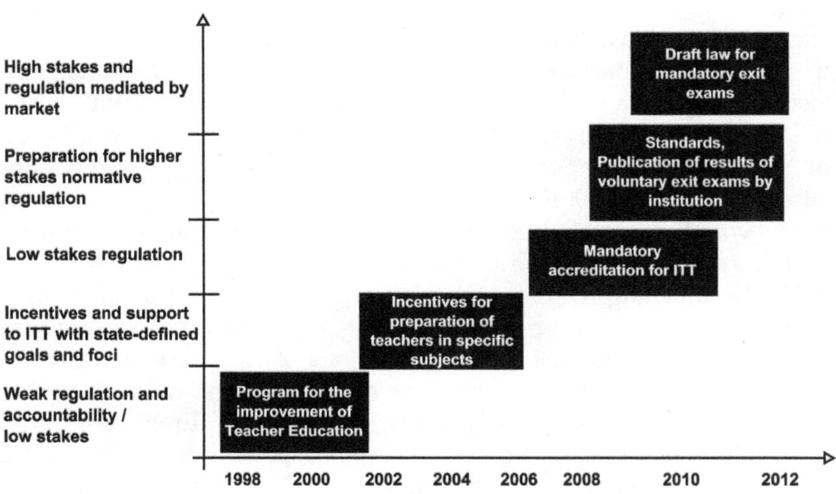

Source: Authors

In the evolution portrayed, we see a visible pattern of continuous attempts to solve a problem that was both complex and strategic for Chilean education, as well as a learning process. We shall expand on this crucial feature, where international influences are relevant and the advocacy coalitions that are confronted do move in their beliefs regarding policy, though without abandoning their core beliefs.

Policy Processes: The Drive towards Regulation as a Learning Process

Between 2004 and 2010, diverse commissions and external reviews pointed out the insufficiency of teacher education in Chile when compared to the demands of the new curriculum that was being implemented in the school system. Four important public reviews of the sector converged as they all diagnosed similar critical features. The most crucial and consequential of these in political terms was an OECD review of Chilean educational policies (OECD, 2004), which – after a systematic review of institutions and practices – bluntly stated that the country was not preparing the teachers that its reformed school system required. The OECD report concluded: "The weak coupling between the reforms and initial teacher education helps create a major 'capacity gap' in the teaching force. This puts most pupils in the country into classrooms with teachers who, through no fault of their own, have been inadequately prepared to teach mathematics, language, and other subjects at the standard required by the new Chilean curriculum" (ibid., p. 267). After this followed reports by the National Commission of Deans of Faculties of Education (2005) and the Presidential Advisory Council on Education (2006). The latter was convened by the government after a widely supported protest movement among secondary students who were demanding quality and equity in education (Donoso Knaudt, 2010). Establishing the external certification of graduates before they were admitted into the profession through a standardized exam was one of the most relevant recommendations of the presidential council. The council was explicit about the need to change the strategy that public policies had followed thus far in this domain: "In the new phase of development of education ... instruments are needed with greater capacities to transform institutions, programs and practices in teacher education. One of them is a system of exams that must be passed to obtain the professional certification" (Consejo Asesor Presidencial, 2006, p. 200). The report also noted, however, that on this issue "there are different visions within the Council."

These diagnostic reviews mirrored the conclusions of the influential *Teachers Matter* report from the OECD (McKenzie et al., 2005), and were very much in tune with the subsequent McKinsey report (Barber & Mourshed, 2008), which highlighted the relevance of teachers and their initial training in the learning outcomes of students, given the pattern shown by the high-performing countries in the Programme for International Student Assessment (PISA). Finally, in 2010 a new government, for the first time in two decades belonging to the "pro-choice" coalition, set up a special panel of experts and ex-ministers of education from both "advocacy coalitions" to diagnose and make proposals regarding the strategic problem of teacher education. The panel's proposal was unequivocal about what was needed: mandatory high-stakes exams in reference to national standards and aligned with best practices abroad, as a mandatory requirement for becoming a teacher in state-funded schools; closure of programs that did not obtain accreditation; and a minimum required score on the national university entrance examinations for education majors (Panel de Expertos, 2010).

Thus – in the span of six years and across three governments[3] – policy diagnoses and debates evolved from raising the key issues in an international report, to a lack of agreement and ongoing discussions about a national examination upon exit from training programs, to an across-advocacy-coalitions proposal that included establishing a minimum-score bar upon entrance to teacher education, high standards within the training programs, and high-stakes mandatory examinations at the end. There is a distinct learning dimension in the sequence on which Eugene Bardach (2006), a theorist from the field of public policy, provides a relevant window. We quote him at length:

> The policy process is in some sense a trial-and-error problem-solving process. Problems arise, citizens complain, and policy makers offer a policy solution. The solution works imperfectly (or not at all), the facts become known and a new policy solution is devised. It too is imperfect, and the process then continues ... Learning in complex and ambiguous problem situations is better thought of as a positive feedback process. The positive feedback element under these conditions has to do with the constantly improving store of information and analytical understanding about both the nature of the problem to be solved and the workability of potential solutions. (p. 350)

In answer to the question of mechanisms or factors that aid learning processes in policymaking, Bardach identifies three, all of which are relevant and distinctively present in the case of the policies under examination. First, the presence of technically minded professionals, which has been a feature of Chilean policymaking in education since 1990, aids in this process. Second, the existence of forums that manage to cut across opposing advocacy coalitions is helpful. Regarding teacher education policies, the two most important such cases are the above-mentioned Presidential Advisory Council of 2006 and the Panel of Experts on Teacher Education, convoked by the minister of education in 2010. Both instances are clear examples of plural forums in which the two "advocacy coalitions" had technically minded professionals working for prolonged periods to devise policy proposals. Third, inter-jurisdictional learning, the intensity of contact with and knowledge of policies or programs applied in other countries, can also help. This, again, has been an acknowledged feature of educational policymaking in Chile over the last two decades. Examples include consistent networking and exchanges with key international figures and experience in the relevant fields; participation in all the most important international studies carried out in different areas by the International Association for the Evaluation of Educational Achievement (IEA) and OECD (TIMSS, PISA, CIVED, ICCS, TEDS-M); subjection of national policies to review and evaluation by multilateral agencies like the OECD (school and higher education systems in 2004 and 2010) and the World Bank along with the OECD (higher education system, 2010).

The evolution of the policies examined were not the result of linear planning derived from a blueprint decided at one point in time, nor did they result from the decision making of one government or "advocacy coalition." Instead, the observed evolution derives both from compromises between the confronted visions and from iteration and learning by the whole of the field of forces at play in the policymaking process. As argued, in this "field-wide" learning, international trends played an important role. Standards occupy such a central role in the new configuration that it is important to trace the process of their construction and adoption in Chile's teacher education.

Configuration of Standards for Teacher Education: Focal Point of International Influence

Defining standards for teachers is one of the central components of the international trend in quality assurance mechanisms in different countries' teaching policies (Kleinhenz & Ingvarson, 2007). Specifically, defining standards that graduating and novice teachers who apply for full registration must meet is common in many countries. Based on Charlotte Danielson's (1996) framework, Chile had already defined standards for initial teacher training in 2000. However, these standards were generic (i.e., they did not detail the specific knowledge and skills that teacher graduates needed to demonstrate to teach specific subjects or particular key stages in schooling), and they were not used to assess or certify newly graduated teachers. Therefore, in 2008 and 2009, the Ministry of Education commissioned the development of specific standards for newly graduated primary teachers, secondary teachers of different subjects, and early-childhood teachers.

In Chile, as in most countries, the development of new policies usually begins with an international review of "best practices." Moreover, one of the criteria for high-quality standards is that these should be "internationally benchmarked" (Kuan et al., forthcoming). At least, this is the case for learning achievement standards, and international experts usually offer advice during their development. Chile was no exception, and at different stages in the development of Chilean teaching standards, experts in the field presented their frameworks (Charlotte Danielson from the Educational Testing Service [ETS], in the early versions) or provided feedback to the Chilean teams (Lawrence Ingvarson from the Australian Council of Educational Research [ACER]).

The dimensions or content considered by the teaching standards, the purposes that the official documents claim underpin their development, and the bodies that have commissioned or are in charge of writing them are all strikingly similar across countries and subnational systems. In spite of their different levels of specificity, most standards describe the *subject knowledge* that teachers must have and the kind of teaching *practices* they should be able to demonstrate; they also stress the attitudes and values that support high-quality teaching. This is shown in table 17.2, which summarizes the dimensions and content observed in the standards we reviewed for several countries and states, including Chile.

As standards have started to be used in formal quality assurance processes within countries and states, the bodies commissioning and developing these standards have moved from professional associations and subnational agencies to state and federal bodies that take on the responsibility of developing standards or providing a national framework for state development (as in the case of the standards developed by the Australian Institute for Teaching and School Leadership [AISTL] in Australia or by the Council of Chief State School Officers' Interstate Teacher Assessment and Support Consortium [InTASC] in the United States). In the case of Chile, the Ministry of Education is leading the national effort in this domain by commissioning and publishing these standards for teacher education.

Policy measures such as the introduction of standards for teachers finishing their initial course of study, a new test to assess their achievement, the institution of mandatory accreditation of teacher education programs, and the introduction of a scholarship scheme to attract high school graduates with better qualifications are all in tune with international trends in the field of teacher education and certification. However, as we will argue in what follows, these policies have adopted particular characteristics in Chile, which, in turn, are the result of the ways in which the country has negotiated different ideological perspectives and managed the gap between international models and national realities in their implementation.The fast dissemination of standards-based policies and the similarities observed among the dimensions considered by these instruments across the different countries could be viewed as

Table 17.2 Contents considered and emphasized by teaching standards in different educational systems*

	Au	Qn	Vc	BC	Ch	US NBPTS	US InTASC	Cl	Tx	En	Mx	NZ
Disciplinary knowledge												
Know and understand the subject (expressed in general terms)	x	x	x	x	x		x	x		x	x	x
Know and understand the subject (specified for each particular subject and stages of schooling)					x[a]	x			x			
Pedagogic practice												
Know, value, and teach according to student characteristics (different cultures, past experience, educational needs, etc.)	x	x	x		x	x	x	x	x	x	x	x
Understand and use knowledge about how students learn, (theories of learning and development)	x	x	x	x	x[a]	x	x	x	x	x		x
Hold high expectations about all students	x		x	x	x	x	x	x	x	x		x
Know how to teach disciplinary content	x		x	x	x	x	x	x	x	x	x	x
Develop higher-order critical thinking and skills	x	x	x	x	x	x	x	x	x		x	x
Plan, implement and assess teaching and learning	x	x	x	x	x	x	x	x	x	x	x	x
Create and sustain an environment that encourages learning	x	x	x		x	x	x	x	x	x	x	x
Value the family's role in student development	x	x	x	x	x	x	x	x	x	x		x

	Au	Qn	Vc	BC	Ch	US NBPTS	US InTASC	Cl	Tx	En	Mx	NZ
Promote social values and ethics among students		x		x		x			x			
Know how to use ICT for learning	x	x	x		x[a]	x	x	x	x	x		x
Incorporate democratic values in classroom teaching practice						x						
Values and professional teaching practice												
Be committed to students' learning and development			x	x	x[a]	x						
Reflect on one's own teaching practice	x	x	x	x	x	x	x	x	x	x		x
Know the rationale for implementation of current educational policies				x					x	x		x
Commitment to professional learning (continuous learning)	x	x	x	x	x	x	x	x	x	x		x
Contribute and be committed to the school community	x	x	x		x	x		x	x	x		x
Contribute to development of the teaching profession	x	x	x	x			x	x		x		
Know and apply guidelines for ethical behaviour		x	x	x				x	x	x		x
Be capable of performing administrative tasks (e.g., registration etc.)	x		x						x			

*Au = Australia, Qn = Queensland, Vc = Victoria Au, BC = British Columbia, Ch = Chile, US = United States, Cl = California, Tx = Texas, En = England, Mx = Mexico, NZ = New Zealand, NBPTS = National Board of Professional Teaching Standards.

[a] In the case of Chile, these areas that were further specified in standards for graduate teachers developed between 2009 and 2011. See http://www.cpeip.cl.

Source: Centre of Study for Policies and Practices in Education (2013)

a manifestation of the global institutionalization of education, and the growing isomorphism of its basic structures and contents (Meyer, Kamens, & Benavot, 1992). Indeed, "it seems evident that educational agendas are increasingly similar in the whole world, regarding both the educational framework in which some important problems are outlined, as well as the educational solutions given to them" (Meyer & Ramírez, 2002, p. 103). Educational systems in the developing world are faced with the problem of how to relate to such a clear isomorphic pressure from different national contexts and levels of development, and how to manage the resulting gap between their specific educational situations and international frameworks and emphases.

Although regulations for university-level pedagogical training are weak or non-existent in most cases in Latin America, over the last few years there have been efforts made in some countries (such as Mexico, Colombia, Brazil, and Chile) to implement accreditation systems, graduation and licensing tests, and standards to provide guidance for the development of training curricula (OREALC/UNESCO, 2012). In many Latin American countries, the very term "standard" is seen as suspicious and is strongly rejected by teaching professionals, since it suggests standardization or the aim of controlling and homogenizing teaching practices. Further, those at universities argue that making training curricula uniform would mean their impoverishment through the curtailment of the autonomy of academic institutions in developing their own projects. Thus, many teachers' organizations and experts have strongly questioned these external interventions because they see them as eroding the teaching profession, and subordinating the education field to technical or bureaucratic agents – sometimes externalized to private agents – whose initiatives may be very disconnected from the needs of schools or even determined by private economic interests. Besides the progress needed in initial and continuing teacher education in most Latin American countries, managing the gap between international trends and national contexts also entails attaining a balance between trust in the work of teachers and their responsibility for their own performance, and between an increasing degree of autonomy and of monitoring/support to ensure that the autonomy is used in a way that is most appropriate for student learning (MacBeath, 2012).

A closer examination of recent Chilean teachers and teacher-preparation-related policies shows how this gap was managed. The standards for newly graduated teachers in Chile reveal a compromise, because, on one hand, the Ministry of Education has declared that these standards constitute the framework within which the final exit exam is currently being developed, but at the same time their official title (Estándares orientadores para las carreras de Educación) suggests that they are just an "orientation" that can be used by teacher education programs in a context of freedom and autonomy (MINEDUC, 2012, p. 4). The ambivalence inscribed in joining the terms "standards" and "orientations" in the naming of the new instrument is the result of an unsolved divergence between competing visions on how to approach the need to make teacher education reach the levels of quality required by society's demands and a more ambitious curriculum in schools. Now, however, in stark contrast to 2006 and earlier, the division between pro- and anti-regulation visions operates *within* a framework that establishes regulations that have consequences. This is clearly a case of "structural movement," where there is, simultaneously, a conservation of the opposition lines that characterize the two advocacy coalitions, and a movement of the whole field of competing options and decisions towards stronger external regulation of the sector. This process resulted in a *hybrid* set of policies, where ambivalence in the orientation, of course, means a risk of incoherence in implementation. This seems to be an unavoidable feature of Chilean public policies at present, which are so clearly embedded in the political conditions of strong advocacy coalitions with comparable political force and differing policy approaches. Their interaction, nonetheless, has produced a convergent pattern and the noted major shift towards regulation.

What has been observed regarding the standards for teacher education operates similarly with other instruments and definitions in the new regulatory framework that has been put in place. Thus, the aforementioned new scholarship scheme to attract secondary school graduates with high scores on their admissions exams seems to resemble the selective policies of high-performing countries, as described by the McKinsey report. A scholarship can only be awarded to applicants who choose to study in one of the eligible teacher preparation programs, which must be accredited and selective (they can receive students only from the top 30 per cent of applicants). However, this is an incentive to attract the best, and not a common minimum standard for the admission of students entering teacher education (as had been proposed by the previously mentioned politically plural panel convoked by the Ministry of Education in 2010). In this way, more selective institutions receiving this incentive coexist with those that can prepare teachers without any entry requirement.

The same ambivalence is evident in the new exit exam that has been established. While the government has presented a law to be discussed in parliament to establish that passing the test will be mandatory for new teachers who want to be hired in schools that receive public funds, at the moment the exam is still voluntary for both institutions and their graduates, and passing it is not yet required in order to enter the teaching profession. However, the results for each teacher preparation program are published. Thus, a combination of central regulation (verifying that teacher graduates meet established standards) and market regulation (public information about institutions' results on the exam, to guide future applicants' decisions and employers' recruitment of new teachers) is achieved.

The Impact of Recent Policies and Standards in Teacher Education

It is too early to assess the impact of this recent move towards a more active role of the state in regulating teacher education and establishing incentives to improve the intake of applicants entering teacher preparation programs. However, there is some evidence that can be interpreted as the initial response of teacher training institutions. As shown in figure 17.1, the overall expansion of enrolment continued after 2008 – that is, after compulsory accreditation and after the introduction of (voluntary) final exams and standards. However, a closer and more disaggregated view of this expansion shows that market forces and the demands of new generations of less-prepared high school graduates pushing to enter higher education have found their way through the heterogeneous maze of teacher preparation programs and are discovering avenues that have not been affected in the same way by the new regulatory policies. For example, final exams were implemented for primary teacher programs first, starting in 2008, followed by final exams for early-childhood teachers in 2010, and exit exams for prospective secondary teachers to be implemented in 2013. In contrast, there is no final exam for graduates of programs in special education.

In another arena, the selectivity of teacher education programs has been stimulated by recent policies, but selectivity is not mandatory for teacher preparation programs to be authorized to admit students. Thus, in order to be eligible to enrol high school graduates with the best admission scores who apply for full tuition grants, teacher education programs must be accredited for a minimum of two years and must change their admission policies to be in line with more selective procedures and cut-off scores for the national university admission test. Consequently, primary and secondary teacher programs that were closer to these new selectivity requirements joined this program, but those that had traditionally set the bar lower for their applicants (programs

Table 17.3 Growth rates in selective and non-selective teacher education programs, 2005–2011

	2005–8			2008–11		
	Selective institutions*	Non-selective institutions*	Total	Selective institutions*	Non-selective institutions*	Total
Programs' growth rate						
Primary education	0.0%	3.5%	3.3%	120.0%	−1.4%	6.3%
Special education	33.3%	84.1%	80.0%	50.0%	65.4%	64.4%
Secondary education	9.4%	20.7%	17.7%	72.0%	−15.1%	6.0%
Early childhood education	25.0%	11.9%	12.2%	80.0%	36.3%	37.6%
Total	10.5%	21.8%	20.1%	75.0%	13.1%	21.6%
Enrolment growth rate						
Primary education	−11.2%	22.3%	17.3%	96.3%	−27.5%	−13.5%
Special education	4.5%	53.5%	46.6%	62.2%	78.1%	76.5%
Secondary education	21.1%	47.9%	36.8%	59.2%	−15.8%	11.8%
Early childhood education	−1.7%	7.8%	6.9%	20.6%	49.9%	47.5%
Total	14.3%	32.7%	27.8%	61.4%	5.7%	18.9%

*Selective institutions are those in which the average admission score of their students is in the top 30% of the scores' distribution (550 points). Those institutions below this measure, with no entrance requirements or without information, are considered non-selective.

for special education teachers and early-childhood education teachers) did not. This is because meeting these new selectivity requirements directly would have meant closing their admissions, as they typically serve groups with lower scores on the entrance examinations or those that do not even take these examinations. As a consequence, the rate of growth of enrolment in non-selective institutions for primary and secondary teachers is negative, but non-selective institutions have expanded (post-2008) their programs preparing teachers for early-childhood education and for special education needs. Table 17.3 provides evidence regarding this pattern, comparing the years 2005–8 (pre-impact of regulatory measures) with the years 2008–11.

Conclusion

Since 2008, policies in Chile have clearly moved in the direction of increased regulation and control in each of the crucial thresholds of the teaching career – incentives to attract more qualified candidates to teacher education, standards to be attained by newly graduated teachers, and a final exam and incentives for those who perform better. However, these changes were introduced late, slowly, and after the decline of selectivity had already occurred as a result of the explosive growth in the number of programs and enrolment.

The speed of teacher education expansion that resulted from market forces and from the demand for social mobility found no barriers to lowering the standards for the admission of new candidates. In contrast, the government's introduction of policies for the regulation of teacher education showed a remarkably slow rhythm (Cox, Meckes, & Bascopé, 2010). As a result, the problem confronting the attempts to improve the quality of teacher education has been compounded substantially, as the numbers of programs, enrolment, financing, and interests at stake have increased enormously.

We can say that over the past two decades in Chile, there has been a political "tie" between government and opposition coalitions regarding educational policies in general and teacher education policies in particular. This "tie" has been evident in educational policies throughout the governments of a centre-left coalition (between 1990 and 2010) and during the right-wing coalition that has been in power since 2010. In particular, when analysing teacher-education-related policies over the last fifteen years in Chile, it is clear that despite the observed evolution towards regulation, each measure is a compromise and contains the ambiguity of these two opposed belief systems, as well as an attention to the interests and social demands involved. Hence, the installation of mandatory accreditation of teacher education programs during the centre-left coalition government combined the introduction of state regulation with the limitation of state power in such regulation (no national accreditation agency was established, fostering instead a "market" of agencies;[4] accreditation bodies are not allowed to close programs that are not accredited), and preserving the role of the market in such regulation (through informing the public of the accreditation status awarded to applicants to these programs). In this way, the economic interests of the higher-education institutions that offer these low-quality teacher preparation programs were protected, and the demand for social mobility of the students applying for such programs was not frustrated.

The same ambivalence was manifest in the establishment of standards for recently graduated teachers, including a final national exam. These measures were inherited from the centre-left coalition by the new right-wing government that implemented them, even though it was not comfortable with the idea of limiting the academic freedom of teacher education programs or with state intervention and regulation. The title of the standards document (*estándares orientadores*) and the delay in its publication for over a year are symptoms of these doubts.

Nevertheless, together with the hybrid nature of these policies, as observed, there has undoubtedly been an evolution towards a more active state role. Indeed, we conclude that there has been a double movement in the evolution of policy regarding teacher education in Chile. First, there is the noted dynamics of hybridization of the policies themselves, which is the result of compromises between advocacy coalitions with comparable influence. At the same time, there is a noticeable structural shift of policy options, from the absence of state regulation to an agenda focused on regulation perceived as a systemic need by both coalitions. As argued above, this change came about through continuous policy discussions about the quality of teacher education institutions and processes for over a decade. The disappointing results, coupled with a marked receptivity to international trends, has been decisive in moving policies from institutional self-regulation to those that involve prescription and assessment (with consequences) of educational training outcomes.

NOTES

1 Research supported by the Center for Research on Educational Policy and Practice, Catholic University of Chile, Grant CIE01-CONICYT.

2 "Advocacy coalitions" consist of "actors from a variety of … institutions at all levels of government who share a set of basic beliefs … and who seek to manipulate the rules, budgets, and personnel of governmental institutions in order to achieve these goals over time." Sabatier & Jenkins-Smith (1993), p. 5. A belief system can be seen as organized into three tiers: a "deep core" of normative belief or ideology, to hold across domains; a "policy core" of

more specific commitments within a domain; and then non-essential or secondary matters. Sabatier & Jenkins-Smith (1999).

3 President Ricardo Lagos's government (2000–6); President Michelle Bachelet's government (2006–10); and President Sebastián Piñera's government (2010–14).

4 Agencies which, in competing for universities to serve, are marred by conflicts of interest. Dominguez, Bascopé, Carrillo, Lorca, Olave, & Pozo (2012b).

18 Internationalization in Canadian Higher Education: The Ontario Experience

KEN SNOWDON

Over the past fifteen to twenty years, considerable efforts have been made to begin incorporating internationalization into all facets of academe in Canada: teaching, research, and service (Association of Universities and Colleges of Canada [AUCC], 2007). The emergence of internationalization as a higher-education public policy imperative occurred against a background of major challenges that affected, and continue to affect, the capacity of institutions to realize internationalization aspirations. This chapter will explore one aspect of the internationalization of higher education in a Canadian province, Ontario, with specific reference to the role of government in the public policy arena and the consequent impacts on international enrolment in higher education.

To the extent that Ontario's economic well-being is inextricably linked to its active presence on the international stage and the quantity and quality of its human capital, the internationalization of higher education is a key vehicle for success, in terms of both expanding the human capital asset base and improving and providing a major stimulus for quality improvement in an increasingly competitive environment. Yet, in Ontario the public policy aspect of internationalization in the post-secondary arena has often taken a back seat to political imperatives. Over the past thirty years, government policy regarding the funding of international students, tuition for international students, and priority accorded international admissions has all the characteristics of a roller-coaster ride – up, down, and bumpy – with major periodic interventions that have had a significant impact on international enrolment.

The public policy environment for internationalization is a microcosm of the larger post-secondary environment that has witnessed the creeping (some would say galloping) presence of government in virtually all realms of higher education. While government has long controlled funding levels, tuition levels, enrolment levels, and program approvals, and set minimum academic admission standards (through eligibility for operating grants), in more recent times the intrusiveness has been extended into the composition of the student body, online education, credit transfer, and forced partnerships. Short-term political considerations tend to trump visionary policy and Ontario's record reflects that reality, especially with regards to one particular aspect of internationalization: the recruitment of international students. And recent policy changes may be the harbinger of an even more interventionist foray into managing the international file.

The story of international recruitment and international students in Ontario's universities and colleges is one that is inextricably linked to capacity and funding issues and therefore linked to government. It is also, interestingly, a story that demonstrates the commitment and evolution of universities' involvement in internationalization and the power and transformative nature of deregulation and funding flexibility.

Setting the Context

Canada comprises ten provinces and three territories. Post-secondary education (PSE) is the purview of the provinces, and the post-secondary landscape in each province differs markedly, reflecting local circumstances and different approaches to the provision of post-secondary opportunities. Those differences in approach affect all aspects of higher education and shape the post-secondary sector and post-secondary institutions in a multitude of ways, from the "structure" of the PSE "system," through institutional mission and program "mix," to admission policy and graduation rates, and from governance to government relations to quality assurance and degree accreditation.[1]

The federal government, although not responsible for higher education, operates a set of post-secondary related programs (like research, training, and student assistance) that have a labour market and economic rationale that cuts across provincial boundaries. The federal programs tend to generate provincial responses that range from full embrace to outright rejection, once again reflecting history, local circumstances, and a constant tension in federal–provincial relations. Provinces react differently to the federal presence and federal initiatives, and the consequent impact on funding arrangements for higher education can differ significantly as a result. In terms of PSE internationalization, there is a federal presence through a number of initiatives and programs, although the success of federal initiatives has been quite mixed (FAITC, 2010).

The province of Ontario is Canada's largest in terms of population (13.5 million), representing close to 40 per cent of the Canadian population and 40 per cent of the country's Gross Domestic Product (Statistics Canada, 2012). The province's capital, Toronto, is the largest city in the country and Canada's capital city, Ottawa, is located in the province as well. Ontario's population has benefited from immigration over the years, and approximately 30 per cent of the population is foreign born (Ontario Ministry of Finance, 2012). Toronto's ethnic diversity is somewhat greater than the rest of the province's, with over 45 per cent of the population now reporting a language other than English as their first (Statistics Canada, 2011b).

The post-secondary "system" in Ontario is essentially a binary system composed of a community college sector and a university sector. While private vocational institutions operate in the province, the private sector role in tertiary education is limited. The public university sector includes twenty separate autonomous institutions ranging from specialized universities to regional comprehensive universities, to five full-service medical/doctoral institutions. The public college sector is made up of twenty-four Colleges of Applied Arts and Technology (CAAT) and includes some with degree-granting authority for specific applied degrees (Institutes of Technology and Advanced Learning). Unlike a number of other PSE "systems," the CAATs were not established as transfer institutions. Over the past decade or so, greater attention has been paid to establishing some program articulation between the sectors and expanding credit-transfer arrangements.

Through much of the past thirty years, the province has experienced major growth in university and college enrolment, and access for Ontarians was, and still is, the major PSE objective. Basic research ranks a distant second behind access issues in the eyes of the principal funding and regulatory agency (the Ministry of Training, Colleges and Universities), and arguably has been eclipsed in more recent times by an expected institutional role as a regional economic innovator and social catalyst. An overriding emphasis on access has been the predominant policy driver and has had major implications for Ontario's policy stance(s) on international education and, more specifically, for providing opportunity to undergraduate international students.

The history of international activities in Canadian higher education stretches back many years and has been documented elsewhere (Friesen, 2009). Through to the late 1970s, it essentially reflected an "aid" approach to the developing world, with scholarships and support programs for students from underdeveloped countries and post-colonial Commonwealth countries. Over time, the emphasis on "aid" shifted from aid to "trade," with more attention devoted to the role afforded Canada's higher-education industry in providing education services to other countries and, in more recent times, to providing education services to international students – here and abroad. Providing opportunities for Canadian students to study abroad has also been a major component of international activity, one initially focused on developing countries and development projects, but recently also incorporated into the curriculum in a number of programs in the form of exchanges and study-abroad opportunities.

Within a given institution, the rationale for internationalization focuses on several aspects, as illustrated in the following excerpt from one Ontario university's strategic plan:

> Within the University, internationalization has generally come to mean that: 1) research and advanced training is undertaken in collaboration with colleagues in other countries in pursuit of both new knowledge and/or with the goal of improving the social and economic well-being of citizens in countries less affluent than our own; 2) teaching in all disciplines is undertaken in a global context, in an environment welcoming of students, postdoctoral fellows and trainees from other countries who enrich the learning experience; 3) the student experience is enhanced through provision of structured opportunities to travel, study, and conduct research abroad, thus contributing to students' understanding of their own and other cultures, as well as their ability to compete in the global marketplace. It should be noted that these objectives are frequently complementary. (University of Western Ontario, 2009)

In Canada, greater interest in internationalization and actively recruiting international undergraduate students evolved over a long period. The level of interest in international recruitment varied by region, with those regions experiencing demographic decline in the traditional PSE 18–24 age group considerably more interested in international recruitment – both to bolster enrolments in their institution and further their internationalization agenda and, as a secondary consideration, to attract potential immigrants to the region. In Ontario, where institutional capacity constraints served to limit the interest in international enrolment, more recent changes in the funding environment ultimately sparked greater activity (by financing capacity growth) that helped institutions realize the multifaceted benefits of internationalization to themselves and the community as a whole. That was not always the case.

Ontario: A Review of Major Policy Developments Affecting International Students

To understand Ontario government policy towards universities and "internationalization," it is important to recognize how public opinion shapes the government's agenda and priorities. In the 1960s through part of the 1970s, Canadian higher education was characterized by a significant increase in immigrants who were hired as professors to accommodate the "baby boom" (CAUT, 2011). By the end of the 1960s, the "De-Canadian issue" began to dominate the political agenda, with expressed concerns from many quarters about the takeover of Canadian universities by foreign academics, "mostly Americans, who understood little and cared less about Canadian affairs and culture" (Monahan, 2004, p. 34). That phenomenon carried through the 1970s until "almost one out of four full-time faculty members had been recruited abroad. Concerns with the 'citizenship question' led to efforts to Canadianize both university faculty and the university curriculum" (AUCC, 1990, p. 77). The concern about "Americans" in higher education reflected larger concerns – social, cultural, and economic – about Canada's relationship to the United States.

The emphasis on "Canadianizing" the professoriate and the curriculum (along with the province's economic circumstances) affected funding policy and marked the starting point of a differential tuition fee policy for international students in Ontario. Beginning in 1977, the government introduced a differential fee for international students – more than double the rate charged to Canadian students – so that "a greater share of the financial burden of educating foreign students be shifted from the shoulders of Ontario citizens" (Parrott, 1976). At the time, the number of students from the United States and the United Kingdom was actually quite small – and considerably less than the largest group of international registrants identified as "Asian."

The introduction of a differential fee for international students appeared to have an immediate impact on demand from both the United States and the United Kingdom. First-year registrations from those two countries dropped significantly but were partially, and then more than fully, offset by increases in undergraduate first-year registrants from two other countries – Malaysia and Hong Kong.[2] Between 1977 and 1981, undergraduate international enrolment increased by over 70 per cent (from approximately 6900 students to 11,800 students) with over 90 per cent of the increase attributed to those two Commonwealth members.

The increase in international undergraduate enrolment happened to coincide with a decline in participation rates in Ontario that resulted in domestic undergraduate enrolment decreases in the same period. The increase in international enrolment, coupled with a decline in domestic enrolment, led to misguided concerns about access for Canadians (Ontarians) and triggered a further change in differential tuition for international students (Council of Ontario Universities, 1986). Once again, the economy – or rather, poor economic circumstances – added to the mix of factors that influenced the differential tuition decision.

In 1982 the government announced that "visa students who register for the first time in a program at an Ontario university will be asked to pay a higher proportion than formerly of their education" (Stephenson, 1982). For 1982, "visa tuition" was set at 50 per cent of the estimated program cost[3] and increased to two-thirds of the program cost the following year. By 1983, a Canadian student enrolled in an arts program was paying approximately $1000 in tuition; the international counterpart paid $3600. In more expensive programs such as engineering, the Canadian student paid $1000, while an international student was charged almost $6000. To ensure that individual institutions did not unduly increase their visa enrolment in the pursuit of additional revenue, the additional fee income was pooled and distributed to all institutions based on their share of what was known as Basic Operating Income – essentially, the grant income plus tuition income. That mechanism effectively reduced the financial incentive for an institution to recruit more visa students. Coupled with the relative size of the increase in international tuition, the overall result was a major dampening of undergraduate international enrolments; when the year's tuition was increased, first-year visa student registrations plummeted by 27 per cent (Monahan, 2004, p. 129).

At the graduate level, the tuition increases also had a major impact as institutions struggled to find the necessary support to recruit and retain students. At that time, Ontario's graduate programs had capacity for more students (OCUA, 1988), and a decrease in international enrolments threatened the sustainability of some programs. Pressure mounted to do something to help offset the impact of the increased tuition for international graduate students. A change in government led to further discussion about the merit of attracting high-calibre international graduate students, and in 1987 the government announced a program of tuition "waivers" for 1001 international students at the graduate level.

For the remainder of the 1980s, Ontario's universities occupied themselves with accommodating a major domestic enrolment expansion such that by 1990, total enrolment had increased by 50,000 students (approx. 25%) relative to 1980. The new government invested in increased enrolment with additional operating and capital monies. Moreover, it introduced a major faculty renewal initiative and formally acknowledged the importance of research and innovation through the investment of new funds. The spotlight on international undergraduates subsided as the institutions focused attention on accommodating a significant increase in domestic enrolment, building research capacity, faculty renewal, and, as the decade came to a close, staking out their aspirations in a major planning exercise with the government's higher-education agency, the Ontario Council on University Affairs (OCUA). With respect to undergraduate international enrolment, the 1980s ended with international student first-year registrations at less than half the peak level (1981), but above the low point in the middle of the decade. The decade ended with international registrations, as a proportion of total first-year registrations, continuing a decade-long decline even though the absolute number of registrations had increased from the mid-1980s.

Early in the 1990s, the Ontario fiscal situation deteriorated in the face of a major economic recession. A newly elected government developed a multifaceted approach to restrain public expenditures including, with respect to PSE, reductions in operating grants, tuition increases, and a change in the eligibility of international students for health coverage in Ontario. Beginning in 1994 all "temporary residents" in the province were required to pay for health insurance and the change in policy contributed to a perception of Ontario as a province that was, at best, ambivalent towards international students. The province's economic circumstances continued to deteriorate and were exacerbated by cutbacks in federal transfer payments – a major source of provincial income.

In late 1995, yet another government was elected and declared that, in addition to a major reduction in operating grant support to universities and colleges, international student enrolments would no longer qualify for operating grants. Rather, international fees would be deregulated with the expectation that institutions would adjust their fees for international students accordingly. However, to ensure that individual institutions did not attempt to address their financial challenges by increasing the number of international students at the expense of Ontarians, it was also noted that "protection of places for domestic students will be a feature of any new policy" (Snobelen, 1995). The cutbacks in operating support, in general, and specific policy direction vis-à-vis international students cast a pall over the sector for a few years, and international enrolments in the universities continued to decline.

From 1996/7 onward, universities were allowed to set tuition for international students and retain the revenue. The government's emphasis on protection of places for domestic students was an explicit part of its desire to ensure that access for Ontarians would not be affected by any attempt to increase international enrolment, even though the change in policy meant institutions would retain the international tuition revenue rather than pool it for redistribution through the formula operating-grants mechanism. Those changes represented a major shift in university financing. Reeling from the effects of the major cutbacks in operating grants (15%), the university community in Ontario took a few years to sort out the implications of the change with respect to international students. Sparked by the severity of the operating grant cutbacks and a major change in tuition policy, some universities began to rethink their international enrolment situation in light of the changed environment.

Ontario universities had been involved in international activities for many years, and as noted previously, there was a distinct emphasis on "aid"-related initiatives. By the mid-1980s, research collaborations with international partners were beginning to raise the interest in internationalization to a new level. New investment in the university sector fuelled faculty renewal, research, and enrolment expansion. Governments at the provincial and federal levels were more receptive to economic arguments about investing in human capital *and* research. By 1990, a number of formal international university exchanges were in place, in some cases with formal sponsorship by government.[4] The term "international" was making its way into strategic plans and mission statements. Within a decade, over 80 per cent of Canadian universities referenced the "international dimension" in their strategic plans (AUCC, 2007, p. 5).

The deregulating of international tuition in 1996 provided the opportunity for institutions in Ontario to begin realizing their internationalization aspirations. The chilly climate of government-imposed tuition and funding regulation gave way to an environment where institutions could determine their own international plan, set strategy, and rely – to a greater extent – on their own business acumen to make the plan work. International enrolments boomed, especially at the undergraduate level.

While operating grants from the province remained constrained in the mid-1990s, the federal government (having balanced its budget on the backs of the provinces via major reductions in transfer payments and thus contributing to provincial constraints) began to invest directly in PSE through student assistance and research initiatives. Many institutions had been actively lobbying for more investment by the federal government, and saw the federal initiatives in research as capacity building with a focus on faculty recruitment and capital investment. Early on in the new millennium, the federal government introduced partial support for the indirect costs of research. In Ontario, the universities welcomed the federal initiatives, much to the chagrin of provincial officials who would have preferred the restoration of transfer payments and resented the federal government setting the agenda in the research arena and attempting to dictate student-assistance policy.

At the same time (late 1990s–early 2000s) Ontario's universities began to plan for another challenge: the "double cohort." Government's decision to eliminate the fifth year of secondary school meant that once the decision was implemented, there would be a double cohort of secondary school graduates looking for a place in post-secondary education. The double cohort challenge was seen as a major access issue, and government was determined to ensure that the double cohort would not create access problems for Ontarians. Accordingly – although the process to obtain additional government funding was tarnished by politics and the pettiness of bureaucrats, while the funding mechanics hindered planning efforts – additional funding did arrive and ultimately allowed for a major expansion of capital facilities, faculty, and staff to accommodate the increased enrolment. However, by that point it was clear that enrolment demand was forecast to increase further as a result of basic demographics and increased participation rates.

In the mid-2000s, greater interest in immigration and the labour market became more prevalent as a newly elected government turned its attention to improving Ontario's global competitiveness as the linchpin for improving prosperity. In the PSE sector, one of the government's early initiatives was to commission a report on higher education that ultimately became a guide for PSE developments for the remainder of the decade. Former premier Bob Rae's report, *Ontario: A Leader in Learning*, led to multiyear investments in PSE. In the case of internationalization initiatives, the Rae report urged (1) greater investment in marketing to "ensure that Ontario remain[ed] an important educational destination for international students," and (2) the establishment of an Ontario International Study Program to increase study abroad opportunities for Ontario students (Rae, 2005, pp. 56–7). Government delivered. In its 2005 budget, the government announced *Reaching Higher: The McGuinty Government Plan for Postsecondary Education*. Among the many initiatives included in the plan was specific reference to "a strategy to attract more international students and encourage study abroad for Ontario students" (Sorbara, 2005, p. 97).

As the first decade of the twenty-first century came to a close, Ontario universities could look back on a period of transformative change. Total enrolment had surpassed 400,000 students, an increase of 125,000 in the decade. Government operating funding increased markedly in absolute terms over the decade and all institutions benefited from significant capital investments. An infusion of research funding from the federal and provincial governments resulted in expanded and updated research infrastructure, new faculty positions, more investment in research and technology transfer, and greater appreciation of the research role in Ontario universities.

International enrolment had never been higher and the growth rate was impressive – especially in light of the other demands of the decade. Increasingly from many quarters, internationalization and international enrolment was heralded as a positive, needed development deserving of public support and investment. International competitiveness became the watchword and competing for the best international students became part of the mantra (Institute for Competitiveness and Prosperity, 2008).[5]

In the 2010 Speech from the Throne, the Ontario government heralded a new era for the province by setting out a five-year plan to "Open Ontario" to new jobs and economic growth. Part of the plan was to "seize new global opportunities and turn them into jobs for Ontarians," and in the case of post-secondary education, the government committed to "aggressively promote Ontario postsecondary institutions abroad, and increase international enrollment by 50 per cent while maintaining spaces for Ontario students" (Ontario, 2010). Ontario's PSE system was clearly seen as an "export industry" with growth potential.

Bolstered by various reports that lauded the multiple benefits associated with increased international enrolments, the political value attributed to expanded internationalization (i.e., international recruitment) increased markedly (Institute for Competitiveness and Prosperity, 2011). Later in 2010, the government followed up on its Open Ontario Plan by announcing the Ontario Trillium Scholarships (OTS) program to help attract and support the best international doctoral students to Ontario. The program, seventy-five scholarships worth $40,000 annually and renewable for four years, was a clear signal that Ontario, along with its universities, was taking a bold step to recognize the importance of attracting the best international doctoral students.

Opposition to the OTS announcement was swift and vocal from opposition parties, students, and parents alike. In an era of supposed financial austerity, when the government acknowledged that "Ontario families are still feeling pinched financially" (Duncan, 2010, p. ix) and Ontario students were faced with tuition increases, critics latched onto the issue as evidence that the government was out of touch with the populace. While university presidents supported the government's announcement with a series of media initiatives, the intensity of the public reaction ultimately led the government to focus its next PSE initiative directly on Ontarians.

Less than a year after the OTS announcement, an election was called and one of the government's main platform pieces was to promise a grant that would translate into a 30 per cent reduction in tuition for a large majority of Ontario college and university students. If re-elected, the grant would be in place by the winter term of the 2011/12 academic year. The funding commitment was extraordinary (about $400 million) in light of the economic circumstances and the government's own straitened finances, and in light of the significant improvements in student assistance that had occurred over the previous several years.

In the 2012 budget the following spring, the government's election commitments ran head-on into fiscal realities. While keeping its promise to deliver a grant to students representing a 30 per cent reduction in tuition, the government also announced measures to reduce operating grants to institutions and introduced a $750 "head tax"[6] on non-PhD international students effective in 2013/14. Explicit in the follow-up documentation was reference to the institutions' ability to increase tuition to offset the loss of operating grants: "Institutions may need to adjust their international student tuition fees as appropriate to manage the funding revenue reduction" (Naylor, 2012). In addition, the government made a series of other adjustments related to international students and subsidies for international recruitment and study-abroad scholarships that translated into an apparent shift in direction from the Open Ontario proclamation and earlier initiatives. The policy changes sent a sobering signal to Ontario's universities and colleges about the priority accorded internationalization. There is little doubt that international students will bear the brunt of the "head tax" via increased tuition; the impact on international enrolment will bear careful monitoring.

The "head tax" has spawned an entirely new government initiative to collect more detailed information about international activities, ostensibly for accountability and transparency purposes. No longer is government simply interested in ensuring that Ontario's universities remain accessible to Ontarians. Education as an "export industry" has garnered government attention; the "industry" will never be the same.

To help clarify the relationship between Ontario government policy initiatives and international student demand (applicants) and actual international enrolment (registrants), figure 18.1 provides a historical picture of first-year international applicants and registrants from the mid-1970s.

The graph clearly indicates the spike in applicants and registrants that preceded the introduction of differential fees for international students (1977), the subsequent sharp decline, and then the significant increase (from Malaysia and Hong Kong) that peaked in 1981 and led to the introduction of much higher "visa fees." From that point through much of the 1980s, the number of applicants declined, as did the number of first-year registrants. Applicant demand picked up in the latter part of the 1980s, as a new government reinvested in higher education and universities expanded to accommodate increased enrolment demand. A small part of the overall expansion included international enrolment and coincided with the decision to introduce visa fee waivers for international graduate students. Nevertheless, while the actual number of international registrants increased in the late 1980s, the percentage of total first-year registrants continued to decline. The 1990s were characterized by a decline in applicant demand that coincided with the economic downturn and a government decision to make international

Figure 18.1 First-year international applicants and actual registrants 1973–2010

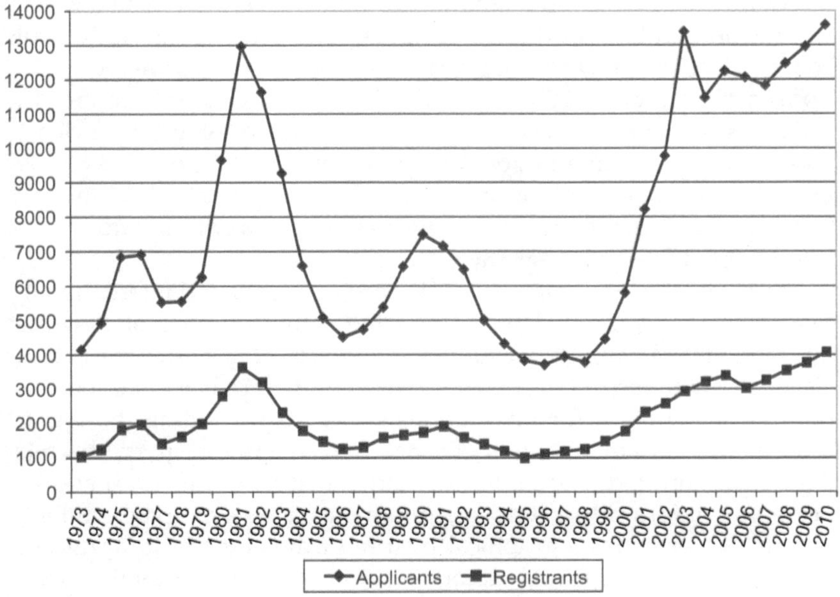

Source: Council of Ontario Universities, Application Statistics, 1973–2010

students ineligible for health coverage during their stay in Ontario. The chilly climate was exacerbated by the further cut-backs of yet another government in 1995 and the deregulation of international tuition the following year. First-year international undergraduate student registrants reached its low point in 1995, at fewer than 1000 new students.

At that point, applicant demand essentially levelled off and international intake remained stable for a few years until it began increasing in 1999. The increase in 1999 coincided with the implementation of the government's new Access to Opportunities Program (ATOP) aimed at increasing the number of computer science and electrical engineering graduates – program areas that tended to attract international students. Further, by that point universities had experienced multiple years of essentially no grant increases and the initial promise of greater tuition deregulation for domestic students was, in fact, muted somewhat by the reality of additional government regulation. In that environment, enrolment expansion under the auspices of ATOP became pretty much "the only revenue game in town." Nevertheless, despite the increase in international applicant demand, institutions responded in a conservative fashion, in light of the looming reality of the impending "double cohort." In 1999, one in three international applicants ultimately ended up as a registrant. In 2003, the official year of the double cohort, the ratio was one in five. The accommodation of the double cohort clearly had an impact on international recruitment efforts from 2003 to 2007 and played a major role in institutional developments. Beginning in 2008, applicant demand began to increase again, as did the number of international first-year registrants.

There are, of course, many other factors – national and international – that affected applicant demand and the actual number of first-year international registrants, including the effects of government actions elsewhere with respect to changes in immigration policies, student visa policies, and tuition for international students (including the impact of exchange-rate fluctuations – a major consideration given the relatively concentrated sources of international student demand) and the perceived nature of the local environment for international students. Figure 18.1 provides a graphical picture of the end result (applicants and registrants) of myriad factors – but also highlights the impact of Ontario government actions that have had a major influence (positive and negative) on international recruitment and the translation of applicants into actual registrants.

Figure 18.2 provides another perspective on the first-year registrant information by indicating the change over time in the international proportion of first-year students. Using five-year time periods, we see the increase in the late 1970s (students from Malaysia and Hong Kong) followed by a dramatic decline in the period between 1980 and 1985 (the introduction of a 50 per cent and then two-thirds cost-recovery tuition differential) and a continued decline through to 1995. Between 1995 and 2000, first-year international student enrolments began to increase and have continued to do so through to 2010, to the point where, as a percentage of first-year students, they are similar to levels in the mid-1970s.

Enrolment data provided by the Council of Ontario Universities (figure 18.3) illustrates the change in international enrolment from the mid-1980s onward in Ontario.[7] The decline in international enrolment is evident in the mid-1980s, followed by an increase through 1991 as university capacity improved and, at the graduate level, the government of the day introduced its tuition waivers for some international graduate students. From the early to mid-1990s, the impact of government cutbacks took a toll on institutional capacity and enrolments, in general,

Figure 18.2 First-year international students as percentage of all first-year students (Ontario universities)

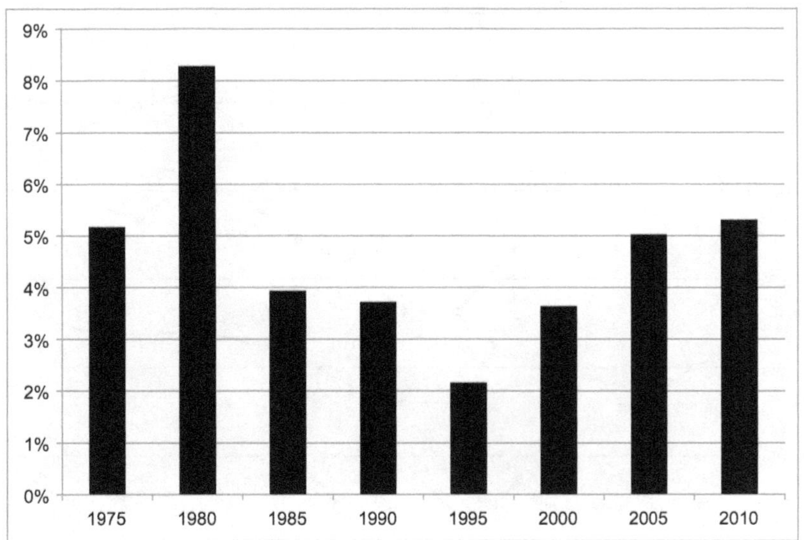

Source: Council of Ontario Universities, Application Statistics, various years

Figure 18.3 International enrolment by level, Ontario universities, full-time and part-time students

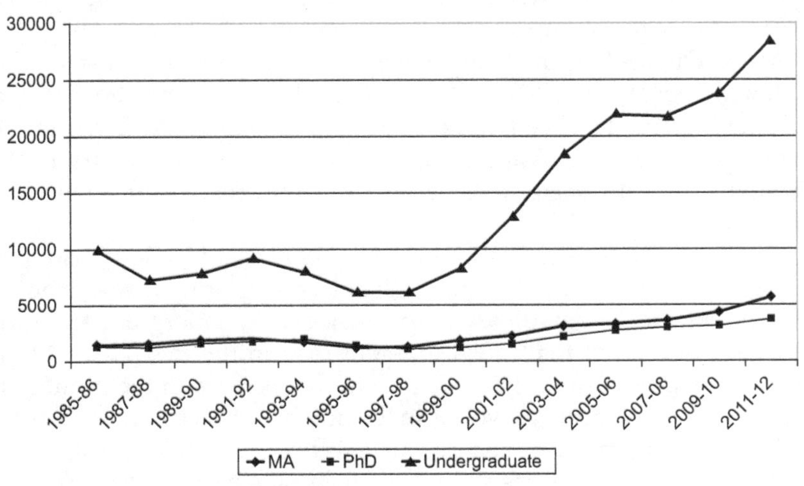

Source: Council of Ontario Universities

Figure 18.4 International enrolment by level, Ontario universities, as a percentage of total enrolment* by level

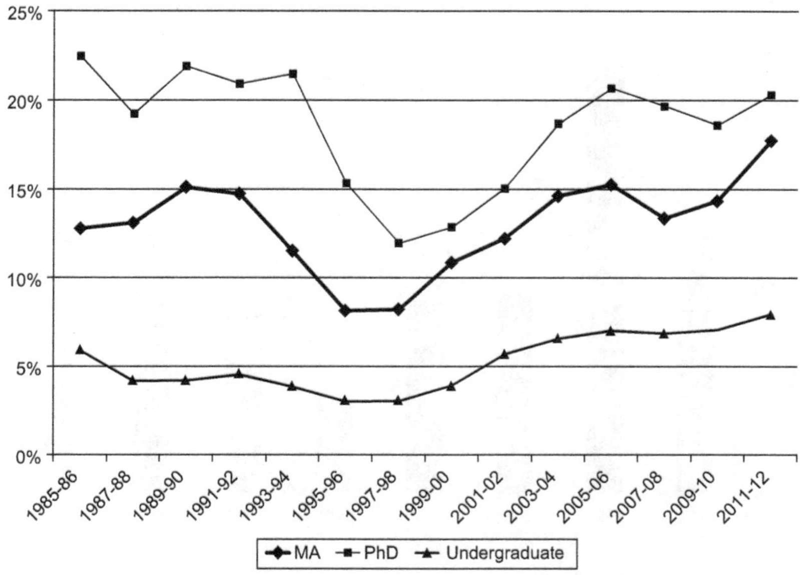

* Total international enrolment (full-time plus part-time) divided by total full-time enrolment

declined. The change in health insurance coverage introduced in early 1994 had a negative impact on applications and admissions.

All of Ontario's growth in international enrolment occurred after tuition deregulation (1996). In terms of absolute numbers, the most significant increase has been at the undergraduate level. At the graduate level, the number of MA and PhD students were very similar from 1985 through 1997, but began to diverge a bit from that point onward, as illustrated in figure 18.3.

Figure 18.4 illustrates the international enrolment by level as a percentage of total enrolment. International undergraduate enrolment in Ontario now represents about 7–8 per cent of *total* undergraduate enrolment – a figure not that much different than in the mid-1980s. Moreover, some part of the increase is due to the increase in the number of exchange opportunities as well as in the number of exchange students at all levels – undergraduate and graduate. While trend data are difficult to find, over 10 per cent of the international enrolment in 2010 is estimated to be related to exchange/study-abroad programs (Ministry of Training, Colleges and Universities [MTCU], 2011).

At the graduate level, international PhD students represent about 20 per cent of total PhD enrolment – again, a number not much different than in the mid-1980s. International master's students represent about 15 per cent of the total master's enrolments – and again, not much different than in the mid-1980s. What is striking in figure 18.4 is the decline in the mid-1980s and in the early to mid-1990s – periods when government policies and the funding environment had a major impact on international recruitment at all levels.

The other striking aspect of figure 18.4 is the increase in the level of activity in international enrolment since the latter part of the 1990s and especially since 2000. As noted previously, universities have expressed an interest in "internationalization" for many years, but it appears that from the latter part of the 1990s onward there was a concerted effort to translate international aspirations into reality at all levels.

International Enrolment in Canada

Before turning to the discussion of the preceding overview of major policy initiatives that have affected the environment for internationalization in Ontario's universities, it is important to put the Ontario experience in context relative to the rest of the country.[8]

As displayed in table 18.1, since the early 1990s, full-time international enrolment in Canadian universities has increased from approximately 31,000 in 1992 to 82,000 in 2009, an increase of 167 per cent. That figure refers to all full-time students studying in Canada, including those on exchange agreements. Total full-time enrolment in Canada increased by 55 per cent over the same period, and consequently the significant increase in international enrolment has resulted in an increase in the percentage of total enrolment attributed to international students, from 5 to 9 per cent.

Ontario experienced a greater increase in total enrolment over the period (67%), but the percentage increase in full-time international enrolment (144%) was less than that for Canada as a whole. However, it is clear that from a relative low point in 1996 there has been a marked increase in absolute terms, from approximately 7600 to 28,500. The change in the percentage of international students since 1992 varied across the country, with some provinces such as New Brunswick, Nova

Table 18.1 Enrolment trends, Canada and Ontario*

			1992/3	1996/7	2000/1	2004/5	2009/10	Change 1992–2009 (%)
Canada	A	Total	569,481	573,636	607,854	759,030	882,621	55
	B	Canadian	538,749	547,935	570,648	694,716	800,637	49
	C	International	30,735	25,698	37,206	64,317	81,987	167
	D	C/A	5%	4%	6%	8%	9%	
Ontario	A	Total	230,571	226,998	242,748	333,216	384,324	67
	B	Canadian	218,904	219,387	230,748	309,627	355,809	63
	C	International	11,664	7,608	11,997	23,589	28,512	144
	D	C/A	5%	3%	5%	7%	7%	
Canada excluding Ontario	A	Total	338,910	346,638	365,106	425,814	498,297	47
	B	Canadian	319,845	328,548	339,900	385,089	444,828	39
	C	International	19,071	18,090	25,209	40,728	53,475	180
	D	C/A	6%	5%	7%	10%	11%	
Ontario international as % of total enrolment			38%	30%	32%	37%	35%	

*Full-time students only
Source: Statistics Canada, PSIS

Scotia, Manitoba, and British Columbia registering significant increases such that international students now account for a relatively large percentage (about 10%) of total enrolment. In Ontario, the percentage of international students in the early 1990s was similar to the Canadian average, and by 2009–10 it had increased to 7 per cent, but was still below the Canadian average.

Considerations and Concluding Comments

Some may argue that the increase in international enrolment is simply related to revenue generation, and that the universities (and colleges) have tapped into a boundless revenue source. Tuition for international students in Ontario is "deregulated" and since the mid-1990s there have been significant increases in international tuition, which is generally higher in Ontario than in other provinces.[9] However, unlike other provinces where international student enrolment is either explicitly or implicitly included in the public funding available to support an institution, international students are not eligible to be counted for provincial operating-grant purposes in Ontario and have not been eligible since the mid-1990s.

Yet, the added costs associated with international students have a significant claim on institutional resources. International marketing and recruitment, coupled with special student services for international students, are additional costs beyond the norm for domestic students, and the student aid demands are generally the responsibility of the institution. In the case of graduate students, there is little or no *financial* incentive for an institution to recruit an international student because the tuition is generally offset by student support costs and the institution provides additional support to help with living expenses. While it may be argued there is an economic rationale for institutions to recruit international students, the reality may be somewhat different. Over the past decade the government's funding policy provided, in general, considerably more revenue for domestic enrolment expansion, yet the expansion in international enrolment in Ontario coincided with – and, in fact, outpaced – the major increase in domestic enrolment. Either institutions had considerable unused capacity, or other factors were influencing institutional decisions to invest in internationalization initiatives and international enrolment.[10]

Over the past quarter-century, internationalization has evolved to encompass a host of activities on Ontario's campuses and Ontario campuses abroad. In more recent times, both the federal and provincial governments have recognized the increasing importance of internationalization and international students to the economic and social well-being of the province and the country. The economic impact of international students is now a bestseller – seen as good for business for the province and the country (Roslyn Kunin & Associates, 2009). But it is also being seen, by some, as an increasingly important portal for attracting highly skilled potential immigrants to Canada and Ontario.

The link between immigration and PSE institutions has been a reality for many years, but more recently has attracted greater attention. The Ontario government's more recent proposed commitment to increase international student enrolment by 50 per cent is driven by a combination of interests such as the financial contribution of international students, interest in attracting more potential immigrants, and providing opportunity for international students to study in the province and thereby strengthening ties with other countries. One could argue, of course, that the provincial government saw the political virtue of endorsing reality; the 2011 census simply reinforced the reality of the continuing ethnic diversification of the province. Unfortunately, the government may have overplayed its hand with some of its Open Ontario initiatives. And then, in the face of political and financial pressure, it introduced a "head tax" – appearing either to make universities pay for their international success or, more specifically, make international students pay.

In fact, the capacity of universities to admit more international students and to provide the necessary support systems to help some of those students pursue landed immigrant status are stretched. As noted previously, universities in Ontario do not receive operating grant support for international students, and in a period of operating grant cutbacks it is unlikely institutions will have discretionary resources to invest in an expansion of such capacity.

Tuition for international students in Ontario is already at the top end relative to other provinces, and the imposition of the "head tax" will simply push fee levels higher. As we look to the future, we should be mindful of the fact that there are many factors that influence the decision by international students to choose to study in Canada and, for that matter, in a particular province. Moreover, in terms of transnational education arrangements, the imposition of a "head tax" on program enrolments may well significantly influence the economic viability of programs.[11]

This chapter has illustrated the apparent impact of government policy as it relates to international students in universities in one province over more than a quarter-century. For roughly one half of the period, the Ontario government[12] played an active role in limiting the degree of international enrolment in higher education by adopting a differential fee policy that was designed to ensure that Ontarians would be served first in the name of access and opportunity. By the latter part of the 1980s, the tide had turned a bit at the graduate level, and the Ontario government introduced tuition waivers for graduate international students in an attempt to maintain international graduate enrolments in areas where there was acknowledged capacity. Meanwhile, at the undergraduate level, international enrolments continued to decline. When a new government took office in late 1995, funding to universities and colleges was slashed, operating grants for international student enrolments were eliminated, and tuition for international students was deregulated. In an environment of tuition flexibility, institutions began implementing tuition policies that acknowledged some semblance of full-cost recovery for international undergraduate students and began to pursue their own internationalization strategies.

Tuition flexibility for international enrolments, along with other aspects of deregulation in the international arena, one could argue, has allowed institutions to pursue an internationalization agenda that is in the best interests of the institution and the province. As institutions have embraced internationalization as a strategic theme for development, more resources have been allocated to internationalization portfolios within institutions and international student recruitment has become a major undertaking for some. At the same time, governments – both provincial and federal – have identified various aspects of PSE internationalization as a high priority and have taken steps to encourage an increase in the level of internationalization.

Government initiatives can have a major impact on international enrolment and on internationalization initiatives – both negative and positive. Furthermore, recent government interest and initiatives in the international arena should be seen for what they are: a new interest in internationalization as an export industry. To that end, government's role should be redefined – not to manage the industry or provide oversight or "tax," but to facilitate and encourage Ontario's institutions to compete in an increasingly competitive market and to provide a buffer to the inevitable downturns in the "export industry" caused by circumstances far beyond the control of the institutions.[13] Recent initiatives, unfortunately, may mark a turning point in international education activity in the province, a potential casualty of creeping (galloping) intrusiveness.

NOTES

1 See Jones (1997).

2 A major part of the apparent increase in popularity of Ontario universities for Hong Kong and Malaysian students was a 1980 introduction of full-cost tuition for international (visa) students in Britain – a destination for many students from the Commonwealth, including Hong Kong and Malaysia.

3 Program cost was estimated based on the existing program funding

weights and the value of the funding unit associated with the Ontario funding formula.

4 The Ontario/Baden-Württemberg program (1990) and Ontario/Rhône-Alpes program (1991) were introduced and offered a range of overseas exchange opportunities to undergraduate and graduate students.

5 By the end of the decade, the province had also introduced two new formal exchange programs – the Ontario/Jiangsu program in 2009 and the Ontario/Maharashtra-Goa program in 2007 – recognizing the growing interest and importance of China and India.

6 The reference in the budget papers was somewhat less clear: "The ministry has identified a reduction in indirect support, through operating grants that the government provides to non-PhD international students." See Ontario Ministry of Finance (2012), Addendum to the 2012 Budget (p. 48). In fact, the government had stopped providing support to universities for most international enrolments in 1996.

7 Readers should note that the data from the COU includes both full-time and part-time international student enrolments to provide a more complete picture of the number of international students. The vast majority of international students are, in fact, full-time, but reporting conventions may categorize the student as part-time if the course load drops below a certain threshold (60–80% of the "normal course load" as set by the institution).

8 The main source for the international enrolment overview is the Statistics Canada report *A Changing Portrait of International Students in Canadian Universities* (McMullen & Elias, 2011). Additional information has been provided by Citizenship and Immigration Canada (CIC) and Statistics Canada's Post Secondary Information System (PSIS).

9 See AUCC for a summary of international tuition by institution across the country: http://www.aucc.ca/canadian-universities/facts-and-stats/tuition-fees-by-university.

10 For example, the expansion of research activity in the sciences drove up demand for graduate students; international students tend to focus in science, technology, engineering, and mathematics (STEM) disciplines – along with business.

11 Programs offered in other countries may be quoted in local currencies and may reflect local economic circumstances. Accordingly, a "head tax" levied at Canadian rates may, in fact, have a major impact on the cost as expressed in local currency.

12 From the mid-1970s through 2012, the "government" changed on a number of occasions as follows: 1985 Progressive Conservative,

1985–7 Coalition Liberal and New Democratic, 1987 Liberal, 1990 New Democratic, 1995 Progressive Conservative, 2003 Liberal.

13 To the extent the "export industry" generates an increasing percentage of operating funding for the institutions, the financial risk increases. The development of programs and services is an on-going expenditure and major disturbances in international demand due to circumstances beyond the institutions' control, such as exchange rate fluctuations, economic downturns in other parts of the world, and civil strife or war, can have a marked impact on international demand for education services.

Conclusion: A Reflection on Contemporary Understandings and Future Directions of Teacher Education in a Transnational World

YVONNE HÉBERT

At the very core of this book, teacher education in a transnational world is not only a vital part of education in all its dimensions of knowledge and action, but also a critical part of the development and survival of the world, as we know it today and hope it to be tomorrow. This notion of *transnational education* – that is, education within border-crossing programs in institutes of learning – is a powerful one, as it assumes that educators and students alike can cross over or into other nation states, and thus live educational, sociocultural, and linguistic experiences that influence them personally and professionally, and that spread horizontally among citizens throughout the nation state. Transnational education goes well beyond the Internet, which already influences and adjusts perceptions of social and educational access, in light of enduring economic contractions in post-secondary and educational institutions of all types, harnessing technological opportunities as well as structural changes needed at all levels, benefiting from local, national, and international provision and attitudes.

Of particular interest to theoretical and methodological considerations are themes that go beyond narrow neoliberal perspectives set within globalization, so as to consider what is involved in becoming well-educated active citizens of this world. As a theory, cosmopolitanism[1] posits that "our political and moral existence should be played out on a world stage and that each of us belongs to a community of human beings that transcends the particularities of local affiliation" (Kymlicka & Walker, 2012, p. 1). In other words, "being a good Canadian citizen includes or entails being a good citizen of the world" (ibid.) – and similarly, in other countries, to be a good citizen of Chile, Germany, and the Ukraine, for example, also entails being a member of the global community, beyond being a member of one's own country.

Transnational education, however, cannot possibly succeed without *cosmopolitanism*. Common to all cosmopolitan views is the notion that all human beings belong to a single community, reflecting a positive moral ideal of a universal community (van Hooft, 2010). In other words, all humans are of equal moral standing and this community should be cultivated. Various forms of cosmopolitanism envision this ethical standard and global community in different ways, with some focusing on political institutions and others on shared moral, ethical, or cultural expressions. A cosmopolitan is not just someone who feels at home in a globalized world, travels widely, and enjoys the cultural products of a global market (Vanderkerckhove & van Hooft, 2010). The term cosmopolitanism is widely used in various disciplines, especially global ethics, political science, international relations, political philosophy, sociology, cultural studies, and history (Hébert, 2013).

A cosmopolitan is a *citizen of the world*. This notion of citizenship implies a commitment and responsibility extended towards all peoples of the world, and a readiness to express such a commitment through political action in the context of institutions with a global reach (Dower, 2003). For example, the Calgary Centre for Global Community (CCGC) has as its first principle: "All of us are citizens of the world. We are all interconnected and cooperation is vital to create a future in which we can all thrive." And yet, this view does have its limits: as global citizens, we do not have a right to reside, vote, express opinions, associate, or travel anywhere we choose. We do, however, have some obligations, such as the obligation to pay taxes, obey laws, and respect authority. In some countries, there might also be an obligation to serve in the military. With the belief that we are all *global citizens*, we are, however, invested in assuring well-governed, well-functioning countries around the world, communicating these views by way of example, discourse, and diplomacy.

Cosmopolitan perspectives as part of civic education could counter excessive patriotism[2] with genuinely open listening to others, without judging or evaluating, to allow oneself to be moved by empathy and an understanding of others. With these words, we take up a transformationalist perspective of globalization (Shultz & Jorgenson, 2007),[3] as a complex set of international, national, and local relationships that have generated new kinds of inclusion and exclusion, according to which the global citizen seeks to "include and engage others based on a common humanity, a shared planet, and a shared future" (Shultz, 2007, p. 255), while also including explicit teaching which takes the local context into account as part of global citizenship (Watson, 2013).

For a deeper understanding of the need for rootedness, moving beyond the suspended state of an "American in Paris," we turn briefly to philosophical considerations. For Kant and other Enlightenment thinkers, there was a sense of "light" patriotism, a sense of rootedness that was important to them and that still finds a voice today in Habermas. The question of "rootedness" is at the heart of cosmopolitanism.[4] Being localized, having local attachments somewhere, and knowing how to get around are very important to all human beings (Hébert, 2013). From an anthropological perspective, Bauman (1996, 2006) recognizes that migrants undergo a process of localization in new contexts, a finding also supported by Hébert's analysis (2013), involving openness towards an Other; a relational attachment to a locality; a recognition of the smallness of one's milieu; a capacity to integrate oneself in a milieu; establishment and maintenance of mutual relationships, interconnecting with other similar persons; awareness of living in multiplicity, in a larger world, with the possibility of relational subtleties and positionings; a moral obligation towards the Other, especially towards those less fortunate; and critical awareness of the major contemporary questions (e.g., economic and ecological crises, and hyper-consumption). With such local attachments, a person is unlikely to be rootless or at risk of being itinerant (Hébert, 2013). Upon such solid concepts serving as pillars for grounding transnational teacher education within an explicit and yet localized cosmopolitan perspective, we weave in transdisciplinarity, citizenship, and globalization (Shultz & Jorgenson, 2007), concepts which are particularly applicable for students engaging in studies abroad, in a state other than their usual or original locus of residency and rights.

The key concepts of *transnationalism*, *cosmopolitanism*, and *the global citizen* traverse this collection of chapters, intertwining in interesting ways with neoliberal programs – programs that are, however, attempting to situate education, educators, and educated persons as economic beings having only instrumental interactions and relationships with others. In an attempt to see where knowledge may lead us in the future, this concluding chapter comments on theoretical and methodological considerations to complexify certain issues. This is done so as to stimulate further thought on the notion of the "cosmos"[5] and our own relationships with Others that may lead us to become cosmopolitan and to engage in transnational projects and programs that support us, each and all, as global citizens for the benefit of others, our countries, and ourselves.

Transnational Teacher Education and the Future of the World

Part of teachers' intellectual and practical education could possibly be undertaken in another country, with emphases on appropriate curricular and pedagogical preparation, as well as on linguistic and intercultural competencies. Such high expectations would benefit not only the candidates, but also future young pupils and their parents. Bilateral projects, cross-border partnerships, and interregional schemes could, each in their own way, further this agenda with respect to teacher education. New models of integration could draw on older forms of training and fellowship, as well as transnational efforts to stimulate a more efficient labour market than one operating only within national boundaries. Although the Erasmus[6] program and the Leonardo[7] project support students who wish to study abroad – that is, at other institutions in other countries within the European Union – these projects have also prompted institutions to clarify their pedagogical objectives and course offerings. In particular, the Bologna Process[8] encouraged the provision of comparative, compatible courses of instruction and programing, whereas the Leonardo project was specifically reserved for apprenticeships in the trades as part of achieving an outstanding professional education.

Such voyages entail an education to alterity that is an ambivalent, incomplete, and tentative process of making a place for the Other in one's identity (Cicchelli, 2007, 2008). In a great majority of cases, Cicchelli's (2012, 2013) research participants claimed a strong national identification that coexisted with a strong interest for other European ways of living. This "cosmopolitanism consists in recognizing and appreciating the other as a stranger. That means that he/she is not completely a stranger, nor an exact copy of oneself. Re-conciliating community and alterity, identity and difference, finding the universal in the particular and the particular in the universal, that is not only the definition of the dialectic but the condition of all authentic dialogue" (Hassner, 2002).

Key to all three types of programs is the notion of cosmopolitanism, understood as being able to live in another "world" where life and society are organized in compatible but rather different ways of being, doing, and becoming. Key to this notion is the attachment that one develops: becoming a "global citizen" means having broader views of the human race beyond one's own city to see oneself as a caring, responsible, and active human being – thus, a "citizen" of this world and, in other words, a citizen of the cosmos. All of us are citizens of the world. We are all interconnected and cooperation is vital to create a future in which we can all thrive.

The cross-border implications for teacher education may not seem obvious at first glance, as teachers are usually prepared for their home nation's schools, rarely with an international component. Exceptions do arise, however; for example, the past and current teacher education programs at the University of Calgary continue to offer a semester abroad, the fourth and final semester, with extensive Internet contact with a mentor, usually a highly seasoned instructor. In this model, basic skills and knowledge are presumed to have been acquired in the previous semesters, on campus and in practica in schools. Returning student teachers have high praise for these experiences, although, in a few cases, cultural egocentrism had not been eradicated or attenuated by international experiences. However, in most such programs, cross-cultural competences are part of the curriculum, to be mastered as part of a teacher's becoming an effective, knowledgeable professional.

In contrast, Canadian post-secondary institutions receive international students, who have been subject to variable provincial policies over several decades, although visa requirements for entry into the country are within federal jurisdiction. Nonetheless, provincial policy in Ontario ranged widely from pecuniary to altruistic motivations, rarely allowing for the possibility and value of equal exchanges of ideas and experiences. Only recently did the province acknowledge the value of such experiences, in terms of internationalization, for receiving institutions and their students. This renewed perspective opened up to a positive allocation of institutional and student funding, rather than maintaining higher fees for international students. Issues involved possible complementarity in exchanges with colleagues at other universities, possible participation in the global marketplace, and possible enrichment of learning experiences among undergraduate students.[9]

Teachers, as leaders in their communities and as pillars of democracy,[10] could well learn from examples in this book, by going beyond narrow national interests to draw lessons from border-crossings and to think smart on teaching and learning. The result would be education allied to an active sense of social justice and of acceptance of others, broadening participation from all groups so as to encourage practical and intellectual education for all of their students. Not only promoting and living democracy, teachers can educate their students about the valuable role of democracy in enhancing and sustaining the quality of life of all citizens. Standing up for democracy means listening to all voices, with decisions made in respectful consultations and interactions, in an ongoing dialogue with all sectors of democracy. Recognizing that their students need to play an active role as engaged citizens in their classroom as preparation for continuation in their adult years, teachers can be artful in having their young charges learn to take up roles as elected classroom officials, such as class president and class secretary, in which all classmates have a voice and get to vote. Later on, such students will take up similar democratic service roles with the student union, in community advocacy, and, more broadly, in society (CIRCLE, 2013). Teachers' work is vital to the sustenance of democracy, to practically and intellectually stimulating lives, to enhancing the common good, and to living in civilized society. And yet, even in this book, there are many negative images of teachers and few positive views. Nonetheless, a 2013 advertisement from the Canadian Teachers' Federation portrays teachers as pillars of democracy!

Rethinking Ways to Wisdom

The Socratic principle of wisdom as a moral horizon places its focus not only in the past but elsewhere, in the discovery of and attention to the other as a real subject, enabling deep knowledge that one must achieve by oneself, following a path for intellectual and political emancipation – for wisdom has to be embodied in a life as a project of service towards a better present and desirable future. To have good teachers, teacher educators must be good people themselves so that they may teach others to be good people.

At the confluence of influential forces, teacher education reflects the changing nature of the relationship between capitalism and Western modernity as two different historical processes, of regulation and of emancipation (Santos, 2002, pp. 1–2). The rules and practices of the market, exposed as it is to the demands of neoliberal capitalism, dominate the modern university as higher education is redefined as a key economic and social driver, while governments reduce their funding and require greater institutional efficiency. Governments require submission to various forms of quality assurance; participation in global, national, regional and local markets; as well as fundraising from the private sector, all while endeavouring to maintain academic values and forms of knowledge (Henkel, 2002, pp. 30–1). Within such modern, neoliberal university settings, teacher quality does matter. Yet, there are few if any indications of awareness regarding possible misunderstandings within the hierarchies of modern neoliberal universities, given linguistic and cultural differences, and little is spoken of the serious need for cross-cultural competences to thrive in the new economy. How then can scholars and students create greater understanding and collaboration towards wisdom across borders?

Teachers are crucial to the implementation of the school improvement agenda, as the agents who will ensure the production of skilled and knowledgeable students for the global economy. In modern, neoliberal educational settings, teacher practice has changed and its quality is now defined in reference to cultural competence, ethical practices, and responsiveness to learners within a broad definition of curriculum assessed through high-stakes testing (Ell & Grudnoff, 2013, p. 82). Interestingly, students in Alberta, a western Canadian province, typically score among the top three jurisdictions on the PISA (Program for International Student Assessment). Why might this be? In this province, a convergence of forces – including province-wide initiatives for school improvement, as well as regional consortia focusing on teachers' professional development – are bringing about increasingly similar pedagogical approaches. Here, an incremental alignment of teacher practice arises in a globalizing, neoliberal societal environment (Farrell, 2011). Assuming the validity of international standardized tests to define and measure student success, these findings make it plausible to link the alignment of teacher practice to students' better learning abilities and to their enhanced cognitive processes. Thus, we see how very crucial teachers are to student success, as measured on international standardized tests. The linkages between such results and academic success, then, ought to have an impact beyond high school and translate into continuing successes within post-secondary studies and the world of work – although there is not yet any evidence to support or deny this hypothesis.

However, quantitative results, such as the PISA, do not reveal the answers to four seemingly simple questions: Whose knowledge counts? What does effective teaching look like? How do the best teachers become effective? What do great teachers think of their profession? Suggestive responses may be found in a reflexive study of a teacher's evolution over a long time span, which suggests five incremental professional steps: moving from novice to advanced beginner, to competent performer, to proficient performer, and finally, possibly, to expert (van Doorn, 2010). The combination of effective teaching with an ecological and cosmopolitan view, allowing oneself to teach with wisdom and to be moved by empathy and understanding of others, may indeed lead to student success with the promise to reap benefits for all concerned.

Inter-Connection with the Earth and Indigeneity

Focusing on the benefits of difference – that is, different ways of becoming, of being, of learning, and of community – makes possible diverse forms of integration. Possibilities for appropriate pedagogies and curricula are grounded in the meaning of the term "indigenous," as being original to a place over time. Such an understanding grounds the notion in different modes of being, while focusing on community as well as the integration of the ancestral knowledge of the indigenous population. The inclusion of Indigenous spaces for learning embodies and locates an argument for culturally appropriate learning on university campuses, with consequent infrastructural organizational changes.

What is of most benefit to both modern Western culture and Aboriginal people is Indigenous knowledge, based on a different ontology – a different way of being in the world. The social, spiritual, intellectual, epistemological, and political aspects of Aboriginal cultures and their ends are of great service to an Aboriginal community. However, the enactment of Indigenous knowledge focuses on the mode of learning in an ontologically co-created "place," an important Indigenous concept (Chambers, 1999, 2008). Having both a literal and figurative reference of connection to land, the term *indigeneity* can be understood as referring to all manner of pedagogies that re-establish the human relationship with place and to being original to the place over the long term. Similarly, the term *decolonizing* refers to or is linked to an explicitly environmental education per se. Through these two terms, sensitive, progressive pedagogy can be premised on re-establishing human connection with place, by means of deep engagement with indigenous modes of being. But how is indigenous education to be enacted in practice? The Indigenous learner knows that when the human world is silenced, it is possible to attend to non-human forces (listening to the wind in the willows), to meander and to experience moments of uncontrolled time and direction, accessible to everyone, but incompatible with the mechanistic world view that predominates in Western society. The essence of this inter-connection occurs in actions in the world that spring from the soil and point to a very different way of inhabiting the world. Autochthony recognizes the deep interconnection between the earth and human beings.

Given the relevance of higher education to the emancipation and survival processes of indigenous communities and cultures, the process, the challenges, the purpose, and the outcomes of indigeneity at the basis of education are richly documented in this book, which thus makes an important contribution to an increasingly rich and detailed body of knowledge.[11] However, much more evidence is available for germane discussion; for example, two important publications set out the goals and direction of the change that has taken place in Canada: the position paper *Indian Control of Indian Education* (National Indian Brotherhood, 1972) and the subsequent comprehensive survey and analysis *Tradition and Education: Towards a Vision of Our Future* (Assembly of First Nations, 1988). The importance of Indigenous knowledge cannot be undervalued, especially in Canada, where there are more than six hundred First Nations/Indian bands and over sixty Aboriginal languages reported by First Nations people – an indication of the diversity of First Nations people across the country (Statistics Canada, 2011a).

Given this diversity, efforts to incorporate Aboriginal approaches to education into formal schooling began to gain acceptance in the 1970s and emerged more fully in the next decade , as described in a 1987 volume by Barman, Hébert, and McCaskill. Seeking to resolve the issues posed in that book, the writings in *First Nations Education in Canada: The Circle Unfolds* (Battiste & Barman, 1995) are organized around the concept of the Sacred Circle, to emphasize the unity, continuity, and interconnectedness of each issue. In a timely fashion, educational innovations had matured to the point where they provided persuasive evidence of the effectiveness of Aboriginal leadership and control. The *Report of the Royal Commission on Aboriginal Peoples* (RCAP, 1996, pp. 433–584) is rich with case examples and statistics that point to recent achievements, with selected papers drawn from studies for the RCAP published in Castellano, Davis, and Lahache (2000). Supported by the Social Science and Humanities Research Council, the 1996 International Summer Institute, held in Saskatoon, challenged entrenched orthodoxies with papers focused upon reclaiming Indigenous voice and vision (later published as a collection by Battiste [2000]). Furthermore, drawing from her place-based research, Chambers (1999, 2008) developed thoughtful, innovative ways of centring "place" into daily curriculum and pedagogical practice. Represented by wise persons of Indigenous and non-Indigenous backgrounds and by valid knowledge, higher education – including research – continues to play a key role in the maintenance, renewal, and continuation of Indigenous cultures and communities.

Knowledge-Making and Methodology

Knowledge is typically studied with some method in mind, and yet, in this book on knowledge making, there is no explicit debate on research methodology for a neoliberal market economy, nor is there any debate on the research methodology required to create new knowledge befitting a neoliberal world in tension with a transnational view of educational services and of a fusion or federation of the various educational views. Nonetheless, the chapters take up theoretical perspectives – be these philosophical,[12] historical,[13] or sociological[14] – producing position papers without much discussion of their method of knowledge making, however necessary this may be. A few others[15] explicitly take up a qualitative methodology to carry out enticing case studies with interviews of educators, students, and parents – that is, agents of interest to specific research topics.

Under international and national pressure to change, teacher education in Chile must produce prospective teachers who are capable of implementing the new national curriculum and of responding to the complex demands of the knowledge society and globalization.[16] Unfortunately, graduating teacher candidates have historically scored very low on university exit exams. Moreover, Chilean teachers have done poorly on the international Teacher Education and Development Study in Mathematics, revealing low levels of subject and pedagogical knowledge. Policymakers and the public have been equally concerned with such poor showings, although solutions are proving to be both difficult and complex. Policymakers want both national policies and the quality outputs of teacher education programs to improve, whereas these institutions are under pressure to increase their student intake, given greater demand from parents, sons, and daughters for access to tertiary institutions for reasons of social mobility.

Of the many possible threads or pathways to knowledge throughout this volume, it becomes quite clear that an important one is the quest not only for knowledge, but also for truth, justice, democracy, participation, voice, and recognition, as well as self in community. Binding laws and international acts/charters create rules for living, learning, and loving. Nonetheless, multilinearity and pluralism acknowledge the complexities of life today in a multimodal world. Other possible threads may indicate tensions, truths, and mistruths: linearity versus complexity; simplistic solutions versus complexity; authority versus collaboration; individuality versus obliged communal attachments and truths.

Theoretical Omissions

In spite of its length and complexity, this book does not cover all manner of views of transnational education, cosmopolitanism, and global citizenship. What then is missing? Curiously, there is no mention of the influence of social class – and yet, teaching and schooling are mostly middle-class activities, and thus issues of mobility and poverty may not necessarily have touched the daily lives of teacher candidates. How then can teachers be credible when assigned to schools in neighbourhoods marked by poverty, when they lack experience with that struggle? Or to schools of linguistic, cultural, social, and economic differences or, in another phrasing, schools richly characterized by diversity?

Only one chapter discusses the impact of poverty,[17] whereas there is limited mention of gender in terms of four possible usages: gender as a new community,[18] gender as a blind spot coupled with race,[19] gender as a boundary,[20] and gender as a phenomenon.[21] Equally surprising, there is no mention of resistance, as demonstrated through art, dance, drama, literature, and music, except for the chapters on Indigenous education. Furthermore, there is no mention of youth in revolt, of a crying lack of decent jobs, of Giroux's (2009, 2012) powerful commentary on the cultural neglect and victimization of today's youth and their low levels of employment. Nor is there a mention of Côté & Allahar's (2006) challenge of the societal phenomenon of delayed adulthood for socio-economic causes. A paucity of employment opportunities for youth is the culprit – in other words, the neoliberal market economy is to blame. If you cannot meet the rent or make monthly mortgage payments with your earnings, if you rely upon your parents' assistance to do so, then are you truly an adult (Gaudet and Quéniart, 2008)? Given youth's inability to obtain reasonably well-paying employment and, thus, their inability to take up the level of responsibility that characterizes adulthood, these youth can hardly quest for transnational educational services.

Glaringly, there is no mention of or realization that most of the chapters are set within a neoliberal era that dwells upon economic matters when transnational intellectuals seek exchanges, desirous of collaboration in the production of knowledge. But here, too, institutions of learning tend to treat scholars and students alike, as *homo economicus* in instrumental relationships, thus conveying a lack of trust and respect for scholarship and a lack of wisdom. Moreover, the students are considered to be clients for services, with administrations tending to cater to the demands of their clients.

The heavy hand of the state is frequently seen – for example, in the Chilean government in publishing test results or in federated bodies adopting possible priorities – and although non-compulsory programs are more attractive, it is seen everywhere in the neoliberal era, as the state does not trust Others. The OECD publishes the PISA test results and spreads the findings all around the world, to less and less avail, although in some jurisdictions, educators gather together to discuss how each is handling teaching and learning in international comparative initiatives. But why does this occur in reinforced societies and with international questions?

Mobility and Poverty

Mobility in a neoliberal environment – movement towards new truths, new lives, and towards social justice – starts with getting enough money to buy food, shelter, and schooling. Tensions between parents of immigrant background, schooled in other traditions, and their children, born in the "new world," lead the parents to try navigating school systems, be it in inner-city schooling or in the suburbs. The cyclical nature of these issues, experienced by many if not most immigrant families, is not often discussed among immigrants, researchers, or service providers.

The poverty of transnational migrants to and within Europe is also apparent, but is certainly not part of the academic and professional programs and projects of the European Union. Transnational merchants, crossing from the Adriatic and Mediterranean Seas, who bring their knowledge of marketing and a selection of goods for particular clients in certain countries and cities, typify poor-to-poor migration (Tarrius, Missaoui, & Qacha, 2013). The merchants travel from source countries in the Middle East and Northern Africa to southern Europe.

Yet in this book there is no mention of poor-to-poor migration – that is, of the movement of the poor from such source countries, often by boat in the dark of night, to host countries (e.g., France, Germany, and elsewhere in Europe), guided by experienced hands, usually part of the underground. Passengers arrive in a "better" part of the world where, as merchants of carpets, technological equipment, and so forth, they can sell their wares in certain European cities, a very favourable outcome to the benefit of their extended families in their countries of origin. Usually protected by observant family males, women may set up in the sex trade, often returning home when they have attained the hoped-for financial savings. Goods may go to different ports than the migrant-merchants. In Europe, other family members take them in as part of the mercantile family chain. This type of migration was first observed in the 1970s, no doubt based on the routes and knowledge of able seamen and mercantile-adventurers travelling this way for centuries, so knowledgeable that travelling in the dark is possible (Tarrius, Missaoui, & Qacha, 2013). The young people involved do not seem to have accumulated much schooling – most certainly not at the post-secondary level – and yet, there is so much to learn, so much good to do in this world. Whose knowledge counts? Why? How is this question to be debated and answered?

Social and Professional Networks

The role of social networks in the world of work, in professional lives, in making good friends at school, and in gathering new information is noted in Burbules's discussion of ubiquitous learning as being situated within the growth of collaborative learning communities. These are viewed as a part of wider social and cultural changes involving the Internet in an ethos of generosity, and hence a generous extension of their social networks within a faceless online community. Such is the power of ubiquitous resources, as these reside in the aggregated contributions made by many. Although the process of book-making herein is built upon professional networks, only one contributor recognizes the significance of social networks to online shared learning as part of professional lives.

Not all authors in this volume recognize the usefulness of theories and theory making in discussions of teacher education in transnational contexts, although others situate theorization at the very heart of their scholarly production. Following a brief discussion of theory making in the introductory chapter, Johnston dwells upon critical theory, post-structuralism, and pragmatism as rival philosophies, battling one another in order to capture what might count as "truth." Such a dynamic rendering of theory making will surely sustain the reader through any theoretical desert towards a land of plenty.

Theory as Power

The concept of *critical* theory is seen to have the power to free people, especially among those who are working towards crisis intervention – for example, in support of Māori in their struggle to gain more control over their lives.[22] Freeing themselves from various layers and formations of oppression, exploitation, and containment is a result of self-critical examination. Also characteristically of critical theory, a linear model is often voiced as being the only way in which to address intervention of this nature, and yet, within the components of *kaupapa Māori*, the flexibility to change and the need to move depend on the variables required to make things happen. Inscribed within the Frankfurt school of critical theory, such flexibility is related to the need for powerful critical interventions as nourishment for the collective and for the recognition of others.[23]

Both post-structuralism and critical theories share a critical view of subjectivism, but both also turn away from the self and towards the Other to glorify differences to the detriment of unities. A third approach – that is, pragmatism – recognizes, theorizes, and synthesizes differences as well as unities, thus avoiding extreme subjectivity.[241] And yet, an intersubjective theory of the self and community is needed to account for globalization in its various dimensions, be these social, political, or economic. Similarly, teachers need scientific and rationalist narratives to account for life patterns, as well as statistical analyses – rather than moral and religious narratives – so as to quantify a situation, to make a point, and to act according to strictly rational and scientific criteria.[252]

Philosophical, logical, qualitative, and case-study approaches are considered to be particularly useful in attempting to redress inequities and to relate social anti-subjective stories of "truth." What is missing, however, is an explicit discussion of spirituality, taking up the question: where does religion fit in? In many areas of the world, daily life is organized around religious beliefs and observances which may or may not be shared or acted upon, whether pervasively or not, in other areas of the world (Willis, 2012). A student abroad could then find herself/himself in a country where life is organized around religion, which would be difficult for a person from a secular society. Religion can make a person better or much worse; what it takes up, though, is the question of how to live seriously (Willis, 2012). In that regard, study abroad, the study of other ways of living, can well be a life-changing experience.

Thus, the purposes of theorizing teacher education in transnational contexts have shifted to preparation for life in a complex but well-developed world, wherein there is no one method of doing, of being, of thinking of oneself and the other as global citizens via transnational higher education. There is, however, sufficient creativity and coexistence, reflection and relativity, and singularity and collaboration to be able to teach, learn, and live reasonably well in a disorderly world of anxiety and uncertainty.

NOTES

1 See, for example, Noddings, in this volume.
2 As Noddings proposes in her chapter.
3 The other two perspectives of global citizenship distinguish between (1) a neoliberal approach to globalization that positions an individual in a privileged position to travel across national borders, and (2) a radical approach to globalization that examines global structures that create and perpetuate global inequality (Shultz & Jorgenson, 2007, p. 24).
4 I give thanks to James Scott Johnston, co-editor of this book, for bringing into the conversation the enlightened concept of "rootedness" (and its long philosophical roots) with respect to cosmopolitanism.
5 Meaning "order" or "world" in the original Greek.
6 See Toporkoff, this volume.
7 See Robinson, this volume.
8 Also in this volume, see chapters by Martínez Valle, Kutsyuruba, and Jover and Geraldo, respectively.
9 See Snowdon, in this volume, for a discussion of the various policy shifts over the years and their motivations.
10 The 1 October 2013 release by the Canadian Teachers' Federation, "World Teachers' Day" proclaimed that teachers are "pillars of democracy," as part of the celebrations of teachers everywhere and in acknowledgment of their work as vital for students and for democracy. First inaugurated in 1994, October 5 is World Teachers' Day, representing a significant token of the awareness, understanding, and appreciation displayed for the vital contribution that teachers make to education and development. See Canadian Teachers' Federation (CTF) (2013).

11 See the chapters of Beeman, Merino-Dickinson, and Robust.
12 See the chapters by Johnston, Noddings, Russell, and Burbules for examples of philosophical perspectives.
13 See the chapters by Whitehead, as well as Bruno-Jofré and Cole, for examples of historical approaches.
14 See Dale's chapter for an example of a sociological approach to globalization, higher education, and teacher education. Of some relevance here is the work of sociologists Pierre Bourdieu and Jean-Claude Passeron, who recognized the significance of the role of the social and cultural milieu in the appropriation and integration of mass (popular) culture.
15 See, for example, Merino-Dickinson's chapter for a case-study, narrative approach to knowledge making.
16 See Cox, Meckes, and Bascopé chapter for an example of policy analysis.
17 See Robinson chapter.
18 See Johnston chapter.
19 See Bruno-Jofré and Cole chapter.
20 See Noddings chapter.
21 See Toporkoff chapter.
22 See Robust chapter.
23 See the work of Smith (1997), described in the chapter by Robust.
24 As discussed by Johnston, this volume.
25 As Whitehead emphasizes in this volume.

Bibliography

Accenture. (2012). *Turning the Tide: How Europe Can Rebuild Skills and Generate Growth*. Retrieved from http://www.accenture.com/SiteCollectionDocuments/PDF/Accenture-Turning-the-Tide-How-Europe-can-Rebuild-Skills-and-Generate-Growth.pdf.

Acker, S. (2000). Traditions and Transitions in Teacher Education: The Development of a Research Project. *Historical Studies in Education/Revue d'histoire de l'éducation, 12*(1/2), 143–154.

Adora-Hoppers, C. A. (2000). Globalization and the Social Construction of Reality: Affirming or Unmasking the "Inevitable?" In N. P. Stromquist & K. Monkman (Eds.), *Globalization and Education: Integration and Contestation across Cultures* (pp. 99–121). Lanham, MD: Rowman and Littlefield.

Adorno, T. (1973). *Negative Dialectics* (E. B. Ashton, Trans.). New York: Continuum.

Albom, M. (2005). *Martes con mi Viejo Profesor*. Mexico City: Océano.

Altbach, P., & Knight, J. (2007). The Internationalization of Higher Education: Motivations and Realities. *Journal of Studies in International Education, 11*(3–4), 290–305. http://dx.doi.org/10.1177/1028315307303542

Alves, R. (1996). *La Alegría de Enseñar*. Barcelona, Spain: Octaedro.

Anderson, B. (1991). *Imagined Communities: Reflections on the Origins and Spread of Nationalism* (2nd ed.). London and New York: Verso.

Anderson, B. (2006). *Imagined Communities: Reflections on the Origins and Spread of Nationalism* (3rd ed.). London: Verso.

Apple, M. (2001). *Educating the Right Way: Market Standards, God and Inequality*. New York: Routledge.

Arendt, H. (1994). The Ivory Tower of Common Sense. In H. Arendt (Ed.), *Essays in Understanding: 1930–1954* (pp. 194–196). New York: Harcourt, Brace & Co.

Argyris, C. (1990). *Overcoming Organizational Defenses*. Boston: Allyn & Bacon.

Argyris, C., & Schön, D. A. (1974). *Theory in Practice: Increasing Professional Effectiveness*. San Francisco: JosseyBass.

Armengol Asparó, C., et al. (2011). El Practicum en el Espacio Europeo de Educación Superior: Mapa de Competencias del Profesional de la Educación. *Revista de Educación, 354*, 71–98.

Arnold, E., & Reh, S. (2005). Bachelor-und Master-Studiengänge für die Lehrerbildung: Neue Studienstrukturen als Professionalisierungschance? *Die Hochschule, 1*, 143–156.

Artyomenko, A. (2005, 25 June). Live and Learn: About the Terms and the Essence. *Zerkalo Nedeli*, 15–17.

Ash, M. G. (2006). Bachelor of What, Master of Whom? The Humboldt Myth and Historical Transformations of Higher Education in German-Speaking Europe and the US. *European Journal of Education, 41*(2), 245–267. http://dx.doi.org/10.1111/j.1465-3435.2006.00258.x

Assembly of First Nations. (1988). *Tradition and Education: Towards a Vision of Our Future*. Ottawa, Canada: Assembly of First Nations.

Association of Universities and Colleges of Canada (AUCC). (1990). *Trends: The Canadian University in Profile, 1990 Edition*. Ottawa, Canada: AUCC.

Association of Universities and Colleges of Canada (AUCC). (2007). *Internationalizing Canadian Campuses*. Ottawa, Canada: AUCC.

Atlantic Information Centre for Teachers (AICT). (1969). *Teaching about the American Impact in Europe*. Report of an international seminar for teachers organized at Füssen, Germany, by the Atlantic Information Centre for Teachers, 23–28 November 1969, ed. J. R. Huntley. Reading, England: Lamport Gilbert Printers.

Atlantic Information Centre for Teachers (AICT). (1971). *Teaching about Collective Security and Conflict*. Report of an international seminar for teachers organized at Rungstedgaard, near Copenhagen, by the Atlantic Information Centre for Teachers, 28–31 October 1971, ed. J. R. Huntley. London: Atlantic Educational Publications.

Auding, I. (2011). Bologna-Reform: Verband fordert einheitliche Lehrerausbildung. *Bildungsklick*. Retreived from http://bildungsklick.de/a/76712/verband-fordert-einheitliche-lehrerausbildung

Autorengruppe Bildungsberichterstattung. (2012). *Bildung in Deutschland 2012*. Köln: Statistische Ämter des Bundes und der Länder. Retreived from http://www.bildungsbericht.de/daten2012/bb_2012.pdf

Avalos, B. (2002). *Profesores para Chile: Historia de un Proyecto*. Santiago, Chile: Ministerio de Educación.

Axelrod, P. (1989). Higher Education, Utilitarianism, and the Acquisitive Society: Canada, 1930–1980. In M. S. Cross & G. S. Kealey (Eds.), *Modern Canada: Readings in Canadian Social History* (pp. 179–205). Toronto, Canada: McClelland & Stewart.

Axelrod, P. (1997). *The Promise of Schooling: Education in Canada, 1800–1914*. Toronto, Canada: University of Toronto Press.

Axelrod, P., & Reid, J. G. (1989). Introduction. In P. Axelrod & J. G. Reid (Eds.), *Youth, University and Canadian Society: Essays in the Social History of Higher Education* (pp. xiv–xv). Kingston and Montreal, Canada, and London: McGill-Queen's University Press.

Baer, M. (2000). Schulen zu Schulen für Schülerinnen und Schüler weiterentwickeln. *Beiträge zur Lehrerinnen- und Lehrerbildung, 18*(1), 23–25.

Barber, B. (1996). Constitutional Faith. In J. Cohen (Ed.), *M. C. Nussbaum, For Love of Country?* (pp. 30–37). Boston: Beacon Press.

Barber, M., & Mourshed, M. (2008). *How the World's Best-Performing School Systems Come Out on Top*. London: McKinsey and Company. Retreived from http://mckinseyonsociety.com/downloads/reports/Education/Worlds_School_Systems_Final.pdf.

Bardach, E. (2006). Policy Dynamics. In M. Moran, M. Rein, & R. E. Goodin (Eds.), *The Oxford Handbook of Public Policy* (pp. 336–366). Oxford, England: Oxford University Press.

Bargel, T. (2011). Nach der Reform ist vor der Reform – Studienqualität vor und nach Bologna. In S. Nickel (Ed.), *Der Bologna-Prozess aus Sicht der Hochschulforschung* (pp. 218–25). Gütersloh, Germany: CHE-Arbeitspapier 148.

Barman, J., Hébert, Y., & McCaskill, D. (Eds.). (1987). Indian Education in Canada (Vol. 2). *The Challenge*. Vancouver, Canada: UBC Press.

Barnett, R., & Maxwell, D. (Eds.). (2008). *Wisdom in the University*. London: Routledge.

Bartz, O. (2007). Expansion und Umbau: Hochschulreformen in der Bundesrepublik Deutschland zwischen 1964 und 1977. *Die Hochschule, 2*, 154–170.

Basso, K. (1996). *Senses of Place*. Santa Fe, NM: School of American Research Press.

Battiste, M. (Ed.). (2000). *Reclaiming Indigenous Voice and Vision*. Vancouver, Canada: UBC Press.

Battiste, M., & Barman, J. (Eds.). (1995). *First Nations Education in Canada: The Circle Unfolds*. Vancouver, Canada: UBC Press.

Battiste, M., & Henderson, Y. (2000). *Protecting Indigenous Knowledge and Heritage: A Global Challenge*. Saskatoon, Canada: Purich.

Bauman, Z. (1996). From Pilgrim to Tourist – or a Short History of Identity. In S. Hall & P. du Gay (Eds.), *Questions of Cultural Identity* (pp. 18–36). London: Sage.

Bauman, Z. (2006). *Liquid Times: Living in an Age of Uncertainty*. Cambridge, England: Polity Press.

Baynazarova, O. (2005). Efficiency of Method Service Work: Monitoring of Method Service Activities in Kharkiv Oblast. In O. Lokshyna (Ed.), *Education Quality Monitoring Development in Ukraine: Educational Policy Recommendations* (pp. 166–181). Kyiv, Ukraine: Ministry of Education and Science of Ukraine.

Beckmann, H. K. (1968). Zur Problematik der Lehrerausbildung. In H. K. Beckmann (Ed.), *Zur Reform des pädagogischn Studiums und der Lehrerausbildung* (pp. 1–10). Basel, Switzerland: Beltz.

Beeman, C. (2006). *Another Way of Knowing and Being*. Doctoral thesis, Queen's University, Kingston, Canada.

Beeman, C. (2010). When Aboriginal Education Becomes Learning, Aboriginally. *Queen's Education Letter*, Spring/Summer (pp. 3–4). Kingston, Canada: Queen's University.

Beeman, C., & Blenkinsop, S. (2008). Might Diversity Also Be Ontological? Considering Heidegger, Spinoza and Indigeneity in Educative Practice. *Encounters on Education, 9*, 95–107.

Belich, J. (1986). *The New Zealand Wars and the Victorian Interpretation of Racial Conflict*. Auckland, New Zealand: Auckland University Press.

Bell, D. (1960). *The End of Ideology: On the Exhaustion of Political Ideas in the Fifties*. Glencoe, IL: Free Press.

Bell, D. (1973). *The Coming of Post-Industrial Society: A Venture in Social Forecasting*. New York: Basic Books.

Beneitone, P., et al. (Eds.). (2007). *Reflexiones y Perspectivas de la Educación Superior en América Latina. Informe Final Proyecto Tuning-América Latina 2004–2007*. Deusto, Spain: Universidad de Deusto.

Benkler, Y. (2002). *Coase's Penguin, or Linux and the Nature of the Firm*. http://www.benkler.org/CoasesPenguin.html

Berg, C., Herrlitz, H.-G., & Horn, K.-P. (2004). *Kleine Geschichte der Deutschen Gesellschaft fuer Erziehungswissenschaften*. Wiesbaden, Germany: VS.

Bernhard, P., & Rohstock, A. (Forthcoming). Learning from Each Other? A Transnational History of Fascist Education in Italy, Spain and Nazi-Germany, 1922–1945.

Berry, W. (1995). *Another Turn of the Crank*. Washington, DC: Counterpoint.

Bess, M. (2006). *Moral Dimensions of World War II*. New York: Alfred A. Knopf.

Best, E. (1986). *The Māori School of Learning: Its Objects, Methods, and Ceremonial*. Wellington, New Zealand: Government Printer.

Bienefeld, S., & Almqvist, J. (2004). Student Life and the Roles of Students in Europe. *European Journal of Education, 39*(4), 429–441. http://dx.doi.org/10.1111/j.1465-3435.2004.00195.x

Biesta, G., & Peters, M. (2007). *Derrida, Deconstruction, and the Politics of Pedagogy*. New York: Peter Lang.

Birtwistle, T. M. (2009). Towards 2010 (and Then Beyond): The Context of the Bologna Process. *Assessment in Education: Principles, Policy & Practice, 16*(1), 55–63.

Bishop, R. (1996). *Collaborative Research Stories / Whakawhanaungatanga*. Palmerston North, New Zealand: The Dunmore Press Ltd.

Blasi, P. (2006). The European University: Towards a Wisdom-based Society. *Higher Education in Europe, 31*(4), 403–407. http://dx.doi.org/10.1080/03797720701303616

Blass, E. (2012). Is Bologna Sustainable in the Future? Future Testing the Bologna Principles. In A. Curaj, P. Scott, L. Vlasceanu, & L. Wilson (Eds.), *European Higher Education at the Crossroads* (pp. 1057–1072). Dordrecht, Netherlands: Springer. http://dx.doi.org/10.1007/978-94-007-3937-6_53

Boden, M. A. (2006). *Mind as Machine: A History of Cognitive Science*. 2 vols. Oxford, England: Oxford University Press.

Bölling, R. (1983). *Sozialgeschichte der deutschen Lehrer*. Göttingen, Germany: Vandenhoeck & Ruprecht.

Bologna National Report Ukraine. (2009). *European Higher Education Area*. Retrieved from http://www.ehea.info/Uploads/Documents/National_Report_Ukraine_2009.pdf

Bontis, N., & Fitz-enz, J. (2002). Intellectual Capital ROI: A Causal Map of Human Capital Antecedents and Consequents. *Journal of Intellectual Capital, 3*(3), 223–247. http://dx.doi.org/10.1108/14691930210435589

Börzel, T. A. (2003). *Shaping and Taking EU Policies: Member State Responses to Europeanization*. Queen's Papers on Europeanisation 2. Boston: Houghton Mifflin.

Bourdieu, P. (1984). *Distinction: A Social Critique of the Judgement of Taste*. Cambridge, MA: Harvard University Press.

Bourdieu, P. (1992). Thinking about Limits. *Theory, Culture & Society, 9*(1), 37–49. http://dx.doi.org/10.1177/026327692009001003

Bourdieu, P., & Passeron, J. C. (1964). *Les Héritiers: Les Étudiants et Leurs Études*. Paris: Éditions de Minuit.

Breyer, A. (2007, December 4). Kinderkrankheiten künftiger Lehrer. *Frankfurter Allgemeine Zeitung*.

Brizzi, G. P. (1999). Les Universités Européennes à l'Époque Moderne: Premières Synthèses. *Revue de l'Histoire de l'Éducation, 81*, 23–24.

Bromme, R. (1992). *Der Lehrer als Experte: Zur Psychologie des professionellen Wissens*. Bern, Switzerland: Huber.

Bruner, J. S. (1960). *The Process of Education*. Cambridge, MA: Harvard University Press.

Bruner, J. S. (1980). Jerome S. Bruner. In G. Lindsey (Ed.), *History of Psychology in Autobiography* (Vol. 7, pp. 75–151). San Francisco: W. H. Freeman.

Bruner, J. S. (1983). *In Search of Mind: Essays in Autobiography*. New York: Harper & Row.

Bruner, J. S. (2006). *In Search of Pedagogy: The Selected Works of Jerome S. Bruner* (Vol. 1). New York: Routledge.

Brunner, B., & Oester, K. (2010). Doing Identity in Transnationalized Space: Adolescents' Self-Representation in Urban Switzerland. Centre on Migration, Citizenship and Development. Working Papers, 75. T. Faist (General Ed.). Bielefeld, Germany: COMCAD.

Brunner, J. J. (2009). *Educación Superior en Chile. Instituciones, Mercados y Políticas Gubernamentales (1967–2007)*. Santiago, Chile: Ediciones Universidad Diego Portales.

Bruno-Jofré, R. (1993). The Manitoba Teachers' Federation, 1919–1933: The Quest for Professional Status. In R. Bruno-Jofré (Ed.), *Issues in the History of Education in Manitoba: From the Construction of the Common School to the Politics of Voices* (pp. 325–368). Lewiston, NY: Mellen Press.

Bruno-Jofré, R. (1998). Citizenship and Schooling in Manitoba, 1918–1945. *Manitoba History, 36*(Autumn/Winter), 26–36.

Bruno-Jofré, R., & Henley, D. (2001). Public Schooling in English Canada: Addressing Difference in the Context of Globalization. In R. Bruno-Jofré & N. Aponiuk (Eds.), *Educating Citizens for a Pluralistic Society* (pp. 49–70). Calgary, Canada: Canadian Ethnic Studies Journal.

Bruno-Jofré, R., & Jover, G. (2008). Los Estudios de Formación Docente y Pedagógica en Canadá y España: Cambios Programáticos e Institucionales en el Escenario de Internacionalización de la Educación. *Revista de Educación, 347*, 397–417.

Bruno-Jofré, R., & Jover, G. (2011). The Publication of the Pedagogical Creeds in The School Journal, 1896–97, the Transatlantic Movement of Ideas, and the Intersection of Religion with the Intellectual Currents of the Time. Presented at a panel organized by the Theory and History of Education Research Group, History of Education Society, 51st Annual Meeting, November 3–6. Chicago.

Bucharest Communiqué (2012). *Making the Most of Our Potential: Consolidating the European Higher Education Area*. Communiqué of the Conference of European Ministers Responsible for Higher Education. 26–27 April,

Bucharest, Romania. http://www.ehea.info/Uploads/%281%29/Bucharest%20Communique%202012.pdf

Budapest-Vienna Communiqué (2010). *Budapest-Vienna Declaration on the European Higher Education Area*. Communiqué of the Conference of European Ministers Responsible for Higher Education. 12 March, Budapest/Vienna. http://www.ehea.info/Uploads/Declarations/Budapest-Vienna_Declaration.pdf

Bundesministerium für Bildung und Wissenschaft (BMBW). (1992). *Das soziale Bild der Studentenschaft in der Bundesrepublik Deutschland. 13. Sozialerhebung des Deutschen Studentenwerkes*. Bonn, Germany: Deutschen Studentenwerkes.

Bundesministerium für Bildung und Forschung (BMBF). (2010). *Internationalisierung des Studiums* (pp. 13, 26, 27, 30, 31). http://www.studentenwerke.de/pdf/Internationalisierungbericht.pdf

Burbules, N. C. (2005). Rethinking the Virtual. In J. Weiss, J. Nolan, & P. Trifonas (Eds.), *The International Handbook of Virtual Learning Environments* (pp. 3–24). Dordrecht, Netherlands: Kluwer Publishers.

Burbules, N. C. (2006). Self-Educating Communities: Collaboration and Learning through the Internet. In Z. Bekerman, N. C. Burbules, & D. Silberman-Keller (Eds.), *Learning in Places: The Informal Education Reader* (pp. 273–284). New York: Peter Lang Publishing.

Burbules, N. C. (2009). Meanings of Ubiquitous Learning. In B. Cope & M. Kalantzis (Eds.), *Ubiquitous Learning* (pp. 15–20). Urbana: University of Illinois Press.

Burbules, N. C., Callister, T. A., Jr., & Taaffe, C. (2006). Beyond the Digital Divide. In S. Y. Tettegah & R. C. Hunter (Eds.), *Technology and Education: Issues in Administration, Policy and Applications in K-12 Schools* (pp. 85–99). New York: Elsevier. http://dx.doi.org/10.1016/S1479-3660(05)08007-8

Burbules, N. C., & Linn, M. C. (1988). Response to Contradiction: Scientific Reasoning during Adolescence. *Journal of Educational Psychology, 80*(1), 67–75. http://dx.doi.org/10.1037/0022-0663.80.1.67

Burbules, N. & Torres, C. A. (Eds.). (2000). *Globalization and Education: Critical Perspectives*. New York: Routledge.

Burkhardt, K. (2004). What Coyote and Thales Can Teach Us: An Outline of American Indian Education. In A. Waters (Ed.), *American Indian Thought: Philosophical Essays* (pp. 15–26). Malden, MA: Blackwell.

Butler, N. M. (1912). *The International Mind: An Argument for the Judicial Settlement of International Disputes*. New York: Scribner.

Butt, G. (2000). *The Continuum Guide to Geography Education*. London: Continuum.

Cajete, G. (1994). *Look to the Mountain: An Ecology of Indigenous Education.* Durango, CO: Kivaki Press.

Calderhead, J. (1992). The Role of Reflection in Learning to Teach. In L. Valli (Ed.), *Reflective Teacher Education: Cases and Critiques* (pp. 139–146). Albany: State University of New York Press.

Calgary Centre for Global Community (CCGC). *Our Principles.* http://www.calgarycgc.org/our-principles.html

Canadian Association of University Teachers (CAUT). (2011). *Almanac of Post-Secondary Education in Canada, 2011–12.* Table 2.21 and Figure 2.14.

Canadian Teachers' Federation (CTF) (2013). *World Teachers' Day.* http://www.ctf-fce.ca/en/Pages/Events/WTD-2013.aspx

Carabaña, J. (2009, May 25). Bolonia: Rectificar a tiempo. *El Pais.* Retrieved from http://sociedad.elpais.com/sociedad/2009/05/25/actualidad/1243202402_850215.html

Carson, R. (1962). *Silent Spring.* Boston: Houghton Mifflin.

Carter, B., Stevenson, H., & Passy, R. (2010). *Industrial Relations in Education: Transforming the School Workforce.* London: Routledge.

Carter, S. (2007). Reflection on Best Practice: A Kiwi Perspective on "New Dimensions for Doctoral Programmes in Europe." In C. Fraser & L. Ayo (Eds.), *Anchoring Our Practice: Perspectives, Partnerships, Projections* (pp. 21–34). Auckland, New Zealand: ATLAANZ.

Carter, S., Fazey, J., González Geraldo, J. L., & Trevitt, C. (2010). The Doctorate of the Bologna Process Third Cycle: Mapping the Dimensions and Impact of the European Higher Education Area. *Journal of Research in International Education, 9*(3), 245–258. http://dx.doi.org/10.1177/1475240910379383

Castellano, M. B., Davis, L., & Lahache, L. (2000). *Aboriginal Education: Fulfilling the Promise.* Vancouver, Canada: UBC Press.

Castillejo Brull, J. L. (1982). Los ICEs y la formación del profesorado. *Revista de educación,* no. 269: 43–54.

Castillo, J., & Cabezas, G. (2010). Caracterización de Jóvenes Primera Generación en Educación Superior: Nuevas Trayectorias hacia la Equidad Educativa. *Calidad en la Educación, 32,* 44–76. Retrieved from http://www.cned.cl/public/secciones/seccionpublicaciones/doc/67/cse_articulo900.pdf

Catalán Fernández, A., & Forteza, D. (2011). La formació inicial del professorat d'educació secundària: Passat i present. *Innovib: Recursos i Recerca Educativa de les Illes Balears, 2,* 99–108.

Center for Information and Research on Civic Learning and Engagement (CIRCLE). (2013). Commission on Youth Voting and Civic Knowledge Releases Report. http://www.civicyouth.org/commission-on-youth-voting-and-civic-knowledge-releases-report/

Centre for Higher Education Policy Studies (CHEPS). (2008). Progress in Higher Education Reform across Europe. Governance Reform. (Vol. 1). *Executive Summary, Main Findings*. Enschede, Netherlands: CHEPS.

Centre of Study for Policies and Practices in Education (2013). Learning Standards, Teaching Standards and Standards for School Principals: A Comparative Study. *OECD Education Working Paper*. Paris: OECD.

Cerych, L., & Sabatier, P. (1986). *Great Expectations and Mixed Performance: The Implementation of Higher Education Reforms in Europe*. Trentham, England: European Institute of Education and Social Policy.

Chabbott, C. (2003). *Constructing Education for Development: International Organizations and Education for All*. New York: Routledge Falmer.

Chambers, C. (1999). A Topography for Canadian Curriculum Theory. *Canadian Journal of Education, 24*(2), 137–150. Retreived from http://www.csse-scee.ca/CJE/Articles/FullText/CJE24-2/CJE24-2-Chambers.pdf

Chambers, C. (2008). Where Are We? Finding Common Ground in a Curriculum of Place. *Journal of the Canadian Association for Curriculum Studies, 6*(2), 113–128. Retrieved from https://pi.library.yorku.ca/ojs/index.php/jcacs/article/viewFile/18099/16865

Charbonneau, L. (2009, February 9). The Bologna Conundrum. *University Affairs*. Retrieved from http://www.universityaffairs.ca/the-bologna-conundrum.aspx

Christensen, J., McDonald, R., & Denning, C. (2012, January 27). Ecological Urbanism for the 21st Century. *The Chronicle Review, 58*(21), B9–B11.

Cicchelli, V. (2007). Des Identités Meurtrières aux Identités Plurielles: Quand l'Autrui Est une Composante de Soi. In M. Breviglieri & V. Cicchelli (Eds.), *Adolescences Méditerranéennes: L'espace Public à Petits Pas* (pp. 409–445). Paris: L'INJEP-L'Harmattan.

Cicchelli, V. (2008). Connaître les Autres pour Mieux Se Connaître: Les Séjours Erasmus, une Bildung Contemporaine. In F. Dervin & M. Byram (Eds.), *Mobilités Académiques* (pp. 101–124). Paris: L'Harmattan.

Cicchelli, V. (2012). *L'Esprit Cosmopolite: Voyages de Formation des Jeunes en Europe*. Paris: Presses de Science Po.

Cicchelli, V. (2013). The Cosmopolitan "Bildung" of ERASMUS Students Going Abroad. In Y. Hébert & A. A. Abdi (Eds.), *Critical Perspectives on International Education* (pp. 205–208). Rotterdam, Netherlands, and Taipei, Taiwan: Sense Publishers.

Clement, M., McAlpine, L., & Waeytens, K. (2004). Fascinating Bologna: Impact on the Nature and Approach of Academic Development. *International Journal for Academic Development, 9*(2), 127–131. http://dx.doi.org/10.1080/1360144042000334627

Clifford, G. J. & Guthrie, J. W. (Eds.). (1988). *School: A Brief for Professional Education*. Chicago: University of Chicago Press.

Cline, Z., & Necochea, J. (2006). Teacher Dispositions for Effective Education in the Borderlands. *Educational Forum, 70*(3), 268–282. http://dx.doi.org/10.1080/00131720608984902

Cochran-Smith, M. (2005). The New Teacher Education: For Better or for Worse? *Educational Researcher, 34*(7), 3–17. http://dx.doi.org/10.3102/0013189X034007003

Cochran-Smith, M., et al. (Eds.). (2008). *Handbook of Research on Teacher Education: Enduring Questions in Changing Contexts* (3rd ed.). New York: Routledge.

Cochran-Smith, M. (2009a). The New Teacher Education in the United States: Directions Forward. In J. Furlong, M. Cochran-Smith, & M. Brennan (Eds.), *Politics and Policy in Teacher Education: International Perspectives* (pp. 9–21). London: Routledge.

Cochran-Smith, M. (2009b). Toward a Theory of Teacher Education for Social Justice. In M. Fullan, A. Hargreaves, D. Hopkins, & A. Lieberman (Eds.), *The International Handbook of Educational Change* (pp. 122–163). New York: Springer Publishing.

Cohen, D. (Ed.). (1973). *New Trends in Integrated Science Teaching*. Vol. 4: *Evaluation of Integrated Science Education*. Paris: UNESCO.

Cole, M. (2005). New Labour, Globalization, and Social Justice: The Role of Education. In G. Fischman, P. McClaren, H. Suncker, & C. Lankshear (Eds.), *Critical Theories, Radical Pedagogies, and Global Conflicts* (pp. 1–21). Lanham, MD: Rowman and Littlefield.

Coleman, H. T. J. (1920). Queen's University Faculty of Education, Report of Dean. Principal's Report 1919–20. Kingston, Canada: Queen's University Archives.

Colom Cañellas, A. J., & Rincón i Verdera, J. C. (2004). Epistemología neoidealista y fracaso fundacional del saber educativo. *Teoría de la educación, 16*, 19–48.

Commission Européenne. (2007). *Le Magazine* (28).

Compayré, G. (1883). *Histoire de la Pédagogie*. Paris: P. Delaplane.

Compton, M., & Weiner, L. (2008). *The Global Assault on Teaching, Teachers and Their Unions: Stories for Resistance*. London: Palgrave.

Consejo Asesor Presidencial para la Calidad de la Educación (CAPCE). (2006). *Informe Final de Consejo Asesor Presidencial para la Calidad de la Educación*. Santiago, Chile. http://mt.educarchile.cl/MT/jjbrunner/archives/libros/ConsejoAsesor/Inf_def.pdf

Cook, D. (2004). *Adorno, Habermas, and the Search for a Rational Society*. New York: Routledge.

Côté, J. E., & Allahar, A. (2006). *Critical Youth Studies: A Canadian Focus.* Toronto, Canada: Pearson Education Canada.

Council of Ontario Universities (COU). (1986). *Bottoming Out, Review 1982–83 to 1985–86.* Toronto, Canada: COU.

Cox, C. (2007). Educación en el Bicentenario: Dos Agendas y Calidad de la Política. *Revista Pensamiento Educativo,* 40, 175–204. Retrieved from http://pensamientoeducativo.uc.cl/files/journals/2/articles/404/public/404-902-1-PB.pdf

Cox, C., Meckes, L., & Bascopé, M. (2010). La institucionalidad Formadora de Profesores en Chile en la Década del 2000: Velocidad del Mercado y Parsimonia de las Políticas. *Pensamiento Educativo,* 46–47, 205–245. Retrieved from http://pensamientoeducativo.uc.cl/index.php/pel/article/view/468

Craig, G. (1978). *Germany, 1866–1945.* Oxford, England: Clarendon Press.

Crawford, M. B. (2009). *Shop Class as Soulcraft.* New York: Penguin Press.

Cronon, W. (Ed.). (1995). *Uncommon Ground: Toward Reinventing Nature.* New York: W. W. Norton.

Crosier, D., Purser, L., & Smidt, H. (2007). *Trends V – Universities Shaping the European Higher Education Area: An EUA report.* Brussels, Belgium: European University Association.

Cruickshank, D. (1987). *Reflective Teaching.* Reston, VA: Association of Teacher Educators.

Cummins, J. (1995). *Brave New Schools.* New York: St Martin's Press.

Curaj, A., Scott, P., Vlasceanu, L., & Wilson, L. (Eds.). (2012). *European Higher Education at the Crossroads: Between the Bologna Process and National Reforms* (Vol. 1). Dordrecht, Netherlands: Springer. http://dx.doi.org/10.1007/978-94-007-3937-6

Curtis, I. (1988). *Building the Educational State: Canada West, 1836–1871.* London, Canada: The Althouse Press.

Dale, R., & Robertson, S. L. (2012). Towards a Critical Grammar of Education Policy Movements. In G. Steiner-Khamsi & F. Waldow (Eds.), *World Yearbook of Education 2012: Policy Borrowing and Lending in Education* (pp. 21–40). London: Routledge.

Dale, R. (1989). *The State and Education Policy.* Milton Keynes, England: Open University Press.

Dale, R. (1997). The State and the Governance of Education: An Analysis of the Restructuring of the State-Education Relationship. In A. H. Halsey, H. Lauder, P. Brown, & A. S. Wells (Eds.), *Education: Culture, Economy and Society* (pp. 273–282). New York: Oxford University Press.

Dale, R. (2009). Studying Globalisation and Europeanisation: Lisbon, the Open Method of Coordination and Beyond. In R. Dale & S. L. Robertson (Eds.), *Globalisation and Europeanisation in Education* (pp. 121–140). Wallingford, England: Symposium.

Dale, R. (2003). Globalization: A New World for Comparative Education? In J. Schriewer (Ed.), *Discourse Formation in Comparative Education* (pp. 87–110, 2nd ed.). Frankfurt am Main, Germany: Peter Lang.

Danielson, C. (1996). *A Framework for Teaching*. Alexandria, VA: Association for Supervision and Curriculum Development. Retrieved from http://dvandkq.net/images/CPC/20120305%20CPC%20Ed%20cmte%20Danielson,%20C%20Enhancing%20Professional%20Practice%20-%20A%20Framework%20for%20Teaching.pdf

Darling-Hammond, L. & Baratz-Snowden, J. (Eds.). (2005). *A Good Teacher in Every Classroom: Preparing the Highly Qualified Teachers Our Children Deserve*. San Francisco: Jossey-Bass.

Deloria, V. (2004). Philosophy and the Tribal Peoples. In A. Waters (Ed.), *American Indian Thought: Philosophical Essays* (pp. 3–11). Malden, MA: Blackwell.

Delors, J. (1996a). *La Educación Encierra un Tesoro*. Madrid, Spain: Santillana/UNESCO.

Delors, J. (1996b). *L'Éducation Est un Trésor Caché Dedans*. Paris: UNESCO.

Demorgon, J. (2000). *L'Histoire Interculturelle des Sociétés* (2nd ed.). Paris: Economica.

Denzin, N., Lincoln, Y. S., & Smith, L. T. (2008). *Handbook of Critical and Indigenous Methodologies*. Los Angeles: Sage.

Derrida, J. (1993). *Margins of Philosophy* (P. Kamuf, Trans.). New York: Columbia University Press.

Descartes, R. (1998). *Discourse on Method and Meditations on First Philosophy* (D. Cress, Trans.). Indianapolis, IN: Hackett.

Dewar, K. C. (2006). Hilda Neatby's 1950s and My 1950s. *Journal of Canadian Studies / Revue d'Études Canadiennes, 40*(1), 210–231.

Dewey, J. (1915). *The School and Society*. Chicago: University of Chicago Press.

Dewey, J. (1933). *How We Think: A Restatement of the Relation of Reflective Thinking to the Educative Process*. Lexington, MA: Heath.

Dewey, J. (1937). John Dewey's Page: President Hutchins' Proposals to Remake Higher Education. *The Social Frontier, 3*(22), 103–104.

Dewey, J. (1976). Intelligence and Morals. In J. A. Boydston (Ed.), *John Dewey: The Middle Works* (Vol. 4, pp. 3–74). Carbondale: Southern Illinois University Press.

Dewey, J. (1981). Experience and Nature. In J. A. Boydston (Ed.), *John Dewey: The Later Works* (Vol. 1, pp. 1–326). Carbondale: Southern Illinois University Press.

Dewey, J. (1982). The Public and Its Problems. In J. A. Boydston (Ed.), *John Dewey: The Later Works* (Vol. 2, pp. 235–372). Carbondale: Southern Illinois University Press.

Dewey, J. (1986a). How We Think. In J. A. Boydston (Ed.), *John Dewey: The Later Works* (Vol. 8, pp. 105–352). Carbondale: Southern Illinois University Press.

Dewey, J. (1986b). Logic: The Theory of Inquiry. In J. A. Boydston (Ed.), *John Dewey: The Later Works* (Vol. 12, pp. 1–527). Carbondale: Southern Illinois University Press.

Dewey, J. (1987). Experience and Education. In J. A. Boydston (Ed.), *John Dewey: The Later Works* (Vol. 13, pp. 1–62). Carbondale: Southern Illinois University Press.

Dietz, T. (2008). Ohne gute Lehrer gibt es keine guten Schulen. *Informationsdienst Wissenschaft*. Retrieved from http://idw-online.de/pages/de/news273343

Dittes, F. (1871). *Geschichte der Erziehung und des Unterrichts: Für dt. Volksschullehrer*. Leipzig, Germany: Klinkhardt.

Dominguez, M., Bascopé, M., Carrillo, C., Lorca, E., Olave, G., & Pozo, M. (2012a). Procesos de Acreditación de Pedagogías: Un Estudio del Quehacer de las Agencias. *Calidad en la Educación*, 36, 54–84. Retrieved from http://www.cned.cl/public/secciones/SeccionRevistaCalidad/doc/73/cse_articulo1024.pdf

Dominguez, M., Bascopé, M., Carrillo, C., Lorca, E., Olave, G., & Pozo, M. (2012b). Procesos de Acreditación de Pedagogías: Un Estudio del Quehacer de las Agencias. *Final report, Consejo Nacional de Educación*. Retrieved from http://www.cned.cl/public/Secciones/SeccionInvestigacion/investigacion_estudios_y_documentos_de_la_sectec_pdf.aspx?strArt=Procesos%20de%20acreditaci%F3n%20de%20pedagog%EDas:%20un%20estudio%20del%20quehacer%20de%20las%20agencias&idArticulo=1032

Donoso Knaudt, S. (2010). *Dynamics of Change: The Chilean Pingüino Movement and its Impact on the Education Agenda*. M.Phil. thesis, Oxford University.

Dow, P. (1991). *Schoolhouse Publics: Lessons from the Sputnik Era*. Cambridge, MA: Harvard University Press.

Dower, N. (2003). *An Introduction to Global Citizenship*. Edinburgh, Scotland: Edinburgh University Press.

Duncan, The Honourable D. (2010). *Ontario Economic Outlook and Fiscal Review*, ix.

Editorial Notes: University Degrees in Pedagogy. (1894). *Educational Journal, Toronto*, *8*(4), 56.

Education, Audiovisual and Culture Executive Agency (EACEA P9 Eurydice). (2012a). *The European Higher Education Area in 2012: Bologna Process Implementation Report*. Brussels, Belgium: EACEA.

Education, Audiovisual and Culture Executive Agency (EACEA). (2012b). *State of Play of the Bologna Process in the Tempus Countries, 2012*. Tempus Study, no. 9. Brussels, Belgium: EACEA. doi: 10.2797/90379

Edwardson, R. (2008). *Canadian Content: Culture and the Quest for Nationhood*. Toronto, Canada: University of Toronto Press.

Egan, K. (2010). *Learning in Depth*. Chicago: University of Chicago Press.

Elken, M., Gornitzka, Å., Maassen, P., & Vukasovic, M. (2010). *European Integration and the Transformation of Higher Education*. Oslo, Norway: University of Oslo, Department of Educational Research. Retrieved from https://www.uv.uio.no/iped/forskning/prosjekter/eie-utd2020forprosjekt/HEIK-Utd2020-Part1-EI_and_transformation_of_HE.pdf

Ell, F., & Grudnoff, L. (2013). The Politics of Responsibility: Teacher Education and "Persistent Underachievement" in New Zealand. *Educational Forum, 77*(1), 73–86. http://dx.doi.org/10.1080/00131725.2013.739023

Elshtain, J. B. (1987). *Women and War*. New York: Basic Books.

Eraut, M. (1995). Schön Shock: A Case for Refraining Reflection-in-action? *Teachers and Teaching: Theory and Practice, 1*(1), 9–22. http://dx.doi.org/10.1080/1354060950010102

Erickson, P. (2006). *The Politics of Game Theory: Mathematics and Cold War Culture*. Madison: University of Wisconsin–Madison.

Escudero Muñoz, J. M. (2009a). Las Competencias Profesionales y la Formación Universitaria: Posibilidades y Riesgos. *Revista de Docencia Universitaria, 2*(1–2), 7–26.

Escudero Muñoz, J. M. (2009b). La Formación del Profesorado de Educación Secundaria: Contenidos y Aprendizajes Docentes. *Revista de Educación, 350*, 79–103.

Essbach, W. (2004, March 20). Unterm Rad der Panierraupe. *Süddeutsche Zeitung* (p.16).

Estall, H. M., & Department of Philosophy. (1965, October 20). Correspondence to Miss Jean Royce, Secretary of the Senate, Queen's University. Appendix C to the Queen's University Senate, Minutes from September 1965 to May 1966, session of November 1965.

Esteve, J. M. (2003). *La Tercera Revolución Educativa: La Educación en la Sociedad del Conocimiento*. Barcelona, Spain: Paidós.

Esteve, J. M. (2010). *Educar: Un Compromiso con la Memoria*. Barcelona, Spain: Octaedro.

European Association for Quality Assurance in Higher Education (EAQAHE) (2005). *Standards and Guidelines for Quality Assurance in the European Higher Education Arena*. Retrieved from http://www.ond.vlaanderen.be/hogeronderwijs/bologna/documents/Standards-and-Guidelines-for-QA.pdf

European Commission. (1989). *Communication from the Commission to the Council. Education and Training in the European Community. Guidelines for the Medium Term: 1989–1992*. COM (1989) 236 final. Brussels, Belgium: European Commission.

European Commission (2002). *From Prague to Berlin: The EU Contribution. Progress Report*. Document no. A2/PVDH (1–8-2002). Brussels, Belgium: European Commission. Retrieved from http://www.bologna-berlin2003.de/pdf/updated_report.pdf

European Commission. (2003). *From Prague to Berlin: The EU Contribution. Second Progress Report*. Document no. A2/PVDH (15–2-2003-rev). Brussels, Belgium: European Commission. Retrieved from http://www.bologna-berlin2003.de/pdf/Text2_KOM.pdf

European Commission. (2011a). Implementation of the European Neighbourhood Policy in 2010: Country Report on Ukraine. Joint Staff Working Paper. COM (2011) 303. Brussels, Belgium: European Commission.

European Commission. (2011b). *Supporting Growth and Jobs – An Agenda for the Modernisation of Europe's Higher Education Systems*. COM (2011) 567 final. Brussels, Belgium: European Commission.

European Commission. (2011c). *DG Education and Culture Management Plan 2012*. Retrieved from http://ec.europa.eu/atwork/synthesis/amp/doc/eac_mp.pdf

European Communities. (2008). *ERASMUS: Mobility Creates Opportunities. European Success Stories*. Luxembourg: Office for Official Publications of the European Communities.

European Council (2000). Presidency Conclusions: Lisbon. *Bulletin of the European Union, 3*.

European Ministers of Education. (1999). *The Bologna Declaration of 19 June 1999. Joint Declaration of the European Ministers of Education*. Retrieved from http://www.ond.vlaanderen.be/hogeronderwijs/bologna/documents/MDC/BOLOGNA_DECLARATION1.pdf

European Union (2012). *2012 Joint Report of the Council and the Commission on the Implementation of the Strategic Framework for European Cooperation in Education and Training (ET 2020)*: Education and Training in a Smart, Sustainable and Inclusive Europe. OJ C 70, 8.3.2012, 9–18.

Eurydice. (1997). *La Educación Secundaria en la Unión Europea: Estructuras, Organización y Administración*. Brussels, Belgium: Eurydice.

Eurydice. (2001). *Glosario Europeo sobre Educación, vol. 3: Profesorado*. Brussels, Belgium: Eurydice. Retrieved from http://www.mecd.gob.es/redie-eurydice/dms/redie-eurydice/doc/Glosarios/Glosario-2001/Glosario%202001.pdf

Faculty of Education, The. (1907, November 5). [Kingston, Canada: Queen's University Archives.]. *Queen's University Journal, 35*(2), 65.

Fahrni, M., & Rutherdale, R. (2008). Introduction. In M. Fahrni & R. Rutherdale (Eds.), *Creating Postwar Canada* (pp. 1–20). Vancouver, Canada: UBC Press.

Fallis, G. (2007). *Multiversities, Ideas, and Democracy*. Toronto, Canada: University of Toronto Press.

Farrell, M. (2011). *Under Surveillance: Teachers and Educational Change in Alberta.* PhD dissertation, University of Calgary, Canada.

Faure, E. (1973). *Aprender a ser*. Madrid, Spain: UNESCO.

Fendler, L. (2003). Teacher Reflection in a Hall of Mirrors: Historical Influences and Political Reverberations. *Educational Researcher, 32*(3), 16–25. http://dx.doi.org/10.3102/0013189X032003016

Fennema, E., Carpenter, T. P., & Peterson, P. (1989). Teachers' Decision Making and Cognitively Guided Instruction: A New Paradigm for Curriculum Development. In N. F. Ellerton & M. A. Clements (Eds.), *School Mathematics: The Challenge to Change* (pp. 174–187). Geelong, Victoria, Australia: Deakin University Press.

Fernandez, B. (2001). L'Homme et le Voyage, une Connaissance éprouvée sous le Signe de la Rencontre. In R. Barbier (Ed.), *Éducation et Sagesse: La Quête de Sens*. Paris: Albin Michel.

Fichte, J. G. (2005). *The Foundations of Natural Right* (M. Baur, Trans.). Cambridge, England: Cambridge University Press.

Fichte, J. G. (2008). *Addresses to the German Nation (1808)*. Cambridge, England: Cambridge University Press.

Fimyar, O. (2008). Educational Policy-Making in Post-Communist Ukraine as an Example of Emerging Governmentality: Discourse Analysis of Curriculum Choice and Assessment Policy Documents (1999–2003). *Journal of Education Policy, 23*(6), 571–594. http://dx.doi.org/10.1080/02680930802382920

Fischer, T., et al. (2004). *Föderalismusreform in Deutschland: Ein Leitfaden zur aktuellen Diskussion und zur Arbeit der Bundesstaatskommission*. Gütersloh, Germany: Bertelsmann Stiftung. Retrieved from http://www.gew.de/Binaries/Binary26323/ew_070806.pdf

Fleming, W. G. (1971). *Ontario's Educative Society* (Vol. 1–5). Toronto, Canada: University of Toronto Press.

Floud, R. (2006). The Bologna Process: Transforming European Higher Education. *Change, 38*(4), 8–15. http://dx.doi.org/10.3200/CHNG.38.4.8-15

Floud, J., & Scott, W. (1962). Recruitment to Teaching in England and Wales. In A. H. Halsey, J. Floud, & C. A. Anderson (Eds.), *Education, Economy and Society* (pp. 527–544). New York: The Free Press.

Folvarochnyi, I. (2011). Comparative Perspective of Professional Teacher Training in Ukraine. Paper presented at the European Conference on Educational Research, Berlin, Germany, September.

Ford, L. R. (2000). *The Spaces between Buildings*. Baltimore: Johns Hopkins University Press.

Foreign Affairs and International Trade Canada (FAITC). (2010, May). Inspector General Office Evaluation Division, Summative Evaluation of the International Education and Youth Programs.

Foro ANECA (Ed.). (2007). Es Posible Bolonia con Nuestra Actual Cultura Pedagógica? Propuesta para el Cambio. VIII Foro ANECA. Madrid, Spain: ANECA.

Foucault, M. (1980). Truth and Power. In C. Gordon (Ed.), *Power/Knowledge: Selected Interviews and Other Writings 1972–1977* (pp. 109–133). New York: Pantheon Books.

Foucault, M. (1988). The History of Sexuality (Vol. 3). *The Care of the Self* (R. Hurley, Trans.). New York: Vintage.

Fox, W. (1990). *Toward a Transpersonal Ecology: Developing Foundations for Environmentalism*. Boston: Shambala.

Freire, P. (1970). *Pedagogy of the Oppressed*. New York: Continuum.

Freire, P. (1992). *Pedagogía del Oprimido*. Madrid, Spain: Siglo XXI.

Friesen, R. (2009). The Growth and Development of Internationalization at Canadian Universities: An Overview. Retrieved from http://umanitoba.ca/faculties/education/media/Friesen-09.pdf

Fuchs, E. (2006). Kinderschutz und Völkerbund. Zur Formierung des Edukativen Multikulturalismus in der Zwischenkriegszeit. In E. Fuchs (Ed.), *Bildung International: Historische Perspektiven und Aktuelle Entwicklungen* (pp. 163–180). Würzburg, Germany: Ergon-Verlag.

Fuchs, E. (2007). The Creation of New International Networks in Education: The League of Nations and Educational Organizations in the 1920s. *Paedagogica Historica, 43*(2), 199–209. http://dx.doi.org/10.1080/00309230701248305

Furlong, J., Cochran-Smith, M., & Brennan, M. (Eds.). (2009). *Politics and Policy in Teacher Education: International Perspectives*. London: Routledge.

Gaudet, S., & Quéniart, A. (Eds.). (2008). *La Sociologie de l'Éthique*. Montreal, Canada: Éditions Liber.

GHK. (2011). *Study on Teacher Education for Primary and Secondary Education in Six Countries of the Eastern Partnership: Armenia, Azerbaijan, Belarus, Georgia, Moldova and Ukraine. Final Report*. Agreement no. EAC-2011–0301

(Negotiated procedure EAC/28/2011). European Commission, Directorate-General for Education and Culture.

Gidney, R. (1999). *From Hope to Harris: The Reshaping of Ontario's Schools.* Toronto, Canada: University of Toronto Press.

Gimeno, J. (Ed.). (2008). *Educar por Competencias ¿Qué Hay de Nuevo?* Madrid, Spain: Morata.

Giroux, H. A. (2009). *Youth in a Suspect Society: Democracy or Disposability?* New York: Palgrave-Macmillan.

Giroux, H. A. (2012). *Disposable Youth, Racialized Memories, and the Culture of Cruelty.* London and New York: Routledge.

Gollnick, D. M., & Chin, P. C. (2006). *Multicultural Education in a Pluralistic Society* (7th ed.). Upper Saddle River, NJ: Merrill Prentice Hall.

González Geraldo, J. L. (2014). *Hacia una Universidad Más Humana. ¿Es Superior la Educación Superior?* Madrid: Biblioteca Nueva.

González Riaño, X. A., & Hevia Artime, I. (2011). El Practicum de la Licenciatura de Pedagogía: Estudio Empírico desde la Perspectiva del Alumnado. *Revista de Educación, 354*, 209–236.

González Sanmamed, M., & Fuentes Abeledo, E. (2011). El Practicum en el Aprendizaje de la Profesión Docente. *Revista de Educación, 354*, 47–70.

Goodlad, J. (1966). *The Changing School Curriculum.* New York: Fund for the Advancement of Education.

Goodman, B. A. (2010). Ukraine and the Bologna Process: Convergence, Pluralism, or Both? Paper presented at the 12th Berlin Roundtables on Transnationality, Berlin, Germany, February.

Granatstein, J. L. (2004). Second World War. In G. Hallowell (Ed.), *The Oxford Companion to Canadian History* (pp. 572–573). Don Mills, Canada: Oxford University Press.

Grissell, E. (2001). *Pursuit of a Garden Ecology.* Portland, OR: Timber Press.

Habermas, J. (1987). *The Philosophical Discourse of Modernity: 12 Essays* (F. Lawrence, Trans.). Cambridge, MA: MIT Press.

Habermas, J. (1992). *Post-Metaphysical Thinking* (W. M. Hohengarten, Trans.). Cambridge, MA: MIT Press.

Halász, G. (2004). *Anwerbung, berufliche Entwicklung und Verbleib von qualifizierten Lehrerinnen und Lehrern. Länderbericht: Deutschland.* Berlin: OECD.

Hampton, E. (1995). Toward a Redefinition of Indian Education. In M. A. Battiste & J. Barman (Eds.), *First Nations Education in Canada: The Circle Unfolds* (pp. 5–46). Vancouver, Canada: UBC Press.

Hansen, D. (2011). *The Teacher and the World: A Study of Cosmopolitanism as Education.* London and New York: Routledge.

Harriss, K., & Osella, F. (2010). Educational "Transnationalism" and the Global Production of Educational Regimes. In T. Faist et al. (Eds.), *Transnationalisation and Institutional Transformations* (pp. 140–163). Centre on Migration, Citizenship and Development. Working Papers, 75. Bielefeld, Germany: COMCAD.

Hartman, A. (2008). *Education and the Cold War: The Battle for the American School*. New York: Palgrave Macmillan. http://dx.doi.org/10.1057/9780230611023

Hartmann, E. (2010). The United Nations Educational, Scientific and Cultural Organisation: Pawn or Global Player? *Globalisation, Societies and Education, 8*(2), 307–318. http://dx.doi.org/10.1080/14767721003780645

Hassner, P. (2002). Le Cosmopolitisme entre Chaos et République. *Revue de Synthèse, 123*(1), 193–199. http://dx.doi.org/10.1007/BF02963327

Hatton, N., & Smith, D. (1995). Reflection in Teacher Education: Towards Definition and Implementation. *Teaching and Teacher Education, 11*(1), 33–49. http://dx.doi.org/10.1016/0742-051X(94)00012-U

Haug, G. (2009). El Futuro de las Universidades se Juega en los Nuevos Títulos de Máster. In X Foro ANECA (Ed.), *Los Nuevos Títulos de Máster y la Competitividad en las Universidades* (pp. 13–20). Madrid, Spain: ANECA.

Healy, T., & Cote, S. (2001). *The Well-Being of Nations: The Role of Human and Social Capital, Education and Skills*. Paris: OECD.

Hébert, Y. (2013). Cosmopolitanism and Canadian Multicultural Policy: Intersection, Relevance, and Critique. *Encounters on Education, 14*, 3–19.

HEFCE. (2001). *Risk Management: A Guide to Good Practise for Higher Education Institutions*. Bristol, England: HEFCE.

Heffron, J. M. (1995). Toward a Cybernetic Pedagogy: The Cognitive Revolution and the Classroom, 1948–present. *Educational Theory, 45*(4), 497–518. http://dx.doi.org/10.1111/j.1741-5446.1995.00497.x

Hegel, G. W. F. (1969). *Science of Logic* (A. V. Miller, Trans.). Highlands, NJ: Humanities Press.

Hegel, G. W. F. (1977). *Phenomenology of Spirit* (A. V. Miller, Trans.). Oxford, England: Oxford University Press.

Heinze, T., & Knill, C. (2008). Analysing the Differential Impact of the Bologna Process: Theoretical Considerations on National Conditions for International Policy Convergence. *Higher Education, 56*(4), 493–510. http://dx.doi.org/10.1007/s10734-007-9107-z

Henkel, M. (2002). Emerging Concepts of Academic Leadership and Their Implications for Intra-Institutional Roles and Relationships in Higher Education. *European Journal of Education, 37*(1), 29–41. http://dx.doi.org/10.1111/1467-3435.00089

Henrich, D. (1992). The Origins of the Theory of the Subject. In A. Honneth, T. McCarthy, C. Offe, & A. Wellmer (Eds.), *Philosophical Interventions in the Unfinished Project of Enlightenment* (pp. 29–87). Cambridge, MA: MIT Press.

Hobsbawm, E. (2004). *Age of Extremes: The Short Twentieth Century, 1914–1991*. London: Abacus.

Holmes Group, The. (1986). *Tomorrow's Teachers: A Report of the Holmes Group*. East Lansing, MI: Holmes Group.

Holowinsky, I. Z. (1995). Ukraine's Reconstructive Process in Education: School Reform, Teacher Education, and School Psychology. In N. K. Shimahara & I. Z. Holowinsky (Eds.), *Teacher Education in Industrialized Nations* (pp. 195–223). New York: Garland Publishing.

Hörisch, J. (2006). *Die ungeliebte Universität*. Munich, Germany: Carl Hanser.

Horkheimer, M. (1993). *Max Horkheimer between Philosophy and Social Science: Selected Early Writings*. Cambridge, MA: MIT Press.

Horn, K. P. (2002). Lehre und Studium im Spiegel der Disziplin. Stellungnahmen erziehungswissenschaftlicher Gremien zu Ausbildungsfragen (1956–1998). Eine Dokumentensammlung. In H. U. Otto, T. Rauschenbach, & P. Vogel (Eds.), *Erziehungswissenschaft: Lehre und Studium* (pp. 245–278). Opladen, Germany: Leske. http://dx.doi.org/10.1007/978-3-322-93238-9_19

Hornberger, N. H. (Ed.). (2003). *Continua of Biliteracy: An Ecological Framework for Educational Policy, Research, and Practice in Multilingual Settings*. Clevedon, England: Multilingual Matters.

Huber, C. (2009). Risks and Risk-Based Regulation in Higher Education Institutions. *Tertiary Education and Management, 15*(2), 83–95. http://dx.doi.org/10.1080/13583880902869554

Huber, M. (2011, July). *The Risk University: Risk Identification at Higher Education Institutions in England*. CARR/LSE Discussion Paper 69.

Hübner, P. (1994). Entwicklungstendenzen der Schulreform und der Kulturföderalismus. In P. Hübner (Ed.), *Lehrerbildung im vereinigten Deutschland* (pp. 149–160). Frankfurt, Germany: Lang.

Hudson, B., & Zgaga, P. (Eds.). (2008). *Teacher Education Policy in Europe: A Voice of Higher Education Institutions*. Ljubljana, Slovenia: Littera picta.

Huisman, J. (2009). Institutional Diversification or Convergence? In B. Kehm, J. Huisman, & B. Stensaker (Eds.), *The European Higher Education Area: Perspectives on a Moving Target* (pp. 245–262). Rotterdam, Netherlands: Sense Publishers.

Hume, D. (1978). *A Treatise of Human Nature* (P. Nidditch, Ed.). Oxford, England: Oxford University Press.

Hunt, E. S. (2010). *Bologna 1999–2010: Achievements, Challenges and Perspectives. Budapest, Hungary, and Vienna*. Vienna, Austria: EHEA.

Husén, T., & Postlethwaite, N. (1985). *International Encyclopedia of Education.* Oxford, England: Pargamon Press.

Hutchins, R. M. (1936). *The Higher Learning in America.* New Haven, CT: Yale University Press.

Institute for Competitiveness and Prosperity (ICP). (2008). *Flourishing in the Global Competitiveness Game.* Working paper 11. Toronto, Canada: ICP.

Institute for Competitiveness and Prosperity (ICP). (2011). *Report on Canada 2011.* Toronto, Canada: ICP.

Instituto Nacional de Estadística. (2009). Censo. Government of Chile.

International Labour Organization. (1989, June). 76th Conference, Geneva, Switzerland.

Ireland, D., & Russell, T. (1978). The Ottawa Valley Teaching Project. *Journal of Curriculum Studies, 10*(3), 206–208.

Issaurat, C. (1886). *La pédagogie: Son évolution et son histoire.* Paris: C. Reinwald.

Jacoby, S. (2004). *Freethinkers.* New York: Metropolitan Books.

Jacotot, J. (1841). *Enseignement Universel. Langue Maternelle.* Paris: Au Siège de l'École de Jacotot.

James, W. (1956). *The Will to Believe and Other Essays in Popular Philosophy.* New York: Dover.

Janda, R. (2005). Toward Cosmopolitan Law. *McGill Law Journal / Revue de Droit de McGill, 50,* 967–984.

Jaspers, K. (2003). *Way to Wisdom.* New Haven, CT: Yale University Press.

Jenkins, K. (1991). *Te Ihi, Te Mana, Te Wehi o te Ao Māori: Literacy, Power and Colonisation.* MA paper. Auckland, New Zealand: University of Auckland.

Johnston, J. S. (2011). The Dewey-Hutchins Debate: A Dispute over Moral Teleology. *Educational Theory, 61*(1), 1–16. http://dx.doi.org/10.1111/j.1741-5446.2011.00388.x

Jones, G. A. (Ed.). (1997). *Higher Education in Canada: Different Systems, Different Perspectives.* New York: Garland Publishing.

Jover, G. (2002). Rethinking Subsidiarity as a Principle of Educational Policy in the European Union. In J. A. Ibáñez-Martín & G. Jover (Eds.), *Education in Europe: Policies and Politics* (pp. 3–22). Dordrecht, Netherlands; Boston, MA; and London: Kluwer Academic.

Jover, G. (2008). Bildung versus Competencies: A View from the Gestation of Theoretical Knowledge of Education in Spain. *Zeitschrift für Pädagogische Historiographie, 14*(1), 33–35.

Judt, T. (2010). *Ill Fares the Land.* London: Penguin Books.

Jukier, R. (2006). Transnationalizing the Legal Curriculum: How to Teach What We Live. *Journal of Legal Education, 36*(2), 172–189. Retrieved from http://papers.ssrn.com/sol3/papers.cfm?abstract_id=2002272

Kalekin-Fishman, D. (2010). Bringing Teachers Back In: Dilemmas of Cosmopolitan Education in the Context of Transnationalism. In T. Faist et al. (Eds.), *Transnationalisation and Institutional Transformations* (pp. 164–192). Centre on Migration, Citizenship and Development. Working Papers, 87. Bielefeld, Germany: COMCAD.

Kassel: Eignungstest für Lehramtsstudierende. (2008). *Lehrer-Online*. http://www.lehrer-online.de/683698.php

Kath, G., Oehler, C., & Reichwein, R. (1966). *Studienweg und Studienerfolg: eine Untersuchung über Verlauf und Dauer des Studiums von 2000 Studienanfängern des Sommersemesters 1957 in Berlin, Bonn, Frankfurt/Main und Mannheim*. Berlin: Institut für Bildungsforschung der Max-Planck-Gesellschaft.

Keanne, M. & Villanueva, M. (Eds.). (2009). *Thinking European(s): New Geographies of Place, Cultures and Identities*. Newcastle upon Tyne, England: Cambridge Scholars Publishing.

Kehrein, J. (1873). Überblick der Geschichte der Erziehung und des Unterrichts: für Zöglinge der Lehrerseminare und zur Vorbereitung auf die Allg[emeinen] Bestimmungen angeordnete Prüfungen. Paderborn, Germany: Schöningh, 1887.

Keiner, E., & Schriewer, J. (2007). Erneuerung aus dem Geist der eigenen Tradition? Über Kontinuität und Wandel nationaler Denkstile in der Erziehungswissenschaft. In J. Schriewer (Ed.), *Weltkultur und kulturelle Bedeutungs-welten* (pp. 321–348). Frankfurt, Germany: Campus.

Kellner, L. (1872). *Kurze Geschichte der Erziehung und des Unterrichtes mit verwaltender Rücksicht auf das Volksschulwesen*. Freiburg im Breisgau: Germany: Herder.

Kerr, C. (1982). *The Uses of the University* (3rd ed.). Cambridge, MA: Harvard University Press.

Keuffer, J., & Oelkers, J. (2001). *Reform der Lehrerbildung in Hamburg*. Basel, Germany: Beltz.

Khagram, S., & Levitt, P. (2008). Constructing Transnational Studies. In S. Khagram & P. Levitt (Eds.), *The Transnational Studies Reader* (pp. 1–18). New York and London: Routledge.

Khustochka, O. (2009). *Teacher Training in Finland and Ukraine: Comparative Analysis of Teacher Training Systems*. Master's thesis, University of Oslo, Norway.

King, J. (2008). Critical and Qualitative Researching Teacher Education: A Blues Epistemology, a Reason for Knowing for Cultural Well-Being. In M. Cochran-Smith, S. F. Nemser, & J. McIntyre (Eds.), *Handbook of Research on Teacher Education: Enduring Issues in Changing Contexts* (pp. 1094–1135). Mahwah, NJ: Lawrence Erlbaum.

Kiuppis, F., & Waldow, F. (2008). "Institute University" meets Bologna Process: The German System of Higher Education in Transition. In D. Palomba (Ed.),

Changing Universities in Europe and the "Bologna Process": A Seven Country Study (pp. 73–99). Rome: Aracne.

Klees, S., Samoff, J., & Stromquist, N. (Eds.). (2012). *The World Bank and Education: Critiques and Alternatives.* Rotterdam, Netherlands; Boston, MA; and Taipei, Taiwan: Sense Publishers. http://dx.doi.org/10.1007/978-94-6091-903-9

Kleinhenz, E., & Ingvarson, L. (2007). Standards for Teaching: Theoretical Underpinnings and Applications. Australian Council for Educational Research, Teaching Standards and Teacher Evaluation. Retrieved from http://research.acer.edu.au/cgi/viewcontent.cgi?article=1000&context=teaching_standards

Kliebard, H. (1986). *The Struggle for the American Curriculum 1893–1958.* Boston, London, and Henley, England: Routledge & Kegan Paul.

Klinzing, H. G. (2002). Wie effektiv ist Microteaching? *Zeitschrift fur Padagogik, 48,* 194–221.

KMK (2003). Lehrämter in der Bundesrepublik Deutschland. In *Lehrereinstellungsbedarf und-angebot in der Bundesrepublik Deutschland. Modellrechnung 2002–2015.* Bonn, Germany: Sekretariat der Ständigen Konferenz der Kultusminister der Länder. Retrieved from http://www.uni-kl.de/Lehramt/KMK%20Statistik%20lehrerbedarf.pdf

KMK (2005). Beschluss der Kultusministerkonferenz vom 02.06.2005. Eckpunkte für die gegenseitige Anerkennung von Bachelor- und Masterabschlüssenin Studiengängen, mit denen die Bildungsvoraussetzungen für ein Lehramt vermittelt warden. Retrieved from http://www.kmk.org/fileadmin/veroeffentlichungen_beschluesse/2005/2005_06_02-Bachelor-Master-Lehramt.pdf

KMK (2008a). Ergebnisse der 323. Retrieved from http://www.kmk.org/no_cache/presse-und-aktuelles/meldung/ergebnisse-der-323-plenarsitzung-der-kultusministerkonferenz-am-16-und-17-oktober-2008-in-saarbr.html

KMK (2008b). *Rahmenvorgaben für die Einführung von Leistungspunktesystemen und die Modularisierung von Studiengängen* und die Beschluss am 16./17.10.2008 von der Kultusministerkonferenz Ländergemeinsamen Strukturvorgaben gemäß § 9 Abs. 2 HRG für die Akkreditierung von Bachelor- und Masterstudiengängen. Retrieved from http://www.kmk.org/fileadmin/pdf/PresseUndAktuelles/2000/module.pdf

KMK (2010). *Ländergemeinsame Strukturvorgaben für die Akkreditierung von Bachelor- und Masterstudiengängen* - Beschluss der Kultusministerkonferenz vom 10.10.2003 i.d.F. vom 04.02.2010. Retrieved from http://www.kmk.org/fileadmin/veroeffentlichungen_beschluesse/2003/2003_10_10-Laendergemeinsame-Strukturvorgaben.pdf

Kononenko, P. P., & Holowinsky, I. Z. (2001). Educational Reform and Language Issue in Ukraine. In N. K. Shimahara, I. Z. Holowinsky, & S. Tomlinson-Clarke (Eds.), *Ethnicity, Race, and Nationality in Education* (pp. 213–232). Mahwah, NJ: Lawrence Erlbaum.

Koshmanova, T. (2006). National Identity and Cultural Coherence in Educational Reform for Democratic Citizenship: The Case of Ukraine. *Education, Citizenship and Social Justice, 1*(1), 105–118. http://dx.doi.org/10.1177/1746197906060716

Koshmanova, T. (2007). Post-Soviet Reconstruction in Ukraine: Education for Social Cohesion. In Z. Bekerman & C. McGlynn (Eds.), *Addressing Ethnic Conflict through Peace Education: International Perspectives* (pp. 231–243). New York: Palgrave MacMillan.

Koshmanova, T., & Ravchyna, T. (2008). Teacher Preparation in a Post-Totalitarian Society: An Interpretation of Ukrainian Teacher Educators' Stereotypes. *International Journal of Qualitative Studies in Education, 21*(2), 137–158. http://dx.doi.org/10.1080/09518390701256415

Kotmalyova, O. (2006). Bologna Process and Its Progress in Ukraine. *Zeszyty Naukowe Zakladu Europeistyki, 2*(2), 41–44.

Kovtun, O., & Stick, S. (2009). Ukraine and the Bologna Process: A Case Study of the Impact of the Bologna Process on Ukrainian State Institutions. *Higher Education in Europe, 34*(1), 91–103. http://dx.doi.org/10.1080/03797720902747066

Krawchenko, B. (1997). Administrative Reform in Ukraine: Setting the Agenda. Discussion paper, no. 3. Budapest, Hungary: Local Government and Public Service Reform Initiative.

Kremen, V., & Nikolajenko, S. (2006). *Higher Education in Ukraine*. Bucharest, Romania: UNESCO-CEPES Monographs on Higher Education.

Krücken, G., & Meier, F. (2006). Turning the University into an Organizational Actor. In G. Dori, J. Meyer, & H. Hwang (Eds.), *Globalization and Organization: World Society and Organizational Change* (pp. 241–257). Oxford, England: Oxford University Press.

Kuan, L., Leinwand, S., Molotosky, A., Reeves, H., & Williams, H. (2012). *Learning Standards: What Matters Most for Quality Education*. Workshop presented at CIES 2012. San Juan, Puerto Rico, 23 April.

Kuehl, W. F., & Dunn, L. (1997). *Keeping the Covenant: American Internationalists and the League of Nations*. Kent, OH: Kent State University Press.

Kuhn, T. S. (1962). *The Structure of Scientific Revolutions*. Chicago: University of Chicago Press.

Kühne, A. (2012, March 3). Mehr Praxis fürs Lehramt. *Der Tagesspiegel*.

Kutsyuruba, B. (2008). *Teachers' Work in Times of Uncertainty: Post-Soviet Change and Teacher Collaboration*. Saarbrücken, Germany: VDM Verlag.

Kutsyuruba, B. (2011). Education in the Period of Post-Soviet Transition in Ukraine. *Demokratizatsiya: Journal of Post-Soviet Democratization, 19*(3), 287–309.

Kvit, S. (2012, April 8). New Dawn for Higher Education in Ukraine? *University World News*. Retrieved from http://www.universityworldnews.com/article.php?story=20120405132528872

Kwiek, M. (2004). The Emergent European Educational Policies under Scrutiny: The Bologna Process from a Central European Perspective. *European Educational Research Journal, 3*(4), 759–776. http://dx.doi.org/10.2304/eerj.2004.3.4.3

Kymlicka, W. (2009). *Multicultural Odysseys: Navigating the New International Politics of Diversity*. Oxford, England: Oxford University Press.

Kymlicka, W., & Walker, K. (Eds.). (2012). *Rooted Cosmopolitanism: Canada and the World*. Vancouver, Canada: UBC Press.

Labaree, D. (2005). An Uneasy Relationship: The History of Teacher Education in the University. In M. Cochran-Smith, S. D. Feiman-Nemser, & J. D. McIntyre (Eds.), *Handbook of Research on Teacher Education: Enduring Questions in Changing Times* (pp. 290–306). Mahwah, NJ: Lawrence Erlbaum Associates.

Labaree, D. (2008). An Uneasy Relationship: The History of Teacher Education in the University. In M. Cochran-Smith, S. Feiman Nemser, & J. McIntyre (Eds.), *Handbook of Research on Teacher Education: Enduring Issues in Changing Contexts* (3rd ed., pp. 290–306). Washington, DC: Association of Teacher Educators.

Lagemann, E. C. (2000). *An Elusive Science: The Troubling History of Education Research*. Chicago: University of Chicago Press.

Lange, D. (1988). *Tomorrow's Schools: The Reform of Education Administration in New Zealand*. Wellington, New Zealand: Government Printer.

Larrivee, B. (2000). Transforming Teaching Practice: Becoming the Critically Reflective Teacher. *Reflective Practice, 1*(3), 293–307. http://dx.doi.org/10.1080/713693162

Latorre Gaete, E. (1984). El Museum de Alejandría: Primera Universidad en el Mundo. *Comunicación y Medios, 4*, 29–40.

Laurie, S. S. (1891). *Rise and Early Constitution of Universities*. New York: Appleton and Company.

Lažetić, P. (2010). Managing the Bologna Process at the European Level: Institution and Actor Dynamics. *European Journal of Education, 45*(4), 549–562. http://dx.doi.org/10.1111/j.1465-3435.2010.01451.x

Le Goff, J. (1985a). *Les Intellectuels au Moyen-Âge*. [Intellectuals in the Middle Ages] Paris: Seuil.

Le Goff, J. (1985b). *Naissance des Universités Médiévales XIIIe siècle*. Paris: Centre National de la Recherche Scientifique / CNRS.

Leslie, S. W. (1993). *Cold War and American Science: The Military-Industrial-Academic Complex at MIT and Stanford*. New York: Columbia University Press.

Leuven Communiqué. (2009). *The Bologna Process 2020: The European Higher Education Area in the New Decade*. Communiqué of the Conference of European Ministers Responsible for Higher Education, Leuven and Louvain-la-Neuve, April 28–29. Retrieved from http://www.ehea.info/Uploads/Declarations/Leuven_Louvain-la-Neuve_Communiqu%C3%A9_April_2009.pdf

Lewin, K. (1999). Studienabbruch in Deutschland. In M. Schröder-Gronostay & H. D. Daniel (Eds.), *Studienerfolg und Studienabbruch* (pp. 17–50). Berlin: Luchterhand.

Lewis, R., & Doorlag, D. (2011). *Teaching Students with Special Needs in General Education Classrooms* (8th ed.). Boston, MA: Pearson.

Lin, N. (1999). Building a Network Theory of Social Capital. *Connections, 22*(1), 28–51.

Linn, M. C. (1982). The Importance of Cognitive Psychology in Curriculum Development and Teacher Education. Paper presented at the National Commission of Excellence in Education's site visit to Lawrence Hall of Science, University of California (Berkeley).

Lortie, D. A. (1975). *Schoolteacher: A Sociological Study*. Chicago: University of Chicago Press.

Lozano, J. F., Boni, A., Peris, J., & Hueso, A. (2012). Competences in Higher Education: A Critical Analysis from the Capabilities Approach. *Journal of Philosophy of Education, 46*(1), 132–147. http://dx.doi.org/10.1111/j.1467-9752.2011.00839.x

Luchinskaya, D., & Ovchynnikova, O. (2011). The Bologna Process Policy Implementation in Russia and Ukraine: Similarities and Differences. *European Educational Research Journal, 10*(1), 21–33. http://dx.doi.org/10.2304/eerj.2011.10.1.21

Lunyachek, V. (2011). Problems of the Education System Development of Ukraine in Times of Crisis. *Public Policy and Administration, 10*(1), 67–78. http://dx.doi.org/10.5755/j01.ppaa.10.1.229

Lütgert, W. (2008). Das Jenaer Modell der Lehrerbildung. In W. Lütgert, A. Gröschner, & K. Kleinespel (Eds.), *Die Zukunft der Lehrerbildung* (pp. 36–47). Weinheim, Germany: Beltz.

Luzzatto, G., & Moscati, R. (2005). University Reform in Italy. In A. Gornitzka, M. Kogan, & A. Amaral (Eds.), *Reform and Change in Higher Education* (pp. 153–168). Dordrecht, Netherlands: Kluwer. http://dx.doi.org/10.1007/1-4020-3411-3_10

Lytvyn, Y. (2009, December 24). Bologna Process: Failure or Fresh Start? Students Suggest Their Own Approach. *Day*. Retrieved from http://www.day.kiev.ua/en/article/society/bologna-process-failure-or-fresh-start

MacBeath, J. (2012). Future of Teaching Profession. *Educational International Research Institute*. University of Cambridge, Faculty of Education. Cambridge, England. Retrieved from http://download.ei-ie.org/Docs/WebDepot/EI%20Study%20on%20the%20Future%20of%20Teaching%20Profession.pdf

Makogon, Y. V., & Orekhova, T. V. (2007). Ukraine Education System Transformation under Conditions of European Integration Processes. *Facta Universitatis, 4*(1), 1–7.

Manzi, J. (2010). Programa INICIA: Fundamentos y Primeros Avances. In C. Bellei, D. Contreras, & J. P. Valenzuela (Eds.), *Ecos de la Revolución Pingüina* (pp. 285–310). Santiago, Chile: Editorial Pehuén.

Marcel, G. (1954). *The Decline of Wisdom*. London: The Harvill Press.

Marchenko, G. (2010, May). Training Teachers in Ukraine. Paper presented at the 9th International Scientific Conference: Engineering for Rural Development, Jelgava, Latvia.

Marga, A., Berchem, T., & Sadlak, J. (Eds.). (2008). *Living in Truth: A Conceptual Framework for a Wisdom Society and the European Construction*. Cluj-Napoca, Romania: Cluj University Press.

Maroy, C. (2009). Convergences and Hybridization of Educational Policies around "Post-Bureaucratic" Models of Regulation. *Compare: A Journal of Comparative Education, 39*(1), 71–84. http://dx.doi.org/10.1080/03057920801903472

Martin, A. K., Russell, T., Bullock, S., O'Connor, K., & Dillon, D. (2012, May). Alternative Conceptual Frameworks for Teacher Education Programs in Canada. Paper presented at the meeting of the Canadian Association for Teacher Education, Wilfrid Laurier University, Waterloo, Canada.

Marx, K. (1964). *Economic and Philosophical Manuscripts of 1844*. New York: International Publishers.

Massey, V. (1951). *Royal Commission on Arts, Letters and Sciences*. Ottawa, Canada: King's Printer.

Maxwell, N. (2007). From Knowledge to Wisdom: The Need for an Academic Revolution. *London Review of Education, 5*(2), 97–115. http://dx.doi.org/10.1080/14748460701440350

McDougall, W. A. (1985). *The Heavens and the Earth: A Political History of the Space Age*. New York: Johns Hopkins University Press.

McIntosh, A. (2001). *Soil and Soul: People versus Corporate Power*. London: Aurum.

McKay, I. (2000). The Liberal Order Framework: A Prospectus for a Reconnaissance of Canadian History. *Canadian Historical Review, 81*(4), 617–651. http://dx.doi.org/10.3138/CHR.81.4.617

McKay, I. (2009). The Liberal Order Framework: A Prospectus for a Reconnaissance of Canadian History. In J. F. Constant & M. Ducharme (Eds.), *Liberalism and Hegemony: Debating the Canadian Liberal Revolution* (pp. 35–63). Toronto, Canada: University of Toronto Press.

McKay, I. (2010). The Canadian Passive Revolution, 1840–1950. *Capital and Class, 34*(3), 361–381. http://dx.doi.org/10.1177/0309816810378722

McKenzie, P., Santiago, P., Sliwka, P., & Hiroyuki, H. (2005). *Teachers Matter: Attracting, Developing and Retaining Effective Teachers*. Paris: OECD.

McKillop, A. B. (1994). *Matters of Mind: The University in Ontario, 1791–1951*. Toronto, Canada: University of Toronto Press.

McMullen, K., & Elias, A. (2011). *A Changing Portrait of International Students in Canadian Universities. Education Matters: Insights on Education, Learning and Training in Canada, 7*(6). Tourism and the Centre for Education Statistics Division. Ottawa: Statistics Canada.

McMurtrie, B. (2006, February 24). Europe's Education Chief Seeks Transatlantic Cooperation. *Chronicle of Higher Education, 52*(25), A39.

Mead, G. H. (1934). *Mind, Self, and Society from the Standpoint of a Social Behaviorist* (Vol. 1). Chicago: University of Chicago Press.

Meckes, L., & Bascopé, M. (2012). Uneven Distribution of Novice Teachers in the Chilean Primary School System. *Education Policy Analysis Archives, 20*(30), 1–27. Retrieved from http://epaa.asu.edu/ojs/article/view/1017

Meetz, F., & Sprütten, F. (2004). *Teilarbeitsmarkt Schule – Arbeitsmarktbericht für das Jahr 2004*. Essen, Germany: AG Bildungsforschung/Bildungsplanung.

Meller, P. (2010). *Carreras Universitarias: Rentabilidad, Selectividad y Discriminación*. Santiago, Chile: Centro de Investigación Avanzada en Educación, Universidad de Chile.

Merino, M. E., & Mellor, D. (2009). Perceived Discrimination in Mapuche Discourse: Contemporary Racism in Chilean Society. *Critical Discourse Studies, 6*(3), 215–226. http://dx.doi.org/10.1080/17405900902974902

Merzyn, G. (2004). *Lehrerausbildung – Bilanz und Reformbedarf*. Baltmannsweiler, Germany: Schneider.

Meyer, J. W., Kamens, D. H., & Benavot, A. (1992). *School Knowledge for the Masses: World Models and National Primary Curricular Categories in the Twentieth Century*. Washington, DC: The Falmer Press.

Meyer, J. W., & Ramírez, F. O. (2002). La institucionalización mundial de la educación. In J. Schriewer (Ed.), *Formación del discurso en la educación comparada* (pp. 91–11). Barcelona, Spain: Ediciones Pomares.

Miguel Díaz, M. (Ed.). (2006). *Metodologías de Enseñanza y Aprendizaje para el Desarrollo de Competencias: Orientaciones para el Profesorado Universitario ante el Espacio Europeo de Educación Superior*. Madrid, Spain: Alianza.

Milewski, P. (2008). "The Little Gray Book": Pedagogy, Discourse and Rupture in 1937. *History of Education, 37*(1), 91–111. http://dx.doi.org/10.1080/00467600701315114

MINEDUC. (2012). *Estándares Orientadores para Egresados de Carreras de Pedagogía en Educación Básica*. Santiago, Chile: Centro de Perfeccionamiento, Experimentación e Investigaciones Pedagógicas / CPEIP del Ministerio de Educación de Chile.

Ministerio de Educación (2012). *Evaluación Inicia: Presentación de Resultados 2011*. Santiago, Chile: CPEIP. Retrieved from http://www.mineduc.cl/usuarios/mineduc/doc/201205071337570.RESULTADOSINICIA2011.pdf

Ministerium für Bildung, Wissenschaft und Kultur Mecklenburg-Vorpommern. (2000). *Lehrerprüfungsverordnung – LehPrVO 2000 M-V*. Retrieved from http://www.isp.uni-rostock.de/uploads/media/Lehrerpruefungsverordnung_2000_M-V.pdf

Ministerium für Kultus Jugend und Sport – Baden-Württemberg. http://www.km-bw.de/,Lde/Startseite

Ministry of Education of Chile. (2010). *Panel de Expertos para una Educación de Calidad: Informe final. Propuestas para Fortalecer la Profesión Docente en el Sistema Escolar Chileno*. Santiago, Chile: Ministry of Education. Retrieved from http://mt.educarchile.cl/mt/jjbrunner/archives/Informe_Finaldef.pdf

Ministry of Education of Chile. (2011). *Evaluación, INICIA*. Santiago: Government of Chile.

Ministry of Education of Ukraine. (1994), *State National Programme of Ukraine 'Education' ('Ukraine of the XXI Century')*. Kyiv, Ukraine: Veselka.

Ministry of Education of Ukraine. (1999). *Education for All 2000 Assessment*. Kyiv, Ukraine: Institute of Content and Methods of Education.

Ministry of Training, Colleges and Universities (MTCU). (2011). *Colleges and Universities – Ontario: Multi-year Accountability Agreement Summary*. Toronto, Canada.

Minks, K. H., & Schaeper, H. (2002). *Modernisierung der Industrie- und Dienstleistungsgesellschaft und Beschäftigung von Hochschulabsolventen*. Hannover, Germany: HIS GmbH.

Mitchell, T. (1986a). Forging a New Protestant Ontario on the Agricultural Frontier: Public Schools and the Origins of the Manitoba School Question, 1881–1890. *Prairie Forum, 2*(1), 33–51.

Mitchell, T. (1986b). In the Image of Ontario: Public Schools in Brandon 1881–1890. *Manitoba History, 12*(2), 25–34. Retrieved from www.mhs.mb.ca/docs/mb_history/12/brandonpublicschools.shtml

Mitchell, T. (1996). The Manufacture of Souls of Good Quality: Winnipeg's 1919 National Conference on Canadian Citizenship, English-Canadian Nationalism, and the New Order and the Great War. *Journal of Canadian Studies / Revue d'Études Canadiennes, 31*(4), 21.

Monahan, E. J. (2004). *Collective Autonomy: A History of the Council of Ontario Universities, 1962–2000*. Waterloo, Canada: Wilfrid Laurier University Press.

Montaigne, M. de (1595). Sur l'Institution des Enfants. *Livre I.*

Mora, J. G., & Vidal, J. (2005). Two Decades of Change in Spanish Universities: Learning the Hard Way. In A. Gornitzka, M. Kogan, & A. Amaral (Eds.), *Reform and Change in Higher Education: Analysing Policy Implementation* (pp. 135–152). Dordrecht, Netherlands: Springer.

Morton, D. (2004). First World War. In G. Hallowell (Ed.), *The Oxford Companion to Canadian History* (pp. 224–226). Don Mills, Canada: Oxford University Press.

Multrus, F., Ramm, M., & Bargel, T. (2010). *Studiensituation und studentische Orientierungen 11. Studierendensurvey an Universitäten und Fachhochschulen*. Bonn, Germany: Bundesministerium für Bildung und Forschung. Retrieved from http://www.bmbf.de/pub/studiensituation_studentetische_orientierung_elf.pdf

Musset, P. (2010). Initial Teacher Education and Continuing Training Policies in a Comparative Perspective: Current Practices in OECD Countries and a Literature Review on Potential Effects. *OECD Education Working Papers, no. 48*. OECD Publishing. http://dx.doi.org/10.1787/5kmbphh7s47h-en

Mutu, M. (1998). Barriers to Research: The Constraints of Imposed Frameworks. Keynote address to Te Oru Rangahau Māori Research and Development Conference, Massey University (Wellington, NZ), 7–9 July 1998.

Naess, A. (1989). *Ecology, Community and Lifestyle: Outline of an Ecosophy*. Cambridge, MA, and New York: Cambridge University Press. http://dx.doi.org/10.1017/CBO9780511525599

National Indian Brotherhood. (1972). *Indian Control of Indian Education*. Position paper. Ottawa, Canada: National Indian Brotherhood.

Naylor, N., & Ministry of Training, Colleges and Universities. (2012, April 3). Memorandum to Executive Heads of Ontario Universities.

Neatby, H. (1953). *So Little for the Mind: An Indictment of Canadian Education*. Toronto, Canada: Clarke, Irwin & Company.

Neatby, H. (1978). *Queen's University, Volume 1, 1847–1917*. Kingston and Montreal, Canada: McGill-Queen's University Press.

Neave, G. (1987). *La Comunidad Europea y la Educación*. Madrid, Spain: Fundación Universidad-Empresa.

Nebot, I. J. (2009). El desconocimiento de los másteres en España. In X Foro ANECA (Ed.), *Los Nuevos Títulos de Máster y la Competitividad en las Universidades* (pp. 23–32). Madrid, Spain: ANECA.

Nelles, W. C. (1995). From Imperialism to Internationalism in British Columbia Education and Society, 1900 to 1939. Unpublished PhD thesis, Department of Social and Educational Studies, University of British Columbia.

New Degrees in Pedagogy, The. (1907, January 15). *Queen's University Journal, 34*(6), 212–213.

Nida-Rümelin, J. (2008, November 2). Der Bachelor-Bankrott. *Süddeutsche Zeitung*.

Norman, N. (1995). Initial Teacher Education in France, Germany, and England and Wales: A Comparative Perspective. *Compare: A Journal of Comparative Education, 25*(3), 211–226. http://dx.doi.org/10.1080/0305792950250303

Nikitin, V. (2008, September 15). Ukraine Needs a New Educational System. *ICPS Newsletter, 27*(419), 1.

Nikolayenko, S. M. (2007). *Higher Education Reform in Ukraine and Bologna Process: Information Materials*. Kyiv, Ukraine: KNUTE.

Noddings, N. (1984). *Caring: A Feminine Approach to Ethics and Moral Education*. Berkeley: University of California Press.

Noddings, N. (2006). *Critical Lessons: What Our Schools Should Teach*. Cambridge, England: Cambridge University Press. http://dx.doi.org/10.1017/CBO9780511804625

Noddings, N. (2007). *When School Reform Goes Wrong*. New York: Teachers College Press.

Noddings, N. (2012). *Peace Education: How We Come to Love and Hate War*. Cambridge, England: Cambridge University Press.

Norberg-Hodge, H. (1992). *Ancient Futures: Learning from Ladakh*. San Francisco: Sierra Club.

Nóvoa, A. (2009). Educación 2021: Para una Historia del Futuro. *Revista Iberoamericana de Educación, 49*, 181–199.

Núñez, I., Weinstein, J., & Muñoz, G. (2010). ¿Posición Olvidada? Una Mirada desde la Normativa a la Historia de la Dirección Escolar en Chile (1929–2009). *Psicoperspectivas: Individuo y Sociedad, 9* (2), 53–81. Retrieved from http://www.psicoperspectivas.cl/index.php/psicoperspectivas/article/viewFile/117/111

Nussbaum, M. C. (1996). *For Love of Country?* J. Cohen (Ed.). Boston: Beacon Press.

Nussbaum, M. C. (2010). *Not for Profit: Why Democracy Needs the Humanities.* Princeton, NJ: Princeton University Press.

Observatory on Borderless Higher Education (OBHE). (2003). British Universities' Credit Ratings under Scrutiny in New Standard & Poor's Report. London, England: March. Retrieved from http://www.obhe.ac.uk/documents/download?id=607

OECD (1971a). *Teaching Resources and Structural Change.* Conference on Policies for Educational Growth, Paris, 3–5 June. Vol. 5. Paris: OECD.

OECD. (1971b). *Training, Recruitment and Utilization of Teachers in Primary and Secondary Education.* Paris: OECD.

OECD. (1974a). The Teacher and Educational Change: A New Role (Vol. 1). *General Report.* Paris: OECD.

OECD. (1974b). The Teacher and Educational Change (Vol. 2). *Recent Trends in Teacher Recruitment.* Paris: OECD.

OECD. (1977). *Activities of OECD in 1976. Report by the Secretary-General.* Paris: OECD.

OECD. (2004). *Reviews of National Policies for Education. Chile.* Paris: OECD Publishing.

OECD (2005). *Stärkere Professionalisierung des Lehrerberufs: Wie gute Lehrer gewonnen, gefördert und gehalten werden können.* Berlin: OECD. Retrieved from www.oecd/edu/teacherpolicy

Oester, K., Fiechter, U., & Kappus, E. N. (2008). *Schulen in transnationalen Lebenswelten: Integrations- und Segregationsprozesse am Beispiel von Bern West.* Zürich, Switzerland: Seismo.

Olson, D. (2007). *Jerome Bruner: The Cognitive Revolution in Educational Theory.* New York: Continuum International Publishing.

Olsson, M. (2004). Neoliberalism, Globalisation, Democracy: Challenges for Education. *Globalisation, Societies, and Education,* 2(2), 231–275.

Ontario, Government of. (2010, March 8). Open Ontario Plan. *Speech from the Throne.* Retrieved from http://news.ontario.ca/opo/en/2010/03/speech-from-the-throne---open-ontario-plan.html

Ontario Council on University Affairs (OCUA). (1988). Advisory Memorandum 88-V, International Graduate Student Differential Fee Waivers.

Ontario Department of Education. (1966). *Report of the Minister's Committee on the Training of Elementary School Teachers.*

Ontario Ministry of Finance. (2012). *Addendum to the 2012 Ontario Budget: Report on Expense Management Measures.* Toronto, Canada: Queen's Printer for Ontario. Retrieved from http://www.fin.gov.on.ca/en/budget/ontariobudgets/2012/addendum.pdf

Ontario Ministry of Finance. (2012, August). Ontario Fact Sheet.

OREAL/UNESCO. (2012). *Background and Criteria for Teachers' Policies*

Development in Latin America and the Caribbean. Santiago, Chile: Teachers for Education for All, Regional Strategic Project on Teachers.

Orlofsky, D. (2001). *Redefining Teacher Education: The Theories of Jerome Bruner and the Practice of Training Teachers*. New York: Peter Lang.

Ortega y Gasset, J. (1982). Misión de la Universidad. In *Misión de la Universidad y Otros Ensayos Sobre Educación y Pedagogía* (pp. 11–79). Madrid, Spain: Alianza/Revista de Occidente.

Osborne, K. (1998). One Hundred Years of History Teaching in Manitoba Schools. Part I: 1897–1927. *Manitoba History, 36*(Autumn/Winter), 3–25.

Owram, D. (1996). *Born at the Right Time: A History of the Baby Boom Generation*. Toronto, Canada: University of Toronto Press.

Paricio, J. (2007). Implicaciones del Paso de la Docencia Centrada en Contenidos a la Docencia Centrada en Competencias. In VIII Foro ANECA (Ed.), *Es Posible Bolonia con Nuestra Actual Cultura Pedagógica? Propuesta para el Cambio* (pp. 25–29). Madrid, Spain: ANECA.

Parrott, The Honourable H., Minister of College and Universities. (1976, May 4). Letter to Dr. J. S. Dupré, Chair of Ontario Council on University Affairs.

Payne, W. H. (1881). *A Short History of Education*. Syracuse, NY: C. W. Bardeen.

Pedró, F. (1996). Modelos de Enseñanza Secundaria en Europa. *Revista Española de Pedagogía, 204*, 277–291.

Pérez Álvarez, M. P. (2011). *Innovación Metodológica y Espacio Europeo de Educación Superior*. Madrid, Spain: Dyckinson.

Pestalozzi, J. H. (1898). *How Gertrude Teaches Her Children: An Attempt to Help Mothers to Teach Their Own Children and an Account of the Method*. E. Cooke (Ed.). Syracuse, NY: Bardeen.

Peters, M., & Besley, T. (2008). *Subjectivity and Truth: Foucault, Education, and the Culture of the Self*. New York: Peter Lang.

Peterson, P. L., Clark, C. M., & Dickson, P. W. (1989). *Educational Psychology as a "Foundation" in Teacher Education: Reforming an Old Notion*. Issue paper 89-9 of the National Center for Research on Teacher Learning, Michigan State University's College of Education. Retrieved from http://ncrtl.msu.edu/issue.htm

Pickle, J. (1985). Toward Teacher Maturity. *Journal of Teacher Education, 36*(4), 55–59. http://dx.doi.org/10.1177/002248718503600414

Popkewitz, T. (1993). *Changing Patterns of Power: Social Regulation and Teacher Education Reform*. Albany: State University of New York Press.

Popkewitz, T. (2008). Globalisation as a System of Reason: The Historical Possibility and the Political in Pedagogical Policy and Research. In T. Popkewitz & F. Rizvi (Eds.), *Globalization and the Study of Education* (pp. 247–267). New York: NSSE.

Power, M., Scheytt, T., Soin, K., & Sahlin, K. (2009). Reputational Risk as a Logic of Organizing in Late Modernity. *Organization Studies, 30*(2–3), 301–324. http://dx.doi.org/10.1177/0170840608101482

Prado Yepes, C. de. (2007). Regionalisation of Higher Education Services in Europe and East Asia and Potential for Global Change. *Asia Europe Journal, 5*(1), 83–92. http://dx.doi.org/10.1007/s10308-006-0069-z

Preliminary Announcement of the Faculty of Education. (1907). Session of 1907–1908. Kingston, Canada: Queen's University Archives.

Pukhovska, L., & Sacilotto-Vasylenko, M. (2010). Perspectives on Teacher Professional Development in Ukraine: Discourse and Practice. Порівняльно-педагогічні студії [Comparative Education Studies], 3–4, 147–155.

Queen's University. (1921). *Principal's Report 1920–21*. Kingston, Canada: Queen's University Archives.

Queen's University, Board of Trustees. (1964a, August 15–16). Kingston, Canada: Queen's University Archives.

Queen's University, Board of Trustees. (1964b, August 28). Kingston, Canada: Queen's University Archives.

Queen's University, McArthur College of Education. (1968). First Session, 1968–69. Kingston, Canada: Queen's University Archives.

Queen's University, Senate. (1965, March 26). Minutes from October 1964 to June 1965. Kingston, Canada: Queen's University Archives.

Quintriqueo, S., & McGinity, M. (2009). Implicancias de un Modelo Monocultural en la Construcción de la Identidad Sociocultural de Alumnos Mapuches en la Región de la Araucanía, Chile. *Estudios Pedagógicos, 35*(2), 173–188.

Rae, B. (2005). *Ontario: A Leader in Learning*. Toronto, Canada: Queen's Printer for Ontario.

Ramsden, P. (2002). *Learning to Teach in Higher Education*. London: Routledge.

Rancière, J. (2010). *El Maestro Ignorante*. Barcelona, Spain: Laertes.

Rauhvargers, A., Deane, C., & Pauwels, W. (2009). *Bologna Process Stocktaking Report*. Retrieved from http://www.ond.vlaanderen.be/hogeronderwijs/bologna/conference/documents/Stocktaking_report_2009_final.pdf

Razik, T. A. (1972). *Systems Approach to Teacher Training and Curriculum Development: The Case of Developing Countries*. Paris: UNESCO, International Institute for Educational Planning.

RCAP (Royal Commission on Aboriginal Peoples). (1996). Report of the Royal Commission on Aboriginal Peoples. (Vol. 3). *Gathering Strength*. Ottawa, Canada: Canada Communication Group.

Rea, K. J. (1985). *The Prosperous Years: The Economic History of Ontario, 1939–1975*. Toronto, Canada: University of Toronto Press.

Recasens, A. (2001). *Anales de la Universidad de Chile*. Retrieved from http://www.anales.uchile.cl/index.php/ANUC/article/view/2529/2446

Reisenauer, E., & Faist, T. (2010). Introduction: Theorizing Transnationalisation and Institutional Transformations. In T. Faist et al. (Eds.), *Working Papers, 87* (pp. 6–19). Centre on Migration, Citizenship and Development. Bielefeld, Germany: COMCAD.

Reissert, R., & Marziszewski, B. (1987). *Studiennverlauf und Beruseintritt*. Hannover, Germany: HIS.

Report of a Special Committee of the 1954–55 Students' Council, Concerning the OCE Teacher-Training Course. Kingston, Canada: Queen's University Archives.

Rizvi, F. (2008). Towards Cosmopolitan Learning. *Discourse: Studies in the Cultural Politics of Education, 30*(3), 253–268.

Roslyn Kunin & Associates (RKA) Inc. (2009). *Economic Impact of International Education in Canada, Final Report*. Vancouver, Canada: RKA, Inc.

Robertson, S. L. (2000). *A Class Act: Changing Teachers' Work, the State and Globalization*. New York: Falmer.

Robertson, S. L. (2012). Placing Teachers in Global Governance Agendas. *Comparative Education Review, 56*(4), 584–607. http://dx.doi.org/10.1086/667414

Robinson, K. (2009). *El Elemento*. Mexico: Grijalbo.

Robinson, K. (2010). Bring on the Learning Revolution! [Video]. Retrieved from http://www.ted.com/talks/sir_ken_robinson_bring_on_the_revolution.html

Robust, T. T. (2013). Indigenous Space – Ancestral Connections within Contemporary Tertiary Settings: Another Era or Another Error. Canada and New Zealand. Unpublished paper, University of Auckland, Auckland, New Zealand.

Rodgers, C. (2002). Defining Reflection: Another Look at John Dewey and Reflective Thinking. *Teachers College Record, 104*(4), 842–866. http://dx.doi.org/10.1111/1467-9620.00181

Rodríguez Fuentes, A., Caurcel Cara, M. J., & Ramos García, A. M. (Eds.). (2008). *Didáctica en el Espacio Europeo de Educación Superior*. Madrid, Spain: Editorial Eos.

Rohstock, A. (2012). Antikörper zur Atombombe: Verwissenschaftlichung und Programmierung des Klassenzimmers im Kalten Krieg. In P. Bernhard & H. Nehring (Eds.), *Den Kalten Krieg Denken: Beiträge zur sozialen Ideengeschichte seit 1945*. Essen, Germany: Klartext.

Rolyak, A. A., & Ohiyenko, E. I. (2008). Comparative Analysis of Teacher Education Systems in Ukraine and Scandinavian Countries. Paper presented at the European Conference on Educational Research, Göteborg, Sweden, September.

Rorty, R. (2011). *An Ethics for Today*. New York: Columbia University Press.

Rudolph, J. (2002). *Scientists in the Classroom: The Cold War Reconstruction of American Science Education*. New York: Palgrave Macmillan. http://dx.doi.org/10.1057/9780230107366

Russell, T. (2005a). Can Reflective Practice Be Taught? *Reflective Practice, 6*(2), 199–204. http://dx.doi.org/10.1080/14623940500105833

Russell, T. (2005b). The Place of the Practicum in Preservice Teacher Education Programs: Strengths and Weaknesses in Alternative Assumptions about the Experiences of Learning to Teach. In G. Hoban (Ed.), *The Missing Links in Teacher Education Design* (pp. 135–152). Dordrecht, Netherlands: Springer. http://dx.doi.org/10.1007/1-4020-3346-X_8

Saarinen, T. (2005). "Quality" in the Bologna Process: From "Competitive Edge" to Quality Assurance Techniques. *European Journal of Education, 40*(2), 189–204. http://dx.doi.org/10.1111/j.1465-3435.2004.00219.x

Sabatier, P. A., & Jenkins-Smith, H. C. (Eds.). (1993). *Policy Change and Learning: An Advocacy Coalition Approach*. Boulder, CO: Westview Press.

Sabatier, P. A., & Jenkins-Smith, H. C. (1999). The Advocacy Coalition Framework: An Assessment. In P. A. Sabatier (Ed.), *Theories of the Policy Process* (pp. 117–166). Boulder, CO: Westview Press.

Sacilotto-Vasylenko, M. (2008). Lifelong Learning Strategies in Teacher Education and Training: Examples from France and Ukraine. Paper presented at the European Conference on Educational Research, Göteborg, Sweden, September.

Safina, C. (2011). *The View from Lazy Point*. New York: Henry Holt.

Santos, B. S. (2002). *Toward a New Legal Common Sense*. London: Butterworths.

Sarason, S. B. (1971). *The Culture of the School and the Problem of Change*. Boston: Allyn and Bacon.

Sartorelli, S. (2009). Una Perspectiva Crítica sobre Interculturalidad y Educación Intercultural Bilingüe: El Caso de la Unión de Maestros de la Nueva Educación para México (UNEM) y Educadores Independientes en Chiapas. *Revista Latinoamericana de Educación Inclusiva, 3*(2), 77–90.

Savater, F. (1999). *Las Preguntas de la Vida*. Barcelona, Spain: Ariel.

Sayer, J. (2009). European Perspectives of Teacher Education. In J. Furlong, M. Cochran-Smith, & M. Brennan (Eds.), *Politics and Policy in Teacher Education: International Perspectives* (pp. 155–168). London: Routledge.

Schaeper, K. (2008). Lehrerbildung nach Bologna. In W. Lütgert (Ed.), *Die Zukunft der Lehrerbildung* (pp. 27–35). Weinheim, Germany: Beltz.

Schellack, A., & Große, S. (Eds.). (2007). *Bildungswege: Aufgaben für die Wissenschaft – Herausforderungen für die Politik*. Münster, Germany: Waxmann.

Schleicher, K., & Weber, P. (Eds.). (2002). Zeitgeschichte europäischer Bildung 1970–2000 (Vol. 3). *Europa in den Schulen*. Münster, Germany: Waxmann.

Schmoldt, B. (1989). *Zur Geschichte des Gymnasiums: Ein Überblick.* Baltmannsweiler, Germany: Schneider.

Schmoll, H. (2004, January 14). Bachelor ist nicht gleich Bachelor. *Frankfurter Allgemeine Zeitung.*

Schön, D. A. (1983). *The Reflective Practitioner: How Professionals Think in Action.* New York: Basic Books.

Schön, D. A. (1987). *Educating the Reflective Practitioner: Toward a New Design for Teaching and Learning in the Professions.* San Francisco: Jossey-Bass.

Schön, D. A. (1995). The New Scholarship Requires a New Epistemology. *Change, 27*(6), 27–34. http://dx.doi.org/10.1080/00091383.1995.10544673

Schön, D. A. (Ed.). (1991). *The Reflective Turn: Case Studies in and on Educational Practice.* New York: Teachers College Press.

School of Pedagogy, A. (1906, December 3). *Queen's University Journal,* 34 (4), 130.

Schorn, A. (1873). *Vorbildern und Bildern.* Leipzig, Germany: Dürr.

Schratz, M. (2011). Die Internationalisierung von Bildung im Zeitalter der Globalisierung. In M. Ruep (Ed.), *Bildungspolitische Trends und Perspektiven* (pp. 19–54). Baltmannsweiler, Germany: Schneider.

Schriewer, J. (1998). Études Pluridisciplinaires et Réflexions Philosophico-herméneutiques: La Structuration du Discours Pédagogique en France et en Allemagne. In P. Drewek & C. Lüth (Eds.), *History of Educational Studies* (pp. 57–84). Ghent, Belgium: CSHP.

Schriewer, J. (2007). "Bologna" – Ein neu-europäischer "Mythos"? *Zeitschrift fur Padagogik, 53*(2), 182–199.

Schriewer, J., & Martínez Valle, C. (2004). Constructions of Internationality in Education. In G. Steiner-Khamsi (Ed.), *The Global Politics of Educational Borrowing and Lending* (pp. 29–53). New York: Teachers College Press, Columbia University.

Schriewer, J., & Martínez Valle, C. (2007). ¿Ideología Internacional o Reflexión Idiosincrática? El Discursos Pedagógico en España, Rusia (Unión Soviética) y China del siglo XX. *Revista de Educación, 343,* 531–557.

Schroeder, W. (2005). *Continental Philosophy: A Critical Approach.* London: Blackwell.

Schubarth, W. (2007). *Endlich Praxis.* Frankfurt, Germany: Lang.

Schuck, S., Aubusson, P., Buchanan, J., & Russell, T. (2012). *Beginning Teaching: Stories from the Classroom.* Dordrecht, Netherlands: Springer. http://dx.doi.org/10.1007/978-94-007-3901-7

Schuck, S., & Russell, T. (2005). Self-Study, Critical Friendship, and the Complexities of Teacher Education. *Studying Teacher Education, 1*(2), 107–121. http://dx.doi.org/10.1080/17425960500288291

Schulte, B. (2005). El Sistema Educativo Alemán. In J. Prats & F. Raventós (Eds.), *Los Sistemas Educativos Europeos ¿Crisis o Transformación?* (pp. 149–176). Barcelona, Spain: Fundación "la Caixa."

Schultheis, F., Cousin, P. F., & Roca i Escoda, M. (Eds.) (2008). *Humboldts Albtraum: Der Bologna-Prozess und seine Folgen*. Konstanz, Germany: UVK Universitätsverlag.

Schultz, T. (1961). Investment in Human Capital. *American Economic Review, 1*(2), 5.

Sergiovanni, T. J., Kelleher, P., McCarthy, M., & Fowler, P. (2009). *Educational Governance and Administration* (6th ed.). Boston: Pearson Education.

Serrano Mérida, R. (2006). Nueva Percepción de la Identidad Profesional del Docente Universitario ante la Convergencia Europea. *Revista Electrónica de Investigación Educativa, 8*(1). Retrieved from http://www.redalyc.org/pdf/155/15508105.pdf

Seth, J. (1917). Memorandum by the Superintendent of Education, Re: Queen's Faculty of Education. Date added May 1917, with a question mark.

Shaw, M. A., Chapman, D. W., & Rumyantseva, N. L. (2011). The Impact of the Bologna Process on Academic Staff in Ukraine. *Higher Education Management and Policy, 23*(3), 71–90.

Shaw, M. A., Chapman, D. W., & Rumyantseva, N. L. (2013). Organizational Culture in the Adoption of the Bologna Process: A Study of Academic Staff at a Ukrainian University. *Studies in Higher Education, 38*(7), 989–1003.

Sheehan, N. M., & Wilson, D. J. (1994). From Normal School to the University to the College of Teachers: Teacher Education in British Columbia in the 20th Century. *Journal of Education for Teaching, 20*(1), 23–37. http://dx.doi.org/10.1080/0260747940200104

Sheffield, E. (1971). The Post-War Surge in Post-Secondary Education: 1945–1969. In J. Wilson, R. Stamp, & L. P. Audet (Eds.), *Canadian Education: A History* (pp. 416–443). Scarborough, Canada: Prentice-Hall.

Shestavina, O. (2004). Interaction of Ukrainian Educational Policy and the EU Neighbourhood Policy in the Context of the Bologna Process. In F. Attina & R. Rossi (Eds.), *European Neighbourhood Policy: Political, Economic, and Social Issues* (pp. 131–144). Catania, Italy: Jean-Monnet Centre Euro-Med, Department of Political Studies, University of Catania.

Shiva, V. (2005). *India Divided: Diversity and Democracy under Attack*. New York: Seven Stories Press.

Shuell, T. J. (1986). Cognitive Conceptions of Learning. *Review of Educational Research, 56*(4), 411–436. http://dx.doi.org/10.3102/00346543056004411

Shulman, L. S. (1986). Those Who Understand: Knowledge Growth in Teaching. *Educational Researcher, 15*(2), 4–14. http://dx.doi.org/10.3102/0013189X015002004

Shultz, L. (2007). Educating for Global Citizenship: Conflicting Agendas and Understandings. *Alberta Journal of Educational Research, 53*(3), 248–258.

Shultz, L., & Jorgenson, S. (2007). Global Citizenship Education in Post-Secondary Institutions: A Review of the Literature. Retrieved from http://www.uofaweb.ualberta.ca/uai_globaleducation/pdfs/GCE_lit_review.pdf

Sieber, P., & Mantel, C. (2012). The Internationalisation of Teacher Education: An Introduction. *Prospects, 42*(1), 5–17. http://dx.doi.org/10.1007/s11125-012-9218-x

Simola, H. (1993). Professionalism and Rationalism of Hopes: Outlining a Theoretical Approach for a Study on Educational Discourse. *International Studies in Sociology of Education, 3*(2), 173–192. http://dx.doi.org/10.1080/0962021930030202

Simola, H. (1998). Constructing a School-Free Pedagogy: Decontextualization of Finnish State Educational Discourse. *Journal of Curriculum Studies, 30*(3), 339–356. http://dx.doi.org/10.1080/002202798183648

Slote, M. (2007). *The Ethics of Care and Empathy*. New York: Routledge.

Smith, G. H. (1997). *The Development of Māori Philosophy and Practices: Theory and Praxis*. Doctoral dissertation, University of Auckland, Auckland, New Zealand.

Smith, G. H. (2002). *Presentation to Māori and Indigenous Graduate Studies Centre (MAI)*. Auckland, New Zealand: University of Auckland.

Smith, L. T. (1999). *Decolonizing Methodologies: Research and Indigenous Peoples*. London: Zed.

Snobelen, J. Operating Support, 1996–97. (1995, November 30). Memorandum to Chairs, Board of Governors, and Executive Heads of Provincially-Assisted Universities.

Sorbara, The Honourable G. (2005). *Paper B: Progress towards a New Generation of Economic Growth. Budget 2005*. Toronto, Canada: Queen's Printer for Ontario.

Sorbonne Communiqué. (1998). *Joint Declaration on Harmonisation of the Architecture of the European Higher Education System*. Retrieved from http://www.ehea.info/Uploads/Declarations/SORBONNE_DECLARATION1.pdf

Sotelo, I. (2009, April 16). Cara y Cruz del Proceso de Bolonia. *El Pais*.

Spring, J. (2001). *Globalization and Human Rights: An Intercivilizational Analysis*. Mahwah, NJ: Lawrence Erlbaum.

Spring, J. (2006). *Pedagogies of Globalization: The Rise of the Educational Security State*. Mahwah, NJ: Lawrence Erlbaum.

Stamp, R. (1982). *Schools of Ontario, 1876–1976*. Toronto, Canada: University of Toronto Press.

Statistics Canada. (2011a). *Aboriginal Peoples in Canada: First Nations People, Métis and Inuit National Household Survey.* Report prepared by A. Turner, S. Crompton, & S. Langlois. Catalogue no. 99-011-X2011001. Retrieved from http://www12.statcan.gc.ca/nhs-enm/2011/as-sa/99-011-x/99-011-x2011001-eng.pdf

Statistics Canada. (2011b). Toronto: City Census Profile, Census 2011. Retrieved from http://www12.statcan.ca/census-recensement/index-eng.cfm

Statistics Canada. (2012).Quarterly Demographic Estimates – January to March 2012, Table 1-1. Quarterly population estimates, national perspective – Population, Selected economic indicators, provincial economic accounts, annual. Table 384-0013.

Statistisches Bundesamt. (2001). *Studierende an Hochschulen Wintersemester 2010/2011.* Wiesbaden, Germany: Statistisches Bundesamt.

Stein, S. (1993). *Noah's Garden: Restoring the Ecology of Our Own Back Yards.* Boston: Houghton Mifflin.

Steinberg, T. (2002). *Down to Earth.* Oxford, England: Oxford University Press.

Steiner-Khamsi, G. (2012). For All by All? The World Bank's Global Framework for Education. In S. Klees, J. Samoff, & N. Stromquist (Eds.), *The World Bank and Education Critiques and Alternatives* (pp. 3–20). Rotterdam, Netherlands: Sense Publications. http://dx.doi.org/10.1007/978-94-6091-903-9_1

Stephenson, B. (1982, February 18). Letter to Principal R. L. Watts, as quoted in R. J. Hand, *Report on the 1982/83 Operating Budget.* Kingston, Canada: Queen's University Archives.

Stevenson, A. (Ed.). (2010). *Oxford Dictionary of English* (3rd ed.). Oxford, England: Oxford University Press.

Stevenson, H. (1971). Developing Public Education in Post-War Canada to 1960. In J. D. Wilson, R. M. Stamp, & L. P. Audet (Eds.), *Canadian Education: A History* (pp. 386–415). Scarborough, Canada: Prentice-Hall.

Stewart, I. (1980). *Organizing Scientific Research for War.* New York: Arno Press.

Stromquist, N. (2002). *Education in a Globalized World: The Connectivity of Economic Power.* Lanham, MD: Rowman and Littlefield.

Tan, S., & Whalen-Bridge, J. (Eds.). (2008). *Democracy as Culture: Deweyan Pragmatism in a Globalizing World.* Albany: State University of New York Press.

Tanner, D., & Tanner, L. (1987). *Supervision in Education: Problems and Practices.* New York: Macmillan.

Tarrius, A., Missaoui, L., & Qacha, F. (2013). *Transmigrants et Nouveaux Étrangers: Hospitalités Croisées entre Jeunes des Quartiers Enclaves et Nouveaux Migrants Internationaux.* Toulouse, France: Presses Universitaires du Mirail.

Task Force on Teaching as a Profession. (1986). *A Nation Prepared: Teachers for the 21st Century*. New York: Carnegie Forum on Education and the Economy.

Tatto, M. T., et al. (2012). *Policy, Practice, and Readiness to Teach Primary and Secondary Mathematics in 17 Countries: Findings from the IEA Teacher Education and Development Study in Mathematics (TEDS-M)*. Amsterdam, Netherlands: International Association for the Evaluation of Educational Achievement (IEA). Retrieved from http://www.iea.nl/fileadmin/user_upload/Publications/Electronic_versions/TEDS-M_International_Report.pdf

Taylor, C. (1992). *The Ethics of Authenticity*. Cambridge, MA: Harvard University Press.

Taylor, M., Scheirer, H., & Ghiraldelli, P. (Eds.). (2008). *Pragmatism, Education, and Children: International Philosophical Perspectives*. Amsterdam, Netherlands: Rodolphi.

Telpukhovska, V. (2006). *Bologna Process in the National Context of Ukraine: Tribute to Fashion or Necessary Step?* Master's thesis, University of Tampere, Tampere, Finland.

Tenorth, H. E. (2007). Inhaltliche Reformziele in der Lehrerbildung. In E. Bosbach & P. Martini (Eds.), *Von Bologna nach Quedlinburg* (pp. 34–46). Bonn, Germany: HRK.

Tenorth, H. E. (2008). Bildungstheorie Angesichts von Basiskompetenzen. *Zeitschrift für Pädagogische Historiographie, 14*(1), 26–31.

Tenorth, H. E. (2012, June 20). Akademisierung der Lehrerbildung – Perspektiven eines ambivalenten Programms. Vortrag zur Eröffnung der "Akademie für Bildungsforschung und Lehrerbildung" der Johann Wolfgang Goethe-Universität, Frankfurt am Main. Retrieved from http://www.abl.uni-frankfurt.de/42269961/Keynote_Prof_-Dr_-Heinz-Elmar-Tenorth.pdf

Terhart, E. (1996). Berufskultur und professionelles Handeln bei Lehrern. In A. Combe & W. Helsper (Eds.), *Pädagogische Professionalität: Untersuchungen zum Typus pädagogischen Handelns* (pp. 448–471). Frankfurt am Main, Germany: Suhrkamp.

Terhart, E. (2000). *Perspektiven der Lehrerbildung in Deutschland: Abschlussbericht der von der Kultusministerkonferenz eingesetzten Kommission*. Weinheim, Germany: Beltz.

Terhart, E. (2001). *Lehrerberuf und Lehrerbildung*. Weinhem, Germany: Beltz.

Terhart, E. (2005, May 10). Universität und Lehrerbildung: Perspektiven einer Partnerschaft. Presentation at the Universität zu Köln.

Thierack, A. (2002). Darstellung der konzeptionellen Diskussion um BA-/MA-Abschlüsse in der Lehrerausbildung (pp. 19–21). Paderborn, Germany. Retrieved from http://www.uni-paderborn.de/fileadmin/plaz/PLAZ-Organisation/PLAZ-Forum/Thierack2002.pdf

Thierack, A. (2007). Bachelor- und Masterkonzepte im deutschen Lehramtsstudium. In E. Bosbach & P. Martini (Eds.), *Von Bologna nach Quedlinburg* (pp. 47–61). Bonn, Germany: HRK.

Thomas, J. B. (1990). *British Universities and Teacher Education: A Century of Change*. London: Falmer Press.

Torres, C. A. (2009). *Education and Neoliberal Globalization*. New York: Routledge.

Transformation of Higher Education. (2010). *Pre-Project Report. Higher Education and Professional Learning: The Effects of European Integration*. Oslo, Norway: University of Oslo, Department of Educational Research.

Tribó i Traveria, G. (2006). Os Títulos de Educación e a Súa Adaptación á Construción do Espazo Europeo de Educación Superior. In X. M. Cid Fernández (Ed.), *Repensar a Educacion e a Sociedade: Realidades e Desafíos* (pp. 195–208). Vigo, Spain: Universidade de Vigo.

Tröhler, D. (2006). The Formation and Function of Histories of Education in Continental Teacher Education Curricula. *Journal of the American Association for the Advancement of Curriculum Studies, 2*, 1–17. Retrieved from http://www2.uwstout.edu/content/jaaacs/vol2/trohler.htm

Tröhler, D. (2010). Harmonizing the Educational Globe: World Polity, Cultural Features, and the Challenges to Educational Research. *Studies in Philosophy and Education, 29*(1), 5–17. http://dx.doi.org/10.1007/s11217-009-9155-1

Tröhler, D. (2011a). Concepts, Cultures, and Comparisons: PISA and the Double German Discontentment. In D. Tröhler (Ed.), *Languages of Education: Protestant Legacies, National Identities, and Global Aspirations* (pp. 194–207). New York: Routledge.

Tröhler, D. (2011b). *Languages of Education: Protestant Legacies, National Identities, and Global Aspirations*. New York: Routledge.

Tröhler, D., Popkewitz, T. S., & Labaree, D. (2011). *Schooling and the Making of Citizens in the Long Nineteenth Century*. New York: Palgrave Macmillan.

True, M. (1995). *An Energy Field More Intense than War*. Syracuse, NY: Syracuse University Press.

Tyack, D. B. (Ed.). (1967). *Turning Points in American Educational History*. Waltham, MA: Blaisdell Publishing Company.

Tyler, R. W. (1949). *Basic Principles of Curriculum and Instruction*. Chicago: University of Chicago Press.

United Nations Development Programme / UNDP (2005). *Human Development Report*. New York: UNDP.

Universität Rostock. (2012). Organisation des Lehramtsstudiums in Rostock. Retrieved from http://www.isp.uni-rostock.de/studium/schulpaedagogik

University of Western Ontario. (2009, May 25). Board of Governors, *Strategic Plan for Internationalization, 2009–2012*.

Urban, W. (2010). *More than Science and Sputnik: The National Defense Education Act of 1958*. Tuscaloosa: University of Alabama Press.

Valli, L. (Ed.). (1992). *Reflective Teacher Education: Cases and Critiques*. Albany: State University of New York Press.

Vanderkerckhove, W., & van Hooft, S. (2010). Introduction. In S. van Hooft and W. Vandekerckhove (Eds.), *Questioning Cosmopolitanism*. Vol. 6: *Studies in Global Justice* (pp. xv–xxviii). Heidelberg, Germany; London; and New York: Springer Dordrecht.

van Doorn, F. (2010). *Teacher Phronésis and Habitus Formation: An Auto-Ethnographic Study of Beginning to Becoming to Being*. MA thesis, University of Calgary, Canada.

van Hooft, S. (2010). Cosmopolitanism, Identity and Recognition. Introduction. In S. van Hooft and W. Vandekerckhove (Eds.), *Questioning Cosmopolitanism*. Vol. 6: *Studies in Global Justice* (pp. 37–47). Heidelberg, Germany; London; and New York: Springer Dordrecht.

Veiga, A., & Amaral, A. (2006). The Open Method of Coordination and the Implementation of the Bologna Process. *Tertiary Education and Management, 12*(4), 283–295. http://dx.doi.org/10.1080/13583883.2006.9967174

Verger, J. (1999). *Histoire des Universités au Moyen-Âge*. Paris: PUF.

Verrier, C. (2004). Enseignement Supérieur et Sentiment Européen au Moyen-Âge. *Journal des Chercheurs*.

Vilches, A., & Gil-Pérez, D. (2010). Máster en Formación del Profesorado de Enseñanza Secundaria. Algunos Análisis y Propuestas. *Revista Eureka sobre Enseñanza y Divulgación de las Ciencias, 7*(3), 661–6.

Viñao Frago, A. (2009). El grado de Pedagogía y la Formación del Profesorado ante el Espacio Europeo de Educación Superior. *Cuestiones Pedagógicas, 19*, 97–113.

Voegtle, E., Knill, C., & Dobbins, M. (2011). To What Extent Does Transnational Communication Drive Crossnational Policy Convergence? The Impact of the Bologna-Process on Domestic Higher Education Policies. *Higher Education, 61*(1), 77–94. http://dx.doi.org/10.1007/s10734-010-9326-6

Vygotsky, L. S. (1978). *Mind in Society*. Cambridge, MA: Harvard University Press.

Waitangi Tribunal. (1999, April 22). *The Wānanga Capital Establishment Report*. Wai 718. Wellington, New Zealand: GP Publications.

Waitangi Tribunal. (1989). *Report of the Waitangi Tribunal on Te reo Māori Claim (Wai 11)* (2nd ed.). Wellington, New Zealand: The Tribunal.

Walker, M. (2012). Universities and a Human Development Ethics: A Capabilities Approach to Curriculum. *European Journal of Education, 47*(3), 448–461. http://dx.doi.org/10.1111/j.1465-3435.2012.01537.x

Wanner, C. (1998). *Burden of Dreams: History and Identity in Post-Soviet Ukraine*. University Park: Pennsylvania State University Press.

Ward, J., & Peppard, J. (2006). *Strategic Planning for Information Systems*. Bedford, England: Wiley and Sons.

Watson, S. (2013). An Exploration into the Teaching of Cosmopolitan Ideals: The Case of "Global Citizenship." *Citizenship, Social and Economics Education, 12*(2), 110–117.

Weegen, M. (2004). Bachelor und Master: Übergänge zwischen strukturellen Verwerfungen und kapazitären Fallstricken. *Das Hochschulwesen, 6*, 206–208.

Weimar Constitution. (1919). Retrieved from http://www.documentarchiv.de/wr/wrv.html

Weinberger, D. (2004, 15 November). The Digital Future. Retrieved from http://www.c-span.org/video/?184427-1/digital-future-web-logs-knowledge

Westerheijden, D., et al. (2010). *The First Decade of Working on the European Higher Education Area: Executive Summary, Overview and Conclusions*. Enschede, Netherlands: Centre for Higher Education Policy Studies (CHEPS).

Whitaker, R., & Marcuse, G. (1994). *Cold War Canada: The Making of a National Insecurity State, 1945–1957*. Toronto, Canada: University of Toronto Press.

Wiebke, E., et al. (2011). Lehre unter den Forschungshut bringen ... – Empirische Befunde zu multipler Zielverfolgung und Zielkonflikten aus Sicht von Hochschulleitungen und Nachwuchswissenschaftler(inne)n. In S. Nickel (Ed.), *Der Bologna-Prozess aus Sicht der Hochschulforschung* (pp. 192–203). Gütersloh, Germany: CHE-Arbeitspapier 148.

Wilkinson, R., & Pickett, K. (2009). *The Spirit Level: Why More Equal Societies Almost Always Do Better*. London: Allen Lane.

Willis, O. (2012). The Study Abroad Experience: Where Does Religion Fit? *Journal of Global Citizenship & Equity Education, 2*(1), 1–18. Retrieved from http://journals.sfu.ca/jgcee/index.php/jgcee/article/view/58/31

Wilson, E. O. (2002). *The Future of Life*. New York: Alfred A. Knopf.

Winter, M. (2007). *PISA, Bologna, Quedlinburg – Wohin treibt die Lehrerausbildung?* Wittenberg, Germany: Institut für Hochschulforschung (HoF).

Winter, M. (2009). *Das neue Studieren*. Wittenberg, Germany: Institut für Hochschulforschung (HoF).

Winter, M. (2011). Die Revolution blieb aus. In S. Nickel (Ed.), *Der Bologna-Prozess aus Sicht der Hochschulforschung* (pp. 20–35). Gütersloh, Germany: Centrum für Hochschulentwicklung.

Wissenschaftsrat. (1992). Empfehlungen zur Lehrerbildung in den neuen Ländern. In *Empfehlungen zur künftigen Struktur der Hochschullandschaft in den neuen Ländern und im Ostteil von Berlin* (pp. 81–159). Cologne, Germany: Wissenschaftsrat.

Wissenschaftsrat. (2008). *Empfehlungen zur Qualitätsverbesserung von Studium und Lehre*. Berlin: Wissenschaftsrat. Retrieved from http://www.wissenschaftsrat.de/download/archiv/8639-08.pdf

Witte, J. (2004). The Introduction of Two-Tiered Study Structures in the Context of the Bologna Process: A Theoretical Framework for an International Comparative Study of Change in Higher Education Systems. *Higher Education Policy*, *17*(4), 405–425. http://dx.doi.org/10.1057/palgrave.hep.8300065

Witte, J., Rüde, M., Tavenas, F., & Hüning, L. (2004). *Ein Vergleich angelsächsischer Bachelor-Modelle: Lehren für die Gestaltung eines deutschen Bachelor?* Gütersloh, Germany: Centrum für Hochschulentwicklung. Retrieved from http://www.che.de/downloads/AP55.pdf

Wolczuk, K. (2004). *Integration without Europeanisation: Ukraine and Its Policy toward the European Union*. Birmingham, England: Centre for Russian and East European Studies, University of Birmingham.

World Bank. (2011). *Equal Access to Quality Education in Ukraine Project: Implementation Completion and Results Report (no: ICR00001701)*. Washington, DC: World Bank.

World Bank. (2012). *Knowledge Assessment Methodology 2012*. Retrieved from http://go.worldbank.org/JGAO5XE940

World Federation of Education Associations. (1929). *Proceedings of the Third Biennial Conference held in Geneva, Switzerland, from July 29th to August 4th, 1929*. Geneva, Switzerland.

Yates, A. (1970). *Current Problems of Teacher Education: Report of a Meeting of International Experts*. Paris: UNESCO Institute for Education.

Yin, R. (1984). *Case Study Research: Design and Methods* (1st ed.). Beverly Hills, CA: Sage Publishing.

Yin, R. (1989a). *Case Study Research: Design and Methods* (rev. ed.). Beverly Hills, CA: Sage Publishing.

Yin, R. (1989b). *Interorganizational Partnerships in Local Job Creation and Job Training Efforts*. Washington, DC: COSMOS Corp.

Yin, R. (1993). *Applications of Case Study Research*. Beverly Hills, CA: Sage Publishing.

Yin, R. (1994). *Case Study Research: Design and Methods* (2nd ed.). Beverly Hills, CA: Sage Publishing.

Zadja, J. (Ed.). (2010). *Globalisation, Education, and Social Justice*. Dordrecht, Netherlands: Springer.

Zaspa, H. (2008). Bologna Process and Higher Technical Education in Ukraine. Paper presented at the 19th EAEEIE Annual Conference, Tallinn, Estonia, June–July.

Zeichner, K. (1996). Teachers as Reflective Practitioners and the Democratization of School Reform. In K. Zeichner, S. Melnick, & M. L. Gomez (Eds.), *Currents of Reform in Preservice Teacher Education* (pp. 199–214). New York: Teachers College Press.

Zgaga, P. (2008). Mobility and the European Dimension in Teacher Education. Paper presented to TEPE Conference, Ljubljana, Slovenia, February 21–23.

Zgaga, P. (2009). The Bologna Process and Its Role for Transition Countries. *Revista de la Educación Superior, 38*(2), 83–96.

Zhulynsky, M., Kis, T., Makaryk, I., & Weretelnyk, R. (Eds.) (1997). Cultural, Educational and Linguistic Policy in Ukraine, 1991–1996. In T. Kis, I. Makaryk, & R. Weretelnyk (Eds.), *Towards a New Ukraine I: Ukraine and the New World Order, 1991–1996. Proceedings of a conference held on March 21–22, 1997 at the University of Ottawa*. Ottawa, Canada: Chair of Ukrainian Studies, University of Ottawa.

Contributors

Martín Bascopé received an M.Sc. in Economics from the Pontificia Universidad Católica de Chile. He is an associate researcher at the Centre for Research on Educational Policy and Practice (CEPPE) at the same university. His main research interests are policies and processes regarding teacher education, educational policy, and comparative educational research.

Christopher Beeman has recently published contributions to *Encounters on Education, Journal of Experiential Education, The Trumpeter,* and *Paideusis*. At the Queen's University (Kingston, Ontario, Canada) Faculty of Education, he has recently taught courses in undergraduate programs, including "Art in an Aboriginal Context" and "Philosophy of Education," and as well as graduate courses in the Aboriginal and World Indigenous Education Studies program. Through Simon Fraser University, he is a research associate with the CURA-sponsored green school in Maple Ridge, British Columbia (Canada).

Rosa Bruno-Jofré, PhD (University of Calgary, Alberta, Canada), is professor at and former dean (2000–10) of the Faculty of Education, cross-appointed to the Department of History, Faculty of Arts, Queen's University (Kingston, Ontario, Canada). She is the author of *Methodist Education in Perú* (Wilfrid Laurier University Press, 1988) and *The Missionary Oblate Sisters* (McGill-Queen's University Press, 2005); co-author of *Democracy and the Intersection of Religion and Traditions* (McGill-Queen's University Press, 2010); and co-editor (with Natalia Aponiuk) of *Educating Citizens for a Pluralistic Society* (Canadian Ethnic Studies Association, 2001) and (with Jürgen Schriewer) of *The Global Reception* *of Dewey's Thought* (Routledge, 2011). In 2010, she received a Group Santander award to serve as a Distinguished Visiting Professor at the Universidad Complutense de Madrid, Spain. She is founding co-editor of *Encounters/Encuentros/Rencontres on Education*, associate editor of *Historical Studies in Education*, and guest editor of *Paedagogica Historica, Bordón*, and *Pensamiento Educativo*, among others.

Nicholas C. Burbules is the Gutgsell Professor in the Department of Educational Policy, Organization and Leadership at the University of Illinois, Urbana-Champaign, USA. He is the director of the Ubiquitous Learning Institute, dedicated to the study of new models of "anywhere, anytime" teaching and learning. He is currently the education director for the National Center on Professional and Research Ethics, located at the University of Illinois.

Josh Cole is a PhD candidate in the Department of History at Queen's University (Kingston, Ontario, Canada). His scholarship lies on the border between educational history and social and cultural history, and deals with education and modernity in the broadest sense. His SSHRCC-CGS-funded dissertation is entitled "Children, Schools, and Utopias: Education and Modernity in Ontario's Long 1960s." He has published papers based on this research in the journals *Sembrando Ideas* and *Historical Studies in Education/Revue d'histoire de l'éducation*.

Cristián Cox received a PhD in sociology from the University of London, England. He is the dean of Faculty of Education at Pontificia Universidad Católica de Chile (Santiago). In the 1990s he was a policymaker at the Ministry of Education of Chile, responsible for a major reform of the country's school curriculum. He has served as a consultant to the OECD, UNESCO, the World Bank, and the Inter-American Development Bank, and was Tinker Visiting Professor at Stanford University (2005).

Roger Dale is professor in the Centre for Globalisation, Education and Societies at the University of Bristol, England, and Visiting Professor of Education at the University of Auckland, New Zealand, where he was a professor (1989–2004). He is the co-founder/editor of *Globalisation, Societies and Education*, and was scientific coordinator of the European Union's Network of Experts in Social Science and Education. His main research interests are in the global governance of education, with a particular interest in European education policy.

José Luis González Geraldo is a lecturer in the Department of Education at the University of Castilla–La Mancha (UCLM), Albacete, Spain. Interested in the field of the theory and history of education among other research, he studies the methodological change of the European Higher Education Area and how it could foster and improve the quality of the *teaching-learning* process in order to move it towards a *learning-teaching* process. In sum, he is focused on what really makes higher education "higher."

Yvonne Hébert is professor emerita at the University of Calgary (Alberta, Canada). She is interested in immigration, citizenship education, youth, identity, democracy, minority studies, bilingualism and second-language education, policy, and educational reform. Her publications include *Critical Perspectives on International Education* (Sense Publishers, 2012); *Negotiating Transcultural Lives* (University of Toronto Press, 2006); and *Indian Education in Canada* (University of British Columbia Press, 1987, 2 vols.); as well as articles on second-generation youth and their mobilities and identifications. In recognition of her scholarly leadership and research contributions to education and community, she has been awarded the Roger Motut prize as well as the commemorative Queen Elizabeth II Diamond Jubilee Medal.

James Scott Johnston is jointly appointed associate professor of education and philosophy at Memorial University (St John's, Newfoundland, Canada) and adjunct associate professor of education at Queen's University (Kingston, Ontario, Canada). He has published several books and articles on various aspects of philosophy of education, including on John Dewey, German Idealism, and progressivist thought.

Gonzalo Jover is professor of education at the Complutense University in Madrid, Spain. At present, he is the coordinator of the master's degree on secondary education teacher training and adviser to the vice-chancellor of postgraduate programs and continuing education. His major research areas are educational theory, the politics of education, and professional ethics.

Benjamin Kutsyuruba has, throughout his career, has worked as a teacher, researcher, manager, and professor in the field of education in Ukraine and Canada. He is currently an assistant professor in educational policy and leadership and associate director of the Social Program Evaluation Group at the Faculty of Education, Queen's University (Kingston, Ontario, Canada). His research interests include educational policymaking; educational leadership; mentorship; trust, moral agency, and ethical decision-making; the transnationalization of higher education; school safety/climate; and educational change, reform, and restructuring.

Carlos Martínez Valle teaches history of education, educational policy, and comparative education at the Universidad Complutense of Madrid, Spain. He studied political science and sociology and worked at the Centre for Comparative Education at Humboldt University, Berlin, and at the Faculty of Education, Queen's University (Kingston, Ontario, Canada). His work focuses on the processes of resistance against and filtering of globalized trends and standards in specific contexts.

Lorena Meckes, M.Sc., studied psychology at the University of London, England. She is a researcher at the Centre for Research on Educational Policy and Practice (CEPPE) at Pontificia Universidad Católica de Chile (Santiago). From 2002–8 she led Chile's national assessment system of learning outcomes (SIMCE). She has served as consultant on standards and educational assessments for the OECD and the World Bank in Latin American and Middle Eastern countries.

María Eugenia Merino-Dickinson is senior professor of linguistics and discourse analysis at the School of Teacher Education, Faculty of Education, Catholic University at Temuco, Chile. Dr Merino holds a PhD in human sciences with specialization in discourse analysis. Her research area is interethnic and intercultural relations, with particular emphasis on racism and discrimination against ethnic minorities and their impact on educational settings. She has conducted research on prejudice and discrimination against Mapuches in Chile.

Nel Noddings is Lee Jacks Professor of Education Emerita, Stanford University (California, USA). She is a past president of the National Academy of Education, Philosophy of Education Society, and John Dewey Society. In addition to 19 books, she is the author of more than

200 articles and chapters on various topics ranging from the ethics of care to mathematical problem solving. Her latest book is *Peace Education* (Cambridge University Press, 2012).

Andrew Robinson. Dr Robinson's career and current spectrum of responsibilities cover senior faculty posts in British universities, including director for Europe at the Open University, executive experience in regional economic development, and consultancy for European private and public sectors. As Honorary Consul for France in the North East of England, he created the first joint Franco-German consulate in the European Union, and was awarded the Légion d'honneur in 2010 for services to Franco-British understanding.

Te Tuhi Robust conducted doctoral research at the University of Auckland, investigating and examining the development of indigenous infrastructure in the university institution. He was a teaching fellow of the Woolf Fisher Research Centre; Research Fellow of the International Research Centre for Maori and Indigenous Education; senior research fellow at the Institute of Earth Science and Engineering, and former director of the James Henare Maori Research Centre, University of Auckland, New Zealand; and associate professor in indigenous education, Te Whare Wananga o Awanuiarangi.

Anne Rohstock, PhD, is a postdoctoral research and teaching fellow at Universität Tübingen, Germany. Her areas of expertise are history of education, history of science, and contemporary history. She has published on the history of higher education systems in the Cold War era, the student revolt of 1968, curriculum development, student migration, and the history of education ideals. Recent book chapters include "The History of Higher Education" (2011); "'Some Things Never Change': The (Re)Invention of Humboldt in Western Higher Education Systems" (2012); and "Tomorrow Never Dies: A Socio-Historical Analysis of the Luxembourgish Curriculum" (2013, with Thomas Lenz and Catherina Schreiber).

Tom Russell is a professor in the Faculty of Education at Queen's University (Kingston, Ontario Canada), where his teaching includes a course in physics for high school teachers. His research interests include reflective practice, action research, learning in the pre-service practicum, and the broad topic of how individuals learn to teach. He is an editor of *Studying Teacher Education* and has been actively involved in self-study of teacher education practices since the field began in the early 1990s.

Ken Snowdon is president of Snowdon & Associates Inc., a consultancy specializing in higher education that provides professional services to universities, colleges, and provincial and national agencies. Before establishing his firm, Ken was Vice-President (Policy & Analysis) at the Council of Ontario Universities from 1998–2002, having spent a number of years in administrative roles at Queen's University (Kingston, Ontario, Canada).

Sylviane Toporkoff is partner and founder of ITEMS International, a company specialized in strategic ICT consulting, and full professor at the University of Paris 8, Institute of European Studies. She received her doctorate in economics from the University of Paris I Panthéon-Sorbonne. She specializes in international research and consulting, including in the areas of the information society, public policy, and economic and strategic international partnerships.

Daniel Tröhler is professor of education and director of the Research Unit Languages, Culture, Media, and Identities and of the Doctoral School in Educational Sciences at the University of Luxembourg. He is also visiting professor of comparative education at the University of Granada, Spain. His latest publications include *Languages of Education: Protestant Legacies, National Identities, and Global Aspirations* (Routledge, 2011) and *Schooling and the Making of Citizens in the Long Nineteenth Century* (edited with Thomas S. Popkewitz and David F. Labaree; Routledge, 2011).

LeRoy Whitehead began his teaching career at a junior high school in Calgary, Alberta, Canada, in 1962. He joined the Faculty of Education at Queen's University (Kingston, Ontario, Canada) in 1977, where he taught school leadership and policy until 2012, serving as associate dean (Pre-Service Teacher Education Programs) for thirteen years. He is currently volunteering in Fiji with an International Teacher Education Program.

Index

www.ingramcontent.com/pod-product-compliance
Lightning Source LLC
LaVergne TN
LVHW090145080826
844660LV00013B/677/J